Burke Davis

GEORGE WASHINGTON
and the
AMERICAN REVOLUTION

Random House New York

Library of Congress Cataloging in Publication Data
Davis, Burke.
  George Washington and the American Revolution.
  Bibliography: p.
  Includes index.
  1. Washington, George, Pres. U. S., 1732–1799.
2. United States—History—Revolution, 1775–1783.
I. Title.
E312.25.D38   973.3'092'4 [B]   75–10274
ISBN 0–394–46388–9

Manufactured in the United States of America

98765432

First Edition

Maps by Rafael Palacios

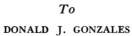

To

DONALD J. GONZALES

Contents

MAPS   *xi*

1   COMMANDER IN CHIEF, JUNE 16, 1775

    "... the Ruin of My Reputation"   *3*

2   THE GENERAL MEETS HIS ARMY

    "... Exceedingly Dirty and Nasty People"   *20*

3   BOSTON BESIEGED

    "We Do Nothing But Watch"   *36*

4   A SURPRISE FOR WILLIAM HOWE

    "Under the Rose"   *61*

5   CAN NEW YORK BE DEFENDED?

    "A Desperate Game"   *78*

6   LONG ISLAND, AUGUST 27, 1776

    "I Will Fight So Long as I Have a Leg or an Arm"   *92*

7   THE LOSS OF NEW YORK

    "Good God! ... Are These the Men to Defend

    America?"   *113*

8   HARLEM HEIGHTS AND WHITE PLAINS

    "I Am Wearied Almost to Death"   *128*

9   THE FLIGHT THROUGH NEW JERSEY

    "... the Game Is Pretty Near Up"   *143*

10   TRENTON, DECEMBER 26, 1776

    "A Glorious Day for Our Country"   *160*

11 PRINCETON, JANUARY 3, 1777

    "A Fine Fox Chase, Boys!"   *177*

12 FOX HUNTER ON THE RUN

    "One of Nature's Geniuses"   *193*

13 BRANDYWINE, SEPTEMBER 11, 1777

    "A Very Hot Evening"   *205*

14 GERMANTOWN, OCTOBER 4, 1777

    "The Day Was Unfortunate"   *224*

15 THE CONWAY CABAL

    "A Weak General and Bad Counsellors"   *238*

16 VALLEY FORGE

    "Starve—Dissolve—or Disperse"   *254*

17 MONMOUTH, JUNE 28, 1778

    "I Expect My Orders to Be Obeyed"   *277*

18 THE DANGEROUS SEASON

    "Idleness, Dissipation and Extravagance"   *300*

19 OUR ENEMIES THE FRENCH

    "The Time Is Precious"   *321*

20 ARNOLD AND WEST POINT

    "Treason Black as Hell!"   *334*

21 MUTINY

    "The American Army Can Furnish But One Arnold"   *352*

22 THUNDER IN THE SOUTH

    "These English Are Mad"   *359*

23 LAFAYETTE IN VIRGINIA, SUMMER, 1781

    "Matters of Very Great Importance"   *371*

24   HOODWINKING HENRY CLINTON

      "The Mask Is Being Raised!"   *382*

25   CONCENTRATION IN THE CHESAPEAKE

      "Keep Lord Cornwallis Safe"   *395*

26   THE SIEGE OF YORKTOWN

      "The Liberties of America Are in Our Hands"   *413*

27   VICTORY

      "The World Turned Upside Down"   *429*

    EPILOGUE: PEACE AT LAST

      "An Affectionate Farewell"   *442*

    SELECTED BIBLIOGRAPHY   *461*

    NOTES   *465*

    INDEX   *482*

Maps

THE SIEGE OF BOSTON   *32*

THE NEW YORK CAMPAIGN   *99*

THE RETREAT THROUGH NEW JERSEY   *145*

TRENTON, DEC. 26, 1776   *167*

PRINCETON, JAN. 2–3, 1777   *185*

PHILADELPHIA CAMPAIGN, 1777   *212*

MONMOUTH CAMPAIGN   *281*

SOUTHERN CAMPAIGNS, 1780–1781   *367*

YORKTOWN, SEPT. 30–OCT. 19, 1781   *419*

GEORGE WASHINGTON
and the
AMERICAN REVOLUTION

1

COMMANDER IN CHIEF,
JUNE 16, 1775

"...the Ruin of My Reputation"

A humid breath from the Delaware docks flowed through the city at dawn, bearing a promise of summer. Wagons from the country clattered over cobbled streets, early-rising servants and housewives emptied the night's pails and chamber pots into the gutters, and metallic screechings rose from the public pumps as water was drawn for the morning's chores.

As it did every day, a familiar bedlam burst upon the State House yard. In the early daylight cooks and scullery boys emerged from Clark's Inn, chasing a pack of small dogs. Whistling and shouting curses, the men seized several dogs, herded them into the tavern kitchen and thrust them into miniature treadmills, where for hours the animals turned revolving spits which roasted meats before an open fire. The odors of wood smoke and cooking beef drifted through a grove of ancient walnuts and over the yard itself. Philadelphia was waking to the warmest day of the young season. It was June 14, 1775.

The workaday sounds of the morning were soon drowned by fifes and drums of militia at drill in vacant lots, where sergeants bellowed as the awkward squads stumbled through their paces.

Though its neat squares of brick buildings occupied but a third of William Penn's plan for his "green country towne," Philadelphia was the largest American city, with a population of almost thirty thousand. It was now on the verge of war, the capital of a nation whose only arm of government was an uncertain Congress of yet untested powers.

The Second Continental Congress had been in session for five weeks, keeping the city in an uproar with its debates over reconciliation or rebellion, war or peace; it had opened with an air of confidence and unanimity, which deteriorated as the awesome task of challenging the military power of Great Britain became clearer.

It was almost two months since British troops and Massachusetts farmers had fought at Lexington and Concord. A New England rabble now surrounded a redcoat army of occupation in Boston, but the siege seemed to be a forlorn cause. The undisciplined rebels lacked arms and uniforms and were clamoring to be paid. Above all, they needed encouragement from other Americans— and a commander who could mold the mob into an army. Each day travel-worn dispatch riders brought pleas from northerners to their congressmen: they must act now or it would be too late, the troops would soon disband. Four thousand disheartened volunteers had already gone home. New England was at the end of its resources.

Among the first men to appear on the streets today were congressmen on their way to the State House, where committees began their interminable meetings at seven-thirty—they would not leave the building until dusk had fallen. One of them, Silas Deane of Connecticut, complained to his wife: ". . . eleven hours at a sitting is too much for my constitution." One of the early arrivals today was John Adams of Massachusetts, an unlikely conspirator with the mild, inoffensive air of a businessman on a holiday, but like his cousin Sam he was one of the firebrands of the Congress. Today their years of secret agitation would begin to bear fruit; the cause of Massachusetts would become a national cause.

Only three weeks earlier Dr. Benjamin Church, an engaging Boston surgeon, had come to Philadelphia with an imploring letter from his fellow patriots of Massachusetts: Would Congress consent to the formation of a new government for the colony—and adopt the army lying outside Boston? The Massachusetts men had become the first to put themselves under the control of Congress, out of the old civilian fear of military power: "We tremble at having an army (although of our countrymen) established here without a civil power to provide for and controul them."

Congress dealt timidly with this unprecedented plea; after a week of debate in committee, Massachusetts was granted permission to hold an election the following year, but of Congress taking over the raffish army, nothing was said. Most delegates, reflecting the views of their constituents, moved cautiously at this step; probably no more than 10 percent of Americans were active in the revolutionary cause, and a country hesitant to proclaim its independence, though it might tolerate the creation of a temporarily free state of Massachusetts, would reject the scheme for raising a Continental army.

But Massachusetts had in John Adams an advocate far more persuasive and resolute than Dr. Church. Outside the State House, in taverns, coffeehouses and on street corners, wherever congressmen gathered, the plump forty-year-old lawyer from Braintree had been agitating for action. Adams had perhaps done more than any other American to bring the country to the brink of war; with his cousin Sam he had led the long struggle against stern British policies in Boston and was now, almost single-handedly, compelling other colonies to come to the aid of New England.

This spring, despite public apathy, Adams detected a subtle difference in the mood of the country. Only a year ago the Massachusetts congressmen had been met on the road by anxious Sons of Liberty from Philadelphia, Dr. Benjamin Rush and Thomas Mifflin among them, men with a stern warning: "You must not utter the word independence nor give the least hint or insinuation of the idea either in Congress or any private conversation. If you do, you are undone, for the idea of independence is as unpopular in Pennsylvania and the Middle States as the Stamp Act itself."

John Adams described himself as a "short, thick Archbishop of Canterbury"; he was a round little man with a girlish complexion and a tiny mouth like a Cupid's bow. He was proud, vain and quarrelsome, highly intelligent and of a painful honesty that often made his contemporaries uncomfortable. To his friends John was warm, open and humane, but toward enemies he was implacable. He had few social graces. One friend said of him, "He cannot dance, game, flatter, promise, dress, swear with the Gentlemen and talk small talk and flirt with the ladies." Adams had deplored violence and bloodshed since his student days at Harvard; he revered the heritage of English civil liberties left by "our British ancestors, who have defended for us the inherent rights of mankind against Kings and cruel priests, in short against the gates of earth and hell."

Still, he was determined that the disorganized American colonies should unite and throw off British rule. Of all rebel leaders, John Adams seemed to see the national issue most clearly. When he realized that his leadership was helping to plunge the country into war with England, he wrote, "I go mourning in my Heart all the Day long," yet John Adams never wavered. On his way to Congress he had visited the misfit army at Cambridge, a mob without uniforms and with scanty equipment, living in crude huts, its food supply dependent upon the bounty of neighboring farmers.

It was an unruly and undisciplined military democracy. Adams had seen a captain, a wrinkled little shoemaker, order a private to fetch a pail of water. "Fetch it yourself Keptin," the man said mildly. "I got the last pail." John had noted that other officers fostered equality in the ranks. Colonel Israel Putnam took raw meat to his mess and cooked it himself, like the most humble of privates.

The commander of this army of sixteen thousand was Artemas Ward, a popular veteran of the French and Indian War, a Harvard man with influential friends. He was now almost fifty, plagued by gallstones, and lacked experience in command. John Hancock, the gouty financier of the rebellion, was a candidate to succeed Ward—though he had never been a soldier, except for serving as colonel of the Boston Cadets on parade.

John Adams left Cambridge convinced that Congress must come to the aid of the New England army or give up the cause. He was one of the first to realize that this local rabble could be instantly transformed into a Continental army, if only a Southerner became its commander. Otherwise, New England must succumb, for it would enlist no recruits south of Connecticut.

John Adams had in mind George Washington of Virginia, who so often presented the final arguments in the meetings of military committees in his calm, reasoned Virginia drawl. He admired Washington's quiet courage, his reserve—his wealth, which would enable him to afford to accept the command. He had first met the Virginian almost twenty years earlier, and had been impressed by his account of the Western frontier. John Adams had convinced himself that the man to unify the army, and the country, was Washington.

Shortly before nine o'clock, when the committees had disbanded for the opening of Congress, Sam Adams appeared in the State House yard, passing briskly beneath the young sycamores at his daily constitutional. He looked even less the part of a conspirator than John, a taller man with a bland, inoffensive expression that masked a daring political radical. A contemporary Tory wrote of Sam: "He understood human Nature so well, that he could turn the Minds of the great Vulgar as well as the small into any Course that he might chuse . . . Mr. (S.) Adams was all serpentine cunning."

John Adams fell into step with his cousin in the yard and took his arm. "I'm going to propose that we adopt the army today," he said. Sam did not reply. "And I'm going to propose Washington as Commander in Chief." Sam merely nodded. "Don't you agree that we must act now, to pull the rest of them along?" Sam nodded. "The Hancock people are all talk," John said. "There's no movement for him—it's mostly jealousy of Virginia . . . If we can make our proposals today we can soon get a nomination."

Sam continued to walk wordlessly. John was not dismayed; he knew that his mercurial cousin could hardly bring himself to speak of war. Sam was a political idealist who pretended that a few bands of militia could win independence of the country. When there was talk of a large standing army, he was apt to snort, "Cromwell!" and launch a tirade on the threat to the liberties of civilians. At last Sam agreed to second the nomination of Washington and they went into the State House.

The East Room was packed with men—fifty-six congressmen crowded about small tables that almost touched one another. From the president's chair, John Hancock frowned in the strong morning

light as if his gout had troubled him during the night. He sat stiffly
upright, looking about with a vain and indolent expression. In odd
contrast a rising sun beamed from the carved back of the chair just
above Hancock's head. The president was fond of ceremony and
allowed none to forget that he was colonel of the Boston Cadets.
His passage through Philadelphia streets was a public spectacle,
with a bodyguard of cavalrymen trotting before his glittering carriage. His fellow congressmen regarded Hancock with a rather
amused tolerance, though he was known as one of the richest men
in America and as a devoted patriot who had given liberally to the
rebel cause. Critics said that the president was the creature of the
radical Sam Adams: "Mr. Hancock was as closely attached to the
hindermost part of Mr. (S.) Adams as the Rattles are affixed to a
Rattle Snake." When Hancock threatened to free himself from
this influence, "Adams, like the Cuttlefish, would discharge his
muddy Liquid, darken the water to such an Hue, that the other
was lost . . ."

Amid the delegates in knee breeches and long-tailed coats at
their tiny tables was the arresting figure of Washington—a tall, expressionless officer in a red and blue uniform, a relic of the French
and Indian War. The colonel sat upright with the ease of a country
fox hunter, strikingly graceful despite broad hips, a sunken chest,
and long thin arms and legs. He was not fat, but he weighed more
than two hundred pounds and was about six feet three inches tall.
Delegates no longer found it odd that the Virginia colonel wore
his militia regimentals in the State House, for he had done so daily,
as if to remind garrulous delegates that rebellion meant war.

Now, in repose, his long face wore an expression described by
one congressman as a "hard countenance." His eyes were set deeply
in enormous sockets. The pale cheeks were pocked and the color-
less skin looked as if it might burn easily in the sun. About his
neck, invisible beneath his stock, the colonel wore a miniature of
his wife. His broad mouth was closed firmly, concealing defective
teeth. It was not a handsome face, nor one that men remembered
clearly. No painter would ever catch this face precisely. It was a
mask that deceived most men. The portraitist Gilbert Stuart was
to write of Washington: "All his features were indicative of the
strongest and most ungovernable passions. Had he been born in the

forests, he would have been the fiercest man among the savage tribes."

Washington's brown hair was pulled tightly over his skull in severe military style, without a queue. His head seemed too small for the great body. Today, as usual, he sat in imperturbable calm, his light blue-gray eyes quietly watchful. He seldom rose to speak in the State House. Though he was a reserved and somewhat humorless man, Washington had inspired confidence in congressmen, Virginia governors and not a few rowdy backwoods soldiers. In conversation, as one friend said, Washington became animated and forceful: "He looks you full in the face, is deliberate, deferential and engaging."

Men did not call Washington by his first name. His friend Gouverneur Morris once joked of this with some companions and accepted their dare to greet the Virginian familiarly. Morris clapped Washington on the back with a cheery "Good morning, George!" and got for his pains a silent, icy glance of reproach. Morris never took such a liberty thereafter. It was one of the rare recorded instances of Washington's having been called George during his manhood.

The colonel was forty-three years old. He had been a civilian for the past sixteen years, and his military experience was limited to the frontier, where his largest command had been a regiment. He had won no battles and had once been captured by the enemy, yet he was known in Congress as an expert on warfare and served on all military committees.

The East Room still hummed with muted voices as John Adams stood. Hancock nodded to his old friend from Massachusetts. The delegates fell silent as Adams looked about. There was something in the speaker's manner and in the roll of his voice, an imperial self-assurance that bordered upon arrogance. He emphasized his points by thumping the floor with a hickory walking stick. Adams had a habit of thinning his lips and sucking his teeth as he drew breath into his large chest, which expanded like a bellows until he cried out. The little lawyer from Braintree proposed that Congress not only adopt the ragged army at Cambridge but also send it a commanding general. Men at nearby tables turned with frowns of disapproval, but Adams continued. After careful consideration of many men, he said, he was ready to nominate a commander in chief: "I declare without hesitation that there is but one gentleman in my mind for this important command."

Smiling expectantly, Hancock leaned back in his chair. Though he had never seen a battle, the cadet colonel fancied himself as the leader of vast patriot armies.

"The gentleman I have in mind," Adams said, "is from Virginia . . ."

Adams saw Hancock's smile vanish: "I never saw a more sudden and sinking Change of Countenance."

Washington rose abruptly from his seat and vanished into the adjoining library. The voice of Adams trailed after him. ". . . A gentleman from Virginia . . . whose skill and experience as an Officer, whose independent fortune, great talents, and excellent universal character would command the approbation of all America."

The colonel did not return for the debate which followed.

Men in the hall may have thought of Braddock's defeat as Washington disappeared—it was almost precisely twenty years since the Virginian had been ambushed in the wilderness with the British commander and escaped unwounded, though he had two horses shot from under him. He had organized survivors of the massacre for the long homeward journey and returned as a hero, with a reputation as an intrepid Indian fighter. Even George II had read of him in a London magazine and muttered over Washington's comment after his first battle in the wilderness: "I heard the bullets whistle, and believe me, there is something charming in the sound."

His frontier adventures had become part of his capital, for he acquired more than twenty thousand acres on the Ohio, some as bounty for his service, but most of them bought from other soldiers. There had been complaints from some veterans that Washington and his friends had taken the valuable bottom lands out of greed and with little regard for the law, and Washington conceded that he had "the cream of the country."

Four years after the Braddock affair, the twenty-seven-year-old Washington had taken a decisive step in creating a fortune by marrying the plump, pleasant and wealthy widow Martha Dandridge Custis. He took a seat in the Virginia House of Burgesses the same year, and though he seldom spoke on public issues, he became one of the most influential members. His reputation had preceded him this spring to Philadelphia, where it was rumored that Washington had made a speech in Virginia's historic convention even more effective than Patrick Henry's call for "Liberty or Death": "I will raise 1000 Men, subsist them at my own Expense, and march my self at their Head for the Relief of Boston." Virginians smiled at this report, but it was repeated often, and added to Washington's prestige in Congress.

He was not the most complex of revolutionaries. The Virginian, respected by congressmen as one of America's great landholders, had a scanty formal education, perhaps two or three years under a country tutor. As John Adams was to say of him years afterward, Washington was no scholar, "he was too illiterate, unlearned and unread." The colonel saw the issues of independence in simple terms, with emphasis on land and money. He had been close to Virginia's intellectual leaders as the colony drifted toward rebellion, but he did not belong to the inner circle. He echoed none of Jefferson's concern for the rights of free Britons in America and gave no sign that he was moved by the eloquence of his gifted compatriot. And yet, on those rare occasions when he turned his methodical mind to the plight of the country, Washington had spoken as forcefully and boldly as any American.

More than six years before, he had become one of the first colonial leaders to speak of war. He had written his neighbor, George Mason, to urge that Virginia join a boycott of British goods in retaliation against restrictive trade policies of Parliament. His reasoning was simple but clear:

> At a time when our lordly Masters in Great Britain will be satisfied with nothing less than the depreciation of American freedom, it seems highly necessary that some thing shou'd be done to avert the stroke and maintain the liberty which we have derived from our Ancestors. . . .
> That no man shou'd scruple, or hesitate a moment to use arms in defence of so valuable a blessing, on which all the good and evil of life depends, is clearly my opinion.

By 1774, when the final break with England approached, Washington felt that war was inevitable. He had signed a resolution condemning "the hostile invasion of Boston" when that port was closed, and had argued that further petitions to London were futile. To Washington it was "as clear as the sun in its meridian brightness, that there is a regular, systematic plan formed to fix the right and practice of taxation upon us."

Today, in a state of confusion at being confronted with the challenge that he had subconsciously sought, Washington fled the State House and left Congress to its debate.

When John Adams sat down, Sam stood at once to second the nomination. Hancock's face darkened with anger; his friends knew how deeply he resented this rebuff, this return for the thousands of pounds he had given Sam Adams to help carry on the work of the rebellion. Voices rose in opposition—Pendleton of Virginia and Sherman of Connecticut said the troops would not fight under a Southerner; the army was already being torn apart by local jealousies over command. Robert Paine of Massachusetts spoke in support of his old friend Artemas Ward. Others spoke for General Charles Lee, the remarkable English veteran who had been hanging about Congress for weeks, offering advice. Lee was at home with soldiers and diplomats of many nations, and was fluent in French, Spanish and Italian; Washington might be a frontier veteran but he lacked Lee's world-wide experience and spoke no foreign languages—he would be at a loss in case European allies came to the aid of the rebels.

Several others spoke in opposition, "more faintly expressed," John Adams observed. When the opposing members had spoken, Congress adjourned without taking a vote.

John and Sam Adams and other friends of Washington canvassed the members overnight. As John Adams said, "pains were taken out of doors to obtain a unanimity," and Washington had such a clear majority that dissenting delegates withdrew their opposition at once. Washington was absent the next morning when Thomas Johnson of Maryland formally nominated him as commander in chief; his election was unanimous. The delegates then voted to raise ten companies of riflemen in Pennsylvania, Maryland and Virginia and send them to the army at Cambridge.

John Adams wrote his wife, Abigail: "They use a peculiar kind of musket called a Rifle. It has circular grooves within the barrell, and carries a ball to great distances. . . . the Rifle Men are very fine fellows, the most accurate Marksmen in the World; they kill with great Exactness at 200 yards Distance; they have Sworn certain death to the ministerial officers. May they perform their oath."

Congress adjourned in the late afternoon and it was only then that Washington learned of his election—when a member shook his hand and called him "General." Washington asked Edmund Pendleton to draft a speech of acceptance; he would refuse the salary of $500 per month offered by Congress so that no critics could claim that he had served his country for profit. He dined at Burn's Tavern near the city and spent the evening with a committee drafting rules and regulations for the army.

The next morning, June 16, when Congress met, John Hancock spoke to Washington from the chair, saying that he had been chosen unanimously as commander in chief, and that Congress hoped he would accept. Washington read the brief speech written by Pendleton, stiffly formal phrases warmed by the colonel's obvious sincerity and made appealing by his insistent modesty:

> Mr. President: Tho' I am truly sensible of the high Honour done me in the Appointment, yet I feel great distress from a consciousness that my abilities and Military experience may not be equal to the extensive and important Trust: However, as the Congress desires I will enter upon the momentous duty, and exert every power I Possess In their Service for the Support of the glorious Cause: I beg they will accept my most cordial thanks for the distinguished testimony of their Approbation.
>
> But lest some unlucky event should happen unfavourable to my reputation, I beg it may be remembered by every Gentn. in the room, that I this day declare with the utmost sincerity, I do not think my self equal to the Command I am honoured with.
>
> As to pay, Sir, I beg leave to Assure the Congress that as no pecuniary consideration could have tempted me to have accepted this Arduous employment [at the expence of my domestt. ease and happiness] I do not wish to make any proffit from it: I will keep an exact Account of my expences; those I doubt not they will discharge and that is all I desire.*

---

* Except for the words in brackets, inserted by Washington, the copy of this speech is in the handwriting of Pendleton.

Congress named a three-man committee to draft a commission and instructions for the general. They then decided to choose two major generals, to be paid $166 a month, and five brigadiers at $125 a month. The pay scale ran down to captains at $20 a month, lieutenants at $13⅓ and privates at $6⅔, salaries approved over the objection of John Adams, who was shocked by their extravagance.

When the long session was over, Washington went out to dine with a friend, Dr. Thomas Cadwalader, and spent the evening alone at his lodgings.

It was perhaps this evening when he met Patrick Henry and talked of the enormous task which lay before him. Henry saw that the colonel was in the grip of strong emotion as tears welled in his eyes: "Remember, Mr. Henry, what I now tell you: from the day I enter upon the command of the American armies, I date my fall, and the ruin of my reputation."

John Adams wrote to Abigail in triumph:

> . . . I can now inform you that the Congress have made choice of the modest and virtuous, the amiable, generous, and brave George Washington, Esquire, to be General of the American army, and that he is to repair, as soon as possible, to the camp before Boston. This appointment will have a great effect in cementing and securing the union of these colonies . . .

Adams wrote soon afterward:

> There is something charming to me in the conduct of Washington. A Gentleman of one of the first fortunes upon the Continent, leaving his delicious retirement, his family and friends, sacrificing his ease, and hazarding all in the cause of his Country!
> . . . His views are noble and disinterested. He declared when he accepted the mighty trust, that he would lay before us an exact account of his expenses and not accept a shilling for pay . . .

Washington began a week of hectic activity—meetings to help plan for the army, seeking ways to feed, supply and pay the troops and raise reinforcements. He had recently bought five military books, probably all those that could be found in Philadelphia, and pored over them in spare moments. He sent home his cumbersome carriage and bought a light phaeton for the trip to Cambridge, bought harness and a saddle, a letter case, a map and glasses "for the use of my command," and noted more hurried purchases in his account book: "&cc &cᵃ &cᵃ." He began to talk with mysterious men who were to form his spy service and advanced them money to begin their work.

Washington observed closely as Congress chose his generals—Artemas Ward, Charles Lee, Philip Schuyler and Israel Putnam as major generals, and nine brigadiers, among them Horatio Gates, an old companion of the Braddock massacre, now settled in Virginia, John Sullivan of New Hampshire and Nathanael Greene of Rhode Island. Many of the new officers were strangers to Washington, and he took no part in the squabbles between delegations as commissions were awarded. John Adams was irritated by the political infighting as each of the old colonies scrambled for its rightful share of commanders, often with little regard for the welfare of the army: "Nothing has given me more torment than the scuffle we have had in appointing the general officers."

Charles Lee, who had been Washington's chief rival for the command, was the most striking of his subordinates. At forty-four, Lee had spent twenty-five years in British and Polish armies. He had come to America to fight in the Braddock campaign, had married the daughter of a Seneca chief, was inducted into the tribe under the name Boiling Water (a tribute to his explosive temper) and became the father of twins. He had frequent fights in the army, had lost two fingers in a duel, and had once been shot by a surgeon whom he had thrashed. He had had more courts-martial "than all the officers of the army put together."

Lee had espoused the rebel cause more than ten years before and written ardently of America as an asylum for free men of all nations. He had not entirely convinced everyone of his American patriotism. Ezra Stiles, who was to become president of Yale, said of Lee: "Whether he is a pimp of the ministry or a sincere friend to public Liberty is to me uncertain." Lee had acted as a consultant to Congress, drawing plans for raising an army and writing anti-British propaganda. He corresponded with Edmund Burke and other English leaders, insisting that America could not be conquered and that the British would be wise to make peace.

Washington chose two young Philadelphia rebel leaders for his staff, Thomas Mifflin as aide and Joseph Reed as secretary. He consulted with Lee and Schuyler, who were to ride north with him. He dined out every evening, at least twice honored by members of Congress.

On June 18 he was entertained at Mullen's Tavern on the banks of the Schuylkill. The party of about fifteen included Franklin, Jefferson, Dr. Benjamin Rush, James Wilson and John Langdon, of New Hampshire—a memorable dinner in a noisy tavern redolent of wood smoke and the odors of good food and rum. After the meal someone proposed a toast: "The Commander in chief of the American Armies."

Rush was struck by the scene as the men rose spontaneously to drink a standing toast: "A silence followed it, as if every heart was penetrated with the awful, but great events which were to follow the use of the sword of liberty which had just been put into General Washington's hands by the unanimous voice of his country." Washington stood "with some confusion" to thank his friends for the honor.

That night, at last, Washington sent the news to his wife:

My Dearest,

I am now set down to write to you on a subject which fills me with inexpressible concern . . . when I reflect upon the uneasiness I know it will give you. It has been determined in Congress, that the whole army raised for the defence of the American cause shall be put under my care, and that it is necessary for me to proceed immediately to Boston to take upon me the command of it.

You may believe me, my dear Patsy, when I assure you, in the most solemn manner, that, so far from seeking this appointment, I have used every endeavor in my power to avoid it, not only from unwillingness to part with you and the family, but for my capacity . . . But as it has been a kind of destiny, that has thrown me upon this service, I shall hope that my undertaking it is designed to answer some good purpose . . . It was utterly out of my power to refuse this appointment, without exposing my character to such censures, as would have reflected dishonor upon myself, and given pain to my friends . . . I shall rely, therefore, confidently on that Providence, which has heretofore preserved and been bountiful to me, not doubting but that I shall return safe to you in the fall. I shall feel no pain from the toil or the danger of the campaign, my unhappiness will flow from the uneasiness I know you will feel from being left alone . . .*

On June 22, as Washington was packing for his journey, a rider brought disturbing news from the North—a sharp battle had been fought outside Boston, on Breed's Hill, an action to become popularly known as Bunker Hill. Casualties had been heavy. The general was now more anxious to be off to join his army.

Friday, June 23, dawned cloudy and cool, with a threat of rain, but a crowd gathered in the early morning to see the commander on his way—troopers of the Philadelphia Light Horse in gaudy uniforms, all of the Massachusetts delegation and other congressmen and many more civilians. Washington detained them to write a hurried note to his wife:

> My Dearest: As I am within a few minutes of leaving this city, I could not think of departing from it without dropping you a line, especially as I do not know whether it may be in my power to write you again till I get to the camp at Boston. I go fully trusting in that Providence, which has been more bountiful to me than I deserve and in full confidence of a happy meeting with you sometime in the Fall. I have no time to add more as I am surrounded with company to take leave of me . . .

The general emerged and made his way through the crowd to his horse, trailed by Generals Lee and Schuyler, and by Mifflin and Reed. Mifflin held a stirrup for Washington as he mounted. The party followed an army band northward through the city, surrounded by cavalry, marching militia, congressmen and civilians in carriages and on horseback. Servants trailed with spare horses and baggage, one of them driving Washington's phaeton behind two white horses.

It was a striking procession. The commander rode with impressive ease despite his bulk; as Jefferson said, he was "the best

---

* Mrs. Washington destroyed all but two of her husband's wartime letters to her, evidently on the ground that they were so intimate in nature that they should not be made public. The general contributed to the frustrations of future historians by abandoning the diary he had kept for years—at the time he took over command of the army. He was to resume his daily entries only when the war was almost over.

horseman of his age and the most graceful figure that could be seen on horseback." Charles Lee rode at Washington's side, his thin, gangling figure erect in the saddle, his horse surrounded by a pack of dogs. As usual, he kept up a constant chatter, obscene, profane, fluent, witty and brilliant—he was given to quoting Shakespeare, Homer, Machiavelli and Rabelais—his stark, bony face alight with fleeting enthusiasms, small hands gesturing rapidly. The face was dominated by an enormous aquiline nose, which was to win him the sobriquet "Naso." He wore a uniform of his own design, expensively cut but already wrinkled and unkempt.

John Adams had reservations about Lee: "He is a queer creature . . . you must love his dogs if you love him and forgive a thousand whims for the sake of the soldier and the scholar."

Philip Schuyler, the second major general, was forty-two years old, a tall, lean New Yorker with a drooping nose and large liquid eyes who rode with the athletic ease of a woodsman; he had spent most of his life as a hunter, fisherman and canoeist. Some found Schuyler arrogant, for his manner was self-assured and austere. He was related to leading New York families, the Van Rensselaers, Van Cortlandts, Beekmans and Livingstons, and was himself a wealthy landholder, lumber and grain merchant and owner of a small fleet on the Hudson. Schuyler was a veteran of the French war, a member of the New York Assembly and delegate to the Second Continental Congress.

Mifflin rode with the generals, a short, handsome, fashionably dressed man with rather sensual features who looked older than his thirty-one years. This wealthy young Quaker merchant had led the movement for independence in Philadelphia, had been active in the Assembly and the militia—and was soon to be dismissed from the Society of Friends because of his army service. Mifflin was an eloquent public speaker and a man of cultivated tastes, a member of the American Philosophical Society—and, most appealing to Washington, an ardent fox hunter. Sam Adams was sorry to see Mifflin leave Philadelphia, though he felt he would "add great spirit to our army"—but one observer, George Lux, said wryly that Mifflin courted popularity "in a low way."

With Mifflin rode his friend Joseph Reed, thirty-four, who had been president of the Pennsylvania Congress, a London-trained lawyer noted for his urbanity and skill as a propagandist. He had become well known after his published correspondence with Lord Dartmouth, Secretary of State for the colonies, in which Reed had forcefully presented the American point of view.

Rain fell as the procession rode through the Delaware River valley farmlands, and the crowd turned back about five miles outside Philadelphia. Washington's party and the cavalry escort rode from sight in the warm shower.

John Adams wore a thoughtful expression on his soft features as he gazed after the commander of his creation. The words of the congressional resolution commissioning Washington must have come to Adams at this moment—that Congress would "maintain and assist him, and adhere to him, the said George Washington, Esq., with their lives and fortunes in the same cause." But Adams had a more personal interest. He had planted his own spy on Washington's staff, his twenty-five-year-old secretary, William Tudor, under orders to report on affairs at headquarters, "for I am determined that I will know that army and the character of all its officers."

Adams was soon back in his lodgings, recording the scene in his diary. He wrote in a mood of bitter envy: "Such is the pride and pomp of war. I, poor creature, worn out with scribbling for my bread and my liberty, low in spirits and weak in health, must leave others to wear the laurels which I have sown; others to eat the bread which I have earned." He had written to his wife, "Oh, that I were a soldier. I will be. I am reading military books. Everybody must, will, and shall be a soldier."

Despite his envy of Washington, Adams helped to prepare the way for him in New England. He urged the patriot leader Joseph Warren to receive the general at Cambridge with honors and said reassuringly, "He is a Gentleman you will all like." John Hancock wrote Elbridge Gerry of the general, "He is a fine man."

And Eliphalet Dyer of Connecticut praised Washington as "discreet and Virtuous, no harum Starum ranting Swearing fellow but sober, steady and Calm." He added, "He is a gentleman highly esteemed by those acquainted with him tho' I don't believe, as to his military and real services, he knows more than some of ours."

2

THE GENERAL
MEETS HIS ARMY

"...Exceedingly Dirty and Nasty People"

A few miles outside Philadelphia the general dismounted and rode in the phaeton behind the white horses, with Lee and Schuyler crowded in beside him. The party halted in the rain to read a message brought by an express rider from the north, a report of the battle of Bunker Hill—and soon afterward met a second messenger, who carried a newspaper account of the battle. These vague reports detained the general only briefly, but an early biographer, tempted by the opportunity to dramatize the incident, was to add to the wartime legends about the general a tale that Washington, when assured that the New England rebels had not flinched before the redcoats, replied melodramatically (and uncharacteristically), "Then the liberties of the country are safe."

The party rode on with the bedraggled Philadelphia cavalrymen in sodden uniforms trailing before and after, the generals surrounded by Mifflin, Reed, William Tudor and several servants, among them black Billy Lee, Washington's companion of innumerable fox hunts. They ferried the Delaware late in the day, spent the night at Trenton and continued northward through New Jersey. Behind them in Philadelphia the radical party, led by the Adamses, pressed a hesitant Congress to prepare for war, with an appropriation of two million dollars in Continental currency and an authorized army of fifteen thousand.

"... *Exceedingly Dirty and Nasty People*"

The road followed by the party was familiar to Washington. He had ridden to New York two years earlier to enter his stepson, Jacky Custis, in King's College, and though he was then a private citizen, his progress through the countryside had been somewhat ceremonious, with halts to dine with the governors of Maryland, Pennsylvania and New Jersey. He had first known the road almost twenty years before, at the end of the French war, when he had ridden to Boston to win assurance from Sir William Shirley that as a Virginia colonel he was not to be outranked by every British regular officer in America.

In the few days since his election as commander, Washington's reputation had preceded him in the villages and towns through which he passed. He was widely, if inaccurately, known as America's richest man. He was, in fact, the hard-working manager of a farm he had inherited fourteen years earlier, whose expansion was made possible only by his marriage to Martha Custis. More than any other experience of his life, perhaps, the demands of plantation management had prepared the general for the years which lay ahead. Almost every act of his life had revealed a strong, almost compulsive, sense of responsibility and devotion to duty. At the age of fifteen he had earnestly transferred from a copybook "Rules of Civility" he had never forgotten: "Every action done in company ought to be with some sign of respect to those that are present . . . Let your countenance be pleasant but in serious matters somewhat grave . . . In speaking to men of quality do not lean nor look them full in the face, nor approach too near them, at least keep a full pace from them . . . Let your conversation be without malice or envy . . . When a man does all he can though it succeeds not well, blame not him that did it . . . Think before you speak . . ."

Washington's accounts of plantation and personal affairs reflected painstaking care and a deliberate, orderly mind; even his records of breeding his pack of foxhounds were models of clarity. Behind him, he had left his beloved Mount Vernon in charge of a twenty-eight-year-old cousin, Lund Washington, with orders to report weekly on livestock, crops, servants, weather, buildings and all else, and in return the general had already determined to set aside time to send instructions for the plantation each Sunday afternoon.

Though meticulous in his dress and attentive to every detail of his uniform, Washington displayed few obvious signs of vanity. At his wife's insistence he had posed for one portrait, by the Philadelphia artist Charles Willson Peale, who had come to Mount Vernon three years earlier.

A former saddler, watchmaker and inventor, Peale was now a fashionable portraitist. John Adams described him as "a tender, soft, affectionate creature," who "has vanity, loves finery, wears a sword, gold lace, speaks French . . ." Peale was to paint one hundred and fifty portraits of Washington, seven of them from life, and was to march with the army in a stirring campaign.

Though he sat reluctantly for Peale, Washington had resurrected his red and blue uniform from the French and Indian War. He had dozed during one sitting and confessed that he had fallen into a mood "so grave—so sullen" that Peale caught his likeness with difficulty. The portrait revealed a tall, sturdy Virginia squire of forty with a complacent air, a provincial war hero apparently at the pinnacle of his career. Peale admired Washington's taciturnity, especially since "he always avoided saying anything of the actions in which he was engaged in the last war. He is uncommonly Modest, very Industrious and prudent." (Washington's modesty and growing reserve were acquired traits, welcomed by those who had known him as an impetuous, aggressively ambitious youth.) Peale had also made a painting of Mrs. Washington on this visit, the miniature which the general now wore about his neck.

The visit had left Peale a vivid memory of Washington's physical prowess. One day at Mount Vernon when the painter and several young men were tossing an iron bar, striving for the longest throw, Washington joined them, and without removing his coat, flung the heavy bar far beyond the most distant mark. "We were indeed amazed," Peale wrote, "as we stood around all stripped to the buff, having thought ourselves very clever fellows . . . the Colonel on retiring pleasantly observed, 'When you beat my pitch, young gentlemen, I'll try again.' "

At almost every turn of the road, every village, tavern or ferry, the procession drew a band of civilians, local dignitaries who insisted upon reading resolutions of praise for Washington, or plain people curious to see him. Though the general was restive at the delay caused "by necessary attentions to successive civilities," he betrayed no impatience. Visitors took away an impression of a friendly but reserved man whose dignity suggested—with some accuracy—an indomitable will and a reservoir of sound judgment and common sense. Only once—in a formal third-person letter to a friend—was the proud, ambitious and self-disciplined Virginian to attempt an explanation of his career, saying that he had "always walked on a straight line, and endeavored as far as human frailties, and perhaps strong passions, would enable him, to discharge . . . duties to his Maker and fellow-men without . . . any indirect or left handed attempts to acquire popularity."

He also once spoke of the deliberate, jealous maintenance of his privacy: "It is easy to make acquaintances, but very difficult to shake them off, however irksome and unprofitable they are found to be after we have committed ourselves to them. . . . Be courteous to all but intimate with few, and let those few be well tried before you give them your confidence; true friendship is a plant of slow growth."

Of those who came to know Washington well, Jefferson left the most revealing estimate of his character:

His mind was great and powerful, without being of the very first order; his penetration strong . . . and as far as he saw, no judgment was ever sounder. It was slow in operation, being little aided by invention or imagination, but sure in conclusion. . . . Perhaps the strongest feature in his character was prudence, never acting until every circumstance, every consideration, was maturely weighed; refraining if he saw a doubt, but, when once decided, going through with his purpose whatever obstacles opposed. His integrity was most pure, his justice the most inflexible I have ever known, no motives of interest or . . . friendship or hatred, being able to bias his decision. He was, indeed, in every sense of the words, a wise, a good, and a great man.

His temper was naturally irritable . . . but reflection and resolution had obtained a firm and habitual ascendency over it. If ever, however, it broke its bonds, he was most tremendous in his wrath. . . . His heart was not warm in its affections; but he exactly calculated every man's value, and gave him a solid esteem proportioned to it. . . .

THE GENERAL MEETS HIS ARMY

The people Washington must lead to war had yet no national consciousness. Like the generals, most Americans thought of themselves not as rebels but as loyal Britons protesting the misguided acts of a perverse ministry in London; Washington also shared with many of his countrymen the vague expectation of a brief conflict, of perhaps six months or so, likely to end in compromise when the king became convinced that Americans would fight for their rights.

As frontier traveler, soldier, farmer, importer and legislator, Washington knew intimately the history of the quarrel between London and the colonists, which had its roots in the French and Indian War. In his young manhood he had carried to French officers from the governor of Virginia a formal demand that they withdraw from the Ohio Valley; he had led the first assault on a French force in the disputed region, and had risen to command all Virginia troops. Like other Americans he had looked longingly toward the Western lands and was angered when George III, after the defeat of the French, had barred settlers from the wilderness to protect the fur trade. As a veteran, Washington had assembled his thousands of acres on the Ohio through his bounty rights and by aggressive purchases from other soldiers.

Though the French had disappeared and the Indian menace had subsided, the British raised a 10,000-man army of occupation for America, and sought to convince colonials that these troops had come to defend them, rather than to forestall a rebellion—and then set about to tax them for support of the army. In the clamor of protest that had greeted early attempts at taxation (notably the Stamp Act and the Townshend Act) Washington spoke his mind only to friends, taking a calm, far-sighted view of each crisis, almost as if he were a neutral spectator. Americans, he said, saw the Stamp Act as "a direful attack upon their liberties," but he accurately predicted repeal of the act, since it would hurt British trade.

Some 95 percent of Americans, like the general, lived in the country, a green land of crystal streams, woodlands and fields stretching from the Atlantic to the Mississippi and from the Great Lakes to Spanish Florida and the Gulf of Mexico. Only twenty-five towns had more than three thousand inhabitants. Fewer than three million Americans were thinly scattered through the thirteen colonies—more than half a million of them black slaves.

". . . Exceedingly Dirty and Nasty People"

Though many whites were doomed to lives of ceaseless labor and struggle, they were self-reliant and independent, skilled in a variety of crafts by which they produced most necessities of life. American farmers were accustomed to hunting and fishing for a livelihood, felling trees, clearing land, making lumber; their countrymen on the frontier were as formidable as their Indian adversaries. A missionary in the South Carolina back country was appalled by what the British, Welsh, Irish, German and French immigrants had become: "The lowest pack of wretches my eyes ever saw . . . as wild as the very deer . . . the females (many very pretty) . . . quite in a state of nature, for nakedness is counted as nothing, as they all sleep together in one room." These people were preyed upon by even wilder outlaw bands, ". . . idle, profligate, audacious vagabonds! Lewd, impudent, abandon'd prostitutes, gamblers . . . horse thieves, cattle stealers, hog stealers . . . united in gangs . . ."

The small cities which had become economic and cultural centers—Savannah, Charleston, Williamsburg, Annapolis, Baltimore, Philadelphia, New York and Boston—were based on a flourishing mercantile trade, but British policy had limited manufacturing. North and South, most menial tasks were performed by blacks or by white indentured servants whose lot was scarcely easier than that of slaves.

As war with England threatened, there was bitter division in every colony, among rich and poor alike, based on differences that were to breed bloody civil war, and those in Congress who clamored for a war of independence were thought to have the support of no more than a third of the people. Many thoughtful men were convinced that the rebel cause was doomed to failure. Washington himself was to look back years later to the day of his departure from Philadelphia with a sense of wonderment that he could have undertaken this adventure with hope of victory:

> It was known that . . . the expense in comparison with our circumstances as Colonists must be enormous, the struggle protracted, dubious and severe . . . the resources of Britain were, in a manner, inexhaustable, that her fleets covered the ocean, and that her troops had harvested laurels in every quarter of the globe. Not then organized as a nation, or known as a people upon

the earth, we had no preparation. Money, the nerve of war, was wanting. The sword was to be forged on the anvil of necessity.

Yet some astute Englishmen were apprehensive at the prospect of war on the rugged continent that lay at least a month away by transport. Adjutant General William Hervey predicted that the rebels would defeat the redcoats by retreating into the wilderness. "Taking America as it at present stands," he wrote, "it is impossible to conquer it with our British army . . . Our army will be destroyed by damned driblets—America is an ugly job—a damned affair indeed." And gouty old William Pitt had shaken his cane and cried to Parliament, "you cannot conquer the Americans . . . I might as well talk of driving them before me with this crutch!"

As Washington's party approached New York the general was warned that he should not take the ferry from the usual crossing at Paulus Hook, since a British warship in the harbor might send a boat's crew to seize him. The party was advised to ride up the Hudson to cross at Hoboken. A committee of the New York Provincial Congress met Washington in Brunswick to report that the divided city was a no man's land. The general would be safe enough on land, though the Royal Navy held the harbor. And William Tryon, the royal governor of New York, planned to enter the city the next day just as Washington did. It would be wise to avoid Tryon, since a meeting of the two leaders might set off a riot. Loyalists were so strong in the New York Assembly that they had prevented the levying of taxes, conscription of soldiers, and even the dispatch of delegates to Philadelphia. This perplexed body reflected the division of the country; only yesterday it had ordered two militia companies to stand by in the city, one ready to greet Washington, and the other Governor Tryon, "whichever shall first arrive."

The generals crossed the Hudson without incident the next morning—before Tryon arrived—and were greeted at a landing which lay near the future Canal Street entrance to the Holland Tunnel. A crowd of thousands—militiamen, assemblymen, local patriot leaders, Tories, and women and children—had gathered, waiting for a glimpse of the new commander. Washington had

". . . Exceedingly Dirty and Nasty People"

never known such a reception, but the expression of dignified calm remained on his long face throughout, as if he had been accustomed to public acclaim from birth. He doffed his hat, a disgusted Tory onlooker said, to "the repeated shouts and huzzas of the seditious and rebellious multitude." The party then rode a short distance to the home of Leonard Lispenard, which overlooked the river from a hill.

While the generals were dining, a dispatch rider from the north arrived with messages for Congress, and when New York assemblymen insisted that the dispatches contained further news of Bunker Hill and should be read, Washington reluctantly opened a letter. He read a description of the little battle, including a report of casualties: sixty or seventy Americans killed and at least one hundred wounded—but though the rebels had been driven from Breed's Hill, they had killed or wounded some 1,000 of the 2,400 redcoats. Enemy losses might be exaggerated, as the Massachusetts leaders hinted, but it was clear that the untrained New England civilians had stood up to the British professionals in open battle. These men might be expected to become good soldiers.

There was also news of a powder shortage in Cambridge, but Washington was assured that an emergency supply had already been sent north, though it left New York defenseless. The general paused to write a dispatch to Congress explaining his opening of the letter, and then, escorted by nine companies of New York volunteers, rode with Lee and Schuyler into the city amid a clangor of drums, bells and shouting crowds.

Mrs. Richard Montgomery, the wife of a newly commissioned general, saw Washington as the most colorful figure in the procession: "He drove a sulky with a pair of white horses; his dress was blue, with purple ribbon sash, a lovely plume of feathers in his hat."

Before this parade had ended, Governor Tryon came ashore from a British ship, astonished at the sight of the throng: "Is this all for me?" The governor was led to Broadway, where, as Mrs. Montgomery noted, "He nearly fainted when he saw the great Washington pass, attended by a crowd of patriots." The governor at first attracted only a small crowd, among them Judge Thomas Jones of the Supreme Court, but later those who had greeted the rebel generals followed Tryon home and welcomed him back to the city. "These very men," Jones wrote, "who had been not five hours before pouring out their adulation and flattery . . . to the Rebel Generals, now one and all joined in the Governor's train . . . what a farce! What cursed hyprocrisy!"

During the night Washington wrote his first order as commander in chief—instructions for Schuyler, who was to be left behind to defend New York: he must hold the recently captured posts on Lake Champlain against the Canadians and northern Indians. Above all, he must keep watch on the resourceful Tryon. If the governor attempted to crush the rebellion in New York City, Schuyler was to ask Congress for instructions. Washington left much to his lieutenant's discretion: "Your own good sense must govern in all matters not particularly pointed out, as I do not wish to circumscribe you within narrow limits."

Washington was anxious to leave early the next morning, June 26, but while Mifflin was out shopping for wine and stationery, the general was asked to appear before the New York Congress. A speaker in the crowded chamber praised Washington at length, but pointedly reminded him of the fears of many Americans:

> Confiding in you Sir . . . we have the most flattering hopes of success in the glorious struggle for American liberty and the fullest assurance that whenever this important contest shall be decided . . . you will cheerfully resign the important deposit committed into your hands and reassume the character of our worthiest citizen.

Washington read his response—probably the work of Reed—deploring the necessity of his appointment and saying plainly that the country need not fear him as a military dictator: "When we assumed the soldier, we did not lay aside the citizen." He looked forward to his return to private life in "a free, peaceful and happy country."

After the Congress had also complimented Lee and Schuyler, the party rode northward, once more accompanied by a caravan of civilians and local militia companies.

The next day they reached New Haven, where Washington reviewed a militia company of Yale students, among them the future philologist Noah Webster. Accompanied for a short distance by three companies of volunteers already raised in the small town, Washington and his officers rode northward, through New London and Wethersfield, to Springfield, Mass., where they were met by a committee from the Massachusetts Congress, including Dr. Benjamin Church, who had so recently visited Philadelphia to plead the cause of the New England rebels.

On Sunday, July 2, the generals reached Watertown, where the provincial Congress was in session. Once more the commander was delayed by a burst of oratory, this time from an earnest speaker who warned that the volunteer soldiers he was to command, though "naturally brave," lacked experience in "things most essential to the preservation of health, and even life." Even more candidly, the speaker conceded that New England troops were dirty and intemperate. The general responded with an odd little speech, expressing his confidence that any shortcomings would be overcome by zealous officers and obedient men. As to his personal sacrifice, he said, he had given up his domestic life in the unselfish spirit of Massachusetts, "a firmness and patriotism without example in modern history."

Charles Lee also spoke, tersely for once, though in a wryly jocular vein that may have baffled his audience, "You may depend, gentlemen, on my zeal and integrity. I can promise you nothing from my abilities."

Later in the morning Washington and his party rode with a troop of cavalry and a few civilians the last three miles into Cambridge, where he was to take command of the army. The Sabbath calm was unbroken, and except for a few loafers around the college buildings no one was in sight. There was no welcome for the commander in chief. Musicians who had been mustered earlier in the morning had been dismissed, since there was no word of the general's approach. Even the siege lines were silent, though a British bombardment had ceased some hours earlier—and it was not long since some Stockbridge Indians had killed half a dozen redcoat pickets with bows and arrows. Washington and Lee went to the home of Samuel Langdon, the president of Harvard, which they took over, except for one room reserved for Langdon. Several camp diarists dismissed the memorable day as laconically as Private John Kettel, who wrote, "Nothing new."

Washington met several of his general officers, among them the man he had come to replace, Artemas Ward, the stern, pious commander of the New Englanders, a Harvard graduate who had won rapid promotion in the French and Indian War. Ward, who was five years older than Washington, and now in ill health, felt his commission as the senior major general should have gone to an abler man, but added firmly, "I am still ready to devote my life in attempting to deliver my native country from insupportable slavery."

The new commander also met Israel Putnam, a barely literate farmer, tavern keeper and Indian fighter who had risen to high station by marrying a rich widow. More than ten years earlier, Old Put, as his troops called him, had founded a future industry by bringing three donkeyloads of Cuban cigars to Connecticut, evidently the first seen there.

New Englanders still told the tale of a British officer bested by Old Put in a duel during the French and Indian War. An irate redcoat had stormed out to challenge Putnam and found him seated on a keg, puffing his pipe. Put said, "I'm no good with pistols. They'd give you an unfair advantage. Here's a powder keg with a fuse in it. If you'll sit down, I'll light the fuse and the one who dares to sit the longest will be the bravest." The fuse sizzled until the flame was an inch from the keg before the Englishman fled— only to discover that the keg contained not gunpowder but onions.

Connecticut's Congressman Silas Deane, a visitor in the Cambridge camp, wrote admiringly of Putnam: "He is the toast of the army. He is no shake-hand body; he is therefore totally unfit for anything but fighting."

Washington gave Putnam his commission as major general, which was eagerly accepted. But the commander passed out no more of the nine brigadier's commissions, for it was soon obvious that Congress had blundered. Senior officers had been superseded by their juniors and the touchy New Englanders had been grumbling since they learned of the new ranks from newspapers. As Ward said, the appointments had "a tendency to create Uneasiness among us." Washington understood that the errors might throw the army "into the utmost disorder." In fact, two new brigadiers, Seth Pomeroy and Joseph Spencer, had left camp in disgust when they learned they were to be ranked below their subordinates, and a third, one of the most valued officers, Lieutenant General John Thomas of Massachusetts, threatened to resign.

In the late afternoon Washington rode with Lee and Putnam to inspect the front where his troops faced the enemy. A nine-mile crescent of trenches stretched from the Mystic River on the north, past Cambridge, to the village of Roxbury on the south. From the mainland side Boston was virtually surrounded, but many British warships lay in the harbor, and since there was no rebel navy to challenge them, the way to the sea was open. The enemy might embark at will. Washington rode to Prospect Hill in the northern sector, looking eastward through his glass across green tidal flats and Back Bay to Boston, on its tongue of land which lay like a misshapen crab's claw in the broad waters.

The small city occupied most of a peninsula which was virtually an island, its southern tip joined to the mainland by a causeway some fifty yards wide. Both rebels and redcoats had fortified lines across this isthmus. Washington saw enemy works about the city, and on the mainland side—no more than a mile from his own lines —he could see British sentries around Bunker Hill and Charlestown, which the enemy had held since the battle in June. Two floating batteries of British cannon were anchored in the Mystic, and a twenty-gun warship lay in Back Bay guarding the foothold on the mainland from rebel attack.

Washington saw that his line had great potential strength. To the north, near the Mystic, it crossed three commanding knolls— Winter, Spring and Prospect Hills; the center was anchored by redoubts near Cambridge; southward, where its trenches shielded Roxbury, the line was dominated by a gun position that looked down on Boston from a steep, rocky hill. To the east of Roxbury, lying so near Boston that they could not have escaped the general's notice, were the unoccupied hills of Dorchester Neck, from which long-range cannon could shell the city, if ever the army had such guns. Washington's first problem as commander in chief was immediately clear: the British were not truly besieged, since they

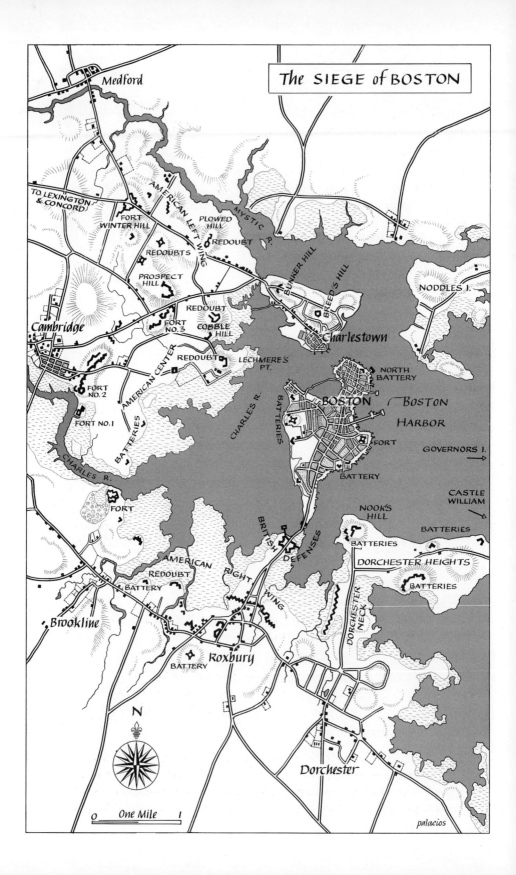

could leave when they wished; they could not be budged until he acquired big cannon, and a bombardment would destroy much of the city; but if the armies settled into a stalemate, the British might assault the mainland once more and scatter the rebel force.

Washington—or perhaps Lee—noted that the siege line might be improved. Some redoubts had been hurriedly built and were vulnerable, and the approaches by water were unfortified; a British night attack might overrun the trenches. If the enemy was to be held in Boston there was work to be done, and as Charles Lee complained, the army's officers knew little or nothing about siege operations: "We were assur'd at Philadelphia that the army was stocked with Engineers. We found not one. We were assur'd that we should find an expert of artillery. They have not a single Gunner." The men in ranks, he said, were "very fine fellows," but were undisciplined.

After his first inspection, Washington, according to army tradition, was entertained at a lively party in Ward's headquarters, where an officer was hoisted, "chair and all, upon the table, and gave the company a rollicking bachelor's song, calculated to make the immobile features of the chief relax. . . . Glasses clinked, stories were told, and the wine circulated." The next morning, July 3, 1775, as forty-two picked fifers and drummers marched and played and three hurriedly assembled regiments stood at attention, Artemas Ward surrendered command of his New England troops to Washington and the Army of the United States was born.

It was, as one lieutenant wrote home, a ceremony of a "grate Deal of grander."

Washington turned to Lee for supervision of the work on the fortifications, and the army was transformed overnight. Thousands of men were at work by 4 A.M. each day and dug until 11 A.M., when the heat compelled a rest. Lee protested that he was pushed almost beyond endurance, attending to chores that should have been performed by others, but he was proud of the accomplishments of the next few days:

> . . . I have scarcely an hour's time in a week upon my hands. Our lines are fourteen miles in extent, and I am scamperer General. I am seldom less than twelve hours on horseback. The want of engineers has occasioned a fatigue to me scarcely credible. . . .

I do not believe there is one capable of constructing an oven. However . . . three or four days more hard labour will make us so secure that I flatter myself not a single post can be forced without a loss of men too great for the enemy to spare.

Washington inspected the lines, then turned to his troops in their hovels behind the trenches and discovered a remarkable camp. An army chaplain, the grandfather of Ralph Waldo Emerson, left a picture of the scene that greeted the commander: ". . . every tent is a portraiture of the temper and taste of the persons that encamp in it. Some are made of boards, some of sailcloth . . . Others are made of stone and turf . . . Birch and other brush. Some are thrown up in a hurry . . . others are curiously wrought with doors and windows done with wreaths and withes, in the manner of a basket." In the midst of this jumble of huts stood precise rows of handsome tents with marquees, homes of the Rhode Island troops of Nathanael Greene, reputed to be the best disciplined regiments of the army.

The commander was dismayed by the appearance of most of the troops, "the most indifferent people I ever saw . . . exceedingly dirty and nasty people." Men wandered through camp as they pleased and shrugged off all attempts at discipline. Washington marveled that the men "regard their officers no more than broomsticks," refused to salute, threatened to shoot them or pulled them from their horses and thrashed them. The general found the spirit of democracy among New England regiments appalling; he was hard put to preserve the dignity of his officers. He reprimanded a lieutenant for "infamous conduct in degrading himself by voluntarily doing the duty of an Orderly Sergeant," and became almost apoplectic with rage when he saw a captain of his bodyguard meekly shaving a private.

Washington was also plagued by challenges to his administration of the army. When a group of soldiers protested the commissioning of young Ebenezer Huntington, saying some senior officer deserved his place, Washington scolded them for interference:

. . . as subversive of all subordination, discipline, and order . . . To yield to it would be in effect to surrender the command of the army to those, whose duty it is, and whose honor it ought to be, to obey. Commissions should ever be the reward of merit, not of age, and I am determined . . . to reward a deserving, active officer, whatsoever may be his standing in the army, or the pretensions of those, who have no other merit than that of having been born or enlisted before him.

Desertion, theft, violence, threats of mutiny and insolence toward officers were common, and corruption was rife among the army's doctors. Washington reported indignantly: "Many of the surgeons are very great rascals . . . often receiving bribes to certify indispositions," and drawing "medicines and stores in the most profuse and extravagant manner for private purposes."

The general turned energetically to the disciplining of his men, putting them to work and punishing shirkers and mutineers. Deserters who were caught were stripped before their regiments, given thirty-nine lashes on their bare backs and then drummed out of the army. Other miscreants were forced to stand in pillories or to sit for hours on wooden horses. Washington cashiered three colonels, one of them for fraudulent accounts. He discovered that some officers drew pay for their minor children, for men who were not on the rolls and for soldiers who had been sent to work on the officers' farms.

After three weeks, Washington concluded that he was molding the mob into an army: "We mend every day and I flatter myself that in a little Time, we shall work up these raw Materials into good Stuff."

3

BOSTON BESIEGED

"We Do Nothing But Watch"

To the thousands of New England civilians who flocked to the Cambridge camps, Washington was the chief attraction, a visible symbol of the rebellion.

In his first weeks some of his troops failed to recognize him. One day after he was refused entry to the camp by a determined sentry, the general bought a blue silk ribbon to wear across his chest as a badge of recognition, "to distinguish myself." In public, Washington invariably wore his new blue and buff uniform, epaulettes, an elegant sword, a black cockade in his hat—and now the shimmering ribbon. Most of those who saw him were reassured by his self-confident air. Dr. James Thacher, a Massachusetts surgeon, was impressed by his first glimpse of the commander: "It was not difficult to distinguish him from all others. His personal appearance is truly noble and majestic, being tall and well proportioned." Abigail Adams, who met the commander about this time, reported to her husband: "You had prepared me to entertain a favorable opinion of him, but I thought the half was not told me. Dignity, with ease and complacency, a gentleman and soldier look agreeably blended in him. Modesty marks every line and feature of his face."

The general was undoubtedly aware that he was the center of attention, but one critic escaped his notice—an anonymous parodist who sketched the camp and its commander to the tune of "Yankee Doodle," a traditional British ballad that was to become so peculiarly the army's own:

> And there was Captain Washington,
>   And gentlefolks about him.
> They say he's grown so tarnal proud
>   He will not go without 'em.
>
> He got him on his meeting clothes,
>   Upon a slapping stallion.
> He set the world along in rows,
>   In hundreds and in millions.
>
> The flaming ribbons in his hat,
>   They look'd so tearin' fine ah,
> I wanted pockily to get
>   To give to my Jemima.

His troops, though they kept watch on him constantly for clues to their future, were slow to penetrate Washington's reserve; the general spoke little but seemed to miss nothing, for his orders catalogued their myriad sins and their needs as well. They saw him frequently on the lines, vigorous and alert, and inevitably with the mulatto slave Billy Lee at his side. By degrees the troops succumbed to his efforts at discipline, and dug his everlasting trenches and shored up small forts in the defenses. They judged the commander was hard but fair, firm in his dealings with officers and, above all, forever vigilant. Gradually they became aware of Washington's iron will. The first Virginia troops in camp undoubtedly brought tales from the general's past, including one of his grim punishment of mutineers in the French War, luckless men he had hanged from gibbets forty feet high as an object lesson to survivors.

Soldiers noted that the general never laughed and his smiles were fleeting, and so they treasured a headquarters story of a rare outburst of his laughter. Washington was drinking wine with officers, according to this tale, when firing broke out along the lines. The generals hurried out, except for Nathanael Greene, who could not find his wig. Charles Lee called, "Look for it behind the mirror," and when Greene turned to the glass he saw that the

wig was on his head. Washington roared with almost uncontrollable laughter.

British propagandists were not slow to attack Washington, first
depicting him as a man of lusty sexual appetite. Someone in Boston added a forged paragraph to an intercepted letter from Benjamin Harrison to Washington:

> As I was in the pleasing task of writing to you, a little noise
> occasioned me to turn my head around and who should appear
> but pretty little Kate, the washerwoman's Daughter over the way,
> clean, trim and rosy as the morning. I snatched the golden glori-
> ous Opportunity, and but for that cursed Antidote to Love,
> Sukey, I had fitted her for my General against his return. We
> were obliged to part, but not until we had contrived to meet
> again; if she keeps the appointment I shall relish a week's
> longer stay. I give you now and then some of these adventures
> to amuse you and unbend your mind from the cares of War.

Tory newspapers delighted in the picture of Harrison ". . . de-
bauching all the pretty girls in his neighborhood on purpose to
raise a squadron of whores to keep his old General warm during
the winter quarters."

This was only the beginning of personal attacks on Washington
by the enemy. The general was frequently assailed for his dis-
loyalty to the king. One such letter from a one-time Virginia friend,
the Tory Jonathan Boucher, denounced Washington:

> . . . I despise the man who, for any motives, could be induced
> to act so mean a part.
> You are no longer worthy of my friendship; a man of honour
> can no longer without dishonour be connected with you. With
> your Cause I renounce you . . .

The general was also under criticism from the army's support-
ers—from armchair strategists in Congress, from newspapers and
assorted civilians, "above all in taverns," men who complained
that the American army was content to lie in camp and consume
public stores. As Washington wrote: "murmurs began to be audi-
ble that the army was inactive; and that a superiority of numbers
might justify an attempt against the town."

"We Do Nothing But Watch"

One of the general's first tasks was to woo the generals who had been offended by Congress. Seth Pomeroy, who had gone home, was probably too old for active service, but John Thomas and Joseph Spencer were valuable officers. Charles Lee seconded Washington in urging Thomas to remain: "For God Almighty's sake, for the sake of everything that is dear . . . for the sake of your country, of mankind, and let me add of your own reputation . . ." Thomas succumbed, but not until another Massachusetts general, thirty-eight-year-old William Heath, agreed to accept him as his senior. Spencer also returned, after a squabble. Fifty of his officers wrote protests in his behalf and the Connecticut Assembly intervened with Congress, but when these maneuvers turned the army against him, Spencer swallowed his pride and rejoined his troops.

John Adams observed from Philadelphia the opening of the war-long struggle for rank and prestige:

> I am wearied to death with the wrangles between military officers, high and low. They quarrel like cats and dogs. They worry one another like mastiffs, scrambling for rank and pay like apes for nuts . . .

Among younger officers, Washington found men who were to serve faithfully to the end. There was Nathanael Greene of Rhode Island, a thirty-nine-year-old fighting Quaker who had been expelled from his church for serving in the militia, a stout, florid former ironworker who walked with a limp. Rejected as a Home Guard officer because of his infirmity, Greene had joined as a private, and after service in the Rhode Island Assembly, had become commander of the state militia. A self-educated soldier, who was seldom without a book in his pocket, Greene was an avid reader of the military historians Saxe and Turenne. The Rhode Islander, an able troop leader and devoted to the cause, quickly won Washington's confidence.

There was also one of Greene's young friends, Henry Knox, twenty-five, a bull-voiced survivor of street fights among South Boston gangs, who weighed almost three hundred pounds. The son of a bankrupt shipmaster, Knox had made his own way as owner of The London Bookstore, which had become a social center in occupied Boston. By reading and with training from British officers Knox had become an expert artilleryman and an amateur engineer. He had married Lucy Flucker, the daughter of the royal secretary of Massachusetts, had rejected the offer of a British army commission, and fled Boston to join the rebels. Despite the frequent braying of his formidable laughter and the faultless cut of his handsome uniforms, Knox was a hard-working soldier. The works built under his direction at Roxbury were the strongest of the entrenchments facing Boston. Oddly enough, though second in command of artillery, Knox was still a civilian.

Another officer who arrived about this time was the Englishman Horatio Gates, whom Washington had known for many years. The illegitimate son of a duke and a godson of Horace Walpole, Gates was also a veteran of the Braddock massacre, a clumsy, near-sighted bear of a man who wore thick spectacles and combed his thin gray hair across his skull to conceal his baldness. Gates had risen no higher than the rank of major during long service in the British army. Though profane and argumentative, he was apt to defer to any challenger out of some sense of inferiority. Nonetheless, his long experience made Gates valuable to Washington in the administration of the new army.

Since his arrival in Cambridge, Washington had sought an accurate count of the army's strength, but returns that should have been made "in an hour" did not reach him for a week. The final returns were alarming—only 13,000 of an expected 20,000 were fit for duty, and though there were but 7,500 British troops in Boston, the commander felt that he needed overwhelming superiority of numbers. Food supply, which had been haphazard since the volunteers had swarmed to Boston in the spring with stuffed pockets and haversacks, was organized under John Trumbull, the son of Connecticut's governor.

Washington was aware that bitter hostility between state troops endangered the army, and on July 4 he reminded the troops that they were colonials no longer, but soldiers of The United Provinces of North America, "and it is hoped that all distinction of colonies will be laid aside, so that one and the same spirit may animate the whole." It was a problem he would never conquer.

One Massachusetts officer reported that his troops "complain very loudly of the partiality of the General to the Virginians"—and accused Washington of court-martialing their officers to make place for newcomers from the South. The intense rivalry between North and South led Nathanael Greene to attempt to allay the fears of Virginians, "I assure the gentlemen from the southward that there could not be anything more abhorrent . . . than a union of these colonies [New England] for the purpose of conquering those of the south."

In the midst of his struggles to improve the army, Washington had a perplexing order from Congress: he was to announce that he was not fighting for independence, but only in self-defense. Congress sent a copy of a petition to George III, called a "Declaration on Taking Up Arms," a timid and conciliatory plea which proclaimed, "we have not raised armies with ambitious designs of separating from Great Britain, and establishing independent states."

Nothing illustrated more clearly the plight of the country in its state of undeclared war than this petition, largely the work of appeasers led by John Dickinson of Pennsylvania. John Adams attacked the proclamation as "a measure of imbecility" and Charles Lee fumed: "What the devil possessed the Congress to send another petition to the callous tyrant?" But when Washington had the declaration read to the troops they were taken by some of its ringing phrases and cheered so lustily as to alarm the British on Bunker Hill, who "being very fearful, paraded themselves in battle array." Washington turned back to his work of preparing the army for battle.

The mercurial Lee, a more impassioned rebel than most natives, was one of the first to insist upon a complete break with Great Britain. He scolded his friend Robert Morris, the Philadelphia banker: "For God's sake, why don't you Pennsylvanians take a firm stand on independence?" and scorned cautious men in Congress: "If they found their wives abed with the Howe brothers they would be too indifferent to interfere."

Lee prodded John Adams: "Now is the time to show your firmness. If the least timidity is displayed, we and all posterity are ruined . . . Do not go hobbling on, like the prince of Lilliput, with one high-heeled shoe, one low one." He urged Congress to confiscate Loyalist property, repress the anti-war Quakers, arrest royal governors, open American ports to European trade, and to enlist the aid of France.

Lee was offended by the least vestige of aristocratic tradition; Massachusetts officials who addressed him as "Your Honor" and Washington as "Your Excellency" made him want to "spew."

When the 7th Connecticut Regiment joined Lee's wing in late September the Englishman found a new friend, Captain Nathan Hale, a Yale-trained schoolteacher and poet who played checkers expertly and starred in football games in camp—he could kick a ball over the treetops. The general was soon teaching the young man the craft of spying, sending him out by night to make his way through the countryside.

The days of siege dragged slowly in the summer heat. Soldiers of both armies were hard put to find amusement. Fifer Caleb Haskell reported: "This morning a bad woman was taken up in the camp, in the afternoon was doused in the river, and drummed out of town." Colonel Jeb Huntington and John Trumbull resorted to a spyglass to get glimpses of women; Connecticut soldiers went into the country in search of "some white-stockinged women"; riflemen released a girl from jail, and tarred and feathered Tories; all troops drank rum when there was money, a rare occasion among the Americans. In the surrounding countryside, life went on almost as usual. The Tory chief justice, Peter Oliver, wrote:

> . . . both Armies kept squibbling at each other, but to little Purpose; at one Time a Horse would be knocked in the Head, and at another Time a Man would be killed, or lose a Leg or an Arm; it seemed to be rather in Jest than in Earnest; at some Times, a shell would play in the Air like a Sky Rocket, rather in Diversion, and there burst without Damage; and now and then, another would fall in the Town, and there burst . . . breaking of a few Panes of Glass: and during the whole Blockade . . . the whole Scene was a idle Business.

In late August Washington reported impatiently that since the enemy would not leave the Boston trenches

> we do nothing but watch each other's motions all day at the distance of about a mile, every now and then picking off a

straggler . . . In return, they often attempt to cannonade our lines to no other purpose than the waste of a considerable quantity of powder . . . which we should be very glad to get.

Nothing seemed to distract Washington's attention from the enemy. He studied their lines through his glass several times a day, alert for signs of movement and puzzled by lack of activity: "Unless the ministerial troops in Boston are waiting for reinforcements, I cannot devise what they are staying for." Washington was unable to provoke the enemy into attacking.

During the night of August 26 he sent thirty-six hundred men under General John Sullivan to dig trenches on the slope of Ploughed Hill, within point-blank range of British guns on Bunker Hill. Enemy gunners shelled the position when they saw the new fortifications, but though they fired on the works for a few days they killed only four rebels, two of whom died in reckless attempts to catch the solid iron shot as they bounded over the ground.

The British continued to puzzle Washington: "Why, as they effect to despise the Americans, do they not come forth and put an end to the contest at once?" He edged closer with his own trenches, taking Cobble Hill and digging new lines on Lechmere Point, but the only response was more harmless cannonading by the British. Washington suspected the enemy of trying "to lull us into a fatal security . . . If this be the drift, they deceive themselves, for if possible, it has increased my vigilance." He had now fortified every approach to his camps, to guard against an attack across the ice when Back Bay should freeze. Whale boats patrolled the beaches each night and saddled horses were tied to trees, ready to carry an alarm to headquarters.

The first reinforcements to join the New Englanders came in July and August: fourteen hundred riflemen from the south, hunters and Indian fighters from western Pennsylvania, Maryland and Virginia. The Virginia company, led by big Daniel Morgan, had marched six hundred miles in twenty-one days. These backwoodsmen wore moccasins, hunting shirts and deerskin leggings, and carried slender long-barreled weapons.

The riflemen astonished the camp with their marksmanship, riddling a target "the shape of a moderate nose" from a hundred and fifty yards or more, and soon made themselves known in Boston as the "shirt-tail men, with their cursed, twisted guns, the most fatal widow and orphan makers in the world." British regulars became so respectful of the long weapons that "nothing is to be seen over the breastworks but a hat."

The riflemen were as formidable in camp as in the field. When one of their unruly sergeants was jailed and set free by other riflemen, one of the rowdies was sent to the prison pen in Cambridge for safekeeping. About thirty outraged riflemen ran into town to release their companion, and Washington subdued the mutineers only by turning out a 500-man guard. The riflemen were fined twenty shillings each, but their behavior did not improve notably. Washington was forced to forbid them to drink cider, and to desist from nude swimming in the Charles River before passing women.

The sharpshooters were increasingly a burden. Artemas Ward wrote: "They do not boast so much of the Riflemen as heretofore. Gen. Washington has said he wished they had never come; Gen. Lee has damned them and wished them all in Boston; Gen. Gates has said, if any capital movement was about to be made the Riflemen must be removed from this camp."

A band of Virginia riflemen who came into camp late in the year had an encounter with the New Englanders that became part of the army's folklore. When Colonel John Glover's Marblehead fishermen hooted with laughter at the sight of the ruffled hunting shirts, fringed breeches and moccasins of the Virginians, the regiments exchanged angry catcalls and the air was suddenly full of snowballs and fistfights broke out.

Washington galloped toward the camp. Billy Lee dismounted to lower fence rails, but the general sailed over the black's head into the field where a thousand troops struggled, men in buckskins grappling with those in blue pea jackets and flopping white trousers. This was the scene, at least as remembered by ten-year-old Israel Trask, a lieutenant's son, who saw Washington at that moment: "He threw the bridle of his own horse into the servant's hands, sprang from his seat, rushed into the thickest of the melee, seized two tall brawny riflemen by the throat, keeping them at arm's length, talking to and shaking them."

"We Do Nothing But Watch"

The boy remembered for years the spectacle of the outraged general shaking the riflemen as if they had been schoolboys, and combatants fleeing Washington's wrath.

For months, even before Washington assumed command, Congress had looked covetously to Canada. When Canadians declined an invitation to join the rebellion, Congress sent an expedition to the north, to strike up the Hudson and Lake Champlain to Montreal. Philip Schuyler and Richard Montgomery were ordered to Fort Ticonderoga, from where they were to launch the invasion, providing that "it will not be disagreeable to the Canadians." Canada was defended by only seven hundred British regulars under General Guy Carleton, but with their Indian allies and civilian reinforcements the redcoats held off Schuyler's two thousand for weeks, surrendering Fort St. John only after a siege. In November, at last, as winter was closing in, Montgomery moved against Montreal.

In midsummer, as he studied the Canadian problem, Washington suggested a second line of attack from the east—up the Kennebec River and down the Chaudière River to the St. Lawrence, and Quebec. He detached a 1,000-man assault force from his army, including a few Virginia riflemen, under the command of Benedict Arnold of Connecticut, a newly commissioned colonel. Second in command was the muscular six-foot Daniel Morgan of Virginia, a veteran who had been a teamster with Braddock. There were also several volunteers, among them the brilliant nineteen-year-old lawyer Aaron Burr. The column left the camp in mid-September.

Rifleman Jesse Lukens, who marched a few miles with the little army, watched wistfully "with a wet eye" as his companions moved northward without him, gone, as he said with a notable lack of prophetic vision, "to scale the walls of Quebec and spend the winter in joy and festivity among the sweet nuns."

The expedition began auspiciously enough at a halt in Massachusetts where the men enjoyed a "three-bear barbecue," pumpkin pies and rum punch prepared by townspeople. The chief attraction was Jacataqua, an Indian beauty, half-French, half-Abenaki, known as the "Queen with the golden thighs," who so captivated Aaron Burr that he took her along on the march to Quebec.

BOSTON BESIEGED

Arnold's little army marched to Newburyport, sailed to the mouth of the Kennebec in sloops and schooners, and began their ascent of the river in two hundred newly made bateaux, clumsy craft unsuited for the portages and rapids that lay ahead. The troops made their way inland with high hopes of surprising Quebec and taking it by storm.

Hardships in the campaign against Montreal were formidable, but when Washington heard that Philip Schuyler and Richard Montgomery threatened to resign because of troubles with undisciplined troops in the north, he wrote Schuyler:

> Let me ask you, sir, when is the time for brave men to exert themselves in the cause of liberty and their country, if this is not? ... God knows, there is not a difficulty, that you both very justly complain of, which I have not in an eminent degree experienced, that I am not every day experiencing; but we must bear up against them, and make the best of mankind as they are, since we cannot have them as we wish.

As August opened, Washington discovered that he had only thirty-six barrels of gunpowder, a fraction of the stock reported a month earlier by inexperienced officers who had included in their inventories all powder ever received in camp, most of it used long since. The troops could fire only nine rounds each. If the British attacked, the army would be overwhelmed.

General John Sullivan, who was at headquarters when the report came, saw that the experience unnerved Washington: "The General was so struck that he did not utter a word for half an hour."

The commander asked his generals to approve raids on British powder magazines at Halifax and Bermuda, and appealed to Congress and the New England states for powder, and for the next few weeks depended on small supplies from colonies to the south and smugglers in the West Indies. The shortage was so severe that the Massachusetts Assembly urged civilians "not to fire a gun at beast, bird, or mark, without real necessity therefor." In camp, morning and evening guns were no longer fired, and the men were awakened by drums rather than cannon. Matters improved on August 20, when "a very seasonable supply" of powder reached the rebel camp from the south, but the situation remained critical.

"We Do Nothing But Watch"

Washington wrote as late as Christmas Day, "our want of powder is inconceivable." A member of the Massachusetts Committee of Safety who deserted told the enemy of the powder shortage, but General Gage was so incredulous as to charge that the deserter was a spy, seeking to lure the British into a trap.

Help was on the way. In December, two Frenchmen, Prenet and Pliarne, came down from Providence offering to smuggle arms to the army, and were sent to Congress with letters of recommendation from Washington. From this beginning a vast flow of French aid was to come.

As early as September 8 Washington proposed to his generals an amphibious attack on Boston on the ground that the country could not afford a winter-long siege. "To sum up the whole," Washington said, "the expence of supporting the army will so far exceed any Idea that was form'd in Congress of it, that I do not know what will be the consequence."

The generals were unanimous in rejecting the proposed attack, but Congress, confident of its military sagacity, urged on the commander by authorizing him to offer a month's extra pay to assault troops in case of success—and in case they were killed, a month's pay to their heirs. Washington's generals rejected this proposal as well.

Washington had reminded Congress that his army would soon melt away, in a plea so urgent that a committee was sent to Cambridge to confer with him:

> . . . my situation is inexpressibly distressing, to see the winter fast approaching upon a naked army, the time of their service within a few weeks of expiring, and no provision yet made for such important events. Added to these, the military chest is totally exhausted. The paymaster has not a single dollar in hand. The commissary-general, he assures me, has strained his credit for the sub-sistence of the army to the utmost . . . The greater part of these troops are in a state not far from mutiny . . . if the evil is not immediately remedied . . . the army must absolutely break up.

The committeemen arrived in mid-October—Benjamin Franklin, Thomas Lynch of South Carolina and Benjamin Harrison of Virginia—bringing $300,000 in Continental currency for the troops. The committee agreed to most of Washington's requests, including a 30,000-man army. If men could not be reenlisted from the old army, Washington should call on the colonies for militiamen.

The general entertained the congressmen at headquarters with a turtle dinner, a memorable occasion for some officers. Nathanael Greene confessed that he could scarcely eat for watching and listening to Franklin "with silent admiration during the whole evening."

The general's table seemed to become more crowded each day. He had now taken over the tall, columned mansion of Major John Vassall, a departed Tory, and the place was busy with the passage of officers, dispatch bearers, visiting civilians, politicians, servants, merchants and men seeking commissions and favors. Since Washington continued the open-handed hospitality of Mount Vernon, he found himself overnight the master of a substantial and expensive official household. The staff included a kitchen maid, a laundress, a tailor and two cooks, one of whom, the Frenchman Adam Foutz, served briefly in the kitchen before joining Washington's bodyguard. Five other servants, two of them blacks, worked in the house at unspecified duties, and three others soon joined the menage, one of them a handsome mulatto seamstress. Expenses were paid by one of Washington's aides who kept accounts for submission to Congress. The steward, Ebenezer Austin, supervised the household.

Wine was a major expense at headquarters. Austin spent £102 for Madeira in September and October, and the rate of consumption grew: one hundred and eight bottles were delivered on October 11, and a larger order arrived on October 22. The army of guests which was to descend upon headquarters throughout the war was almost always to enjoy Madeira, even in the dark days when famine threatened and defeat seemed certain. Washington regarded wine as a necessity, since it brought "cheerfulness" to his table.*

---

* Of a total of $414,000 listed as expenses by Washington during eight years of the war, more than $88,000 went for "Household Expences" of his headquarters, chiefly to serve food and drink to his streams of visitors, official and unofficial, foreign and domestic.

"We Do Nothing But Watch"

Out of lifelong habit the general rose early each morning and began his correspondence before dawn, writing to officers, state officials, congressmen, his wife, friends, Lund Washington. The burden of paperwork was to become enormous, but though he kept a series of secretaries busy, the general's insistence upon writing most letters and dispatches himself kept him at his desk for hours each day.

Civilians who passed through the lines brought Washington news of distress in Boston. More than half of the city's people had fled after the battle of Bunker Hill, and most of those who remained were poor Whig families, despised by the redcoats. Epidemics of fever and smallpox swept the city, and burial parties trailed endlessly to the cemeteries. One British official said, "You meet as many dead folks as live ones in Boston streets."

By late July, when four new regiments arrived, the British had six thousand troops on duty, with fourteen hundred more in hospitals. For weeks after the fight at Bunker Hill, doctors had worked over the wounded, removing "old nails and angular pieces of iron" from the legs of soldiers; the rebels, one surgeon said, had loaded muskets with these deadly scraps and fired low so as not to kill the redcoats, "but leave them as burdens on us."

Fuel was so scarce that many trees were felled. The Liberty Tree, a great elm under which patriots had met, was split into fourteen cords of firewood. The pulpit and pews of Old South Church were ripped out and burned, and one handsome carved pew, upholstered in silk, was split to make a pigsty. Soldiers covered the church floor with tanbark and installed a riding school, heating it with a stove which consumed books and manuscripts of a private library as kindling. The usual ration of saltfish, pork or beef was reduced by midsummer to a scanty supply of pork. The ministry shipped half a million dollars' worth of food to the garrison, but storms scattered the ships, washed cattle overboard and spoiled vegetables. Milk cows were killed for lack of hay, Boston's town bull was slaughtered. Even ranking officers felt the pinch. Lord Percy served the meat of a foal to a dinner party, and a major's fat mare was "stolen, killed and sold in the market for beef."

BOSTON BESIEGED

Jonathan Sewall, the Tory attorney general, was depressed by conditions:

Everything I see is laughable, cursable, and damnable; my pew in the church is converted into a pork tub; my house into a den of rebels, thieves, and lice; my farm in the possession of the very worst of all God's creation; my debts all gone to the devil with my debtors.

Officers struggled to keep the Boston garrison alert, scolding "Languid and Tardy" troops. Whipping posts were kept busy. Soldiers were given six hundred lashes—and sometimes a thousand—for assaulting officers.

Lack of space on transports had reduced the army's supply of Englishwomen to one for each ten men, but these were supplemented by native camp followers. The women were closely watched, their belongings often searched for stolen goods, their "scandalous depredations" in stealing fences for fuel and smuggling liquor condemned.

One officer reported somberly that the outnumbered garrison was "like a few children in the midst of a large crowd." The rebels, he said, "grow daily more and more bold, menacing us most insolently; and we fear when the days shorten, and the dark nights come on, they'll put some of their threats in execution."

Rebel propagandists tempted the redcoats with leaflets, one of them contrasting the lot of soldiers in the two armies:

American	British
Prospect Hill	Bunkers Hill
$7.00 a month	Threepence a day
Fresh provisions and in plenty	Rotten salt pork
Health	The scurvy
Freedom, ease, affluence and a good farm	Slavery, Beggary and want

All told, "it was a miserable life inside Boston for troops who had sailed from England in the belief that they were to take part in a triumphant and leisurely progress through a series of rich and repentant provinces."

The British commander in Boston was Thomas Gage, a survivor of the Braddock massacre, who had served almost twenty years in America and had been Washington's friend and correspondent. Now paunchy, fifty-five, and the father of seven, "Honest Tom" was an able officer, dignified and courteous, though lacking in imagination and aggressiveness. He had been at home in America, as a life member of the American Philosophical Society and owner of lands in New York and Nova Scotia. His wife was Philip Schuyler's cousin, a tall, slender woman of French, Dutch and Greek descent who was said to be "the man of the family." Though alarmed by the ferocity of early American resistance, Gage had expressed none of his fears in official reports to London, probably because he realized his views would be rejected. Curiously enough, he sent insistent confidential warnings to his friend Lord Barrington, the Colonial Secretary, urging that Boston's rebel leaders be seized: "Till they are sent Home Prisoners I fear we shall have no peace." Gage had foreseen that only a huge army could subdue the Americans. "If you think ten thousand Men sufficient, send Twenty, if one Million [pounds] is thought enough, give two, you will save both Blood and Treasure in the end." Lord Barrington's reaction to these reports was equally remarkable, for he honored Gage's trust by withholding them from the War Ministry and concealing them so well that they were to remain undiscovered for more than a century.

Gage's failure to cope with the wily rebel leaders of Massachusetts brought a belated reaction from London. Only six weeks before Washington arrived in Cambridge, as if to urge Gage to greater exertions, three influential major generals had been sent to Boston: William Howe, Henry Clinton and John Burgoyne. Burgoyne had exclaimed on his arrival: "What? Ten thousand peasants keep five thousand of the King's troops shut up? Well, let us get in, and we'll soon find some elbow-room." He was thereafter to be called General Elbow Room.

The four generals had planned a move against the mainland opposite Boston, the occupation of the only two heights from which cannon could threaten the city—Charlestown on the north and Dorchester on the south. Though Gage had clung to the Charlestown peninsula since his costly victory of Bunker Hill, he had refused to move against Dorchester, despite the insistence of

Henry Clinton that he do so. Gage reasoned that no American cannon could reach Boston from the hills to the south, and that if the
rebels attempted bombardment from there, his superior artillery
could blow them to bits.

Gage's report to Dartmouth on the Bunker Hill engagement was
almost laconic, deploring heavy losses but insisting that his attack
had been necessary. Only in his private letter to Barrington did the
veteran Gage concede that Bunker Hill was a foretaste of
catastrophe:

> . . . These people shew a Spirit and Conduct against us, they
> never shewed against the French . . . they are now spirited up by
> a Rage and Enthousiasm, as great as ever People were possessed
> of, and you must proceed in earnest or give the Business up . . .
>
> The loss we have sustained, is greater than we can bear. Small
> Army's can't afford such losses . . . I wish this place was burned!

Gage's report caused such dismay in London that within four
days George III recalled "the mild General" and replaced him
with William Howe. The King then moved to crush the rebellion
despite all opposition. The army and navy were to be substantially
increased and German mercenaries hired; a War Cabinet was installed. The new secretary for the American colonies was a friend
of the King's youth, Lord George Germain, a haughty ex-cavalry-
man who had been cashiered for cowardice in battle; he was reported to be a homosexual.

The recall of Gage was welcomed in Boston by his dispirited
troops, who blamed him for the failure at Bunker Hill. In early
October, accompanied by Thomas Flucker, the father-in-law of
Henry Knox, the ousted commander made a lonely departure for
London, leaving with Howe a strategic plan the generals had
worked out in weeks of consultation: he should hold Boston until
spring, then occupy New York and cut the colonies in two.

William Howe, who was regarded as a cousin by the King, was
an illegitimate grandson of George I and his mistress, the Baroness
Kilmansegg. Howe was tall and dark, and bore a strong resem-
blance to Washington. His troops admired the general for his personal bravery, his indulgent manner and reputation as a gambler

and drinking man, but Charles Lee, who had served with him for years, scorned the new commander as illiterate and lazy, "totally confounded and stupify'd" by the challenging task of conquering America. Like Gage before him, Howe gave no sign that he detected in the observant and diligent Washington an opponent who might become dangerous.

Howe soon took a mistress, Mrs. Joshua Loring, a "flashing blonde" who was frequently seen at card tables in Boston, where she "would gamble away 100 guineas or so with any pretty fellow in love with sport." Her husband, a former high sheriff of Massachusetts, was placed in charge of confiscated property and prisons, posts from which he earned £30,000 a year. Judge Thomas Jones, the Tory historian of New York, declared that Loring acquiesced in his wife's romance with Howe: "He fingered the cash, the General enjoyed Madam . . . Loring was determined to make the most of his commission . . ."

The liaison became a part of rebel folklore in a popular ballad by Francis Hopkinson:

> Sir William he as snug as a flea,
> Lay all this time a snoring,
> Nor dream'd of harm as he lay warm
> In bed with Mrs. Loring.*

The tempting sight of British supply vessels sailing into Boston and his desperate need for munitions led Washington to create a small navy of his own—an army on shipboard. Though he had no authority for this, his ingenuity left Congress no grounds for complaint. On September 2 he sent orders to Nicholas Broughton, of Glover's regiment of Marblehead fishermen:

> You, being appointed a Captain in the Army of the United Colonies of North America, are hereby directed to take the command of a detachment of said Army, and proceed on board the Schooner *Hannah*, at Beverly, lately fitted out and equipped with arms, ammunition, and provisions, at the Continental expense.

* Mrs. Loring had two sons, one of whom became archdeacon of Calcutta and the other a vice admiral in the British navy.

Washington assigned six other floating army detachments to patrol the coast and seize British ships, offering the crews one third of the value of cargoes taken. The privateers were instantly successful. On his first day out, Broughton captured a vessel loaded with fish, lumber and provisions, and in less than a month took three others, one of them laden with 2,200 barrels of flour, "a capital prize." Another vessel took a British ordnance brig from a convoy, and brought in stores Washington had sought in vain: 2,000 muskets, 30 tons of musket shot, 100,000 flints and 30,000 cannonballs. Most welcome of all was a 2,700-pound mortar that fired thirteen-inch shells, a monster whose arrival set off a celebration in camp. Israel Putnam climbed atop the mortar with a bottle of rum and christened it "The Congress," to the cheers of thousands of soldiers.

The general's tiny raiders created havoc with British supply lines into Boston, but Washington found his sailors even more troublesome than his troops ashore: "Our rascal privateersmen," he said, "go on at the old rate, mutinying if they cannot do as they please . . . the plague, trouble, and vexation I have had with the crews of all the armed vessels, are inexpressible. I do believe there is not on earth a more disorderly set." The commander was undoubtedly relieved when Congress, under the leadership of John Adams, created an American navy.

One day in late September Nathanael Greene brought a civilian to headquarters for a private audience with Washington. Greene's companion was Godfrey Wainwood, a baker from Newport, R.I., who brought a coded letter addressed to an enemy officer. Wainwood suspected that the letter, which had come to him from a prostitute, had been written by a spy.

Washington inspected the letter, a sheet covered with ciphers, addressed to "Major Cane in Boston on his majisty's sarvice," and ordered a search for the woman. She was brought to headquarters in the evening—riding horseback behind Israel Putnam, according to one story—a shrewd young woman who for hours refused to identify the writer of the letter, though Washington grilled her as he had many a witness in his career as examining justice in Virginia. The woman maintained her silence throughout the night, and only the next day did she succumb to the general's relentless questioning and threats of hanging to betray the author of the letter. Washington was stunned by her confession: "It was Dr. Benjamin Church."

Since Church was a respected patriot leader, an intimate of Hancock and the Adamses, and director general of the hospitals, Washington moved cautiously. He sent to Watertown for James Warren and other provincial congressmen, told them the story, and had Church seized only upon their advice. The doctor was all smiles when he was taken to headquarters under guard, protesting his innocence. It was indeed his letter, he said—but it was merely a message to his brother-in-law, who was in Boston. The young woman who had acted as messenger was his mistress. But though the doctor proclaimed his loyalty to the patriot cause and said a deciphering of the letter would prove his innocence, he made no offer to translate it.

Washington was positive that he was dealing with the first American traitor: if the letter was harmless, why was it in cipher, and why had it been sent in roundabout fashion through enemy hands when it could have gone openly into Boston? The doctor's replies were unconvincing, and the general held Church until the letter was deciphered by two amateur cryptographers: Church's message revealed the strength of Washington's army and described its equipment, reported the plan to invade Canada and the creation of the fleet of privateers—but also urged his correspondents to "solicit peace, repeal the acts, or Britain is undone." He had sent instructions for a secret reply: "Make use of every precaution, or I perish."

The doctor protested even now—he had the American cause at heart, he said, and had exaggerated rebel strength in the hope of discouraging a British attack. A council of war agreed that Church was lying, but was helpless to deal with the traitor, since hurriedly adopted regulations imposed absurdly inappropriate penalties for communicating with the enemy—thirty-nine lashes, a fine of two months' pay, or discharge. Washington kept Church under guard and awaited instructions from Congress.

Rebel leaders were stunned by the case. John Adams said: "I stand astonished. A man of genius, of learning, of family, of charac-

ter, a writer of liberty songs and good ones, too, a speaker of liberty orations . . . good God! What shall we say of human nature?
What shall we say of American patriots?"

The Massachusetts House sentenced Church to solitary confinement in a Connecticut prison. When he was released because of
illness several months later, the doctor sailed for the West Indies,
and his ship was lost without a trace. Actual proof of Church's
treason was not to come to light until the twentieth century, when
scholars studied the papers of General Gage.

In December, at Washington's urging, his wife undertook her
first northern journey and came to Cambridge, where she arrived
in a four-horse carriage with a coachman and postilion wearing the
red and white Washington livery, accompanied by Jacky Custis
and his wife, two of Washington's cousins of the Lewis family, and
Mrs. Horatio Gates. The flushed and smiling women emerged from
the carriage to the greetings of men at headquarters—"not a bad
supply," in Joseph Reed's phrase, "in a country where wood is
scarce." Mrs. Washington was watched closely, since gossips had accused her of Tory sentiments and whispered that she disapproved
of her husband's role. Martha soon disarmed skeptics with the
warm and unassuming manner of a Virginia gentlewoman.

Mrs. Washington was a tiny, rather shy woman of forty-four
now become fat. (She had recently ordered gloves "to fit a small
hand and pretty large arm.") Though she was not beautiful, there
was a quiet animation on her pleasant face; she had clear blue
eyes, a large hooked nose, a small mouth and a well-rounded chin.
Her clothing, though plain and muted in color, was of fine materials; she was so well groomed as to make overdressed women
acquaintances feel uncomfortable. The unpretentious Martha did
not soon recover from her astonishment at her reception as she
passed through Philadelphia: "I left in as great pomp as if I had
been some great body."

Mrs. Washington's introduction to camp life was unsettling. The
frequent cannon fire, she said, seemed to surprise no one but her:
"I confess I shuder every time I hear the sound of a gun." She
went to an outpost for a look at the enemy and reported on "Pore
Boston" in her highly original fashion: "There seems to be a num-

"We Do Nothing But Watch"

ber of very fine Buildings in Boston, but God knows how long they will stand; they are pulling up all the warfs for fire wood—to me that never see anything of war, the preperations are very terable indeed, but I endeavor to keep my fears to my self as well as I can." She observed other details of camp life with a more practiced eye. To draw the attention of men at headquarters "There are but two Laides in Cambridge," she said, "but neither of them is pritty I think."

Martha entertained in the simple style of the Virginia countryside, as she did when Samuel Cooper and his wife called and she served oranges and wine. But the sophisticated Mercy Warren, an author and political leader, was taken with the easy cordiality of Martha's greeting and impressed by "that politeness and respect shown in a first interview among the well bred." Young officers noted that the pace of social life at the Vassall house grew more hectic. Washington's aide, John Trumbull, the son of Connecticut's governor, was embarrassed by his duty of introducing "many of the first people of the land of both sexes." Women callers were numerous, among them Abigail Adams, Lucy Knox—and Lucy Greene, whose infant son had been named for Washington, the first of many thousands of the general's namesakes.

With the aid of Henry Knox, Washington had begun a search for big guns capable of driving the enemy from Boston. When Knox suggested that he bring the cannon at Fort Ticonderoga which had lain useless since their capture from the British six months before, Washington sent him off with an urgent order to bring back the big guns at all costs, "the want of them is so great that no trouble or expense must be spared to obtain them." He also gave Knox a $1,000 draft on the army's paymaster general. Knox reached Ticonderoga in the first week of December, still a civilian, and without having drawn the money; he would pay the costs of the expedition from his pocket.

Knox found most of the old cannon useless, but loaded sixty of the best on barges and scows, a weight of 120,000 pounds—in addition to a ton of lead and a barrel of musket flints—and with the aid of hired crews floated all down Lake George in windy, freezing weather. Scows sank and had to be raised, and Knox was delayed until his half-frozen men had thawed themselves. When he reached Fort George, where hundreds of horses, oxen and sleds awaited him, Knox wrote Washington, "It is not easy to conceive of the difficulties we have had in getting the cannon over the lake . . . Three days ago, it was very uncertain whether we would have gotten them until next spring; but now, please God, they must go." He promised to deliver a "noble train" of artillery to Cambridge within seventeen days—he was to be forty days on the 300-mile journey over rough country. Knox led the caravan through heavy snows past Glens Falls and Saratoga and into Albany, "almost perished with the cold." Some big guns fell into the Hudson as the caravan ferried the river, and crews labored in freezing spray to recover them.

The sleds turned down the river, then eastward into the Berkshires, over stony passes and through dense evergreen forests, skirting chasms, descending steep slopes where drivers eased the guns to safety with the use of logs and chains. The sleds emerged into the frozen lowlands and moved more swiftly, into Springfield and Framingham, then Cambridge. Knox returned to find himself the army's new chief of artillery, with the rank of colonel, but he was not reimbursed for expenses; it was to be years before he collected the $2,500 with which he had financed the expedition.

The British navy raided New England ports during the winter, but Washington refused to send help, fearful of loosening his grip on Boston. To Governor Trumbull of Connecticut, who reported the bombardment of Stonington and threats to New London and Norwich, Washington replied, "The most important operations of the campaign cannot be made to depend upon the piratical expeditions of two or three men-of-war privateers."

But in December, when he got an appeal from Rhode Island, where Tories were troublesome and British landings were expected, Washington sent Charles Lee with a hundred riflemen and a guard of thirty men. In a whirlwind tour, Lee inspected harbors and planned fortifications, frightened Tories and arrested those who refused to take oaths of loyalty. Lee was soon back in camp, eager for more action. He had urged Washington to send him to New York, where the British were likely to attack. With his usual impetuosity, Lee had declared that the vulnerability of New York made him "uneasy almost to distraction . . . for Heaven's sake why has Congress not fortify'd that city. . . . Not a single instant is to be lost . . . Not to crush the serpents before their rattles are grown would be ruinous."

Washington sent Lee southward to defend New York City while the army held Howe's force at bay in Boston.

Washington's attempt to mold the army into a continental force demanded much of his time, energy and diplomatic skill; for weeks it seemed that the New Englanders would disband rather than accept reorganization. No two state units were alike. The strength of regiments varied from six hundred to one thousand men, but when Washington tried to create regiments of uniform size, there were howls of protest. Since state troops refused to accept strange officers, many field commanders would be left without units, and would be forced out of the army. Soldiers accustomed to electing their own officers would return home if substitutes were placed over them. Washington confessed that of all his burdens, the creation of an effective officer corps "sets heaviest on my mind."

The general wrote Joseph Reed, who had returned to Philadelphia to try some law cases, "Connecticut wants no Massachusetts man in their corps; Massachusetts thinks there is no necessity for a Rhode Islander to be introduced; and New Hampshire says it's very hard, that her valuable and unexperienced officers . . . should be discarded because her own regiments . . . cannot provide for them." He found officers and men of all states unshakably stubborn, and though he made some changes, he was forced to stop short of reform and warned Congress that "the Experiment is dangerous. . . . It is in vain to attempt to reason away the prejudices of a whole army."

The army's mood became apparent when Congress sent up its Continental articles of war, which the troops refused to sign, fearing that it would obligate them to longer service. The time of the Connecticut men would expire on December 10, and the rest of the troops would leave on the last day of the year. A new army must be enlisted.

BOSTON BESIEGED

Washington gave up the attempt to form a national army, made up his new regimental rosters as best he could, and in mid-November tried to reenlist the Connecticut troops for another year. But though chaplains preached and Washington and others harangued them, almost all of the state's men marched away home, hissed and hooted by others in camp and by civilians on the roads. Many of Nathanael Greene's troops also went home, "sick of this way of life." Washington filled the ranks with raw militia from Massachusetts and New Hampshire who were to prove themselves surprisingly good soldiers—older, more settled men, many of whom had fought against the French in their youth.

More than half of the Rhode Island and Connecticut troops deserted the army in the end, leaving Washington with a mixture of new militia and veterans. By mid-December fewer than six thousand had reenlisted, less than a third as many as needed. The soldiers who remained were sometimes more disposed to fight each other than the enemy. Since wood had virtually disappeared from the neighborhood, "different Regiments," as Washington reported, "have been on the point of cutting each other's throat for a few standing locusts near their encampment, to dress their victuals with." Many soldiers ate their rations raw, and Washington feared they would soon demolish nearby houses in their quest for firewood.

Near the end of the year the commander, near the limit of his patience, wrote Reed in an angry outburst:

> Such a dearth of public spirit, and such want of virtue, such stock-jobbing, and fertility in all the low arts to obtain advantages of one kind or another . . . I never saw before, and pray God's mercy I may never be witness to again . . . could I have foreseen what I have, and am like to experience, no consideration upon earth should have induced me to accept this command . . .

4

A SURPRISE FOR
WILLIAM HOWE

"Under the Rose"

Drum rolls turned out the troops in the predawn darkness of the bleak first day of 1776 and the thinned regiments filed into the lines. The trenches were so sparsely manned that when daylight came, soldiers could see few of their companions; one sector of the line was abandoned, and would remain so for three days. More than a quarter of the troops lacked muskets, and guarded the works with crude twelve-foot spears. The challenges of the sentries had a strange ring today. Now and then a soldier called the password "The Congress," and was answered with the countersign "America!"

A new flag was run up on Prospect Hill, the British Union flag, with two crosses in a corner and a field of alternating red and white stripes, symbolic of the colonies. In defiance of the powder shortage thirteen cannon fired a salute to the new army on its birthday. Guardhouse doors were thrown open and prisoners freed. Washington's orders to the troops rang with a confidence he did not feel. He spoke of the need for training and discipline, and the sacrifices that must be made by men of the "entirely Continental army."

The British sent into camp that day a copy of an address by King George, a vigorous message to Parliament which dashed all hopes of reconciliation. The King branded the revolt of the

Americans a "desperate conspiracy," offered pardons to those who would submit to his authority, and announced plans to punish those who did not surrender.

When the British saw the new flag rise over the rebel works, they interpreted it as a sign of submission in response to the King's speech—a thought that moved even the grave Washington to make a small joke: "I presume they begin to think it strange that we have not made a formal surrender of our lines."

The commander denounced the King's address: "It is full of rancor and resentment against us, and explicitly holds forth his Royal will to be, that vigorous measures must be pursued, to deprive us of our Constitutional rights and liberty. These measures, whatever they may be, I hope will be opposed by more vigorous ones . . ." Though Washington still thought of himself as a British citizen, the King's proclamation led him to think more favorably of the move for independence.

Most of the old troops were leaving for home, and Washington could do nothing to hold them: "The same desire of retiring into a chimney-corner seized the troops of New Hampshire, Rhode Island and Massachusetts . . . as had worked upon those of Connecticut." The brief hours of daylight were crowded with the passage of troops—those who were going home, joining new regiments or squabbling with officers over their weapons, the prospect of reenlisting, the lack of pay, fuel, clothing and rum. Officers were ordered to seize all muskets, but most of them were worthless and others were smuggled from camp. Many departing New Englanders were sharply critical of Washington, resentful of floggings for having broken his stern regulations, protesting that he had accomplished no more than Artemas Ward, and that he had prolonged the siege to increase his own importance. There was order and stability only in the ranks of the militia, new regiments of quiet onlookers who for a time would be the army's chief strength.

Washington was unaware of disasters elsewhere on this first day of the year: far to the south, the city of Norfolk, Virginia, was burned by Lord Dunmore, the ousted royal governor who had been Washington's friend. To the north, General Richard

"Under the Rose"

Montgomery lay dead, a casualty of the attack on Montreal. The Canadian campaign was collapsing.

The commander was not confident that he could hold the enemy in Boston. He had raised only half his regular regiments and his five thousand militia had enlisted only until January 15, when they would leave, whatever the crisis: "Thus it is," he wrote, "that for more than two months past I have scarcely emerged from one difficulty before I have plunged into another. How it will end, God in his great goodness will direct." He was skeptical of officers who assured him that the ranks would soon be filled: "I have been told so many things which have never come to pass that I distrust everything."

He missed Reed, and urged him to return; other secretaries and aides were poor substitutes for the resourceful, self-reliant Philadelphian, whose sophistication, quick wit and wide acquaintance among leaders of every state made him invaluable as an aide. Washington complained of the loss: ". . . My time is so much taken up at my desk that I am obliged to neglect many other essential parts of my duty. It is absolutely necessary, therefore, for me to have persons that can think for me, as well as execute orders." It was to be months before Reed returned.

His very weakness led Washington to urge an attack on Boston before all of the army's strength was dissipated, and before the British were reinforced. His generals agreed, but said the army should attack only when it was stronger. He was authorized to call thirteen fresh regiments of militia, which raised Washington's hopes of getting at the enemy by bombardment or headlong assault: "Give us powder, or *ice!*" he once wrote. Stephen Moylan of the headquarters staff perhaps spoke the general's thoughts when he said, "If we had powder, I do believe Boston would fall into our hands." Many of Washington's officers, especially Israel Putnam, were equally eager to attack. Moylan wrote during a spell of warm weather, "The Bay is open, everything thaws here except Old Put. He is still as hard as ever, crying out for powder—'Ye Gods give us Powder!'"

Washington sometimes prowled the lines at night to stare across the black waters to the impregnable defenses of the enemy. He once returned to his writing desk and confessed to a mood of frustration:

> . . . many an unhappy hour when all around me are wrapped in sleep . . . I have often thought how much happier I should have been if, instead of accepting the command under such circumstances, I had taken my musket on my shoulder and entered the ranks; or . . . retired to the back country and lived in a wigwam.

The general's wedding anniversary fell on January 5, and though he felt that the plight of the army was too grave for celebrations, he surrendered to Mrs. Washington's insistence and presided over a festive dinner party on Twelfth Night, at a table laden with delicacies—sweetmeats, limes and oranges furnished by the enemy, with the aid of privateers.

On January 17 Washington had a dispatch from Schuyler reporting the death of Montgomery and heavy casualties among his men at Montreal. There was more bad news—Arnold was wounded, and the attack on Quebec had also failed. Unless Washington could send reinforcements the Canadian expedition must be abandoned, and the British would have an open road to invade New York, isolate New England and conquer the colonies piecemeal. Since he could spare no men "in the present feeble state" of his army, Washington called upon the New Englanders for new regiments and urged that they be sent to Canada before British reinforcements arrived in the spring.

An anonymous tract called *Common Sense* reached camp during the month and was recited and debated—a sensation in the army as it was among civilians. Within a few weeks half a million copies were in print. This was the work of Thomas Paine, a frail, pallid British tax clerk who had migrated to America with the aid of Benjamin Franklin and had become an editor in Philadelphia. His prophetic pamphlet brought a new radicalism to the rebel cause, setting Americans against oppression everywhere:

> O! Ye that love mankind! Ye that dare oppose not only the tyranny but the tyrant, stand forth! Every spot of the old world

is overrun with oppression. Freedom hath been hunted around the globe. Asia and Africa have long expelled her. Europe regards her like a stranger, and England hath given her warnings to depart. O! receive the fugitive, and prepare in time an asylum for mankind.

Washington praised the pamphlet's "flaming arguments . . . sound doctrine and unanswerable reasoning" and said, "I find that *Common Sense* is working a powerful change in the minds of many men."

February 12 was a night of bitter cold, and by morning the narrows of Back Bay were frozen so thickly that soldiers ran out to collect spent musket balls fired by the British. Washington studied the approach to Boston from Lechmere Point, where his lines were nearest the enemy works. In one swift rush, his infantry could be upon the British works, probably before an alarm was given.

The coming of the ice and a report that the rebels were assembling materials for new earthworks stirred William Howe to brief action. At 4 A.M. on February 14 he sent a party of cavalry across the frozen bay to Dorchester. The horsemen drove off seventy rebel sentries and captured two of them, but when they found the place with no signs of fresh fortifications, they burned a few vacant houses and returned. They were back in Boston by 6:30. William Howe was content, convinced that Washington had no plans to fortify Dorchester. The garrison was not threatened by the forbidding hills. From the moment these troops returned, Howe relaxed his vigilance and waited for spring, when he hoped to be reinforced so strongly that he could move against the rebels.

Howe's cavalrymen had hardly returned to their barracks when Washington proposed to his generals an attack across the ice. There were enough troops for the moment, he argued, almost 9,000 Continentals and 7,000 militia. The British were perhaps 5,000 strong. There was no powder for the artillery, but a swift attack with small arms would be feasible—in fact, "a stroke, well aimed . . . might put a final end to the war." They should strike at once, before the ice melted, and before the British seized the initiative.

Artemas Ward opposed the plan strongly and the other generals agreed with him unanimously—an assault would end in disaster. The British force was much stronger than Washington calculated, perhaps ten thousand strong, and in any event, the fire of Howe's superior artillery would shatter the American columns. No attack was feasible until Boston had been bombarded for several days, and the powder magazines must first be filled.

The council proposed an alternative: If Washington occupied the commanding hills on Dorchester Heights, Howe might be drawn out of his trenches and could be driven into the bay. His army might be destroyed.

Washington betrayed his disgust in a letter to Reed: "Behold, though we have been waiting all the year for this favorable event, the enterprise was thought too hazardous."

Even so, the general seemed to realize that the council's decision was fortunate for the army.

He was not yet prepared to overrule his generals, but he was convinced that they were mistaken: ". . . I am sure yet that the enterprise, if it had been undertaken with resolution, must have succeeded . . ." But, though he wrote Governor Trumbull of Connecticut that ". . . a golden opportunity has been lost, perhaps not to be regained again this year," Washington confessed to John Hancock that the frustrations he had faced in Boston—"the irksomeness of my situation"—might have made him reckless. Still, he must make some move—he was acutely aware that "the eyes of the whole continent" had been upon him during the six months he had besieged Boston, accomplishing little or nothing.

Then, as if his patience had melted like the ice in the warming bay, Washington turned with all of his energies to the planning of a move against Dorchester Heights, whose twin hills were obviously keys to the possession of Boston. If the big guns from Ticonderoga were mounted there, within easy range of the city, William Howe could not ignore them. The stalemate would be broken.

It was a move that would test the army, since it must be made in one night, before it was detected by the enemy—fortifications must be built, guns, ammunition and supplies hauled into place, new quarters for troops built. Artemas Ward had made just such a move before the battle of Bunker Hill, but the earth was now frozen to a depth of eighteen inches, and conventional earthworks could not be raised between nightfall and dawn.

Washington called to headquarters Colonel Rufus Putnam, a resourceful engineer from Massachusetts, who devised a way to raise breastworks within a few hours, through the use of chandeliers, wooden frames that could be driven into the ground and filled with bundles of bound sticks known as fascines. Behind this temporary screen, workmen would shovel earth over the fascines, making them proof against artillery fire. Washington discovered that the troops of Ward and Thomas had been making these materials for weeks.

The plan was soon complete: three thousand troops would march from Roxbury to the Dorchester hills after dark one night, guarded by five companies of riflemen, marksmen who would "gald the enemy sorely," Washington thought, if they landed from small boats. To make the new works more formidable, axmen would cut adjoining orchards and stack branches in long rows. Barrels filled with sand and stone would be stacked along the works, ready to be rolled down upon advancing redcoat columns. Doctors and their troops made two thousand bandages. Haystacks were robbed for miles around, and soldiers twisted together huge masses that weighed as much as eight hundred pounds, to be used as a screen for the three hundred oxcarts that would haul material up the hills.

Militia from neighboring towns would be called up to man the vacated works in Roxbury. To divert the attention of the enemy, big cannon scattered along the entire line would bombard Boston for two nights before the move. In case William Howe attacked Dorchester, four thousand troops under Greene and Sullivan, who would be waiting near Cambridge, would counterattack across the bay in boats, to land in exposed North Boston and seize Beacon Hill and Copps Hill.

The council made final plans on February 26. At Thomas

Mifflin's suggestion, the move was set for the night of March 4 so that the new works would confront the enemy at dawn of March 5, the anniversary of the Boston Massacre, when redcoats had first shed American blood. Leaves were canceled, and the lines were closed to all passage. Washington revealed his plan only to the Council of Massachusetts and to Congress. He explained the Dorchester move as a maneuver to "try if the enemy will be so kind as to come out to us . . . I should think if anything will induce them to hazard an engagement, it will be our attempting to fortify these heights." The general also wrote Reed of the plan but cautioned him: "What I have said respecting . . . Dorchester Heights, is spoken *under the rose.*"

General orders of the next day sought to prepare the troops for a supreme effort by forbidding them to gamble or to succumb to other "vice and immorality" that might divert them from the business at hand . . . "It is a noble cause we are engaged in; it is the cause of virtue and mankind . . . freedom or slavery must be the result of our conduct." There was one other matter: "It may not be amiss for the troops to know that if any man in action shall presume to skulk, hide himself, or retreat from the enemy, without the orders of his commanding officer, he will be *instantly shot down . . ."*

News of Washington's plan spread swiftly through the army and into the countryside and on the evening of March 2 reached Abigail Adams in her house at Braintree, not far behind the American lines. Mrs. Adams was writing to her husband of the expected attack: "I have been kept in a continual state of anxiety or expectation ever since you left. It has been said, 'tomorrow' and 'tomorrow' for this month but when the dreadful tomorrow will be, I know not."

At that moment the roar of a cannon shattered the silence. As other cannon fired, Mrs. Adams went to the door and listened. Anxious neighbors gathered to gossip of the siege. A climax was at hand, someone said; the militia from all surrounding towns had been ordered to report to the lines on Monday night. Abigail returned to her letter: "No sleep for me tonight. And if I cannot, who have no guilt upon my soul with regard to this cause, how shall the miserable wretches who have been procurors of this dreadful scene and those who are to be the actors, lie down with the load of guilt . . ."

The first gun, fired just before midnight, was followed by others at long intervals, and though they caused little damage in Boston, the British were astonished by the size of the guns Washington had mounted in his line.

Washington's cannonade was costly. Three of his mortars had burst because of the inexperience of gun crews in bedding the weapons on the frozen ground, or perhaps, as one rumor went, there had been sabotage. In the afternoon the big brass "Congress" mortar was hauled into the line by scores of straining men. Washington repeated to Ward his orders for the occupation of the Dorchester Hills: the troops must move no later than Monday night, for fear the enemy might move first. The work parties and their guards were to be led by John Thomas, under the overall command of Artemas Ward. Washington left details to officers on the front.

The American bombardment was resumed at 9 P.M. on March 3, the guns firing "just fast enough to keep the enemy alarmed." One shell plunged into a church and another whizzed above the roof of Faneuil Hall, where a soldier's farce, *Boston Besieged,* was in progress. For the first time, the city was in real danger. An officer hurried upon the theater stage, halted the actors and ordered officers to their posts.

The "Congress" mortar split on its third shot, about midnight, and Washington became anxious; his bombardment of the city might be ineffectual.

The guns fell quiet during the day of March 4 as the rebels made final preparations, but at 10 A.M. a sudden stir in the British line opposite Lechmere Point brought an alarm. Two or three hundred redcoats waited at the dock for about two hours, and a few of them embarked in small boats, only to turn back when they were near enough to the mainland to see thousands of rebels in the trenches, waiting with ready arms.

The night was ideal for the army's move. The moon rose in the dusk at 5:20 P.M. and shed pale light on the hills, but a fog bank over the water concealed Dorchester from the city. A breeze from the north would carry the sounds of carts and laborers away from Boston. The ground was still frozen, but there was a mildness in the air; the troops would not suffer.

The covering bombardment of Boston opened at seven o'clock, a fury of fire. Washington was not hoarding powder tonight— this was much the heaviest American cannonade of the siege. British gunners retaliated, and the sky was often lit by six or seven shells at once, trailing fiery arcs over Back Bay. In moments of quiet the screams of Boston's civilians could be heard in rebel lines. Lieutenant Samuel Webb of Putnam's staff was moved by the sounds: "Our shell reaks the houses terribly and the Crys of poor women and Children frequently reached our Ears."

The first troops wound out of Roxbury just as the guns opened, a procession oddly suggestive of a medieval siege party—first a band of seven hundred and fifty marksmen who settled at the waterside nearest Boston, to guard working parties on the hills to their rear; next came twelve hundred workmen with their tools, followed by a caravan of three hundred and sixty lumbering oxcarts, loaded with fascines and chandeliers, bales of hay and the stone-filled barrels to be rolled down upon the enemy. Axmen went down into the orchards, felled trees and piled their sharpened branches across the slopes in forbidding rows.

John Thomas rode among the men and carts as they moved back and forth, and Washington soon joined him. Building materials and tools were dumped at marked locations on the hilltops, and the carts turned down into Roxbury to reload. Men struggled silently to unload carts and pile the twists of hay along the route until the movement was screened from the view of Boston sentries; even if the fog lifted, the work on Dorchester should be invisible to the enemy. Despite the wind and the roar of guns from the northern sectors of the line, men on Dorchester whispered to one another, and gave orders to oxen in undertones. The troops worked steadily and well.

The wicker containers went into place, and men with picks began breaking through the eighteen-inch layer of frosty earth, only slightly thawed. Just to the rear, crews erected scores of huts, prefabricated some days before. Teamsters waited with spare carts. Doctors and their assistants unloaded their bandages and litters for carrying the wounded. Thomas looked at his watch and saw with surprise that it was only ten o'clock. The two fortified hills were already strong enough to withstand enemy cannon fire, and the guns themselves would soon be hauled into place.

Like some gigantic ant colony the troops continued their work, each party moving to its assigned task. Three thousand fresh men came up from Roxbury at 3 A.M. to relieve the work parties, and the pace quickened. At the night's end, as a pale curtain rose imperceptibly in the east, men still deepened trenches, rammed earth into fascines and hauled Ticonderoga's guns into place. Six small forts were nearing completion along the hilltops and in the flats below, with flanking works to shield the positions from enemy fire.

In the half-light of dawn came the first sign that the occupation had been detected: a puff of smoke from Boston's southern defenses, a roar shuddering across the water, and the thud of iron shot on a slope below the new forts. John Thomas now saw the people of Boston, soldiers and civilians, faces turned up to Dorchester Heights. The city's wharves and rooftops were black with people. One officer noted that the sight of the new forts threw the crowd into "very great confusion."

In Boston, more than one officer was reminded of the tale of Aladdin's lamp as the work of Washington's troops was revealed. William Howe, so the Americans were soon telling one another, had looked across to Dorchester and said in dismay, "Good God! Those fellows have done more in one night than I could have made my army do in three months!" He estimated that at least twelve thousand to fourteen thousand men had labored to create those menacing earthworks, and Archibald Robertson, one of his engineers, set the figure even higher.

British gunners tried to reach the new forts, but their fire fell short no matter how they dug carriage wheels into the earth and elevated their gun muzzles, and they gave up the attempt after two hours. Howe must drive the rebels from Dorchester by an attack across the water.

Sporadic cheering swept the heights after British cannon fire died away. Washington rode the lines to remind the troops that this was the anniversary of the Boston Massacre, and said they should be ready to avenge the deaths of their countrymen. The general's remark passed ahead of him through the ranks. Washington and his staff waited, aware that Howe could not attack before noon, when high tide would wash the Dorchester beaches; troops disembarking at low tide would be forced to wade across mud flats under fire, exposed at every step.

There was a stir in Boston just before noon as five regiments of redcoat troops left the docks for transports in the harbor. The ships then sailed down from the harbor to the Castle, where they anchored. Four more regiments were held on the docks, ordered to embark at 7 P.M. The night attack, their officers said, would be made with unloaded guns and only their bayonets would be used. An American civilian watched the soldiers on the docks at close range: "They looked pale and dejected, and said to one another that it would be another Bunker's Hill affair or worse."

Thousands of spectators crowded the American lines from the Mystic to Roxbury, settling down to enjoy a spectacle, "a bloody battle," one of them confessed, but as the tide ebbed it became evident that the British would not attack by daylight. The next turn of tide would come after nightfall. The weather worsened before dark. The wind shifted to the south and became chill, and was soon howling with hurricane force, pelting the armies with rain. Some of Howe's transports were driven ashore on an island and the waiting troops on the docks were dismissed. Small boats would not dare the white surf off Dorchester.

British headquarters seemed to have been paralyzed by the American move. Archibald Robertson, who had studied the Dorchester works with mounting apprehension, tried all day to reach William Howe, but was turned away, and was reduced to predicting to junior officers that an attack on the rebels would end in disaster, and that the army should abandon Boston. A council of war at headquarters dragged on until late evening, when Robertson learned with relief that the attack had been canceled. In the next morning's orders Howe told his troops that the night assault had been "unavoidably put off by the badness of the weather"; the army would soon leave the city.

It was after 8 A.M., when the storm had died away, before

Washington learned that British troops had returned to Boston. The general kept his troops on the alert and continued work on the new forts. Putnam's four thousand troops remained in position near their small boats, ready to counterattack in case the enemy struck at Dorchester.

Confirmation of victory came to Washington in the afternoon of March 8 when a British officer and three civilians came from the city under a flag of truce, bearing a message from the selectmen of Boston: the British were evacuating. William Howe had promised to leave the city undamaged if the rebels held their fire until he had gone. Washington and his officers suspected treachery. Howe might have deceived the selectmen, and might well burn the city if Washington relaxed his vigilance. The commander replied that since Howe had not signed the message, he could take no official note of it. He made no promises.

During the day the master of a captured American merchant ship, one Captain Irvine, escaped from Boston and told Washington that Howe was beginning to evacuate. Irvine's story had the ring of truth. It was corroborated by the selectmen's message, and Washington could now see the loading of ships at the Boston docks. The rebels waited two more days, then another— and another.

Evacuation had in fact begun on March 6, when the first of the army's heavy gear went aboard ships. Panic struck the Tories as the loads were trundled to the docks, and Boston's streets filled instantly with "uproar and confusion; carts, trucks, wheelbarrows, coaches, chaises . . . driving as if the devil was after them." Quartermasters and engineers saved only the best of the ordnance, brass guns and mortars which they pulled from the line and replaced with iron ones. Three enormous mortars were dragged to the wharves, but broke the loading tackle and were dumped into the harbor. The commissary general went on shipboard early in the day and left valuable goods scattered throughout the town, at the mercy of the troops.

Though some army transports were only half loaded, Tories were barred, and were forced to hire other vessels. Benjamin Hallowell, the collector of customs, shared a cabin on one ship with thirty-six others, "Men, women and children; parents, masters, and mistresses, obliged to pig together on the floor, there being no berths."

An onlooker saw the distress of Loyalist civilians: "The Torys that went with the enemy carry'd death in their Faces, some run distracted. John Taylor, that infamous Tory, has distroy'd his own life." When Washington, to whom Tories were anathema, was told of this tragedy, he said sternly, "It's what a great number ought to have done long ago."

When the Tories had loaded the ships with all the furniture they could get aboard, the remainder was tossed into the harbor; mahogany chests, desks and beds floated in the bay, to drift ashore on distant beaches many days later. The soldiers looted warehouses and private homes in the last hours, and householders were forced to fight to save their furniture. Even the hardened General James Robertson wrote of "the Soldiers rather acting Licentiously and breaking up some stores." To preserve discipline, barrels of rum were poured into the streets and liquor stores closed. Officers were detailed to sleep in every barracks room to keep watch over the troops. When plundering continued, Howe's provost passed through the city with an executioner and a guard, to hang looters on the spot without trial.

On March 9 the impatient Washington ordered a final move to force Howe from the city—the fortifying of Nook's Hill, on the very tip of Dorchester Neck, a height overlooking Roxbury Neck from a range of two hundred and fifty yards, so close that British positions could be shelled from the rear.

Howe's inaction, so perplexing to Washington, was due to the weather; the British awaited only a favorable wind. The fleet of a hundred and twenty-five ships lay in the harbor with sails furled, bearing 11,000 soldiers and sailors, 1,200 women and children and 1,100 Tories. Ashore, all was in readiness: the redcoats had dug ditches across the Neck, the outer gates were locked, and the largest guns had been spiked, to be abandoned to the enemy. Archibald Robertson noted glumly in his diary on March 14: "Nothing but the Wind, which is foul." The last redcoats were marched to the wharves the next morning but were ordered back to their barracks when the wind turned east.

The final hours of waiting were the most trying for Washington as he watched Howe make ready for his escape to sea. He had insisted more than once: ". . . it is of essential importance, that the troops in Boston should be destroyed . . .," and "No man upon earth wishes more ardently to destroy the nest in Boston than I do." Now it was pointless to shell civilians left behind and force Howe to burn the city.

For still another day, March 16, Howe waited, held by a feeble breeze, but early the next morning, St. Patrick's Day, the first ships moved out of the harbor. As they left, a little comedy was enacted by a Lieutenant Adair of the Marines, a young Irishman sent out to scatter crows' feet—wicked four-pointed iron obstacles that always fell with one sharp spike turned upward to discourage close pursuit. Adair scattered the crows' feet around the gate nearest the rebels, so that he had to pick his way through them on his return and was almost captured. The rebels were close on his heels when he neared the docks.

It was now about 9 A.M. The British rear guard had gone aboard the transports and only engineers remained in the city, ready to set fire to houses if the rebels pressed them too closely. They went aboard at last, and the city was free. Small boys dashed over the causeway on the Neck, leaped the new ditch and tipped gingerly around Adair's crows' feet. Behind them came Boston's selectmen to greet the rebel army.

Colonel Ebenezer Learned led five hundred men into the city all of them soldiers who had been exposed to smallpox. When other troops entered despite orders, guards were posted at the gates to halt traffic until the city was free of smallpox. Bostonians, shouting, sobbing, laughing, thronged the streets to welcome the troops, civilians who had been cooped in the city for eleven months and confined indoors for the past few days. The troops found the streets clean and most houses intact, though the redcoats had damaged the interiors. John Hancock's house was in good condition, its family portraits and furniture undamaged. Except for a hundred or more houses pulled down for fuel, the endless defensive lines and the disfigured Common, the town was largely unchanged.

Suspicious rebels in the line on the mainland who saw British sentries standing motionless on Bunker Hill advanced to fin dummies dressed in redcoat uniforms, with shouldered muskets and fixed bayonets. A note was pinned to the breast of one figure: "Welcome, Brother Jonathan." Other British deceptions were discovered in Boston, one of them an imposing "earthwork" that was only a pile of horse manure.

Washington did not enter the city during the day. He was busy at headquarters in the morning, planning the move of the army to New York, where he expected the enemy to strike. He went to church in the afternoon. When darkness fell he was astonished to see lights at sea—Howe's fleet, anchored in protected waters below Boston, still a threat to the army and the city.

The general went into the city the next morning—his first visit in twenty years—and found it "in not so bad a state as I had expected." He looked over the "almost impregnable" defenses built by the enemy and put his men to work building more, facing seaward. He ordered the troops to be held ready to move or fight at a moment's warning, since the enemy might "have some design of aiming a blow at us before they depart."

The rebels found vast quantities of stores and arms: 250 cannon, 28,000 bushels of grain, 25,000 kettles of coal, 150 horses, warehouses filled with bedding and clothing for troops, and many ships, only slightly damaged. This was only the beginning of the rebel loot, for in the next few weeks British captains, unaware that the port had fallen, would bring to Boston cargoes of powder, guns, food, clothing and fresh troops—all to be captured.

Life in Boston began a return to normal almost at once. Citizens flocked to a town meeting. The Thursday Lecture was resumed. The body of Joseph Warren was exhumed from its grave on Breed's Hill and given a Masonic funeral befitting the hero of the first pitched battle of the war.

When news of the evacuation reached London it was presented by the government as a victory for Howe—a judicious change of base—but critics were not deceived. The Duke of Manchester, snatching at "the veil of silence cast over the disgrace," told the House of Lords:

"Under the Rose"

The mode of retreat may, to the general, do infinite honor, but it does dishonor to the British nation. Let this transaction be dressed in what garb you please, the fact remains that the army which was sent to reduce the province of Massachusetts Bay has been driven from the capital, and that the standard of the provincial army now waves in triumph over the walls of Boston.

CAN NEW YORK
BE DEFENDED?

"A Desperate Game"

Charles Lee and a bodyguard of riflemen descended upon New York on February 4, after a month's journey from Boston; it was hardly a triumphal entry. An attack of gout had delayed Lee in Stamford and he traveled the last miles painfully, by litter and carriage, still surrounded by his dogs and tended by his faithful Italian servant, Guiseppe Minghini. About twelve hundred Connecticut militia shambled in with him, over the protests of local American leaders, who feared British ships in the harbor would bombard New York in retaliation.

The enemy would not dare turn naval guns on the city, Lee said haughtily, since "the first house set in flames . . . shall be the funeral pile of some of their best friends," but the New York Committee of Public Safety and "the accursed Provincial Congress of New York" were difficult, challenging him at every step. Even his troops came into conflict with "that heterogeneous substance known as General Lee," who shouted to disobedient militiamen, "Men, I do not know what to call you. You are the worst of creatures." He threatened to shoot some of his volunteers.

The city's population of some twenty-five thousand had dwindled rapidly as families fled to safety, leaving hundreds of houses to be seized as barracks by rebel soldiers. Governor Tryon had lived for three months in the harbor aboard the H.M.S. *Asia,* where merchants and farmers openly sent goods and food.

Lee arrived just as Henry Clinton entered the harbor with British ships on their way to assault Charleston, S.C.—a fleet that so alarmed the countryside that five militia regiments from New York, Connecticut and New Jersey marched in to help defend the city.

Lee settled comfortably in the tavern of a Mrs. De La Montaine, opened an account with a wine merchant and set about building defenses for a city he regarded as indefensible. He threw up trenches, planted batteries along the Manhattan waterfront and earthworks on the commanding Brooklyn bluff, which towered a hundred feet above the East River. He withdrew British cannon from lower Manhattan, pulled down the stone walls of Fort George to prevent its use by the enemy and posted a guard at Kingsbridge on the Harlem River, the escape northward from the city. He thought these moves might hold a British fleet at bay and make an assault by infantry costly to the enemy. Apparently he did not foresee that the city might become a trap if the enemy seized Long Island and exposed Manhattan's flanks.

When Lee jailed a few Tories and forced others to take loyalty oaths, the state's delegation in Philadelphia protested furiously, and Congress soon called him to a greater task in the Carolinas: to fend off the coming attack led by Henry Clinton. Lee squabbled with the New Yorkers to the last. The Tory judge Thomas Jones said that when Mrs. De La Montaine presented her tavern bill, "He damned her for a Tory, cursed her for a bitch, and left the house without paying her a sixpence." Lee's wine merchant was to make futile efforts to collect his bill throughout the war.

Lee rode to the South on March 9, leaving in command William Alexander, a hard-drinking veteran of the French and Indian War, who insisted upon calling himself Lord Stirling as claimant to a lapsed Scottish title whose princely American land grants included Nova Scotia, New Brunswick, most of Maine as well as Nantucket, Martha's Vineyard and parts of Long Island. The vigorous Stirling drafted every able-bodied man in New York and assigned blacks to work daily and whites every other day.

7

THE LOSS OF NEW YORK

"Good God!...Are These the Men to Defend America?"

The beaten army settled upon New York like a congress of bedraggled scarecrows. Sodden tents, blankets and clothing were draped everywhere, on houses, walks and streets. Order had disappeared.

A touring English civilian was repelled by the ". . . Yankee men, the nastiest devils in creation." Only swine, he thought, could live amid "such a complication of stinks" as rose from their camp. "If my countrymen are beaten by these ragamuffins," he wrote, "I shall be very much surprised."

The Tory parson Shewkirk, who had seen the rebels march blithely toward battle on Long Island to the tune of fifes and drums, noted with satisfaction that they were now mournfully silent. "Everything," he wrote, "seemed to be in confusion." The troops, "sickly, emaciated and cast down," were deserting in droves. It was absurd to suppose that the colonies could win independence by the valor of this army.

For a day, at least, it was virtually a leaderless army. Washington was so near exhaustion that he was physically unable to report to Congress until twenty-four hours after his escape. He apologized for his tardiness:

THE LOSS OF NEW YORK

... The extreme fatigue, which myself and family have undergone ... rendered me and them entirely unfit to take pen in hand.

Since Monday, scarce any of us have been out of the lines till
our passage across the East River . . . and for forty-eight hours
preceding that, I had hardly been off my horse, and never closed
my eyes; so that I was quite unfit to write or dictate till this
morning.

Historians were to charge Washington with decisive errors in
his first set battle: dividing his strength to defend an indefensible base, failing to secure his flanks before his advanced troops
met the enemy, and, in particular, with neglect of the flank at
the Jamaica Pass. The general himself blamed Sullivan's outposts
for the surprise, and was never to concede that he had suffered
a major defeat in the battle, only a "check" to a "detachment" of
his army. His almost casually brief report to Congress offered
no hint that the commander, untested like his troops, had been
victimized by a superior army of professionals.

Washington ended his report to Congress abruptly:

I am much hurried and engaged in arranging and making new
dispositions of our forces . . . and therefore I have only time to
add, that I am, with my best regards to Congress, &c.

The general's "dispositions" left much to be desired, for his
army was evaporating once more, as it had outside Boston.
Volunteers simply marched homeward, unpaid, embittered and
humiliated; in less than a week his Connecticut militia dwindled
from eight thousand to two thousand. Washington realized that
his departing veterans were going home to harvest crops for their
wives and children. He knew intimately the problems of the
farm homestead in this vital season, problems now faced by
thousands of families in every colony; in the absence of their
men, women in Pennsylvania's Brandywine Valley, for example,
were already ploughing fields to put in a wheat crop. "The
impulse for going home," Washington wrote, "was so irresistable
... I have been obliged to acquiesce."

Though he had told Congress in a few modest words that he
had crossed the river from Brooklyn without loss and "in better

order than I expected," Washington gave no indication that he felt he had atoned for defeat by the evacuation. He was unaware of the extravagant praise for him in the enemy camp. Though most of them expected the victory on Long Island to end the war, William Howe's officers thought Washington's retreat remarkable—"astonishing and daring," in the words of a captain, and "particularly glorious," the officer-historian Charles Stedman said. The British historian Trevelyan was to laud the "master stroke of energy, dexterity and caution by which Washington saved his army and his country."

But the vital thing to the Howe brothers was the easy victory over the rabble. William Howe's report, which exaggerated both American strength and casualties, reached London in early October and set off celebrations in many cities, ringing of bells, firing of cannon and blazing bonfires. Tories proclaimed the end of the war. British stocks soared on foreign exchanges.

Black Dick Howe saw the rout on Long Island as a fresh opportunity to press his peace mission. No sooner had he learned of the surrender of Sullivan and Stirling than he invited them to dine aboard the *Eagle*, and the captive generals lounged in the cabin of the flagship, wooed by the admiral while their troops were being rowed to safety through the fog. Howe protested that his earlier peace effort had been misunderstood, insisted that he was not handicapped by limited powers, and that Parliament would ratify any agreements he made. He spoke of the war as senseless and said that Parliament had no right to tax Americans, and that in any event the country could never be conquered by the British army. He argued for a truce so convincingly that his guests were won over—Sullivan, at least, agreed to go to Philadelphia and invite a congressional committee to visit the admiral. Sullivan was paroled so quickly that he was back in New York a few hours after Washington arrived.

The commander was impatient with those who still clamored for negotiations with the British and could not approve Sullivan's mission, but sent him on his way: "I have consented to his going to Philadelphia, as I do not mean . . . to withhold or prevent him from giving such information as he possesses . . ."

By September 2 Sullivan was in Philadelphia, urgently presenting Admiral Howe's views to congressmen in private and talking optimistically of a generous peace settlement, but when he was asked to reduce Howe's offer to writing, Sullivan was more guarded. He was still less persuasive when he addressed Congress from the floor of the crowded meeting room in the State House. The indignant John Adams had heard but a few words from the officer before he whispered to his neighbor, Dr. Benjamin Rush, "I wish that the first ball fired on Long Island had gone through his head." Adams then stood to denounce Sullivan as "a decoy duck, whom Lord Howe has sent among us to seduce us into a renunciation of our independence." Congress accepted Howe's invitation, but doomed the conference to failure by ordering the radical leaders Adams and Benjamin Franklin to serve on the committee. They journeyed north to meet the admiral on Staten Island, accompanied by the moderate Edward Rutledge of South Carolina.

As his troop strength ebbed, Washington became more anxious for news of the enemy, who had made no move since their victory on Long Island. On September 1, he ordered spies sent into the British camp. He urged General Heath, who commanded at Kingsbridge, to "Leave no stone unturned . . . do not stick at expense to bring this to pass, as I was never more uneasy . . ."

Within a day or two, Nathan Hale, a twenty-four-year-old captain in Lieutenant Colonel Thomas Knowlton's new company of Rangers, responded to the call for volunteers and offered to spy on the enemy. Hale realized that capture meant death, but said he was anxious to do something for the country: "For a year I have been attached to the army, and have not rendered any material service . . ." Washington talked with Hale, apparently at headquarters, and a few days later the young spy made his roundabout way to Long Island and was soon within British lines. He had disguised himself as a schoolmaster.

On Long Island, William Howe moved deliberately, as if awaiting the outcome of his brother's peace offensive. On September 2, while Sullivan was on his mission to Congress, General Howe and Henry Clinton rode up the bank of the East River, peering across at the defenses of Manhattan Island, and later in the day a British frigate and some landing craft moved up the river to Newtown Inlet. Clinton argued for an attack north of Manhattan, to close the only rebel escape route at the bridge over the Harlem, but Howe rejected his plan and ordered an assault on the beaches at Kips Bay, some three miles north of New York City, where farmlands stretched away northward to the Harlem River and beyond. During the next few days redcoats gathered in strength around the assault fleet at Newtown Inlet and occupied islands in the river. Otherwise, the British did not stir, beyond a few raids to plunder Long Island.

The Americans in New York were puzzled by the British delay. Even when Washington began moving stores to safety north of Kingsbridge, the enemy made no move. Old Put wrote: "Gen. Howe is either our friend or no general. He had our whole army in his power on Long Island and yet suffered us to escape . . . he is still with his army upon Long Island—his long stay there surprises us all. Had he instantly followed up his victory the consequences to the cause of liberty must have been dreadful."

During this delay Washington's generals became more acutely aware of their still-vulnerable island position, open to waterborne attack or an enemy landing in Westchester. Nathanael Greene, who returned to duty after three weeks in bed with fever, urged Washington to burn the city and withdraw to safety. He argued that the loss of New York was unimportant, since Tories owned two-thirds of it. The Quaker was impatient for action: "The country is struck with a panick . . . A general and speedy retreat is absolutely necessary . . . I would burn the city and suburbs . . . if the enemy gets possession of the city, we can never recover . . . without a superior naval force." Others, including Joseph Reed and Chief Engineer Rufus Putnam, agreed with Greene, and John Jay, the owner of much property in New York, also urged the burning.

The commander himself was ready to give up New York: "Till of late I had no doubt in my mind of defending this place, nor should I have yet, if the men would do their duty, but this I despair of." IIe held a council of war on September 7 to review the unpromising prospects of holding the city.

By now openly contemptuous of the militia, Washington urged Congress to create a standing army, "I mean, one to exist during the war." Without such an army, he warned, all might be lost. Congress responded by ordering eighty-eight regiments of regulars—most of them destined to remain paper regiments. Washington also complained that he had no money and that his troops had not been paid for two months.

Most recruits coming to camp were sullen and undisciplined, many of them without muskets, tents or even camp kettles. Washington thus had a warm welcome for two small Continental regiments from Virginia, eleven hundred strong, enlisted for long terms and destined to fight throughout the war. One of these, the 3rd Virginia, was led by the rough and ready Colonel George Weedon, a tavern keeper from Fredericksburg known to his troops as Old Joe Gourd, in tribute to his generous service of rum punch from a gourd.

The general revealed none of his anxieties in his postbattle order to the troops. He pointed out that the army was united once more and that the enemy had broad waters to cross before attacking: ". . . if officers and soldiers are vigilant, and alert, to prevent surprise, and add spirit when they approach, there is no doubt of our success . . . Now is the time for every man to exert himself, and make our Country glorious, or it will become contemptable."

There was no obvious effect upon American discipline, which remained much as it had been in the early days before Boston. A surgeon who had sold certificates of disability for sixpence each was drummed out of camp. A Connecticut captain who forged a pass to go home was dressed in women's clothing, forced to carry a wooden gun and sword and paraded homeward under guard. One soldier, halted by guards as he left camp, was laden with trophies, among them a cannonball. "I'm taking it home to my mother," he said, "so she can pound mustard seed." Most army surgeons, it was said, were "unlettered and ignorant," incompetent to care for the one-fourth of the army now on the sick rolls.

The army was wracked by sectional rivalries, and its discipline was still hampered by a rampant spirit of democracy in the ranks. A general officer said that Pennsylvania and New England troops "would as soon fight each other as the enemy. Officers of all ranks are indiscriminately treated in a contemptable manner."

One marked change in the army during the lull was a growing distrust of the army's leadership—the first such expression since Washington took command. Some officers felt that the general was too often influenced by young men of his staff and did not delegate responsibility to mature soldiers. The veteran Colonel John Haslet of Delaware wrote in early September: "The Genl I revere, his Character for Disinterestedness, Patience and fortitude will be had in Everlasting Remembrance, but the Vast Burthen appears to be much his own. Beardless youth and Inexperience Regimentated are too much about him." Haslet expressed a wish that was to echo in the army's future: "W'd to Heaven Genl Lee were here . . ."

Washington's plans for the defense of the city developed fitfully and by compromise. The council of September 7 voted to leave Putnam's five thousand troops in the city itself, as a concession to Congress. William Heath's nine thousand were to hold the sector from Harlem up to Kingsbridge with their northern flank near a new earthwork called Fort Washington. The intervening space was to be held by Greene's five brigades of fewer than six thousand men, mostly militia, who were posted along the East River front. The Quaker's troops were concentrated at Turtle Bay and Kips Bay, the latter at the end of what is now Thirty-fourth Street. This deployment extended the army in a thin line over sixteen miles, with the weakest force in the center, an open invitation to disaster.

These weaknesses were pointed out by Greene and others in a petition for a second council of war. Washington explained that the original plan was made in light of the congressional wish to defend New York "at every hazard," but he had a prompt response from Philadelphia saying that the army should not remain in the city "a moment longer" than Washington thought wise. Still, only minor changes of the plan were made before the British moved to the attack.

Near sunset on September 14 Washington was called to the

waterfront: six enemy ships were moving to new stations in the East River, and British troops were assembling on nearby islands. As Joseph Reed wrote his wife: "The enemy are evidently intending to encompass us on this island by a grand military exertion . . . I hope they will fail. It is now a trial of skill whether they shall or shall not, and every night we lie down with the most anxious fears for the fate of tomorrow."

Washington, now convinced that Howe would land north of the Harlem in an attempt to isolate and destroy the army, moved to Harlem Heights that night, ready to meet an assault the next morning. He spent the night in the home of Roger Morris, which was to become known later as the Jumel Mansion.

An odd little flotilla crept from the city one evening during this time, borne by the tide toward Staten Island: several whaleboats filled with oarsmen towed a bulky, clam-shaped burden eastward. History's first submarine attack was under way. The strange craft barely broke water and a dim light fell through half a dozen tiny glass disks about the head of the volunteer operator, Sergeant Ezra Lee of Connecticut. The craft was the *American Turtle,* the invention of a young Yale graduate, David Bushnell, commander of a company of explosives experts—sappers and miners. The awkward craft, which had been building in secret for weeks, had emerged to break the British blockade.

Seven hundred pounds of lead ballast was strapped to the bottom of the tiny ship—bars which could be released from within, so that the *Turtle* would rise toward the surface. Lee could also control his depth, sinking beneath the surface by opening a sea cock and rising by forcing water out with a hand pump. There was also a crude fathometer, a glass tube a foot long and an inch in diameter in which a cork and a piece of wood floated—theoretically a one-inch rise in the cork indicated a descent of one fathom.

Lee was cast off near the enemy fleet and pushed his craft forward, steering the *Turtle* with one hand and cranking furiously with the other to turn a pair of foot-long oars that spun slowly before him like a tiny windmill.

Lee was near suffocation before he moved under the stern of H.M.S. *Asia,* where he opened a hatch and gulped fresh air; he saw and heard British sailors on deck. He closed the hatch and submerged beneath the coppered bottom of the warship, where he tried to screw a powder charge into the hull, but could not penetrate the metal. Lee gave up after many attempts, when he realized that dawn was near and that enemy boats would be rowing about the harbor. "I thought the best generalship was to retreat as fast as I could, as I had four miles to go before passing Governors Island." He had a narrow escape on his return.

A British barge came out to investigate as the *Turtle* floated past an island. Lee cut loose his powder magazine, which was set to be exploded by a gunlock within twenty minutes, hoping that if he was captured, "we should all be blown up together." The British lost interest and turned back. Sergeant Lee had almost reached Manhattan when the floating magazine went off harmlessly with a tremendous roar. The failure brought the American submarine venture to an end. The British fleet was unaware that it had survived a threat.

On September 11 the congressional committee—Franklin, John Adams and Edward Rutledge—landed, without consulting Washington, on Staten Island, where they were greeted amiably by Lord Howe, and led to a house that had been used by soldiers. Adams noted that it was filthy, but had been "romantically" decorated by Howe—the floor was covered with moss and the walls hidden by green branches of shrubs. The guests dined on cold cuts, drank claret and conferred fruitlessly for three hours, most of the time listening to Lord Howe's rather rambling but guarded offers of peace. Franklin, who had known Howe well in London and had frequently played chess with his sister, Lady Caroline Howe, seemed to enjoy this occasion as an opportunity to exercise his wit.

The two countries could settle their differences, the admiral said. "I feel for America as if for a brother. If it should fall, I'd lament it like the loss of a brother."

"My Lord," Franklin said dryly, "we will do our utmost to spare Your Lordship that mortification."

The admiral knew that the old man was thinking of a French alliance to save the rebel cause. "I suppose you'll endeavor to give us employment in Europe."

The Americans said nothing, and Howe continued: he regretted that independence had been declared before his arrival. He could not treat with them as members of Congress, but only as "gentlemen of great ability and influence." The Americans agreed to speak as private citizens, and Adams said, "your Lordship may consider me in what light you please . . . except as a British subject."

The admiral turned to the others and smiled humorlessly. "Mr. Adams is a decided character," he said.

Howe's guests seldom interrupted his monologue. He insisted that he could not accept the colonies as independent states, and that Americans must find some way of "treading back this step of independency" to open the way for negotiations. Adams and Franklin replied that they represented free men who would never submit to domination by Great Britain. Rutledge told Howe that England might prosper more from an alliance with an independent America than from its rule of the colonies, and added firmly that South Carolina would never become a colony again, even on the orders of Congress.

Franklin brought the fencing to an end: "Well, My Lord, as America is to expect nothing but upon unconditional submission—" Howe protested that no submission would be required, but little more was said, and the interview ended on a note of confusion.

The committee returned and reported to Congress that Howe's authority was limited to the granting of pardons to submissive Americans, and that he had misled Sullivan. There seemed to be no legitimate grounds for negotiation.

During the night of September 14–15, within a few hours after he had word of his brother's diplomatic failure, William Howe held a council of war in a farmhouse near Newtown Inlet to outline his plan of assault on New York. The movement would begin at 4 A.M. Clinton would command the infantry as it was ferried across the river to Kips Bay, behind a barrage of naval guns—a frontal assault, but one that could not trap the rebels on their island. When Sir Henry urged a flank movement instead, he was brusquely overruled by Howe, but continued to protest. To Howe's arguments Clinton said firmly, "You may make every argument you wish. I will oppose you with all my might until 4 o'clock —but from that moment on I will lead the attack as if I had planned it myself." Sir Henry was then reduced to private disapproval in his notebook a few moments later: "My advice has ever been to avoid even the possibility of a check. We live by victory. Are we sure of it this day? *J'en doute.*"

When Clinton boarded the frigate *Roebuck* just after dawn, he was dismayed by what he saw from only three hundred yards offshore of Kips Bay: there was no open sandy beach like those of Long Island. His troops must clamber over large rocks under fire to reach the rebel trenches, which were "well lined with men whose countenance appeared respectable and firm." To the right, inland from the trenches, rose a slope crowned by a farmhouse which was to be the first objective of the landing troops. To his left, downstream, Clinton saw the town of New York. Rebel works lined the shore between Kips Bay and the city, and stretched out of sight to the north. British landing craft soon crept from the Long Island shore and approached the ships, quartering across the river. Clinton ordered the flotilla to wait for a slack tide, and the eighty-four small boats clustered about the ships until eleven o'clock. Clinton gave the command and the boats moved shoreward under a hot sun, through water as smooth as glass.

All morning a small regiment of Connecticut militia had awaited attack at the lower edge of Kips Bay. Its commnder, Colonel William Douglas, did not expect the army to hold New York: "Our generals are faithful and good, no one can doubt, but we have not got experience which will teach America wisdom in her wars, as it did Peter The Great."

The trenches where the Connecticut militia lay were defenses in name only, Private Joseph Martin noted: "They were nothing more than a ditch dug along on the bank of the river, with the dirt thrown out towards the water." These men had lain there quietly for two nights, flanked downstream by Massachusetts and New York militia and a brigade of Connecticut Continentals. In the early darkness of this Sunday, September 15, sentinels of Private

Martin's command had called to one another along the shore, "All is well"; a British voice rolled out of the darkness, surprisingly near, "we'll change your tune before tomorrow night!"

At dawn rebel troops in the trench saw that four British ships had crept in during the night and were anchored within musket shot of the shore. Gun ports were open and cannon frowned down upon them. In the distance, when the fleet of small boats loaded with troops pulled out from Long Island, Private Martin thought they were like "a large clover field in full bloom." The Connecticut troops watched as the barges clustered about the ships, waiting for the turn of the tide. They stirred apprehensively as the loaded craft turned shoreward.

Lord Rawdon and Henry Clinton, in one of the lead boats, looked shoreward uneasily, where rebels waited behind their works and columns of reinforcements hurried toward the beach. Clinton thought the landing "the most dangerous I ever saw." Rawdon agreed. "As we approached we saw the breastworks filled with men, and two or three large columns marching down in great parade to support them." The Hessians, "exceedingly uncomfortable" in the open craft at such short range, began singing hymns. The British troops, also nervous, cursed "with wonderful fervency." Every sound was drowned by the big guns from the ships.

This broadside opened Private Martin's battle: "All of a sudden, there came such a peal of thunder from the British shipping that I thought my head would go with the sound. I made a frog's leap for the ditch, and lay as still as I possibly could, and began to consider which part of my carcass was to go first." Swivel gunners in the British tops added grapeshot to the barrage.

Benjamin Trumbull, a 1st Connecticut chaplain, watched the shot and shells as they leveled the earthworks and "buried our men . . . almost under sand and sods of earth, and made such a dust and smoke that there was no possibility of firing on the enemy." The left of Colonel Douglas' line crumbled and began to flee.

Douglas lay under the heavy fire on the right wing until one of his captains crawled to warn him that he must retreat. Douglas discovered that he had only ten men left in line, and when they ran, he followed.

The British boats grated ashore without opposition, redcoats and Hessians climbed up the rocks, formed on the beach, and moved inland. They were not fired upon. Captain William Evelyn, who was in a boat, found the attack "one of the grandest and most sublime scenes ever exhibited." Henry Clinton, one of the first ashore, sent an engineer running ahead to wave a white handkerchief and shout, "Surrender! Surrender!" Most of the rebels ran on without a backward glance, but one of them gave up. Clinton led his men inland to the crown of a hill, where he halted, as ordered, fretting because he could not march to the western shore of the island and cut the rebel retreat.

Private Martin and his companions, scrambling under fire across an open field, neared a band of soldiers hurrying in the same direction. They ran to overtake them, but veered off toward Kingsbridge when they saw that the strangers were Hessians. Other rebels came under fire from a few British troops hidden in a cornfield, and fled. Martin wrote: ". . . our people were all militia, and the demons of fear and disorder seemed to take full possession of all and everything on that day." The ground where the militia were fired upon was "literally covered with arms, knapsacks, staves, coats, hats . . ." The retreat was joined by men from the downstream positions and the rout of the army became general. Within a few minutes they had been defeated once more, turned out of their trenches with almost absurd ease. New York had been lost for the duration of the war.

Washington mounted at the first sound of firing and, calling reinforcements, rapidly covered the four miles from Harlem Heights. As he neared the home of a Quaker merchant, Robert Murray, on the heights now called Murray Hill, about the corner of what is now 36th Street and Park Avenue, Washington found militia making a disorderly retreat. When General Parsons and his men came up, Washington told them to form along the Post Road in front of the enemy who were running up from Kips Bay. Washington shouted in a fury: "Take the walls!" "Take the cornfield!" He could not force the scattered troops into line and they began to flee, followed by some Continentals, among them Prescott's veterans of Bunker Hill. Washington turned his horse about in the midst of these flying regiments, shouting. He wrote: "I used every means in my power to rally and to get them into some order; but my attempts were fruitless and ineffectual; and on the appearance of a small party of the enemy, not more than sixty or seventy, their disorder increased, and they ran away in the greatest confusion, without firing a single shot."

The troops, astonished by the general's fit of temper, spread tales of his wrath which were to become part of the army's tradition: men said Washington had drawn his sword and snapped his pistols at the fleeing troops, and that he was saved from capture only by an officer who seized his horse's reins when the enemy were only a few yards away. William Heath and Joe Gourd Weedon reported that the general had thrown his hat to the ground in despair and shouted, "Good God!" Are these the men with which I am to defend America?"

Colonel Robert Smallwood of Maryland left a glimpse of the fleeing Connecticut troops, "wretches who . . . from the Brigadier General down to the private sentinel, were caned and whipped by the Generals Washington, Putnam and Mifflin, but even this indignity had no weight, they could not be brought to stand one shot." Nathanael Greene said that Washington was so exasperated by men who deserted him within eighty yards of the enemy that "he sought death rather than life."

The main body of retreating rebels streamed toward Harlem on the Kingsbridge Road along the lines of modern Park Avenue South and Lexington Avenue, and despite the rout and sting of yet another ignominious defeat, most of the army was safely united north of Manhattan, looking down from the forbidding stony barricades of Harlem Heights. Most of the troops had evaded the enemy advance; aside from the loss of the city itself, the price of the running battle was slight—only three hundred and fifty wounded, captured or killed.

Putnam, fearful for his isolated troops farther south in the city, had ridden back into New York ahead of the advancing Hessians, and with the aid of young Major Aaron Burr led Silliman's brigade along the Hudson shore, beyond sight of the enemy. Knox and his artillerymen escaped with them, but left their guns behind. The British obviously thought the rebels had abandoned the city early in the day, and the troops of Putnam and Knox reached Harlem Heights late in the afternoon without serious challenge. They got a rousing welcome in camp, where they had been given up as lost.

David Humphreys, Putnam's adjutant, felt that the city garrison had been saved by Old Put: "issuing orders, and encouraging his troops, flying on his horse, covered with foam, wherever his presence was most necessary. Without his extraordinary exertions, the Guards must have been inevitably lost and it is probable that the entire Corps would have been cut in pieces."

By late afternoon the British Light Infantry occupied the road near 42nd Street, grenadiers under Cornwallis and Vaughan drove across the island along the line of 34th Street, and Hessians captured about three or four hundred of Wadsworth's Brigade near 23rd Street and Park Avenue South—if they had pressed on faster they might have taken thousands of rebel prisoners.

While Putnam's troops moved past him to the west, Clinton advanced up the Kingsbridge Road and near dusk camped near present 96th Street and Fifth Avenue, where he was halted by Smallwood's Maryland Regiment. When the British tried to outflank him, Smallwood climbed rocky hills in his rear and joined the main army. It was the final movement of the day on the field. The armies settled for the night, about a mile and a half apart, the British crossing the northern end of the future site of Central Park.

During the hours of the drive northward, a detachment from the British fleet had landed at the lower end of the island and occupied the city just as Putnam's men fled. Lord Rawdon rode into New York with the first of the invaders: "The rebels had fortified it very strongly, and we found great quantities of stores of all kinds and a number of cannon, the immense heaps of shot and shells really surprised me."

Mobs hauled down American flags, stamped them in the streets, and ran up the Union Jack in their places. The homes of known or suspected rebels were declared forfeited, their doors painted with the crude letter R, and pillaged to the bare walls.

"And thus," said Parson Shewkirk, who felt that the British had been sent by God, "was the City now delivered from those usurpers who had oppressed it for so long."

8

HARLEM HEIGHTS
AND WHITE PLAINS

"I Am Wearied Almost to Death"

The main body of the army, ten thousand strong, went into camp
on the northern end of Manhattan Island in a rugged defensive
position Washington had chosen long before, on the narrow plateau between the rocky cliffs of the Hudson and the Harlem. This
hill position, soon to be known as Washington Heights, was four
miles deep, crossed by three lines of earthworks, could not be
flanked, and lay beyond the reach of British naval guns. If Howe
advanced, his men must climb the slopes in frontal assault and the
rebels would at last meet the enemy on equal terms. The position
appealed to Joe Gourd Weedon, the old frontier fighter: "I am
more easy in my mind since we have got elbow room . . . Indeed,
I could wish we were three miles further back yet, as it's not our
business to run any risque of being surrounded."

But even here, as he reported to Congress, Washington had
little faith that his soldiers would stand up to the enemy: "We
are now encamped . . . on the Heights of Harlem, where I should
hope the enemy would meet with a defeat in case of an attack if
the generality of our troops would behave with tolerable resolution. But experience, to my extreme affliction, has convinced me
that this is rather to be wished for than expected." He added with
a brief flash of optimism: "However, I trust that there are many

who will act like men and show themselves worthy of the blessings of freedom."

Officers who passed through the camp were not reassured by the look of the men huddled about the fires, exhausted by the day-long rout, depressed by the loss of artillery, baggage and all else except the muskets they carried, their lean haversacks and the sodden rags on their backs. Colonel David Humphreys saw them early in the night, ". . . excessively fatigued . . . their blood chilled . . . their hearts sunk within them" as they settled to sleep "upon their arms, covered only by the clouds of an uncomfortable sky."

The raffish army was now to redeem itself. Before dawn of September 16 Washington sent Captain Thomas Knowlton and one hundred and twenty of his Rangers to scout the enemy. The Rangers were volunteers, most of them from Connecticut, young, vigorous men chosen for hazardous duty, and devoted to the six-foot Captain Knowlton, who had won the army's respect at Bunker Hill and Long Island. The scouts crossed the valley that lay between the armies, aroused British Light Infantry pickets about sunrise, fought four hundred redcoats from the cover of a stone wall for a few minutes and retreated after the loss of ten men. The British followed recklessly, far in advance of Howe's main army, and as the Rangers filed back into their lines a British trumpeter blew the mocking notes of a fox hunter's call, "Gone to earth." Joseph Reed, who had ridden out to meet Knowlton, was stung by the "insulting manner" of the bugle call: "I have never felt such a sensation before," he said, "it seemed to crown our disgrace."

The Virginia fox hunter was also drawn by the taunting call of the bugle, and as if to avenge the army's humiliation, gave hurried orders to cut off the British advance party. He moved a hundred and fifty Rhode Islanders into his front to lure the redcoats downward and sent Reed to circle into the enemy rear with a flanking force—Knowlton's Rangers reinforced by some Virginians, two hundred and fifty men in all. As the British moved into the trap, firing from the cover of trees and fences at the Rhode Islanders, Knowlton's men approached the rocky crest; a few hundred yards farther and they would reach the British rear and isolate the Light Infantry—but at that moment a nervous officer gave the order to fire, the redcoats fell back, and the opportunity was gone. Then, to Washington's astonishment, his troops took matters into their own hands. The two parties joined, climbed after the enemy "with splendid spirit and animation," mounted the ridge and disappeared in woodlands that roared with musketry.

The Rangers exchanged fire with the British at forty yards. Major Andrew Leitch, the Virginia commander, fell with three musket balls through his body and within ten minutes Knowlton was shot; both were mortally wounded. The column did not falter; company officers took the Rangers forward. Washington sent reinforcements—the rest of Weedon's Virginians, troops from Maryland and Massachusetts and the Connecticut regiment of William Douglas that had failed him so miserably at Kips Bay. The Maryland volunteer Tench Tilghman, Washington's aide, who rode with them, said admiringly, "These troops, though young, charged with as much bravery as I can conceive." They drove the enemy from one stand to another.

British reinforcements were now coming up. The small battle that was in the making drew Washington's most aggressive officers from all parts of the front. Three generals went along—Greene and Putnam and George Clinton, who was soon to become governor of New York—and all joined Reed, Tilghman and Weedon in urging on the troops. The few skulkers could hardly run rearward without bumping into an officer. Reed subdued one by whacking his skull and slicing off a thumb with his sword, and only because he had forgotten his pistols had Clinton failed to kill "a puppy of an officer" who retreated.

The British were driven from the woodlands into a buckwheat field on the site of the future Barnard College at Broadway and 116th Street and then pursued for more than a mile before they halted near 110th Street where redcoat reserves gathered—including the tall grenadiers, who had been driven three miles on the run "without a halt to draw breath."

British fire was dwindling when Washington arrived, but since still more of Howe's reinforcements were advancing, he "judged it prudent to order a retreat."

Tench Tilghman, sent to order the men back, found them in no mood to obey. "The pursuit of a flying enemy was so new a scene," he said, that they could hardly be persuaded to leave. The excited young rebels turned back at last, "gave a hurra and left the field in good order."

Captain Knowlton died before his troops returned, gasping for breath. "Did we drive them?" he asked. "Did we drive them?" They were his last words.

The brisk little action of Harlem Heights, hardly more than a skirmish, stunned men of both armies. For the first time British regulars had turned tail in open battle. British prisoners who were led into Washington's lines marveled at the behavior of the rebel troops, whom they had expected to flee as they had before. They had hardly believed their eyes when they saw ragged men rushing to the attack so recklessly as to break the veteran ranks of red-coats and Germans.

There was a heady sense of elation in the camp after the fight: "You can hardly conceive the change it has made in our army," Reed wrote his wife. "The men have recovered their spirits . . . I hope they will now look the enemy in the face with confidence." Joe Gourd Weedon reported to John Page, the president of the Virginia Council, that his Virginians had fought well and that the overconfident enemy had been "cursedly thrashed."

Washington's orders praised the new-found courage of his men:

> The General most heartily thanks the troops . . . who first advanced upon the enemy, and the others who so resolutely supported them. The behavior of yesterday was such a contrast to some of the troops the day before, as must show what may be done where officers and soldiers will exert themselves. Once more, therefore, the General calls upon officers and men to act up to the noble cause in which they are engaged . . .

But the general was troubled by the failure of his ambush. The enemy loss would have been much greater, he said, if his orders had not been countermanded in the field: "Inferior officers . . . however well they mean, ought not to presume to direct." Future orders were to be carried out precisely as he issued them. He would send his orders to the front only by Reed, Tilghman and Stephen Moylan.

Casualties were high for the numbers engaged. Howe reported losses of about one hundred (though a Hessian officer estimated they were three times as great). Rebel losses were about a hundred and thirty.

Washington reported tersely to Congress, emphasizing the fact that stood out above all others: "The troops charged the enemy with great intrepidity, and drove them."

The exultant mood of the rebels was short-lived. The army lay in its camp for a month awaiting the next British move, its generals divided as to whether Howe would try to flank them from Long Island Sound, or strike their front in an all-out assault. Rebel work parties deepened the trenches each day. Washington with his ten thousand held the lines above Harlem Heights; William Heath covered the flank at Kingsbridge, a few miles to the north; and Greene, with six thousand held Fort Constitution on the New Jersey side of the Hudson. The men had no tents, thousands were without blankets, and recruits who joined often came with "not a pan or kettle." The troops stole and pillaged so brazenly that Washington asked Congress for emergency powers to control them:

> Such a Spirit has gone forth in our Army that neither publick or private Property is secure—Every Hour brings the most distressing complaints of the Ravages of our own Troops who are become infinitely more formidable to the poor Farmers and Inhabitants than the common Enemy.

Soldiers stole horses from army herds and ransacked hospital stores, the baggage of officers, even the quarters of generals. Mutinies and defiance of authority became commonplace. Courts-martial, which sat continuously, were so lenient that Washington accused officers of collusion with their rebellious men. He felt that the army was "on the eve of another dissolution."

He complained even more bitterly of "the difficulties which have forever surrounded me since I have been in the service," of the constant mental strain, and of "the wounds which my feelings as an officer have received." He was surprised, he said, that Congress had not demanded his resignation. He wrote his brother John: "Fifty thousand pounds should not induce me again to undergo what I have done." And to his cousin Lund at Mount Vernon: "If I were to wish the bitterest curse to an enemy on this

side of the grave, I should put him in my stead with my feelings."
He had threatened to resign if Congress did not reform the military system, but had inspired only nervous debate in Philadelphia.
As he wrote to Lund: "I am told that if I quit the command inevitable ruin will follow . . ." The general then burst forth in
indignation: "In confidence I tell you that I never was in such an
unhappy, divided state since I was born."

Yet a few lines later his thoughts turned to the Virginia farmhouse he loved, and to the practical details of finishing fireplaces,
doors and windows in the renovation of Mount Vernon.

Reed was also talking of resignation, out of disgust with the
spirit of democracy that undermined the authority of officers:
"Either no discipline can be established, or he who attempts it
must become odious and detestable . . ." When Reed made up
the army's returns he found its strength was largely on paper. In
fact, it was under strength by more than eleven thousand men.
Benjamin Lincoln's Massachusetts militia, for example, estimated
at four thousand men, "are so scattered and ignorant of the forms
of returns, that none can be got." Reed predicted that the army
would not survive the winter unless France intervened, or the
British fell to fighting among themselves.

Even Henry Knox was ready to leave the army rather than "risk
my reputation on so cobweb a foundation." He thought Washington was "as worthy a man as breathes," but that he was failing for
lack of officers. Most of the army's officers, Knox said, were ignorant and stupid; the country must have a military academy, or the
army would remain as it was now, "only a receptacle for ragamuffins."

Washington was called out near midnight of September 20 to
watch a fire in New York, a blaze at first so small that it was like a
candle in the distant darkness, but fanned by a breeze, soon became a holocaust. Flames ran swiftly up the tall steeple of Trinity
Church, and "a lofty pyramid of fire" illuminated buildings below
with the light of day.

The fire had begun on the waterfront and spread under a brisk
wind, until more than a fifth of the city had gone up in flames. No
general alarm was sounded, since church bells had been carried
away by the rebels and melted down for cannon. A few fire com-

pany stragglers tried to fight the blaze but found their pumps out of order and were helpless; British troops and seamen were called out as fire fighters. A shift in the wind about 2 A.M. confined flames to the area between Broadway and the North River, but five hundred houses and several churches had burned, forcing the British to find other quarters for troops.

Several Americans were charged with arson, and one of them, in the act of setting a fire, was knocked down by a grenadier and tossed to his death in the flames. British sailors reported that "some mad-cap Americans" had set the blaze, one of whom they saw "hanging by the heels dead . . . a bayonet wound through his breast." Ambrose Serle reported: "Many others were seized, on account of combustibles found upon them, and secured, and, but for the officers, most of them would have been killed by the enraged populace and soldiery."

Sir William Howe reported that "a most horrid attempt was made by a number of wretches to burn the town . . . we have reason to suspect there are villains still lurking there, ready to finish the work they had begun . . ."

Washington denied that he had ordered this sabotage, but confessed to Lund, "Providence, or some good honest fellow, has done more for us than we were disposed to do for ourselves."

In the evening of September 21, while embers yet glowed in the city and British headquarters were still in an uproar, Nathan Hale was dragged in by guards, dressed like a Dutch schoolmaster, with a round broad-brimmed hat, his only identification his diploma from Yale. In his pockets were found sketches of British fortifications and troop positions. Hale had almost completed his mission when he was arrested at a tavern called The Cedars, where he was denounced by a Tory kinsman, Samuel Hale, of Portsmouth, N.H.

The young captain confessed that he had been sent to spy on the British, and Howe ordered him executed without trial at eleven o'clock the next morning. A British officer who took Hale to his tent to wait for a time before his death admired the young soldier's courage in his last moments: "He was calm, and bore himself with gentle dignity." Hale asked for writing materials and wrote letters to his mother and to a fellow officer. He asked to talk with a minister, but was denied. He was then led to the gallows. As the rope was fixed about his neck Hale spoke to the few British soldiers who had come to witness his end. He urged them to be ready to meet death at any moment. It was many years later before Hale was reported to have said at last, "I only regret that I have but one life to lose for my country."

On October 12, almost a month after the battle of Harlem Heights, William Howe left a strong force to hold New York, embarked four thousand troops in eighty small vessels and moved under cover of a fog toward Throgs Neck, a tempting target on Washington's flank. He met with unexpected difficulties.

As the troops were rowed through the turbulent narrows of Hell Gate several craft were caught in roaring cross currents and flung upon rocks, and a few guns and gunners were lost. The Howes, who were in the leading boat, tried to turn back, but were hurled helplessly forward at dizzying speed. Henry Clinton said, "Nothing, in my opinion, but Lord Howe's obstinacy could have engaged us in that extraordinary water movement, and nothing but his knowledge and intrepidity could have saved us."

The British flotilla emerged into sunlight and calm water, and sailed up the sound to Throgs Neck, where troops landed under fire from a frigate. It was to no avail. Howe discovered that his maps were inaccurate—the neck was an island at high tide, a marshy finger connected to the mainland by a bridge and causeway. Washington had posted sentries there, thirty Pennsylvania riflemen who had stripped planks from the bridge and now opened fire from the cover of a huge woodpile.

The redcoats turned aside, hurrying for the mouth of the creek, but fell back in confusion when they found more rebels there. The Americans, reinforced by two cannon, forced the British to throw up earthworks and settle into an uncomfortable camp on the island, where they lay for six days until their baggage was brought up the sound.

Howe's offensive had opened badly, but he had broken the stalemate; he was in the rebel rear, and Washington must flee or risk his army in open battle. The Virginian was quick to see his danger, but he did not begin to retreat from Harlem Heights for five days.

Charles Lee returned to the army as a hero at this time, hailed
for his defeat of the British in Charleston—"your victory," as Washington said. One officer wrote from camp, "General Lee is hourly
expected, as if from heaven, with a legion of flaming swordsmen."
Fort Constitution, on the New Jersey bank of the Hudson, was re-
christened Fort Lee in the Englishman's honor. Washington
placed half the army under his command and asked him to inspect the terrain for a day or two, so that he might propose a sound
strategy. Lee gave his opinion unhesitatingly—the army should
abandon the entire region, including Forts Washington and Lee,
and retire inland for the winter, beyond reach of the enemy. Otherwise, Lee pointed out, Howe's flanking movement would trap the
army on Manhattan Island. Other officers opposed Lee, among
them Nathanael Greene, who insisted that Fort Washington should
be defended to the last. A council of war on October 16 agreed
with Greene—the fort was defensible—though it would become
vulnerable if the army abandoned its trenches on Harlem Heights.
When Washington explained that Congress had insisted on a defense of the Hudson at all costs, Lee poured out his contempt for
the Philadelphia strategists, ". . . the Congress seem to stumble
every step—I do not mean one or two of the cattle, but the whole
stable . . . in my opinion General Washington is much to blame
in not menacing 'em with resignation unless they refrain from un-
hinging the army by their absurd interference."

The Americans fell back to White Plains, leaving Fort Washington and its 2,500-man garrison fifteen miles in the rear. Stirling's
brigade led the way in a forced march—fifteen miles in four hours
—and the main body of thirteen thousand toiled along behind, as
Washington rode endlessly up and down the procession, keeping
an anxious eye on the flanks and rear. Horses and wagons were so
scarce that wagoners were forced to dump their loads at the end of
each day and turn back for more. Men dragged cannon by ropes
over the rutted roads. Thus, by exhausting labor, the army
dragged itself across the Harlem River and along the Bronx into
White Plains in four days, a march it should have made in one
day.

William Howe abandoned Throg's Neck on the day Washington began his move, proceeded up the sound to Pell's Point and

met a small rebel force under Colonel John Glover at the village of Eastchester. Glover's vanguard, fighting from behind stone walls, inflicted heavy casualties on the British and Hessian attackers before retreating to Dobbs Ferry.

Four nights later the emboldened Americans attacked the enemy near Mamaroneck, where Major Robert Rogers, a hero of the French and Indian War, had camped with some five hundred of the Queen's American Rangers, a body of Tories detested by the Americans. Colonel John Haslet, with seven hundred and fifty troops from Delaware, Maryland and Virginia, crept upon the Ranger camp in darkness and took thirty-six prisoners after a wild hand-to-hand battle, though most of the Rangers escaped the bewildered rebels by shouting imitations of their war cry: "Surrender, you Tory dogs! Surrender!"

The skirmishes of Glover and Haslet, though they inflicted little harm on the British, had slowed their advance and raised the morale of Washington's troops. Howe delayed, moving only seventeen miles in ten days, until reinforced by fresh Hessian regiments. It was now seven weeks since the Howes had assembled their overpowering army and naval force and they had moved only thirty-five miles.

The eccentric Charles Lee was a continual source of amusement to the commander's staff. One day Washington and his officers, returning from a reconnaissance, stopped for dinner at the farmhouse near White Plains where Lee made headquarters. The party was hardly out of earshot before Lee was berating his aides: "You must find me another place, for I shall have Washington and all his puppies continually calling on me, and they will eat me up."

The next day Washington and several officers saw a chalked message on the front door of Lee's house, "No victuals dressed here today," and turned away to dine at headquarters, roaring with laughter.

The army's line skirted the village of White Plains, between the Bronx River and forested Chatterton's Hill, which towered almost two hundred feet above the river. The troops were waiting here on October 28 when Howe's army approached. Five hundred New England skirmishers held off the British and Hessian advance for several hours, falling back when hard pressed, making stands behind stone walls until outflanked. A Hessian column once came so close that it was broken by a volley, to the delight of an American officer: "We . . . scattered them like leaves in a whirlwind . . . so far off that some of the regiment ran out . . . and brought off their arms and accoutrements and rum." The skirmishers drank the rum, the Germans reappeared, and the chase went on as before, from wall to wall, until the New Englanders had scrambled back up Chatterton's Hill.

The American skirmishers passed through a line of veterans on the hilltop, sixteen hundred men of Smallwood's Marylanders, the 1st and 3rd New York, Webb's Connecticut and Haslet's Delaware regiments. These were among the army's most reliable regiments, but their line was thin and their reinforcements were nervous militiamen from New York and Massachusetts.

The British army now appeared below the rebel line and halted in a wheat field, where Howe and his officers, on horseback, inspected the terrain and conferred with field commanders.

Howe sent eight regiments and a few guns to a ridge opposite Chatterton's Hill, and the rest of his army sat in the field below as the guns shelled the heights. A British cannonball struck a militiaman in the thigh and his whole regiment scattered to the rear, to be re-formed only when officers hunted down the men and drove them back into position. A Hessian battalion, led to the river, balked at crossing the flooded stream, and the armies waited as trees were felled; the Hessians went over in single file.

A few Americans then ran down the hill and drove the Germans back, but two cheering British regiments rushed over a lower ford, pushing the rebels ahead of them, moving up the hill with the coolness of professionals, in long lines abreast, just as they had at Bunker Hill. When they were checked by rebel fire the troops re-formed into a column, to present a smaller target.

Howe and his generals, watching from below, saw in astonishment that the column had halted while its commanding officer reloaded his small musket. Men dropped under rebel fire as the loading went on with agonizing slowness. Henry Clinton said, "They're going to break. They won't stand it." A moment later the veteran units fled for cover. Clinton and Cornwallis agreed: "If the battle is lost, that officer is the cause of it."

But the column re-formed and the rebels were soon driven from the field by Colonel Johann Rall's Hessians. The green Massachusetts and New York militia troops returned one round of fire, but broke when dragoons charged with pealing trumpets and throbbing kettledrums. The riders chased them for half a mile, sabering some of the screaming men and capturing most of the survivors. Rall's Germans then struck Haslet's exposed flank, and the Delawaremen fell back stubbornly, "in a great body, neither running nor observing the best of order," bringing with them the one remaining American cannon. It was defeat once more, but once more the tattered veterans had fought stubbornly. Washington could ask no more of them.

The British force halted on the hill. Howe did not pursue; the defenses protecting the village had a formidable look. The Battle of White Plains had ended. Casualties on each side were from two hundred to three hundred men. The brief engagement, fought by insignificant numbers, had saved Washington's army, temporarily. It also paved the way for an American disaster.

Washington left his old lines at White Plains to Howe's twenty thousand and fell back to North Castle, where American work parties threw up imposing earthworks built largely of cornstalks pulled from adjacent fields and lightly covered with earth. Howe turned back toward New York on November 4, to the relief of the Americans, who for a few days enjoyed "good flour, beef and pork a plenty, with grog to wash it down." The troops celebrated; now, it was thought, the frustrated British would retreat into the city. In fact, Howe was moving upon isolated Fort Washington. Ensign William Demont, a deserter from the 5th Pennsylvania Regiment, had taken plans of the fort to the British, exposed its weakness and the orders for its last-ditch defense. "I sacrificed all I was worth in the world," the traitor said.

The riverside fort was a five-sided earthwork crowning a hill above the Hudson, a crude enclosure with no barracks or buildings, without a protective ditch, and without fuel or water supplies; in case of a siege, water must be drawn from the river two hundred and thirty feet below. Nathanael Greene remained confident despite the fort's vulnerability. The garrison could be brought off "at any time" and was in no danger. Washington was dubious, but though he warned against the risk of men and supplies in the fort, he gave Greene full discretion: ". . . as you are on the Spot leave it to you to give such Orders as to evacuating Mount Washington as you Judge best."

On November 14 Washington crossed the Hudson from New Jersey to inspect Fort Washington, just as British cannon fire began to fall on the works. Twenty-one guns shelled the position from the banks of the Harlem and others fired from ships in the Hudson. A British officer had appeared under a white flag a few moments earlier, demanding surrender upon the threat that the whole garrison would be killed, but Colonel Robert Magaw, the commander, had refused, ready to defend the fort "to the last extremity."

The fort itself was now doomed, since Magaw had scattered bands of defenders in a four-mile circle of outposts that had been overrun by Howe's superior force. General Knyphausen led 3,000 Hessians against 250 riflemen from Maryland and Virginia; Lord Percy led nine British battalions and a German brigade against Colonel Lambert Cadwalader's force of 800; and Generals Cornwallis and Matthews, with 3,000 men, fell upon a little band of 200 militiamen from Bucks County, Pa. With these outer defenses swept aside, the British moved against the main fort. Washington left the fort and recrossed the river only moments before the enemy stormed in.

The commander watched helplessly from the New Jersey bank of the Hudson as the overmatched American bands were driven into the fort, one by one. The troops of Cornwallis and Matthews, climbing the steep slopes of Laurel Hill under heavy fire, shot down several American officers and pushed the leaderless militia ahead of them.

Many Germans died in the climb, for riflemen leaned over the precipice to fire, and cannon blasted the rocky face with grapeshot. Rall's men clambered onto level ground amid trees and enormous stones, still under fire. The Hessian drummers and hautboy players sounded a charge and Colonel Rall bellowed, "All that are my grenadiers march forwards!" The cheering Hessians ran into the midst of the rebels and the skirmish ended with a bizarre scene: "Immediately all were mingled together, Americans and Hessians. There was no more firing, but all ran forward pell-mell upon the fortress."

Washington sent messages to Magaw, urging him to hold out until nightfall so that the garrison could be rescued, but it was too late. Magaw surrendered to Knyphausen, and the garrison of twenty-five hundred marched between lines of Hessians to give up their arms. The Americans had lost only 150 dead and wounded, as against some 450 for the British and Germans, but the loss of the garrison, its arms and supplies was one of the great American disasters of the war. Nathanael Greene was plunged into misery. He wrote Knox asking anxiously what was being said of him at headquarters: "I feel mad, vexed, sick, and sorry . . . this is a most terrible event: its consequences are justly to be dreaded." Washington blamed only himself. Greene's confidence and the desire of Congress to hold the fort had "caused that warfare in my mind and hesitation which ended in the loss of the garrison."

Washington saw that other disasters were to follow: Fort Lee was also a trap, and must be evacuated at the first sign of a British move. He returned to Hackensack to organize a retreat, to find but a handful of the Jersey militia he had expected. Howe might cross the river at any moment, and Washington's army was dangerously divided into four detachments: his small band at Hackensack and Fort Lee, Heath guarding the magazines at Peekskill, Lee in White Plains, and Stirling at Rahway and Brunswick. He recited his troubles in a dolorous letter to John Augustine with occasional outbursts of anger—the loss of Fort Washington had been caused by troops who refused to man the lines; the few fresh regiments coming to camp were led by officers who were "not fit to be shoe blacks."

Charles Lee, who had boasted to Dr. Benjamin Rush that he "foresaw, predicted, all that has happened," chided Washington for the loss of the fort with ill-disguised scorn, "Oh, General, why would you be overpersuaded by men of inferiour judgement to your own? It was a cursed affair."

The British herded the rebel prisoners from Fort Washington into New York, where they were beset by a band of women, camp followers who had been told that Washington was among the captives, hags who shouldered into the column, taunting the ragged men, "Which is Washington? Which is Washington?" A British officer shouted, "Away with that woman! Take her away! Knock her down, the bitch! Knock her down!"

Lieutenant Frederick Mackenzie, the Royal Welsh Fusilier who watched the prisoners straggle into the city, surmised that they had not washed during the war: "A great many of them were lads under 15, and old men." Mackenzie recalled the scores of half-naked rebel bodies he had seen recently on the battle-fields: ". . . many were without shoes or stockings & Several were observed to have linen drawers on . . . They are also in great want of blankets . . . It will be astonishing if they keep together 'til Christmas."

9

THE FLIGHT THROUGH
NEW JERSEY

"...The Game Is Pretty Near Up"

At 9 P.M. on November 19, under cover of a cold rainstorm, Charles Cornwallis led four thousand crack British and German troops—guards, grenadiers, light infantry and riflemen—into small boats and across the Hudson. Before dawn, when the rain had ceased, they were marching toward Fort Lee, six miles downstream. Cornwallis was a forty-two-year-old veteran of European combat, an intimate of George III, who, like the Howes, had at first disapproved the American war and voted with the Whigs in Parliament. Cornwallis was more aggressive than William Howe, an able soldier—modest, industrious, energetic—a tall, rather awkward figure who had a cocked eye, a souvenir from the hockey field at Eton. He did not belittle the task confronting the British army: "I never saw a stronger country, or one better calculated for the defensive."

An American patrol stumbled into the head of the Cornwallis column at daylight of November 20 and fled to Fort Lee, where an officer shook Greene awake. Washington galloped in from Hackensack, and just as the British appeared, led two thousand bewildered troops toward the Hackensack River. Greene rode back into the fort to round up stragglers; he lost a hundred and five men of the rear guard, but reported that they were skulkers trying to hide from the fight.

Pursuing British who entered Fort Lee moments later found pots bubbling over breakfast fires. There were also a thousand barrels of flour, about three hundred tents and all the officers' baggage. The victors were unimpressed by the spoils:

> On the appearance of our troops, the rebels fled like scared rabbits, and in a few moments after we reached the hill near their entrenchments, not a rascal of them could be seen. They have left some poor pork, a few greasy proclamations, and some of that scoundrel, *Common Sense* man's letters, which we can read at our leisure, now that we have got one of the "impregnable redoubts" of Mr. Washington's to quarter in. . . . We intend to push on after the long faces . . .

Washington had moved a supply of gunpowder from Fort Lee two days earlier when he concluded the fort was of "no importance," and though he now said his losses were "inevitable," they were also disastrous. In the fall of the twin forts he had lost almost 150 cannon and 12,000 rounds of ammunition, 3,000 muskets and 400,000 cartridges, not to mention tents, entrenching tools and assorted equipment. The commander's failure to act promptly and send peremptory orders to Greene had meant the loss of irreplaceable matériel so painfully collected since the fall of New York.

The loss of the forts shook the confidence of the staff officers. Joseph Reed, whose friendship with Washington had become warm and affectionate, asked to be relieved as adjutant general. Privately, Reed had begun to think of Charles Lee as the ideal commander in chief. He wrote the Englishman:

> I do not mean to flatter, nor praise you at the Expence of any other, but I . . . do think that it is entirely owing to you that this Army and the Liberties of America . . . are not totally cut off. . . .

Reed said he was positive that Lee could have saved the Fort Washington garrison, and that the staff as well as the soldiers "ardently" wished to see him in command of the army.

Reed poured out to Lee his despair over Washington's hesitant and vacillating habits of command:

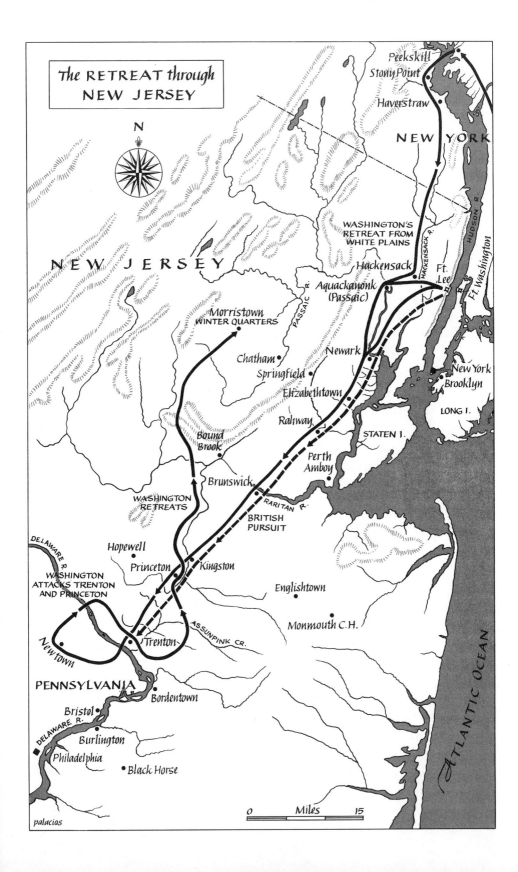

The RETREAT through NEW JERSEY

N

Peekskill
Stony Point
Haverstraw

NEW YORK

WASHINGTON'S
RETREAT FROM
WHITE PLAINS

NEW JERSEY

HACKENSACK R.

HUDSON R.

Hackensack

Aquackanonk
(Passaic)

Ft.
Lee

Ft. Washington

PASSAIC R.

Morristown
WINTER QUARTERS

Chatham

Springfield

Newark

New York

Brooklyn

Elizabethtown

LONG I.

Rahway

STATEN I.

Bound
Brook

Perth
Amboy

WASHINGTON
RETREATS

Brunswick

RARITAN R.

BRITISH
PURSUIT

DELAWARE R.

Hopewell

WASHINGTON
ATTACKS TRENTON
AND PRINCETON

Princeton

Kingston

Englishtown

Monmouth C.H.

Newtown

ASSUNPINK CR.

Trenton

PENNSYLVANIA

Bordentown

ATLANTIC OCEAN

Bristol

DELAWARE R.

Burlington

Philadelphia

Black Horse

0   Miles   15

palacios

Oh! General—an indecisive Mind is one of the greatest Misfortunes that can befall an Army—how often have I lamented it in this campaign . . .

A visitor—a stranger to the staff—appeared at headquarters during the confusion of retreat. He was John Honeyman, a veteran of the French and Indian War who now posed as a butcher and cattle trader in the country near Princeton, where he was known as a Tory. Honeyman was one of Washington's spies, whose secrets were not shared with the staff. The general conferred privately with the butcher and ordered him to follow the army's retreat, keeping watch on British camps, where he passed in and out freely. To further the deception, the general sent to Honeyman's wife a letter addressed to "the good people of New Jersey and all others whom it may concern," an order that Mrs. Honeyman and her children be "protected from all harm and annoyance"—but adding, "this furnishes no protection to Honeyman himself . . . the notorious Tory." This letter was to save the family home from pillage by a patriot mob which came in search of Honeyman. After the butcher's departure from the camp on the Hackensack, Washington offered a reward for his capture. He was to be brought directly to the general's quarters, whatever the hour.

Washington once more found himself between river barriers, and made cautious by his fox hunter's eye for open terrain—or perhaps by the memory of the catastrophe in New York— retreated westward from the Hackensack and across the Passaic on November 21. The enemy did not follow, but there was a danger that Howe would lead reinforcements into New Jersey.

The familiar problem of divided forces still plagued Washington's "wretched remains of a broken army," as Reed described them. Three divisions were at a distance from Washington: Stirling, with a thousand men, still kept watch on the enemy near Brunswick; Heath remained at Peekskill; and Lee, with some fifty-five hundred of the army's finest troops, camped near White Plains. Washington, anxious to concentrate, ordered Lee to cross the Hudson "with all possible dispatch" in case the British moved into New Jersey. When there was no reply, Washington repeated the order, though not in positive terms: ". . . it would be advisable in you to remove . . . your command on this side . . ." and, "I am of opinion . . . that the public interest requires your coming over to this side."

By November 23 Washington had fallen back to Newark, still unhampered by the enemy. He sent Reed to Governor William Livingston of New Jersey and Thomas Mifflin to Congress, begging for money to pay the troops and men to replace those who would soon leave him.

Charles Lee finally responded to pleas from headquarters—with a refusal that bordered on insubordination: ". . . we could not be there in time to answer any purpose . . . withdrawing our troops from hence would be attended with some very serious consequences which at present would be too tedious to enumerate." Instead of bringing his own men to Washington's aid, he had ordered Heath to send two thousand of his own—an order Heath refused.

Washington replied, ". . . you seem to have mistaken my views entirely . . . it was your Division I want to have over." Even on November 26, when Washington learned that Cornwallis was advancing, he wrote mildly to Lee, "I confess I expected you would have been sooner in motion."

Washington retreated from Newark, his rear guard burning a bridge just as the scouts of Cornwallis appeared. The enemy did not pursue. The Americans fell back to Brunswick.

Joseph Reed was still away on his recruiting expedition on November 30, and when a letter for him arrived from Charles Lee, Washington opened it, as he did most official dispatches. A glance was enough to tell the general that Reed had turned against him, and was being encouraged by Lee:

> I received your most obliging, flattering letter—lament with you that fatal indecision of mind which in war is a much greater disqualification than stupidity or even want of personal courage. Accident may put a decisive blunderer in the right, but eternal defeat and miscarriage must attend the man of best parts if curs'd with indecision . . .

Washington's reaction was one of hurt and embarrassment, rather than anger. He sent the letter to Reed with an almost abject apology for having opened a personal message under the impression that it was a routine dispatch:

> . . . This, as it is the truth, must be my excuse for seeing the contents of a letter which neither inclination nor intention would have prompted me to. I thank you for the trouble and fatigue you have undergone in your journey to Burlington, and sincerely wish your labours may be crowned, with the desired success. With best respects to Mrs. Reed . . .

Reed withdrew his resignation at Washington's appeal, and the commander was to say no more of their strained relationship until three months later, when Reed left him to become a cavalry commander: ". . . True, it is, I felt myself hurt by a certain letter . . . not because I thought my judgment wronged . . . but because the same sentiments were not communicated immediately to myself." Washington added that since he had always sought Reed's advice, and acted upon it, he was "not a little mortified" to have him write such criticism to Lee.

British officers were perplexed by the tactics of Washington's little force: "As we go forward into the country the rebels flee before us, and when we come back, they always follow us, 'tis almost impossible to catch them. They will neither fight nor totally run away, but they keep at such distance that we are always above a day's march from them. They seem to be playing at Bo Peep."

The invaders vented their frustrations upon civilians. Colonel Adam Stephen wrote Thomas Jefferson, "The Enemy, like locusts, sweep the Jerseys with the besom of destruction. They, to the disagrace of a civilized nation, ravish the fair sex from the age of ten to seventy."

The Pennsylvania Council of Safety reported British atrocities near Pennytown, N.J.: "Besides the sixteen young women who had fled to the woods to avoid their brutality, and were there seized and carried off, one man had the mortification to have his wife and only daughter (a child of ten years of age) ravished . . . and also . . . another girl thirteen years of age was taken from her father's house, carried to a barn about a mile away, there ravished, and afterwards made use of by five more of these brutes."

The British stripped the country clean: "Everything portable they plunder and carry off, neither age nor sex, Whig or Tory is spared . . . infants, children, old men and women, are left in their shirts without a blanket to cover them . . . Furniture of every kind destroyed or burnt, windows and doors broke to pieces . . . the houses left without provisions, every horse, cow, ox, hogs and poultry carried off, a blind old gentleman near Pennytown plundered of everything, and on his door wrote, 'Capt. Wills of the Royal Irish did this.' "

Washington's ragamuffins also pillaged the country, especially well-stocked cellars. As they passed through Brunswick, according to Lieutenant James McMichael, many soldiers became drunk and rowdy: "They have chiefly got a disorder, which at camp is called Barrel Fever, which differs in its effects from any other fever—its concomitants are black eyes and bloody noses."

The troops found other diversions. One night a neighborhood Tory mistook the camp for that of the enemy and wandered in. Soldiers seized him, took off his breeches, forced him to sit on ice "to cool his loyalty" and put him to work dragging in firewood.

Public resistance to the enemy collapsed in the wake of the army as it retreated southward. About five thousand New Jersey civilians trooped into British camps to take an oath of allegiance. Even Joseph Galloway, a member of the First Continental Congress, joined the British and wrote pamphlets damning the rebels and urging "wholesale pillage and destruction." The prominent Allen brothers of Philadelphia—one a former member of Congress, another a member of the Philadelphia Committee of Safety, and the third a lieutenant colonel of the army —all went over to the enemy.

Thomas Paine, the author of *Common Sense,* now marched with the army as a volunteer aide to Greene. The frail Englishman scrawled new pamphlets on drumheads by the light of campfires, tracts to be known as *The American Crisis,* filled with phrases that had a strange ring in the miserable camps:

THE FLIGHT THROUGH NEW JERSEY

These are the times that try men's souls. The summer soldier and the sunshine patriot will, in this crisis, shrink from the service of their country, but he that stands it *now*, deserves the love and thanks of man and woman. Tyranny, like hell, is not easily conquered; yet we have this consolation with us, that the harder the conflict, the more glorious the triumph . . .

Paine observed Washington closely during the retreat and was reassured. Like some great generals of the past, he thought, Washington was at his best when the outlook was darkest: "There is a natural firmness in some minds which cannot be unlocked by trifles but which, when unlocked, discovers a cabinet of fortitude." Paine thought it a "public blessing" that the Virginian was blessed with "a mind that can even flourish with care."

On December 1, when redcoats appeared in Brunswick, Washington retreated to Princeton in a night march, hurried on by a cannonade across the Raritan River. In a headlong chase, Cornwallis drove his troops twenty miles over boggy roads but failed to catch Washington. The rebels reached Trenton, on the banks of the Delaware, and began collecting small boats. Within a few days a fleet of sturdy boats was hidden along the Pennsylvania shore, most of them Durham boats, so named after an early builder who supplied them for the river trade. These shallow craft, from forty to sixty feet long, carried loads of fifteen tons, and could be rowed or poled across the stream. The vanguard of Washington's army settled in relative safety on the Pennsylvania bank of the Delaware, but as one of his soldiers said, "We are in a terrible situation with the enemy close upon us, and whole regiments of Marylanders and Jerseymen leaving us."

With the enemy only thirty miles from Philadelphia, Congress fled to Baltimore "amid the jeers of Tories and the maledictions of patriots," leaving a panic-stricken capital behind. Shops and houses were boarded and many civilians fled. Israel Putnam, sent to defend the city, declared martial law and called out the militia.

The portrait painter Charles Willson Peale hurried his family out of town and rounded up his 81-man company of the Philadelphia Associators, all of whom lived in the block bounded by Market, Front, Arch and Second streets. The company marched to Washington's camp on the banks of the Delaware with the city brigade of fifteen hundred under Colonel John Cadwalader, a welcome reinforcement despite its shortage of arms—many of these men bore antique muskets or pikes, and others refused to carry their weapons, fearful that the army would not pay for them in case of loss.

These recruits reached camp in darkness, while Washington's bedraggled veterans were still crossing the Delaware into Pennsylvania. It was a scene that was to haunt Lieutenant Peale for the rest of his life—shadowy figures shuffling past the blazing fires on the shore as boatloads of men, cannon, horses and baggage emerged from the blackness, the endless obscenities of the men borne away by a freezing wind. To Peale it was a nightmare vision from *Paradise Lost*: "The most hellish scene I have ever beheld."

Peale was approached by a stranger: "Suddenly a man staggered out of line and came toward me. He had lost all his clothes. He was in an old dirty blanket-jacket, his beard long and his face full of sores. He could not clean it, which so disfigured him that he was not known by me on first sight. Only when he spoke did I recognize my brother James." The Maryland regiment with which James Peale marched had gone into the battle of Long Island with almost a thousand men—it was now reduced to five officers and about a hundred and fifty enlisted men, and its commander, William Smallwood, was at home recuperating from his wounds.

Washington recrossed the river into New Jersey on December 7, hoping to meet Charles Lee and perhaps face the enemy near Trenton, but on his way he met Stirling's rear guard, which was retreating before Cornwallis. Washington turned back reluctantly.

Lieutenant Enoch Anderson of Haslet's Delaware regiment was with the rear guard: "We continued in our retreat—our Regiment in the rear and I, with thirty men in the rear of the Regiment and General Washington in my rear with pioneers, tearing up bridges and cutting down trees to impede the march of the enemy. I was to go no faster than General Washington and his pioneers."

The British, who came stubbornly behind them on the road from Princeton, reached Trenton the next morning—December 8—just as the last of the Americans shoved off into the Delaware.

Washington scattered his men in camps along the Pennsylvania bank of the Delaware, now a force of about five thousand men, "daily decreasing by sickness and other causes." He had ended a desperate retreat of ninety miles in three weeks since the disasters around New York, and "crouching in the bushes" behind the river barrier, still feared that the enemy army of ten thousand would force a crossing. He wrote Congress that he was powerless to prevent the British from invading Pennsylvania.

Now, at last, Washington had word from Charles Lee, who was trailing southward at a leisurely pace on his way from White Plains. "If I was not taught to think that your Army was considerably reenforced," Lee wrote, "I should immediately join you; but as I am assured you are very strong . . ."

In fact, Lee did not relish the thought of leaving his independent command to join Washington, whatever the crisis. He was already displaying an insubordination that was a direct challenge to the commander's authority. Lee proclaimed that he had invaded New Jersey "for the salvation of America," and would attack the exposed British rear.

Lee held the upper hand: even minor victories would bring him public acclaim at the expense of Washington, who could not then discipline him for disobedience. With luck, Lee might win the supreme command for himself.

When a dispatch rider found Lee at Morristown on December 8, the mercurial Englishman shrugged off news that Washington had been driven across the Delaware and wrote the commander somewhat grandly: "It will be difficult I fear to join you; but cannot I do you more service by attacking their rear? I shall look about me tomorrow, and inform you further." He could not conceal his feeling that his military judgment was superior to Washington's. When he learned that the commander was dragging heavy boats along with the army, he wrote with a patronizing air: ". . . I am told you have the gondolas from Philadelphia with you, for Heaven's sake what use can they be of?"

Once more Washington literally begged Lee for obedience: "I cannot but request and entreat you, and this too by the advice of all the general officers with me to march and join me . . . Do come on." He reported his problems with Lee to Congress, but stopped short of charging him with insubordination: ". . . I have wrote to him in the most pressing terms to join me with all expedition."

Still Lee dawdled. Like other Americans in the field, his barefoot troops now marched in "shoes" of bloody beef hides, but even this did not explain Lee's delay. He marched an average of three miles a day, rested for two days at Morristown, and still deaf to Washington's pleas for speed, moved only eight miles the next day, to the village of Vealtown. Only there did Lee reluctantly order his men toward the Delaware. He then left the division with John Sullivan, who had recently been exchanged after his capture on Long Island, and rode three miles from camp on one of his adventures—to spend the night in a tavern kept by a Mrs. White at Basking Ridge. Lee took with him only his bodyguard of fifteen riders and four officers, one of them Major James Wilkinson, who had brought him dispatches from Horatio Gates.

There were women in the house and the party was evidently up late; once during the night Wilkinson heard a woman scream in agony. At ten o'clock the next morning—Friday, December 13 —Lee was at breakfast, in his customary disheveled state, "an old blue coat . . . and greasy leather breeches," writing to Gates, a stinging criticism of Washington:

> The ingenious manoeuvre of Fort Washington has unhing'd the goodly fabrick we had been building—there never was so damn'd a stroke—*entre nous*, a certain great man is damnably deficient—He has thrown me into a situation where I have my choice of difficulties. Unless something which I do not expect turns up we are lost . . .

Lee had hardly finished his letter and passed it to the waiting Wilkinson when British horsemen galloped into sight, killed two sentries, surprised the guard in an outbuilding and surrounded the house. The British shot through doors and windows of the tavern, and though Lee's officers returned fire, the general did not resist. He spurned Mrs. White's suggestion that he hide in a bed and paced the floor until the British threatened to burn the place. When Lee emerged to surrender he was carried away at once by the enemy commander, Lieutenant Colonel William Harcourt. The general had been captured by his old regiment, the 16th Light Horse, which he had once led brilliantly against the Spanish in Portugal.

William Howe called off the chase of Washington on December 13, the day of Lee's capture. Judge Jones, who was enjoying the comforts of home in New York, became caustically critical of Howe: "The only reason I ever heard given for The General not passing the Delaware was that the rebels had carried all the boats across the river. But I have been told . . . that there was a board yard, entirely full, and in back of the . . . headquarters, and which he must have seen every time he looked out of his bedroom window. Besides, there were in Trenton a number of large barns and store houses . . . out of which rafts might have been made . . ."

Washington, incredulous when he was told of Howe's decision, at first dismissed it as a British ruse. Howe's exasperated field officers found little substance in his vague orders: ". . . the campaign having closed with the pursuit of the enemies Army near 90 Miles by Lieut. Gen. Cornwallis's Corps . . . and the approach of Winter putting a stop to any further progress . . ."

Howe established a chain of outposts stretching from Burlington, Bordentown and Trenton on the Delaware, through Princeton, Kingston and Brunswick to the Hackensack River, and led the army back to New York. New Jersey's Hessian garrisons were left under the command of General James Grant, who said with his customary modesty, "I will undertake to keep the peace in New Jersey with a corporal's guard." Henry Clinton, who said that the rebels were "trained to every trick of chicane," warned

Howe that the chain of posts would be attacked, but he was ignored.

News of Lee's capture reached Washington on December 15, a day when he had watched Hessian patrols across the Delaware in a vain search for boats hidden on the New Jersey shore. The general reported "the melancholy intelligence" as a calamity, but said in exasperation that Lee had been captured because of "his own imprudence . . . for the sake of a better lodging."

Even Nathanael Greene, who had warned Washington that Lee would not obey orders, said the capture was "a great loss . . . as he is a most consummate general." Young John Trumbull of Connecticut wrote his father, the governor, that the loss was irreparable, "we have no officer in the army of equal experience and merit." But one youthful soldier, Thomas Rodney of Delaware, saw Lee's capture as a blessing, since Washington, who had so frequently deferred to Lee's judgment, would now be forced to rely upon his own.

Washington ordered Lee's troops to camp and turned to other problems: when neighboring millers refused to grind grain for the army, Washington confiscated both grain and mills; to Congress he reported rumors that Howe had ended his campaign, but warned that the enemy might still cross the Delaware if it froze over.

He besieged congressmen and governors for reinforcements, saying that he would be left with as few as twelve hundred men at the end of the year. He looked ahead to 1777, arguing that even regiments of regulars would be worthless without reliable officers, and that their selection could not be left to politicians from the states, as Congress planned.

On December 18 he wrote his brother, "If every nerve is not strained to recruit the New Army with all possible expedition, I think the game is pretty near up . . . No man, I believe, ever had a greater choice of difficulties and less means to extricate himself from them."

Matters improved two days later when Sullivan brought Lee's troops into camp, though they were only 2,000 strong, rather than the 5,500 Washington had expected. Desertions and expir-

ing enlistments had plagued Lee, too; many were "fit only for
the hospital." Horatio Gates also arrived with 500 men. With
the addition of John Cadwalader's Philadelphia militiamen, the
army now had about 6,000 fit for duty—though it would be
only ten days before the force would melt away once more.

The general sent another plea to Congress, asking for corps of
engineers and artillery, and urging that the army be increased.
He also requested authority to make decisions in the field, since it
was impractical to refer everything to Congress, "at the distance
of 130 to 140 miles, so much time must necessarily elapse as to
defeat the end in view." He added somewhat self-consciously:

> It may be said that this is an application for powers that are
> too dangerous to be intrusted. I can only add, that desperate
> diseases require desperate remedies, and with truth declare, that
> I have no lust after power but wish with as much fervency as any
> man upon this wide extended Continent for an opportunity of
> turning the sword into a plow share.

Washington fortified nine ferry landings and spread his command thinly along twenty-five miles of the Delaware, guarding
"every suspicious part of the river." Only spies were allowed to
cross into New Jersey. The troops kept three days' rations cooked,
ready to move by day or night.

Somehow there was a lingering spirit of optimism in the
army. Samuel B. Webb wrote, "You ask me our situation; it has
been the Devil, but is to appearance better. About 2000 of us have
been obliged to run damn'd hard before about 10,000 of the
enemy. Never was finer lads at a retreat than we are . . . No fun
for us that I can see; however, I cannot but think we shall drub
the dogs . . . Never mind, all will come right one of these days."
He was not alone. A few days earlier Henry Knox had written
his wife that though "unlucky circumstances" had forced the
army to retreat before the British ". . . we shall soon, I hope, be
able to face them."

Rumors of a surprise attack on the enemy had seeped from
headquarters. Washington made no secret of his hopes in his correspondence. He had written Gates while he was on the march,
"If we can draw our forces together, I trust, under the smiles of

"... The Game Is Pretty Near Up"

Providence, we may yet effect an important stroke . . ." To the Governor of Connecticut he wrote that he hoped to strike the enemy, "who lie a good deal scattered, and to all appearances in a state of security."

In fact, an audacious plan of assault that Washington had considered when he first crossed into Pennsylvania again occupied his mind. James Wilkinson found the general distant and distracted, ". . . always grave and thoughtful . . . pensive and solemn in the extreme."

Dr. Benjamin Rush, who rode to camp from Philadelphia on December 23, got no hint of these plans. Joseph Reed, who was hurrying off to scout the enemy, told Rush that the cause seemed hopeless. Rush spent an hour alone with Washington the next morning and was chilled by the general's gloomy manner. "He appeared much depressed and lamented the ragged and dissolving state of his army . . . I gave him assurance of the disposition of Congress to support him . . ."

The general scratched absent-mindedly with a quill upon some scraps of paper, and when a sheet fell to the floor at Rush's feet the doctor read a striking phrase he would not forget: "Victory or Death."

On the same day Reed wrote Washington from Bristol: "We are all of the opinion, my dear General, that something must be attempted to . . . give our cause some degree of reputation. . . . Will it not be possible to make a diversion . . . at or about Trenton?" Washington called Reed to headquarters, told him he had already planned an attack, and sent a militia band back to Bristol with him, to raid smaller Hessian outposts.

The general ordered that the troops be mustered to hear readings of Thomas Paine's new *Crisis*, which had been printed in Philadelphia despite the panic which had swept the "amazingly depopulated" city. The pamphlet was also sent into the countryside, and "flew like wildfire through all the towns and villages."

Washington, who was still his own chief of espionage, dipped often into his fund for secret agents during these days, and wrote to them with invisible fluids, making use of several private codes. From headquarters near the Delaware he urged his officers to bring him detailed reports on the enemy at Trenton:

You will give out your strength to be twice as great as it is . . .
you will keep as many spies out as you can see proper. A number
of horsemen, in the dress of the country, must be constantly kept
going backwards and forwards . . . keep a good look-out for spies
. . . Let me entreat you to find out some person, who can be
engaged to cross the river as a spy . . . Expense must not be
spared . . . and it will readily be paid by me.*

One of the general's most dependable spies, the "Tory butcher"
John Honeyman, reappeared at headquarters just before Christmas. American scouts hiding on the New Jersey side of the river
had captured him when he wandered out of the Hessian lines at
Trenton, driving a single scrubby cow. Honeyman had readily
given his name and was hurried to headquarters, where Washington spent half an hour alone with the spy and heard his report
on the enemy: the Hessians had built no boats, and had not
begun to fortify Trenton. Their commander, Colonel Rall, had
only contempt for the rebel army. He was preparing a traditional
German holiday celebration.

Washington ordered Honeyman held for court-martial as a
Tory spy, but during the night the butcher vanished from his log
hut under mysterious circumstances: a guard had been diverted
when a nearby outbuilding caught fire, and Honeyman escaped
—no one knew how. A few hours later the butcher reported to
Rall in Trenton: there was nothing to fear from the feeble
American army "for some time to come."

A council of war met on Christmas Eve in a crowded room of
Stirling's quarters, the stone farmhouse of the Thompson family
—Washington, Greene, Sullivan, Mercer, Stirling, Roche de Fermoy, St. Clair and several colonels, among them John Glover of
the Marblehead regiment, whose fishermen must once more ferry
the army across a river. Final plans for an attack were made
after long discussion, risky plans that would test the strongest of
armies: three separate divisions would cross the river—Washington would lead the main army of 2,400 men over at McCon-

* As usual, Washington advanced the money to pay his spies, but later
billed the government for large sums under the heading "secret intelligence."

key's Ferry and march to attack Trenton, nine miles downstream. General James Ewing, with about 700 Pennsylvania and New Jersey militia, would cross at Trenton to block the Hessian escape to the south. Farther downstream, at Bristol, General John Cadwalader and his 2,000 men would launch a feint attack. The columns would move on Christmas, after nightfall. Success depended upon precise timing by the columns in crossing the treacherous stream in darkness and uncertain weather. As Washington had written Reed: "Christmas-day at night, one hour before day, is the time fixed for our attempt at Trenton. For Heaven's sake keep this to yourself."

10

TRENTON, DECEMBER 26, 1776

"A Glorious Day for Our Country"

Early in December three regiments of Hessians settled in Trenton, a village of about one hundred scattered houses at the falls of the Delaware. The fifteen hundred Germans occupied many of its deserted buildings; most of them houses on King and Queen streets, which lay parallel to the river.

The Germans were under the command of Colonel Rall, who had won the confidence of his troops in every action since Long Island. The fifty-year-old veteran had once served in the Russian army under Alexis Orloff, the assassin of Czar Peter III, but though brave and experienced, Rall was stubborn, proud and impulsive and lacked experience in general command. Andreas Wiederhold, one of his lieutenants in Trenton, complained: "There was more bustle than business at the post. The men were harassed with watches, detachments and pickets without purpose and without end. Whether his men when off duty were well or ill-clad, whether they kept their muskets clean and bright and their ammunition in good order was of little moment to the colonel, he never inquired about it; but the music! That was the thing! The hautboys—he never could have enough of them." When his band marched near headquarters the colonel followed each changing of the guard to hear the music. Rall gambled or entertained every night and slept late in the mornings. Troops assembled for parade at 10 A.M. often had to wait half an hour until the colonel finished his bath.

Rall disdained the rebels as "nothing but a lot of farmers" and refused to prepare for an American attack, even on December 14, when his superior, Colonel von Donop, ordered him to fortify the main approaches to Trenton. Two of his lieutenants, Wiederhold and Friedrich Fischer, of the artillery, offered to build the breastworks themselves, but Rall refused. "Let 'em come! he said. "We want no trenches! We'll at them with the bayonet."

By December 22 rumors of rebel activity reached Trenton. A Bucks County farmer told Rall that the post would be attacked. "Let 'em come!" Rall repeated. The next day two American deserters told him that the rebels had cooked four days' rations, an infallible sign of movement. Rall scoffed. When a neighbor, Dr. William Bryant, took the colonel a similar report, Rall said, "This is all idle! It's all old woman's talk."

On Christmas Eve a dispatch rider brought a warning from General Grant, saying that Washington was being urged to strike at the Trenton outpost. Grant wrote, "I don't believe he will attempt it, but be assured that my information is undoubtedly true, so I need not advise you to be upon your guard against an unexpected attack . . ." Rall led a patrol nine miles northward during the day, as far as the Delaware ferry opposite Washington's main force, but though his advance drove a few rebels from the ferry, Rall left no outpost to watch the crossing.

As Washington had expected, the Germans celebrated Christmas with feasting, singing and drinking that lasted far into the night. Only the Von Lossberg men, as the regiment of the day, were kept ready for immediate action; they were forbidden to remove their uniforms.

A rattle of musket fire aroused pickets at the northern edge of the village on Christmas night, a few scattered shots which wounded six Hessians. The outpost reported that forty or fifty rebels had attacked and fallen back into the darkness. The alarm spread through the village, all three regiments were called out and Rall left a game of checkers with Stacy Potts, in whose home he made headquarters. Sentries moved two miles up the northern road but found nothing. One officer urged the colonel to send patrols out on all roads and to the ferries. "There'll be time enough in the morning," Rall said. He also brushed aside a suggestion that he pack the baggage wagons to be ready for retreat, and said scornfully, "These country clowns can't whip us!" His troops went back to their bottles and the firesides.

The colonel did not return to headquarters but went to the home of Abraham Hunt on King Street. Postmaster Hunt, a prosperous merchant, held a secret commission as a New Jersey rebel militia officer, but tonight he entertained the German officers as if they were boon companions. After supper Hunt's guests turned to drinking and playing cards. About midnight Jessie Wall, a Tory farmer, knocked at the door and asked for the colonel. When a servant refused to interrupt the gamblers, the farmer scribbled a message of warning—the rebels were coming. Rall stuffed the note into his pocket without reading it and turned back to his game. It was shortly before dawn when the colonel left the card table and went yawning to his bed.

The first of the ice came down the river at noon, jagged floes broken out of the creeks upstream, surging in the swift current —thin, knife-sharp cakes that would pummel the boats in the crossing. Washington's most distant regiments began arriving at the Pennsylvania side of McConkey's Ferry soon after 2 P.M. and waited behind the ridge in deepening cold. The troops were turned out for evening parade just before six o'clock, but tonight they did not march back to their huts; they were turned toward the ferry in the dusk. The wind had risen to a gale, raking across the river from the Jersey shore. John Fitzgerald of Washington's staff, who had just made copies of the marching orders, walked out from the warmth of the ferry house into the chill blast: "It is fearfully cold and raw . . . The wind is northeast and beats in the faces of the men. It will be a terrible night for the soldiers who have no shoes. Some of them have tied old rags around their feet, others are barefoot, but I have not heard a man complain."

Suddenly the boats were there, lumbering among the ice floes in the darkness, dozens of Durham boats built for the peacetime iron ore trade on the Delaware, flat-bottomed craft thirty or forty feet long, sharp-pointed fore and aft like canoes. They had been brought from hiding behind a nearby island by John Glo-ver's Marblehead fishermen and eased against the shore by expert helmsmen with broad stern sweeps. The troops began to load, the Virginians first, and the lead boats pushed off, the blue-jac-keted seamen struggling to pole the craft in the current as they walked the decked gunwales, colliding with other polemen who pushed aside the cakes of ice. The floes were thicker now, grind-ing against the hulls. The lines of waiting troops at the river-side grew longer and men shivered in the freezing wind. The bass voice of Henry Knox rang above the subdued roar of the wind and the river, shouting orders in his flat Boston accent.

As Washington mounted to leave his headquarters James Wilkin-son rode up with a dispatch. The general's temper was short: "What a time to hand me letters!"

Wilkinson apologized. "General Gates asked me to bring it to you."

Washington was incredulous. "General Gates? Where is he?"

"I left him this morning in Philadelphia."

"What was he doing there?"

"I understood . . . he was on his way to Congress."

Washington's voice rose. "On his way to Congress!" He opened the letter and read briefly. Gates was gone, off on a mission to his friends in Congress that was to remain a mystery. Of all the senior officers with whom he had begun the war, only Greene would be with him tonight.

The general halted for a few moments to write to Cadwalader, far downstream at Bristol:

Notwithstanding the discouraging Accounts I have received . . . of what might be expected from the Operations below, I am determined, as the Night is favourable, to cross the River and make the attack upon Trenton in the Morning. If you can do nothing real, at least create as great a diversion as possible.

A final order from headquarters went off to Dr. Shippen at the army hospital in Bethlehem—he was to come up at once with all his doctors and aides. Heavy casualties were expected.

The horses stamped in the cold and troops crowded near them for warmth. Cursing men struggled to load the nervous animals into the boats and dragged cannon to the water's edge. When Washington reached the riverside soon after six o'clock one soldier among the half-frozen scarecrows saw that the general had a red nose, "apt to turn scarlet in the wind . . . He was not what ladies would call a pretty man."

After two or three hours of waiting, as the swirling ice grew thicker and the struggles of the boatmen became more desperate, Washington and Knox boarded one of the boats and were pushed into the current. Knox sat in the stern. The craft lurched, and one gunwale dipped dangerously near the water. Washington shouted to his huge artillery chief—or so the soldiers were soon telling one another: "Shift your tail, Knox, and trim the boat."

The river was barely three hundred yards wide, but it seemed a long crossing. Washington stepped to the New Jersey shore and found that Stephen's men had fanned out in the darkness to form a picket line and seal off the landing; no one was allowed to pass in or out. The general sat on an old beehive to await his horse. Snow began to fall at eleven o'clock, dry flakes lashed by the wind. By midnight, when the army should have been safely across, much of the infantry was still on the Pennsylvania bank, and it was three o'clock before the eighteen guns went over and four o'clock before the army was ready to move southward. For ten hours the seamen had labored to shuttle across the twenty-four hundred men, eighteen guns and the horses. Glover's men were near exhaustion.

Fitzgerald was with the commander in the last moments at the ferry landing: "I never have seen Washington so determined as he is now. He stands on the bank of the river, wrapped in his cloak, superintending the landing of his troops. He is calm and collected, but very determined. The storm is changing to sleet and cuts like a knife. The last cannon is being landed, and we are ready to mount our horses."

The officers around the chief, James Wilkinson thought, were "gloomy and despondent." The army was now four hours late. Dawn would come soon after seven o'clock, before the men could cover the nine miles to Trenton. The enemy would be astir. Washington had lost his chance at a surprise night attack but he did not hesitate. Orders were passed: the men were to march quietly and keep to their places. Any man who left the ranks would be shot. The men were reminded of the password "Liberty or Death." Sentries were called in. Guides took the road and the troops moved inland. The guides were spies, volunteers in farmers' clothing, men who lived in Hopewell and Trenton; Washington had hoped for a dozen guides, but there were only three tonight. Within a mile the vanguard reached Bear Tavern and turned southward, downriver, toward Trenton.

The way seemed easier with the wind at their backs, but freezing rain made the earth like glass and men stumbled across the frozen ruts as the road wound through forests of oak and hickory, past dark farmhouses. The column moved soundlessly in the storm. A rider came to Washington with a message from Sullivan: rain had ruined powder in the muskets, and they could not be fired. "Tell the General to use the bayonet," Washington said. "I am resolved to take Trenton." Greene's officers carried orders through the ranks—the men were to see that firing pans were covered with coats or blankets to keep the powder dry.

Near the head of the army was the New York artillery battery of nineteen-year-old Captain Alexander Hamilton, which was a "model of discipline." The boy captain had dismounted and hitched his horse to one of the guns, and now marched with his men, a slight, erect figure pressing resolutely ahead with a cocked hat pulled down over his eyes, apparently lost in thought. He walked beside a cannon as he often did on the march, "patting it every now and then as if it were a favorite horse or pet plaything."

Other men marked for fame struggled through the night with the miserable column, among them a future President, Lieutenant James Monroe, and the future Chief Justice of the Supreme Court, Private John Marshall. The painter Charles Wilson Peale and his brother James were in the ranks. Another soldier was twenty-five-year-old George Nixon of Wilmington, Del., who was to become the ancestor of the thirty-seventh President of the United States. There was also General Hugh Mercer, a brigade commander who had not long to live; he was to become the great-grandfather of General George S. Patton.

The column halted at the settlement of Birmingham, where

the men ate breakfast from their haversacks. From his farm-house nearby, Benjamin Moore sent out food for the general and Washington ate in the saddle. Many men fell asleep at the roadside and were shaken awake with difficulty when the march resumed; two of them were reported to have frozen to death during the halt.

Washington divided the army into columns in this village. Sullivan led half the troops along the river road by the banks of the Delaware and Greene's column turned to the left, on the parallel Pennington road, a mile or so to the east. Washington ordered both commanders to strike as soon as they met the enemy, and to push into town without waiting for support. By torchlight the general drew out his watch and had his officers set their watches by his own. As the columns separated, Washington joined Greene on the Pennington road.

Private Elisha Bostwick, who marched with the 7th Connecticut, was to remember this night in his old age, most vividly the red light of cannon torches stuck into the touchholes of the plunging guns, where they "sparkled and blazed in the storm all night." Not long before dawn Washington rode past Bostwick's regiment, calling encouragement to the men: "Soldiers, keep by your officers. For God's sake, keep by your officers!" All this, Bostwick said, was "spoke in a deep and solemn voice."

A few minutes later Washington narrowly escaped a fall. His horse slipped as he clambered up an icy bank and the general grabbed the mane of his mount with both hands to save himself. It was now becoming daylight. The head of Greene's column was still two miles from Trenton. Washington looked anxiously at the sky and called as he rode, "Press on, men. Press on." The soldiers moved in silence, unhurrying, as the high singsong voice grew fainter along the ranks.

The column halted abruptly. Washington rode forward to investigate and found a small band of men in a field at the roadside. They were Americans, someone said, who had come out from the village. An officer in the field identified himself as Captain Richard Anderson of the 5th Virginia.

"Where have you been?" Washington said. Anderson explained that General Stephen had sent him across the river early on

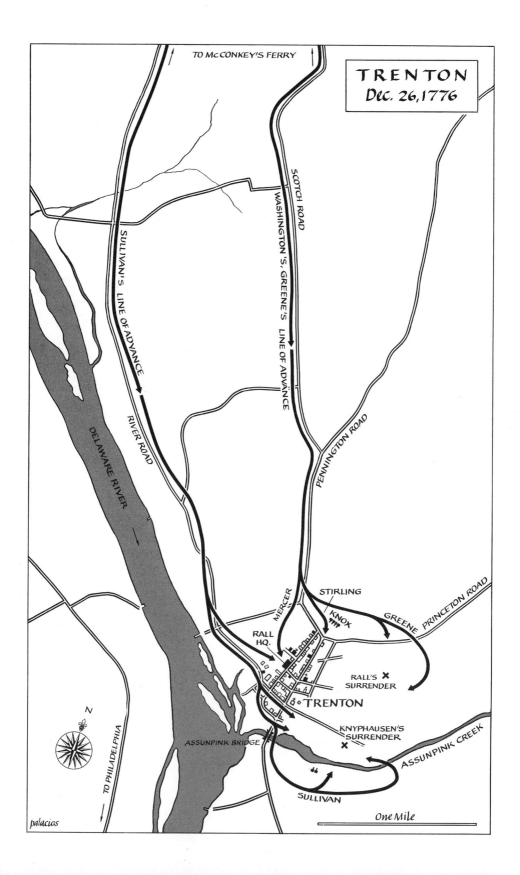

TRENTON, DECEMBER 26, 1776

Christmas Day, to locate enemy outposts at Trenton. He had tried to follow orders by avoiding battle, but his men had stumbled into a Hessian picket in the storm, and had left one body lying in the road. Washington turned furiously upon Adam Stephen, his fellow Virginian, who was nearby: "How dared you send them over the river the day we were to march, without authority? You, sir, may have ruined all my plans by putting them on their guard!" Stephen made no reply. As a blustering parade-ground officer during the French and Indian War, Adam Stephen had been one of the general's early political rivals. Washington told Anderson's weary men to fall in with the vanguard, rather than march to the rear, where the waiting would be cold and interminable.*

It was almost eight o'clock when Greene's advance scattered the first outpost. By now Washington had reined his horse before a house at the edge of the village where a farmer was chopping wood. "Can you tell me where the Hessian picket is?" The man stared dumbly. "Don't be afraid. I'm General Washington." The man's face brightened and he pointed across fields to Howell's shop, where a Hessian ran along the road. At Washington's side Fitzgerald watched the enemy soldier: "He yelled in Dutch and swung his arms. Three or four came out with their guns. Two of them fired at us, but the bullets whistled over our heads."

In Trenton, Friedrich Fischer of the artillery rose at 4 A.M. as usual, ordered horses hitched to two brass cannon before the sentry post on King Street, and sent two gunners to headquarters, where they reported for the early patrol to the nearby river landing. Colonel Rall was still asleep, but Lieutenant Piel, his adjutant, sent the men to Major von Dechow, the officer of the day. The old veteran, who had once fought with Frederick the Great, looked out into the snowstorm and sent back a sleepy reply: "The duty will be omitted this morning." The horses were unhitched and led to their stables. The Germans saw nothing on the road from the north, and took no notice of the stir on the opposite

---

* Captain Anderson became the father of General Robert Anderson, who defended Fort Sumter in Charleston Harbor at the opening of the Civil War.

bank of the river, where General Ewing's force was making a vain effort to cross, blocked by floes of ice which had piled up against the bank like a glacier, a barrier some three hundred feet long.

An hour later, near five o'clock, as it did every morning, a German patrol emerged from a house just north of the village. This morning, instead of the usual twenty or thirty infantrymen and a few cavalrymen, only three jaegers came out, their short rifles slung. They trudged a short distance northward through the blizzard and turned back to report that they had seen nothing. An hour later, and a mile farther, they would have met Washington's advance. Lieutenant Piel went to Colonel Rall's room before six o'clock but found him sleeping so heavily that he left. He returned an hour later, but the commander was still snoring.

The strongest outpost on the Pennington road was at Richard Howell's tiny cooper's shop, which Lieutenant Andreas Wiederhold had reinforced with nine men. Small patrols had gone out at intervals during the night, and the first day patrol had gone its rounds and reported all quiet. It was now about 7:45 A.M.

Wiederhold stepped outside the shop and saw through the woods a band of dark figures moving steadily toward him. Another American raiding party, he thought, no more than sixty strong. Wiederhold's sentinels had seen them by now, and rushed from the shop shouting: *"Der Feind! Der Feind! Heraus! Heraus!"* ("The enemy! The enemy! Turn out! Turn out!")

The picket exchanged volleys with the Americans and ran across fields toward Rall's headquarters, until they were cut off by rebels hurrying in from their right, the men of Mercer's brigade. The Germans turned toward Captain von Altenbockum's company, which had already fallen in across the road. This combined party fired once and then fled. The Americans moved after them at a rapid trot. Stephen's brigade poured into the streets of the village, giving the Hessians no time to make a stand. Two of Altenbockum's men were killed and several wounded as they retreated. The Americans passed Lieutenant Georg Kimm as he lay dying at the roadside, and Captain Samuel Morris of the Philadelphia cavalry halted to help the fallen man, but

Nathanael Greene drove him forward with a sharp command.

In the village Lieutenant Piel hurriedly sent troops to the aid of the picket posts, halted before Rall's house and pounded on the door. The colonel, in his nightshirt, looked down from a window.

"What's the matter?"

"Don't you hear the firing?"

"I'll be out in a minute," Rall said. He was soon in the open, fully dressed. American cannon had already begun to fire down the street.

A few minutes later, at the edge of the village, Washington heard the roar of other cannon from the riverside. Fitzgerald was with him: "General Washington's face lighted up instantly, for he knew it was one of Sullivan's guns." The officers saw hundreds of Germans far down the street, milling about a church to form ranks, a melee of scurrying men, bellowing officers and straining artillery horses. Captain Thomas Forrest wheeled six of his guns into position, Henry Knox gave them the range, and the Pennsylvania gunners opened fire down King and Queen streets. Riflemen ran across fields to cut off retreat by the Pennington road and others overran German cannon, seizing them before they could fire, and shooting down artillery horses. Laughing Americans shouted as they ran through the streets: "These are the times that try men's souls!"

By now Colonel Rall had assembled the Von Lossberg regiment in the graveyard of the Anglican Church. He led one of its battalions into King Street toward the Americans, but cannon fire was already knocking men out of his ranks. Mercer's infantrymen had scattered and fired from houses and from the yard of an old tannery. Colonel Rall saw two cannon standing in the street, already hitched to their horses and shouted, "My God, Lieutenant Engelhardt, the picket is already coming in! Push your cannon ahead!" Drivers shouted and cracked their whips and the guns plunged ahead, but Alexander Hamilton's two guns and sharpshooters from the tannery killed or wounded eight men and five of the battery's horses, and the weapons could not be dragged off the street. Engelhardt's final round of grapeshot rattled harmlessly off the fences and buildings of the tannery.

Some Germans were seen in the streets, desperately packing

loot into wagons for escape; they could not be driven into ranks for defense of the town. The twenty British dragoons of Rall's command scampered southward out of town over the bridge of Assunpink Creek and escaped without firing a shot. Rall's own regiment had begun to melt away as men ran for the stone bridge, but a fresh company of the Von Lossberg troops charged up King Street toward the Americans. The charge carried no more than fifty yards when Hamilton's guns scattered it, driving the troops into a woodland and leaving several wounded lying in the street. Germans were now falling back together near the southern edge of the village, some of them in panic. Lieutenant Engelhardt and a few surviving gunners ran across gardens to the rear. They had taken only a few steps before the Americans seized the guns.

Engelhardt found Rall in the street, standing with his sword drawn, surrounded by a swarm of confused men. Engelhardt shouted, "Colonel Rall, there is yet time to save the cannon!" Rall said nothing, and the lieutenant repeated his plea. The bewildered colonel looked toward the sound of rifle fire from Sullivan's front. "Lord, Lord, what is it?" he said. "What is it?" Another officer told him that the cannon could be saved, but Rall said absently, "Never mind, we'll soon have them back." He waved his sword and shouted, "Forward, men, forward!" The troops about him did not move. Engelhardt and his gunners left the commander and ran toward the rear. As he passed Major von Dechow, Engelhardt told him that the cannon were lost. The old soldier replied with a distracted shout, "For God's sake, I understand!" Under fire from some of John Glover's riflemen, Engelhardt and his party dashed across the stone bridge to safety on the road to Bordentown.

Henry Knox, looking on from a few hundred yards away, thought that the "hurry, fright and confusion" of the Hessians was like a scene from the end of the world. The enemy, fleeing from the streets, hid behind houses, where they came under musket fire.

By now Greene had thrown a double line of troops along the road to Brunswick, cutting off the escape of Hessians to the north. Colonel George Weedon's Virginia regiment then charged down King Street toward the abandoned Hessian guns, with Captain William Washington and Lieutenant James Monroe in the lead. The charge was joined by Sergeant Joe White and his crew of Virginia artillerymen. White said, "I hollowed as loud as I could scream to the men to run for their lives right up to the pieces." White was the first man to reach the German cannon, found a lone gunner there, raised his sword and shouted, "Run, you dog!" The Hessian fled. Captain Washington and Lieutenant Monroe were wounded as they fought for these cannon.

The remnants of two German regiments moved forward in a counterattack, but fell back before Greene's marksmen who fired from houses and from behind fences and trees. By this time Sullivan's advance had moved across the southern edge of the village, led by a fierce little band from John Stark's regiment—an enormously fat captain, Ebenezer Frye, with a sergeant and sixteen men from Derryfield, New Hampshire, who ran ahead throughout the fight, hunting down Hessians wherever they found them. The ragged squad once captured a force of sixty Germans. Sullivan's main column captured Hessian barracks, and Glover's brigade took the Assunpink bridge, closing the last route of escape.

Still the Hessians fought on. Young officers gathered survivors of the Rall and Von Lossberg regiments in low ground south of town and badgered the distracted Colonel Rall until he agreed to an assault. When he was told that they must charge or retreat to the bridge, or be killed to the last man, Rall nodded and rode ahead: "Forward march! Attack them with the bayonet!" The precise ranks were soon torn by artillery and musket fire, but a regimental band began to play, and the forlorn attack carried into Queen Street. Fire now poured down from houses on every side. Rall was shot—a slight wound, he said, but he appeared to weaken from loss of blood. About two hundred of the Von Lossberg regiment fought on, in clouds of bitter smoke which concealed the enemy. The men tried to fire rapidly, but wet powder made many muskets useless. They were told to chip their flints, but still the muskets did not fire. By now fourteen of the Von Lossberg men were down, including several officers.

Rall sent Lieutenant Piel to the rear to inspect the escape route over the Assunpink bridge. In the heavy snowstorm he mistook

John Glover's regiment for Hessians and narrowly escaped capture. He reported to Rall that it was too late. The news seemed to arouse the colonel. He shouted, "All who are my grenadiers, forward!" Once more the men refused to budge. As Rall looked about him uncertainly he was knocked from his horse with two severe musket wounds in his side. He lay in the snow briefly and then was carried into the nearby Methodist Church on the arms of two soldiers, who laid him on a pew.

Many Hessians had already been captured. Major von Dechow, weakened from a hip wound, hobbled into the street and surrendered, to the disgust of his still-defiant men. Command passed to Lieutenant Colonel Francis Scheffler, who led the remnants of two regiments into an orchard, where he hoped to make a stand, but several American brigades now encircled the position, and rebel gunners, only sixty feet away, stood with smoking slow matches, ready to touch off their cannon. Rebel officers shouted, "Surrender! Throw down your guns!"

An ensign, Karl Kleinschmidt, who understood a little English, interpreted these calls and Von Scheffler called out to a mounted American officer, "I think we will surrender." The American horseman came forward—he was Lieutenant Colonel George Baylor of Washington's staff—and talked briefly with the German. Troops of the two regiments dropped their arms and flags, and officers held up their hats on their swords in token of surrender. Some angry men in the ranks flung their muskets into the woods.

Washington was some distance from the orchard, near the guns of Captain Forrest. The general ordered the gunner to load with canister for close-range firing.

"But, sir, they have struck," Forrest said.

"Struck?"

"Yes. Their colors are down."

Washington stared intently. "So they are," he said quietly, and rode toward the orchard.

The Von Knyphausen regiment, penned into a wooded marsh near the creek with the hysterical women and servants of the army, was surrounded by St. Clair's brigade. Men tried to swim the creek, but most of them turned back from the swift waters.

A few were swept downstream and drowned. St. Clair sent an ultimatum: "We hold the bridge, the fords and the roads. Surrender immediately or I will blow you to bits." The Von Knyphausen regiment was surrendered and it was all over. The battle had lasted less than two hours. Sergeant White, the Virginia gunner, walked over the ground where the fight had raged: "My blood chilled to see such horror and distress."

Major Wilkinson rode through the pelting snow and rain to carry the news to Washington, and found him on King Street. The general took the young officer's hand. "This is a glorious day for our country, Major Wilkinson."

Washington's victory was complete except for some four hundred of the enemy who had escaped. More than nine hundred were prisoners, about thirty of them wounded so badly that they must be left in Trenton. Twenty-two Germans were dead. American losses were incredibly light, two officers and two privates wounded, and though they went unreported, two men had probably frozen to death on the march.

As news of the Hessian surrender spread, American troops yelled, flung their hats into the air and capered through the snowy streets. They were soon put to rounding up prisoners and searching the houses of Tories, where more Germans were dragged from hiding. Washington ordered the portmanteaus of Hessian officers and the knapsacks of the men returned, unopened, but collected the German loot and called in civilians to claim it—twenty-one wagonloads of stolen household goods. American officers broke open forty kegs of rum and poured them into the streets, but liquor was found in the barracks and so many troops were soon so roaring drunk that officers reported the army out of control.

Colonel Rall, lying on a church bench, was borne through the streets to his quarters in the Potts house, where he was put to bed. As his wounds were dressed the note of warning from the Tory farmer Wall fell from his pocket and someone translated it for him. Rall grimaced and said quietly, "If I had read this at Mr. Hunt's I would not be here."

Washington and Greene went to the house during the morning to express their sympathy to Rall through the interpreter. The colonel asked that his men be treated kindly and Washington assured him they would be well cared for. Rall died during the night and was buried in the Presbyterian churchyard in an unmarked grave. Major von Dechow died a few hours later.

It was now clear that two of Washington's three assault columns had failed to cross the river, and that only Trenton had been attacked. Ewing had been unable to move a single boat through the towering floes at the Trenton Ferry. Cadwalader had put across some infantrymen farther downstream, but recalled them when heavy ice prevented his artillery from crossing. Other Hessian garrisons were intact, and the enemy might soon march on Trenton in strength. Greene and Knox urged Washington to pursue the panic-stricken Germans who had escaped, but a council of war voted to recross the river, to safety in Pennsylvania. It was about noon when the army straggled off northward on the return march.

It moved more slowly now. Snow and sleet still pelted the troops, and in addition to herding prisoners, there was loot to haul—six brass cannon, seven ammunition and baggage wagons, a thousand muskets and many drums and flags. The Hessians marched awkwardly in their long-skirted coats with stiff upright collars—short, muscular, broad-shouldered men with tow-colored hair pulled tightly over their skulls so that their greased pigtails "stuck straight back like the handle of an iron skillet." Elisha Bostwick noted "a blueish tinge" in their light complexions. The Germans had been told that the Americans killed and ate prisoners, and many of them eyed their captors warily. The prisoners shuffled along silently in their heavy uniforms and leggings, in contrast to Washington's rowdy ragamuffins.

When the column returned to the ferry landing, prisoners were crowded into the first boats. One boatload of German officers almost overturned and was swept two miles downstream, where the Hessians were forced to wade ashore among the ice floes. In other boats the crews stamped their feet to shake ice from the flat-bottomed craft and motioned to the prisoners to help. Bostwick was amused by the response: "They all set to jumping at once with their cues flying up and down and soon shook off the ice." The officers were crowded into the ferry house at McConkey's for the night, and complained that they fared "very miserably without anything to eat or drink." The next day they were marched to the nearby village of Newtown, where their men were placed under guard in the Presbyterian Church and the county jail.

Some Americans with the rear ranks fared worse than the prisoners. Captain William Hull's company did not reach its tents until the following morning, December 27. "Two nights and a day in as violent a storm as ever I felt," Hull wrote. "What can't men do when engaged in so noble a cause?"

All of Washington's troops were badly worn, for many of them had marched thirty or forty miles, and the regiments had been marching or fighting in the raw weather for thirty-six hours or longer. More than a thousand men were reported unfit for duty on the day after the battle. Washington settled near Newtown, five miles east of the Delaware, in the farmhouse of John Harris, where he composed a restrained victory message to Congress:

> I have the pleasure of congratulating you upon the success of an enterprise, which I had formed against a detachment of the enemy lying at Trenton, and which was executed yesterday morning. . . .

He praised his men, and said that every unit had marched and fought bravely and well. He also sent Congress the captured battle flags, handsome silk banners embroidered in gold, the first such trophies of the war. It was only nine days since he had written in despair, ". . . I think the game is pretty near up."

As the army celebrated the victory the general received a message from Congress conferring emergency powers and making him a virtual dictator—for six months. His first thoughts were of the country's future; he seemed to fear that he would be accused of lusting for power: ". . . instead of thinking myself free from all civil obligations," he replied, "I shall constantly bear in mind, that as the sword was the last resort for the preservation of liberties, so it ought to be laid aside, when those liberties are firmly established." The Virginian posed no danger to the civil liberties of his nation—if ever it became a nation.

11

PRINCETON, JANUARY 3, 1777

"A Fine Fox Chase, Boys!"

Back in camp on the Pennsylvania side of the Delaware, Washington entertained twenty-eight Hessian officers at headquarters on December 28, soldierly men in the dark blue of the Von Lossberg and Rall regiments. The German professionals spoke with the staff through interpreters, haltingly at first, but more warmly as the evening wore on, until they lost their air of arrogance and talked of war with the Americans as if they were equals. They studied intently the commander of the rabble which had defeated them. Lieutenant Weiderholt had a lasting impression of the Virginian: "Gen. Washington is a courtly and elegant man, but seems to be very polite and reserved, speaks little and has a sly expression."

Later in the evening four senior officers dined with the general and his staff. The prisoners did not suspect that even as he played host at the dinner table Washington was planning a blow more daring than the assault on Trenton—to recross the Delaware and strike at exposed British forces once more.

It was late in the evening when the general took leave of the four guests* and returned to his work. During the day he had

---

* The German officers were paraded before crowds in Philadelphia and Baltimore before being taken to prisons in western Pennsylvania and Vir-

studied a dispatch from Colonel Cadwalader, who was preparing to cross to Trenton from his position downstream, and urged Washington to join him in blows at other enemy outposts in New Jersey: "We might perfectly surround the troops at Bordentown, so as to prevent one man escaping." Washington and his generals debated their dilemma. The army could not move until the men had rested a day or two and more rations were brought in—but it might be unable to move at all after December 31, when the enlistments of most regiments expired. Troops would soon be flocking homeward, leaving no more than fifteen hundred veterans in the command.

Washington wrote Cadwalader that he would cross the river at McConkey's Ferry once more with the main army and would join him in Trenton, and on December 30 his troops began to cross the stream in bitter weather more forbidding than that of the week before. Snow lay six inches deep in nearby villages. Ice was so thick that many boats were driven back and the army did not finish the crossing until the next day. Many troops were left behind, among them the half-naked gunners of Captain Forrest's battery.

The unshod artillery horses scrambled helplessly on the icy Jersey shore, aided by struggling men. A sergeant who marched with the advance wrote: "Our men, too, were without shoes . . . and . . . the ground was literally marked with the blood of the soldiers' feet."

Washington rode ahead of his troops to Trenton; he found no sign of the enemy on the familiar road. Dispatch riders brought only vague reports of the British and Hessians, who had apparently abandoned the area. Cadwalader had also crossed the river into New Jersey by now and was in Bordentown with about thirty-five hundred troops, half of them Pennsylvania and Delaware recruits led in by General Mifflin. After he reached Trenton, Washington sent a desperate appeal to Robert Morris for money to pay a $10 bounty to men who would agree to serve six weeks longer:

---

ginia. In Philedelphia bands of screaming women attacked the officers and snatched away gifts of bread and liquor brought by other civilians. The officers were exchanged in 1778; enlisted men spent the war in prison, though many escaped to settle on mountain farmlands.

"A Fine Fox Chase, Boys!"

"We have not the money to pay the Bounty . . . If it is possible, sir . . . borrow Money . . . every Lover of his Country must strain his Credit . . . No time, my dear sir, is to be lost." Washington added optimistically, "The bearer will escort the money." He could not wait for a reply from Morris.

The next day, December 31, the general faced the troops on the last day of their enlistment. The drums beat and the sullen men fell into ranks. Washington rode out and sat in the saddle, looking down at the men as he made one of his rare speeches; he was not an orator and his voice did not carry well. He spoke of the victory at Trenton, and told the men that troops were needed as never before. "You can do more for your country now than at any time to come."

At the end, a veteran sergeant remembered, Washington "in the most affectionate manner entreated us to stay." It was in vain.

The general pulled his horse to one side while field officers promised a bounty of $10 to every soldier who would remain in the army. The drums beat for volunteers, but the men stared stubbornly ahead, and not a man stepped forward to volunteer. The hungry and battle-worn troops "had their hearts fixed on home." Washington made a final effort. The watchful sergeant remembered these moments many years later:

> The General wheeled his horse about, rode in front of the regiment and addressing us again said, "My brave fellows, you have done all I asked you to do, and more than could reasonably be expected; but your country is at stake, your wives, your houses and all that you hold dear. You have worn yourselves out with fatigues and hardships, but we know not how to spare you."

He urged the men to stay one month longer.

The soldiers were moved by something in the manner of the general, who had swallowed his pride and put aside his deep reserve to beg them to do their duty. The long, pocked face still wore its somber composure, but his veterans knew the effort that his pleas had cost him. They looked at one another, then one stepped forward to volunteer, others followed, until more than two hundred of the regiment had agreed to stay, most of those still fit for duty.

An officer called: "Shall we enroll them, General?"

"No," Washington said, "men who will volunteer like this need no enrollment to keep them to their duty."

A day later in the nearby town of Crosswicks, the New England veterans of General Daniel Hitchcock were lined up in Cadwalader's camp. Their commander was ill with tuberculosis, and Thomas Mifflin rode out to address them.

Mifflin was a handsome figure in a large fur hat, bundled in a greatcoat made from a rose-colored blanket. The accomplished orator played shrewdly upon the pride of the northern troops. If they would stay another month, not only would they get $10 bounty, their states would send troops to relieve them. They could also share the booty of the battlefield—in the future they could keep the spoils they took from the British. "Every soldier who will stay," Mifflin shouted, "will poise his firelock!" Several men raised their muskets, and others followed until whole regiments had pledged to remain in service.

Other regiments agreed to stay; only the men of John Glover's Marblehead regiment left in large numbers, for many were eager to go home and serve aboard privateers, where they could share the wealth from plundered ships. Only a fragment of this regiment remained behind.

One excited colonel ordered his men to give three cheers and had a gill of rum served to each volunteer. The camps were noisy by nightfall, and the worn troops seemed to be ready for battle. One young officer wrote, "Never were men in higher spirits than our whole Army is."

Washington's dispatch to Congress revealed his relief that "after much persuasion" more than half of the New Englanders had remained in ranks. Within a few days many of these volunteers would lie dead on a battlefield or of smallpox, and the others, it was said, deserted as soon as they had collected their bounty.

Late on December 31 a dispatch rider from Cadwalader rode to headquarters in Trenton with a surprise for Washington, a map of Princeton drawn a few hours earlier by an anonymous spy, "a very intelligent young gentleman" who had noted the British position in detail, its guns, breastworks, outposts, guards and barracks. Most interesting of all was an unguarded road which entered

Princeton from the east. If the army could move swiftly enough it might destroy the Princeton garrison.

When he had learned the position of the enemy, Washington settled his five thousand troops on the ridge overlooking Assunpink Creek, south of Trenton, and sent a main vanguard on the road toward Princeton. These men were commanded by an ambitious soldier of fortune, the French engineer Brigadier General Mathias de Fermoy. They were ordered to feel out the enemy and to delay any British attack.

Charles Cornwallis, who had been called home to England because of the illness of his wife, was in New York, packing for the voyage, when news of the disaster at Trenton reached headquarters. He hurried south with fresh regiments, pushing his horse to cover the fifty miles to Princeton in one day, and arrived in a rainstorm after nightfall of January 1. He spent the night preparing to march against Washington. Cornwallis left behind in Princeton a brigade under Lieutenant Colonel Charles Mawhood and marched out of the village at daybreak of January 2 with a force of almost seven thousand, bound for Trenton.

The British marched in three columns, often toiling calf-deep in the mire, halting frequently to drag their heavy guns until, at 10 A.M., the vanguard met the rebel outposts of Fermoy in the little town of Maidenhead. Cornwallis halted to bring up more men, left another brigade in Maidenhead, and pushed on toward Trenton with a reduced force of fifty-five hundred men. The redcoats advanced painfully, under fire "at every turn of the road, from every flanking thicket and ravine." The long American rifles outranged German rifles and British muskets, and the column halted often, until snipers were flushed from hiding and the vanguard could move on to the next ambush. At last Cornwallis reached Shabbakonk Creek, three miles from Trenton.

General de Fermoy had disappeared. Somewhere along the road, when redcoat flanking parties threatened to overwhelm the thin line of riflemen, the French engineer galloped back to Trenton, unable to explain why he had abandoned his troops. He had been drinking, army gossip said; "A worthless drunkard," Major Wilkinson thought. Colonel Hausegger, the commander of Washington's German battalion, was also lost. The colonel, trailing his Pennsylvania German battalion, fell into the hands of the British —deliberately, some soldiers said. Hausegger went away as a prisoner, and was soon urging other captive Americans in Princeton to give up the hopeless struggle. Israel Hand took over Fermoy's advance force, and resistance stiffened. It was now 1 P.M.

Hand's infantry and a couple of cannon along Shabbakonk Creek halted the British. Six rebels stepped into the open to confront some oncoming Hessians, gesturing and shouting, "We want to surrender! Come and take us in." When the Germans approached, a marksman shot their lieutenant through the chest and the American band scuttled back into the woods. For more than two hours Hand's force held the line of the creek, until the British formed in heavy lines of battle and pushed ahead. Hand withdrew in good order to the outskirts of Trenton. The enemy followed, but for more than an hour the small American force stood them off, and it was after four o'clock, when daylight had begun to fade, before skirmishers fell back through the streets of Trenton, firing from behind houses at pursuing redcoats. The American vanguard retreated southward over the Assunpink Bridge into the lines of the main army. These men who had prevented a daylight attack on Washington's line were near panic at the end.

As the enemy approached down Queen Street, Washington rode to the narrow bridge and tried to slow the retreat of his men, who swarmed across so rapidly that one of them, John Howland, was hurled against the flank of Washington's white horse and tore his arm on one of the general's spurs. Howland remembered how Washington's horse stood with his breast pressed against the bridge rail and "the firm, composed and majestic countenance of the general inspired confidence . . . the horse stood as firm as the rider, and seemed to understand that he was not to quit his post." Washington rode to the rear when the last man had crossed.

Dr. Benjamin Rush, who was tending the wounded, had a glimpse of the general with his aides, riding past "in all the terrible aspects of war," shouting to hurry his men. Rush turned back to tending the wounded, about twenty of them. One who stuck in his memory was an uncomplaining New England boy who held up his right hand, which dangled from a strip of skin.

"A Fine Fox Chase, Boys!"

The oncoming Hessians claimed a victim as the rebels drew back into the lines south of the creek. The Reverend John Rosburgh, a sixty-three-year-old Presbyterian chaplain, was surprised at supper in a tavern and ran for the American lines. As he tried to ford the creek a band of Germans caught him, and "while praying for his captors" the minister was stabbed seventeen times with bayonets and cut with sabers, his clothing stripped from his body, and his money and watch taken by the Hessians.

When the last of the British army reached Trenton, Washington's troops were in line south of the creek on a front almost three miles long, with earthworks overlooking the stone bridge and along the crest of the hills. Rebel supper fires soon sprang up in the darkness. There was an occasional round from an American cannon, as Henry Knox said, "chucked into the town to prevent them enjoying their new quarters," but watchful American sentries saw that redcoats thronged Trenton's streets most of the night.

Near sunset, as soon as he reached Trenton, Cornwallis met with his officers, some of whom urged him to attack the American position across the Assunpink. Colonel Sir William Erskine said, "If Washington is the general I take him to be, you won't find his army there in the morning." The sublimely confident General Grant disagreed. The Americans had no easy route of retreat, he said, and could be overtaken by the veterans of Cornwallis wherever they moved in New Jersey. A British night attack over strange terrain would be folly. They should wait for daylight, when the task would be easy. Erskine and Colonel von Donop urged the earl to send a patrol across the creek to watch the rebel right wing. Cornwallis shook his head. "I'll bag the fox in the morning," he said. The troops were ordered to cook supper and settle into camp.

Young Stephen Olney, who spent the night beside the American fires overlooking the creek, feared what morning would bring: "Our army was in the most desperate situation I had ever known it; we had no boats to carry us across the Delaware, and if we had, so powerful an enemy would certainly destroy the better half of us before we could embark." Olney asked his commander, Lieutenant Bridges, "What do you think now of our independence?"

Bridges grinned cheerfully. "I don't know, the Lord will help us."

Washington met his officers in the early evening at St. Clair's headquarters in the house of Alexander Douglass, who was serving the army as a quartermaster. It was a somber conference in the small room which served the Douglass family as parlor, dining room and kitchen. Knox, Greene, St. Clair, Mercer, Mifflin, Reed and several others were there, among them General Philemon Dickinson of the New Jersey militia. By the flickering light of candles and fireplace logs the officers debated their problem: the army must move—but where? Retreat over the river was impossible, since the boats had been left many miles upstream. If they abandoned the fortified ridge they would be cut to pieces in the open by the disciplined British and German regiments. An attack on Cornwallis in Trenton was out of the question, but to wait on the hillside was only to postpone defeat and surrender until morning.

Many suggestions were discussed and discarded until at last someone—probably Dickinson or Reed, who knew the country—proposed that the army abandon its lines in the darkness and move over back roads to attack the garrisons at Princeton and Brunswick before Cornwallis stirred from Trenton. Washington seemed to have been waiting for just such an audacious proposal. He approved at once. Some officers felt that he had made this plan before he recrossed into New Jersey and led the army into the apparent trap south of Trenton. Already he had sent three Philadelphia cavalrymen to sit in the cold darkness, watching the Quaker Bridge of the Assunpink, several miles to the east on a little-used road to Princeton. The general gave orders to move the baggage and the largest of the cannon southward to safety, to Israel Putnam in Burlington. Washington then called in civilian guides, three men who lived on the route to Princeton and knew the roads in that direction.

There was no time to lose. The army must carry its field guns, and these would move slowly in the mud, but officers who hurried out to prepare for the march emerged from the Douglass house to a pleasant surprise. A chill northwest wind had been blowing and the frozen roads would soon bear artillery. Orders were passed quickly, some of them in voices so low that several colonels did not hear and were confused about the movements of their regi-

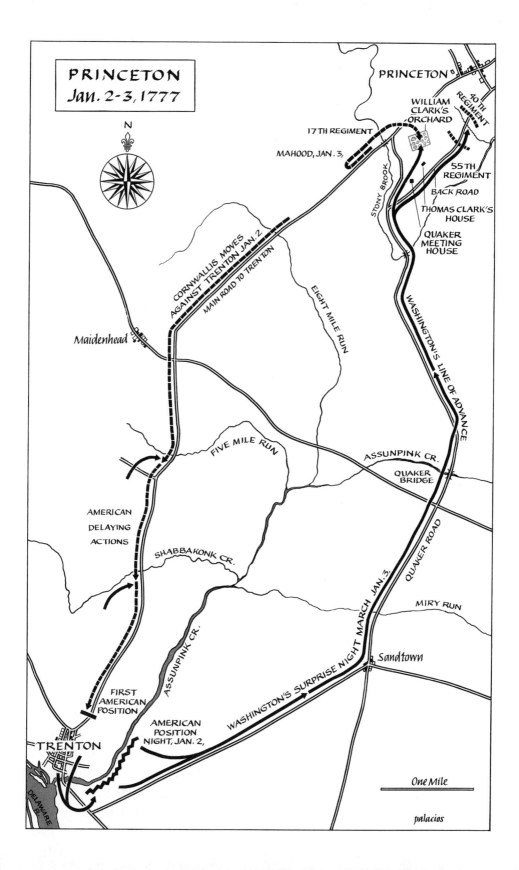

PRINCETON
Jan. 2-3, 1777

N

PRINCETON

WILLIAM CLARK'S ORCHARD

17TH REGIMENT

40TH REGIMENT

MAHOOD, JAN. 3,

55TH REGIMENT

BACK ROAD

THOMAS CLARK'S HOUSE

STONY BROOK

QUAKER MEETING HOUSE

CORNWALLIS MOVES AGAINST TRENTON JAN. 2

MAIN ROAD TO TRENTON

EIGHT MILE RUN

Maidenhead

WASHINGTON'S LINE OF ADVANCE

FIVE MILE RUN

ASSUNPINK CR.

QUAKER BRIDGE

AMERICAN DELAYING ACTIONS

SHABBAKONK CR.

QUAKER ROAD

MIRY RUN

ASSUNPINK CR.

WASHINGTON'S SURPRISE NIGHT MARCH JAN. 3,

Sandtown

FIRST AMERICAN POSITION

AMERICAN POSITION NIGHT, JAN. 2,

WASHINGTON'S SURPRISE NIGHT MARCH JAN. 3,

TRENTON

DELAWARE R.

One Mile

palacios

ments. Field officers were told nothing of their destination. The army merely followed the guides into a back road. On the high ground above Assunpink Creek campfires were built up with cedar rails and a rear guard of five hundred men dug noisily in the frozen earth and chopped saplings in the woods, as if they were raising new breastworks. Picks and shovels and the ringing axes could be heard plainly in British lines only a hundred and fifty yards away. The redcoats also saw rebel sentries pacing back and forth at the bridge and two fords of the creek.

Beyond the fires, out of sight of the enemy, the regiments fell in silently, and by midnight the first of them moved off toward Princeton. Cannon rolled soundlessly on wheels wrapped heavily in rags. The army slipped away so quietly that even its rear guard did not miss it for some hours. Several of Washington's weary officers who had gone to sleep in farmhouses not far away were astonished to find the army gone the next morning, and spent hours in search of their commands.

The American army passed stealthily across the British left flank in the early hours of January 3, moving eastward toward Princeton. There was no alarm in the enemy camp. The night was hazy but cloudless. The way led through an isolated region known as The Barrens, with swamps on either side of the rough road. Stumps in the roadway slowed the guns and bruised the feet of stumbling soldiers. Men were miserable in the aching cold. One private remembered: "We moved so slow on account of the artillery . . . and when ordered forward again one, two or three men in each platoon would stand, with their arms supported, fast asleep."

A brief panic swept the rear when someone shouted that Hessians had surrounded the column; hundreds of militiamen bolted toward Bordentown before officers restored order. The files emerged from deep woodlands in the gray light of dawn and approached Stony Brook, about a mile and a half south of Princeton. The rising sun touched the landscape with fire as Washington's vanguard came into the open. Hoarfrost glistened in the fields and woods, from every fence rail, and in the rimed ruts of the road. The bright morning was bitterly cold. Washington divided the column, sending Sullivan with the main body along the undefended back road which led into Princeton from the east, flanking British defenses. Hugh Mercer was sent toward the Post Road, the main route from Princeton to Trenton, with orders to destroy the Stony Brook bridge and cut off enemy retreat from the village.

Mercer's miniature brigade was no more than three hundred and fifty strong, the remnants of regiments from Maryland, Virginia and Delaware, two guns of a New Jersey artillery battery and stray troops from other units. Some distance in the rear were Cadwalader's militia, followed by Hitchcock's New England regulars. Mercer's men caught the first glimpse of the enemy, a single redcoat horseman who squinted up toward them, shading his eyes with a hand, half blinded by the sun. Mercer ordered riflemen to pick him off, but the rider wheeled and disappeared before the long weapons could be fired. At almost the same moment Major Wilkinson, in the distance with the main column, saw glittering bayonets of a British column as it approached the Stony Brook bridge. It was almost eight o'clock.

Lieutenant Colonel Charles Mawhood rose in the early darkness of January 3, and when his troops had been fed and mustered he led them out of Princeton toward Trenton, to reinforce Cornwallis. He left one infantry regiment behind to hold Princeton. Riding a small brown pony, with two spaniels bounding about him, Mawhood led his 17th Regiment across the Stony Brook bridge. The 55th Regiment brought up the rear, about half a mile behind. The colonel was not far beyond the bridge when the enemy was sighted. Mawhood sent riders to warn the Princeton garrison and call up the 55th Regiment, and then recrossed the bridge at a gallop, leaving the road to ride cross-country. The three hundred men of his vanguard were close behind him. When he saw rebel troops in an orchard only six hundred yards away, Mawhood ordered his infantrymen to pile their packs in a fence corner and led them toward the orchard. The front file loaded behind a fence, then rose and fired. Mawhood's 17th Regiment had collided with Hugh Mercer's brigade.

As the British scout rode from sight General Mercer turned his handsome gray horse toward a commanding hill on his right, leading his men. Colonel John Haslet, the commander of the Delaware regiments, hobbled beside Mercer's horse. Haslet had fallen into the icy river during the crossing Christmas night, but though his legs had swollen painfully he led his men on foot today. He had orders to leave the army on recruiting service, but had disobeyed for fear of missing action. Mercer and Haslet and their men were among the fruit trees when a British volley rattled through the branches, showering twigs about them as the bullets flew harmlessly overhead. Redcoat files had formed in the open, only forty yards away. Mercer's worn men loaded and fired rapidly and smoke from hundreds of weapons rose above the orchard into the wintry sun "in one beautiful cloud." Mawhood's men stood firm under three rebel volleys.

The redcoats then charged into the orchard with bayonets. Two guns of Captain Daniel Neil's New Jersey artillery tore gaps in the enemy line, but the veteran British infantry did not falter. One of Mercer's sergeants was in the midst of this action: "Our fire was most destructive; their ranks grew thin and the victory seemed nearly complete when the British were reinforced. Many of our brave men had fallen and we were unable to withstand such superior numbers of fresh troops." Most of Mercer's men, who had no bayonets, fled from the orchard to the south. The sergeant heard Mercer shout "Retreat!" It was too late for many of the ragged band.

Redcoats speared the scattered Americans, even those who surrendered. A lieutenant hobbled into a nearby farmyard with a broken leg and hid under a wagon, but was dragged out and stabbed to death. Eighteen-year-old Lieutenant Bartholomew Yeates, a Virginian, who gave up and begged for quarter, was shot and clubbed and stabbed thirteen times. Captain Neil was killed, and the British turned his captured battery on Mercer's fugitives. Colonel Haslet fell dead with a bullet through his head. Mercer's horse dropped with a leg wound and the general ran across the open, trying vainly to rally his men. As Mercer stood near the barn of William Clark, not far from the orchard, he was suddenly surrounded by redcoats. Mercer's coat concealed his insignia, and the troopers thought they had captured Washington.

"Surrender, you damned rebel!"

Mercer slashed about him with his sword until he was knocked to his knees by a musket butt. He fell to the ground with seven bayonet stabs in the body, feigning death. The redcoats left him lying beside the barn.

A few yards away remnants of the 1st Virginia were halted and formed into ranks by Captain John Fleming. "Gentlemen, dress the line before you make ready." A redcoat yelled, "Damn you, we'll dress you!" and shot Fleming. The Virginians held their post long enough to fire a deadly volley at close range, so that "the enemy screamed as if many devils had got hold of them," but Captain Fleming was killed and his troops rejoined the flight.

Cadwalader's Pennsylvania militia had come by now. Mercer's fleeing men burst down upon these green troops, pursued by the shouting British. Enemy cannon fired overhead and many rebel bodies lay on the slope. The Pennsylvanians fled in panic, but a handful of artillerymen on the flanks prevented a massacre—the tough Philadelphia longshoremen of Captain Joseph Moulder's battery, who opened on the British with a hail of grapeshot. With the aid of a few sharpshooters with rifles, Moulder continued to fire from between two haystacks, despite British cannon fire and an infantry attack.

The farmyard now began to swarm with American reinforcements. Washington galloped from the rear of Sullivan's column, a flying figure on a tall white horse closely followed by Greene and a dozen other officers. Just behind, at a run, came Israel Hand's riflemen and the veterans of the 7th Virginia. While officers rode among the frightened men of Mercer and Cadwalader, halting their flight, Washington formed a line with Hitchcock's New Englanders, Hand's riflemen and the Pennsylvanians and Virginians. The line was long enough to overlap the British flanks. Within a few minutes the retreat had been halted, and Washington urged the troops forward, shouting above the din: "Parade with us, boys! There's only a handful of them. We'll have them directly."

Washington's presence steadied the troops. The rebels went uphill at a walk, without firing, steady under a British volley. The general halted within thirty yards of the enemy and called: "Halt. . . . Fire!" Major Fitzgerald was sure Washington would be shot from his saddle; he covered his face with his hat so that he could not see him fall. When the smoke of the volley cleared, Fitzgerald saw that Washington was unhurt and shouted, "Thank God, you're safe." Washington said, "Bring up the troops, Major. The day is ours."

Redcoats began falling to the rear. Mawhood and his officers tried desperately to make them stand, but the British regulars ran from the orchard and across the fields beyond, finally fleeing in terror, abandoning cannon and throwing away muskets and knapsacks. Whooping Americans pursued them closely. Washington stood in his stirrups and shouted, "A fine fox chase, boys!" and spurred after the redcoats—his first pursuit of a defeated army on an open field. With only Colonel Stephen Moylan at his side he soon outran the rest of the army. Washington gestured to show how he would surround the disorganized enemy. Moylan said, "But where are your troops?" When the general saw that they were alone, with the British only a few yards ahead, he wheeled and rode to the rear. One of his colonels, James Potter, had already been captured as he rode among the fleeing enemy.

Washington returned to the battlefield to find his officers anxious about his long absence. One of them wrote: "Our army love the general very much, but they have one thing against him, which is the little care he takes of himself in any action." Washington saw Colonel Daniel Hitchcock and stopped to thank him for the charge of his New Englanders. Hitchcock was weak and feverish; ten days later he would be dead.

When the general rode past an American thief who leaned over the body of a wounded British soldier trying to rob him, Washington drove him off and placed a guard over the helpless redcoat until he could be moved. He also prepared for the coming of Cornwallis, who would soon be in pursuit. Washington halted Captain Varnum of a Massachusetts regiment and sent him with a company to destroy the Stony Brook bridge.

A few minutes later the vanguard of Cornwallis appeared at the stream. They were, as Henry Knox said, "in a most infernal sweat, —running, puffing and blowing, and swearing at being so outwitted." The enemy was halted for a time at the stream, and when they did cross it was too late to save the Princeton garrison. By now the British 55th Regiment, which had been blocked from the battlefield by Sullivan's column, had retreated into Princeton to join the 40th Regiment. St. Clair's brigade drove these troops

North Carolinians called, "Put him down and let him die—don't punish him so," but the wounded man's companions bore him from sight, his entrails still dragging the earth.

The British 2nd Light Infantry rushed to the aid of the outpost, soon reinforced by redcoats of the 40th Infantry, led by the grim-visaged Colonel Thomas Musgrave, a veteran with a gaping hole in one cheek, the result of an old wound. Conway's four hundred men were held up for almost an hour before Sullivan's superior forces arrived, with Wayne's Pennsylvanians trotting in advance, shouting for revenge for the victims of Paoli, and cutting down many of Musgrave's men with bayonets. Though Wayne's officers beat at their men in an effort to save "the poor wretches who were Crying for Mercy," the slaughter went on after some of the British had surrendered. Anthony Wayne reported that every redcoat within reach was bayoneted, even the wounded. A number of Musgrave's men could not believe their ears when a bugler called retreat: "This was the first time we had ever retreated from the Americans and it was with great difficulty we could get the men to obey our orders."

Sullivan's divisions drove ahead for more than a mile, but it was slow work, prying the British from each fence and halting to pull down the rails before advancing to the next wall or ditch along the road. Gunsmoke thickened the fog into a blinding, choking cloud in which friends and enemies appeared as drifting specters. As the roar of musketry swelled, Washington sent Timothy Pickering to the front: "I'm afraid General Sullivan is throwing away his ammunition. Ride forward and tell him to preserve it."

Sir William Howe and Mrs. Loring had been abed no longer than an hour, so headquarters gossips said. After a nightlong bout of gambling, the general and his mistress had slept through the roaring of cannon, and Howe was roused only when General Grant forced his way into his bedroom. Otherwise " 'Tis likely our hero might have been surprised in bed, for he was deeply engaged somewhere, or with somebody." Sir William rode into Musgrave's retreat along Skippack Road a few moments later, puffy-faced, red-eyed and irritable. A neighborhood boy who stood nearby heard Howe's plaintive cry of alarm when he saw his men falling back, "My God, what shall we do? We're certainly surrounded," but the British Lieutenant Martin Hunter heard only Howe's bellow: "For shame, Light Infantry! I never saw you retreat before! Form! Form! It's only a scouting party."

Hunter and his hard-pressed men glared resentfully at Howe, and some burst into laughter as a rebel cannon fired a round of grapeshot, a hail of small iron balls that riddled the branches of a large chestnut tree and showered twigs upon Howe and his staff. Hunter could not conceal his pleasure: "I think I never saw people enjoy a discharge of grape before, but we really all felt pleased . . . to hear the grape rattle about the Commander-in-Chief's ears, after he had accused the battalion of having run away from a scouting party. He rode off immediately, full speed."

Colonel Musgrave retreated to his headquarters, a large stone house called Cliveden, the home of Pennsylvania's Tory chief justice, Benjamin Chew. The colonel and his hundred and twenty men ran into the fortresslike house, barred and shuttered doors and windows, and from the windows of the second floor opened a deadly fire against Sullivan's advance. Rebel cannon fired at the house, but the round shot caromed from the massive walls in showers of stone chips. Men who darted across the open to batter at doors and windows were cut down by bayonets. Marksmen from above snarled the ranks of Wayne and Sullivan as they passed on either side of the house, and rebels firing from opposite sides of the lawn shot down some of their own men.

Washington and Knox, who had come up to watch the bizarre struggle, sat their horses nearby, debating whether to take the house by storm or post a guard about it and push forward the attack. Knox had not forgotten his reading of the classics: "It would be unmilitary to leave a castle in our rear," he said. "Summon them to surrender."

Pickering warned that the British would shoot down a messenger, but Knox was so insistent that Washington sent Lieutenant Colonel Matthew Smith of his staff across the yard with a flag, carrying a demand for surrender. One of Musgrave's men felled him with a shot that mangled one knee, a wound that was to prove fatal. Artillery opened on the house once more, but though the guns blew open doors and windows and files of infantry tried to force their way into the house, all were turned back by Musgrave's men, who fought from behind barricades of piled-up furniture on the first floor and kept up a steady fire from the upper windows. Colonel John Laurens and a French volunteer, the Chevalier du Maudit de Plessis, ran to the house with blazing tufts of hay from the stables but were driven back, Laurens with a bullet in his shoulder. Soldiers loaded a wagon with wood, set it ablaze and dragged it to a door of the house, in vain.

After half an hour or longer, when more than fifty American corpses lay in the yard, Washington ordered Sullivan to leave a guard at the house and push forward toward the British camp. At this moment Washington and two aides rode past the waiting Carolina brigade, where the general was challenged by young John Brantly, "an illbred soldier from Deep River, N.C." Brantly moved toward the general somewhat unsteadily, brandishing a jug.

"Won't you drink wine with a soldier?"

"My God, boy, this is no time for drinking wine."

Brantly shouted, "God Almighty damn your proud soul! You're above drinking with soldiers!"

Washington wheeled his horse. "Come," he said, "I'll drink with you." He lifted the jug to his mouth and then held it out to the soldier.

Brantly shook his head. "Give it to your servants," he said. When the two colonels had tasted the wine, Brantly grinned up at the general. "Now," he said emphatically, "I'll be damned if I don't spend the last drop of my heart's blood for you."

Washington rode away into the fog.

It was only now, almost an hour behind schedule, that a roar of muskets signaled the approach of Greene's column from the Limekiln Road. The Quaker's route was four miles longer than Sullivan's, and his guide had led him astray in the darkness. Even on the outskirts of Germantown, Greene's advance was delayed by fences, thickets and marshes; his brigades were out of proper order when they arrived and more time was lost in realigning the units. The delay was too much for the impetuous Adam Stephen, who had been drinking during the march. Drawn by the roll of gunfire from the Chew House, he led his men across fields toward the scene without orders, abandoning Greene's column and altering the plan of battle.

Greene pressed ahead along the Limekiln Road with the brigades of Muhlenberg, Scott and McDougall, drove a British advance from Luken's Mill after a sharp fight, then wheeled to his right and broke into the enemy rear near the Market House. Greene's leading troops charged so impetuously that redcoat infantry units fell back in disorder. Peter Muhlenberg led a bayonet attack that carried past rows of tents in the British camp, taking many prisoners. Virginians had charged "with the greatest intrepidity . . . driving them from their camp, fieldpieces, stone walls. Trophies lay at our feet . . ." British officers, it was reported, had already issued orders to retreat from the field, through Philadelphia to a rendezvous in Chester. Victory was within Greene's grasp.

At this time Wayne, pushing along the Skippack Road to the aid of Sullivan, collided with Stephen's troops, who mistook the approaching Pennsylvanians for the enemy and opened fire. After a few blazing volleys in the smoke and fog, both units broke into flight. Panic spread abruptly through Washington's ranks.

The men of Sullivan's division, now well beyond the Chew House, had almost exhausted their forty rounds of cartridges when they were assailed on both flanks by the enemy. Soldiers began to shout that they were out of ammunition, and the British closed in more swiftly. Already alarmed by the endless roar from the Chew House in their rear, Sullivan's men were stampeded by a cavalryman who rode up at that moment and shouted that they were surrounded. Men ran in all directions through swirling clouds of smoke and fog.

Lieutenant Colonel William Heth felt that the fog itself was the chief cause of this panic, since the troops imagined themselves surrounded and were struck by fear "which like an electrical shock seized some thousands, who fled in confusion, without the appearance of an enemy."

British and Germans who had been fighting Sullivan then turned against the outnumbered Greene. Muhlenberg was a thousand yards away in the enemy rear, but though he broke an encircling British line with a bayonet charge and rejoined Greene, with the loss of an entire regiment, he was too late. The left wing could not hold its ground alone.

It was now Greene's troops who were pressed back from fence to fence, firing from behind walls and houses until their cannon could be drawn off. When the wheels of one gun were shattered, the stubborn Peter Muhlenberg helped to heave it into a wagon and rode in its rear, but Muhlenberg had been in the saddle two nights and a day almost without rest and his weary horse refused a fence. The fighting preacher fell asleep in his saddle while his troops were pulling down the fence rails, and was roused only by the whistling of musket balls past his ears.

Washington sat his horse in the middle of the Skippack Road, trying to halt the rout, "exposing himself to the hottest fire," but his men swept past, holding up empty cartridge boxes in mute explanation. Major Benjamin Tallmadge formed a squad of horsemen across the road to block the retreating men, with little effect. Despite covering fire from a few guns of Greene's and Wayne's artillery, the retreat was disorderly, "past the powers of description, sadness and consternation expressed in every countenance."

Once out of the village the defeated men plodded so slowly in the tracks of the leaders that Thomas Paine feared they might halt entirely. "The retreat was extraordinary. Nobody hurried themselves." The exhausted men could move no faster, for they were nearing the limit of their endurance—but their suffering had only begun.

Cornwallis, who had come up from Philadelphia with three fresh battalions, followed the army for a few miles at "a civil distance," his gunners firing an occasional round. Officers begged Washington to halt and rest the men, but he drove them relentlessly far into the night, to Pennypacker's Mills, more than twenty miles from Germantown and safely beyond the reach of the enemy.

The army discovered only now that it had fought the battle without the militia columns of the outer flanks, the pincers of the attack. John Armstrong had led his Pennsylvanians of the right wing down the Manatawny Road to the crossing of Wissahickon Creek, where he drove back some Hessian riflemen with his small cannon, but instead of charging with his infantry, kept up a leisurely shelling until 9 A.M., when the Hessians turned on him and chased his militia rearward for three miles. Armstrong led his troops out of danger, far from the main battle in the village and unaware of its course.

The militiamen of Smallwood's left wing had been even more impotent; they had made such slow progress over their road that they reached their objective after the fighting was over.

Once more the army had lost heavily, about twelve hundred men, among them Francis Nash of the North Carolinians, mortally wounded by a cannonball that struck his horse and tore off the general's leg. The army lost another general during the retreat when Adam Stephen was found lying in a fence corner, too drunk to ride or walk; he was to lose his command. But the retreat was so wearing, even for officers on horseback, that other generals succumbed; both Thomas Conway and Casimir Pulaski left their troops and fell asleep, exhausted. At eight o'clock that night, when Washington stopped at a farmhouse for a few minutes, he drank a cup of tea and pulled half a biscuit from his pocket—the other half, so he told his hosts, was the only food he had eaten for twenty-four hours.

An orderly sergeant from headquarters came to the camp of the North Carolina brigade the next day, looking for the soldier who had treated Washington to wine, but John Brantly was not to be found; he hid on the outskirts of the camp and did not appear until he was reported to the sergeant, who marched him off toward headquarters. An unsmiling Washington gave the private a salute.

"Are you the man who gave me the jug yesterday?"

"Yes, sir. I thought you were dry. I made up my mind that you'd drink from it, if you passed us during the day, and that's how come me to stop you at a busy time."

"Is the wine all gone?"

"Every drop. Our colonel got hold of it and I saw it no more. I told him he might as well eat the jug since he'd drank the wine."

Washington had a steward bring wine and rum, watched Brantly drink from both bottles, gave him ten dollars and sent him on his way, "The first good spirits you come across, drink my health and yours, too. You're a smart soldier."

Once more the beaten army had left the field with its morale unimpaired, or so Washington insisted. The general told Congress that "the day was unfortunate rather than injurious," and wrote a friend in Virginia, "It is vain to look back to our disappointment . . . at Germantown. We must endeavor to deserve better of Providence, and, I am persuaded, she will smile upon us." He blamed the fog for the sudden retreat of his men "in the midst of the most promising appearances," but did not tantalize himself with what might have been—if either militia wing had reached the field, if Conway's vanguard had not alarmed the enemy, if Sullivan had not run out of ammunition, if Adam Stephen had obeyed orders, if his troops had not collided in the fog, if the Chew House had been bypassed. Washington's ambitious battle plan had demanded too much of tired and poorly trained troops and inexperienced officers, but even so, he thought, the army had come within moments of victory. The army shared his optimism. Anthony Wayne wrote his wife, "Upon the Whole it was A Glorious day—Our men are in the highest Spirits—and I am Confident we shall give them a total Defeat the next Action . . ."

When news of Germantown crossed the Atlantic, military men and politicians of European courts were profoundly impressed. The French court, still debating an alliance with the rebels, equated the defeat at Germantown with the victory at Saratoga. The foreign minister, Vergennes, said "nothing struck him so much" as Washington's turning upon Howe at Germantown: "To bring an army, raised within a year, to this, promised anything."

15

THE CONWAY CABAL
"A Weak General and Bad Counsellors"

Among the captives taken by the British in Philadelphia was the Reverend Jacob Duché, a former chaplain of Congress whose prayers had once moved delegates to tears. Though his patriotic ardor had cooled and he had resigned after the Declaration, donating his salary to widows and orphans of the army's dead, the minister was clapped into jail for one night by William Howe. Duché emerged the next morning as a confirmed Loyalist and propagandist for the British cause.

Duché was a Philadelphia eccentric who was afflicted with an odd sense of humor, "a disposition to laughter" so compelling that he was forced to pinch himself to prevent his laughing aloud in the pulpit. As a popular speaker and writer "full of gush without much principle," he had become an ecclesiastical chameleon, in succession "an Arminian, a Mystic, a disciple of Swedenborg."

Duché now made an effort to end the war through an appeal to Washington, a fourteen-page letter that was carried through the lines to the general's headquarters by Sarah Graeme Ferguson, a prominent Philadelphian whose husband was a well-known Tory. Washington greeted Mrs. Ferguson courteously, but it was with mounting indignation that he read Duché's letter, a plea that the general persuade Congress to rescind "the hasty and ill-advised declaration of Independency" and make peace with the British.

Duché insisted that Washington *was* the Revolution, and that "the Dregs of a Congress" now in office were unworthy successors to the leaders of 1775 and "not the men you engaged to serve . . . 'Tis you, Sir, and you only, that support the Present Congress." And as for the rebel army, "The whole world knows that its very existence depends upon you, that your Death or Captivity disperses it in a moment . . ." Since the army had failed him so frequently, Duché asked, "Can you have the least confidence in a sett of undisciplined men and officers . . . . without Principle, without courage?"

Washington reproved Mrs. Ferguson for having delivered the letter, and passed Duché's appeal to Congress, which rather surprisingly had it published. The "mean, pitiful, contemptible" document caused a sensation, largely, perhaps, because its unpalatable truths expressed the thoughts of many patriotic Americans. After two years of failure and defeat, Washington did seem to be the one steadfast support of Congress and the only inspiration of a hapless army. Americans at large had no such faith in their Congress.

As Duché charged, the Congress that had chosen Washington as commander in chief had virtually disappeared; only six delegates of 1775 were still in office, and within a few days four of those would be gone. Of the shrunken Congress of twenty-two members sitting in York, only two knew Washington: the others had little understanding of the administrative burdens under which he struggled or of his perennial shortage of men, arms, supplies and money, and had had no opportunity to assess his character, judgment or tenacity of purpose.

A noisy faction among the fugitive legislators, embittered by sectional rivalries, saw the commander in unfavorable contrast to Horatio Gates, already the hero of New England. Most of the new congressmen, though fair-minded and responsible men, knew little of the relative troop strength of the opposing armies, nor of Howe's advantages over Burgoyne in communications and supply. Such men tended to judge Washington by his loss of Philadelphia after two disastrous defeats, and Gates by his startling victory at Saratoga, whose details were seeping through the country by rumor.

The delegates were also much impressed by Thomas Conway,

who, with the aid of a few influential friends, appeared as a growing challenge to Washington's leadership of the army. The garrulous Irishman had nagged at Congress for promotion since his
arrival, and when he learned that Baron de Kalb, his subordinate
in France, was now a major general, Conway protested to John
Hancock and demanded a "very speedy and categorical answer" to
his own request for that rank.

Conway described his heroic role at Germantown to Benjamin
Rush, complained that he had been opposed by Washington at
every turn of the battle, and hinted that he would leave the army
at once unless promoted. Rush appealed to John Adams, "For
God's sake, do not suffer him to resign! . . . He is . . . the idol of the
whole army."

In his quest for promotion Conway was not content to expound
upon his talents and experience to all who would listen. He was
also openly scornful of Washington's ignorance of military affairs:
"No man is more of a gentleman than General Washington, or
appears to more advantage at his table, or in the usual intercourse
of life; but as to his talents for the command of an army they are
miserable indeed."

Conway provoked Washington to spiteful comments such as he
made of no other officer in the war on either side. Conway, he said,
had become his "inveterate enemy," who was intriguing against
him because of "an absurd resentment of disappointed vanity."
The Irishman's "ambition and great desire to be puffed off as one
of the first officers of the age could only be equaled by the means
he used to obtain them . . . It is a maxim with him, to leave no
service of his own untold."

About this time Conway wrote to Horatio Gates, outlining more
than a dozen causes for the defeat at Brandywine, most of which
he traced to the ineptness of Washington. It was a letter that was
to bring to light the so-called Conway Cabal and precipitate a
crisis at headquarters that would shake the army for months and
baffle generations of historians. But though this controversy was to
disturb Washington deeply and convince many officers that he was
in danger of losing his command, it was to run its furious course
and fade away, leaving scanty evidence that the general had been
seriously challenged.

"A Weak General and Bad Counsellors"

Just when Washington was faced anew with the collapse of his officer corps, he learned that Congress planned to promote Conway to major general, over the heads of all of the army's twenty-three American brigadiers. Already, within less than a week, twenty officers had asked permission to resign to go home and care for their families, and when Washington heard of the elevation of Conway, he appealed to Richard Henry Lee, the only remaining Virginia congressman from the delegation of 1775. To promote Conway over all other brigadiers, he wrote, would be "as unfortunate a measure as ever was adopted . . . it will give a fatal blow to the existence of the Army." Then, for the first time in a letter to a congressman, he hinted at his own resignation: "I have been a slave to the service: I have undergone more than most men are aware of, to harmonize so many discordant parts; but it will be impossible for me to be of any further service if such insuperable obstacles are thrown in my way."

Lee's reply was not reassuring: he felt that Congress would refrain from promoting Conway if that would produce "the evil consequences you suggest," but Lee then announced a reorganization of the Board of War that would give it broad powers over the army's command and reduce Washington's authority. There was another matter: Thomas Conway was to be assigned to headquarters as his adjutant general. Washington's apprehension over the threatened arrival of Conway was increased by a warning from Lafayette that the Irishman was "an ambitious and dangerous man. He has done all in his power, by cunning maneuvers, to take off my confidence and affection for you."

Lafayette had not been idle during six weeks of convalescence in Bethlehem, Pennsylvania. He studied English and read liberal French philosophers with the ardor of a convert, imbibing radical ideas that would have shocked friends and relatives in Versailles.

Though he had left France only in the hope of making a reputation in the war against the British, the naïve boy was so impressed by his first glimpses of life in America that he was soon declaiming of liberty as if he were a hard-bitten old revolutionary: "The moment I heard of America, I loved her; the moment I knew she was fighting for freedom, I burnt with desire of bleeding for her . . ." He wrote his wife urging her to become a good American: "The welfare of America is bound up with the welfare of all mankind; it is going to become the . . . haven for virtue, honesty, tolerance, and a tranquil freedom." And though he had assured Congress and Washington that he sought no troop command, the ambitious marquis was now yearning for an active post in the field, and had begun to intrigue for it.

Lafayette was already making influential friends, among them Henry Laurens, the new president of Congress, who became his admirer and frequent correspondent. Nathanael Greene said Lafayette was "one of the sweetest-tempered young gentlemen," and Baron de Kalb wrote of the marquis to a friend in Europe, "No one deserves more than he the esteem he enjoys here. He is a prodigy for his age, full of courage, spirit, judgment, good manners, feelings of generosity and of zeal for the cause of liberty on this continent."

Lafayette's relationship with Washington grew warmer despite their separation. The commander had taken the marquis into his councils of war from the start, thought of him as a reliable, mature young man, and confided in him as he did in few American officers. Washington had urged the orphaned French boy to think of him as both a father and a friend, in a manner so simple and sincere that Lafayette was moved to tears.

Though he conceded that other foreign officers did not share his feelings, Lafayette's affection for Washington was virtually boundless. As he wrote his father-in-law: "Our general is really a man made for this revolution, which could not succeed without him. I see him at closer range than any other man in the world . . . Every day my admiration for the beauty of his character and of his soul grows greater . . ."

The one irritant in their friendship was Lafayette's determination to have a command, which he no longer concealed from Washington: "I know well, my dear General, that you will do everything to procure me my one ambition, glory." Washington at first resisted. He wrote Benjamin Harrison: "What the designs of Congress respecting this gentleman were . . . I know no more than a child unborn, and beg to be instructed . . . If . . . it was intended to vest him with all the power of a major-general, why have I been led into a contrary belief . . .?" Harrison replied that Lafayette's commission was only honorary and that Congress had no intention of giving him troops. But it was only a matter of weeks before Washington succumbed. In early November he urged Congress to make Lafayette a major general and give him Adam Stephen's old division: ". . . he is sensible, discreet in his manner, has made great proficiency in our language" and at Brandywine had shown "a large share of bravery and military ardor."

Lafayette was now launched upon an influential career that was to last throughout the war and exert a decisive effect upon Franco-American relations.

The dramatic struggle on the New York frontier that was to bring the French into the war had been decided on October 7, when Burgoyne's army was severely mauled in a second battle at Freeman's Farm, near Saratoga. Though the day found Gates and his officers bickering at headquarters, and Benedict Arnold sulking after his removal from troop command, the Americans were in a fighting mood. Now reinforced by swarms of aroused New England militia, Gates had more than twelve thousand men in camp, at least twice the strength of Burgoyne.

In a foolhardy attempt to circle to the rear of Gates before he had reconnoitered the rebel position, Burgoyne attacked with fifteen hundred of his best troops. Gates ordered Daniel Morgan to "begin the game," the Virginia riflemen burst into the British rear, demoralized the redcoats with heavy fire from the cover of a rail fence, and sharpshooters who had climbed trees picked off almost every enemy officer within sight. At this time New England infantrymen who had stormed entrenchments in the British center had begun to fall back when the impetuous Arnold galloped into the front without orders, recklessly exposing himself and shouting encouragement to his old troops until his leg was shattered by a bullet wound that was to cripple him for life. When darkness fell, Burgoyne had lost almost half of his attack force and withdrew, with the exultant rebels pressing closely behind.

By October 12 the British had fallen back to the heights of Saratoga, where they were surrounded. By now Burgoyne had learned that Henry Clinton had taken two rebel forts on the Hudson not far below, and had brief hopes that his army would be rescued, but it was too late. Rebel militia parties "swarmed around . . . like birds of prey," dead horses and wounded men lay everywhere, and American shells and bullets were fired into the camp day and night. After two days of this, Burgoyne proposed an armistice while terms were discussed, but Gates demanded unconditional surrender, with the defeated troops to give up their arms to the Americans at once and become prisoners of war. Burgoyne replied defiantly that he would fight to the last man rather than have his troops ground arms under orders from the rebels.

He insisted that, instead, his survivors march out of their camp, give up their arms under commands of their own officers, and that his troops were not to be prisoners of war, but should be marched to Boston and then sent to England, to serve no more during the war.

To the astonishment of the officers of both armies, Gates accepted these terms, probably because he feared that Clinton would attack his rear. Gates approved even Burgoyne's insistence that the agreement be called a convention rather than a surrender. In any case it was a dazzling rebel victory and the roll of prisoners was truly impressive: seven generals, a thousand other officers, noncoms and musicians, and more than forty-eight hundred privates, all with their arms and equipment. News of the triumph was to stampede the French into an alliance with the rebels. Within two days of its report in Paris, Louis XVI signed a brief note of recognition of the rebel government, and diplomats felt that a formal declaration of war against England was not far away.

Washington first heard incomplete news of the victory at Saratoga on October 14, and passed it on to Congress, though it was little more than gossip. Four days later an express rider halted at headquarters in a farmhouse on Skippack Creek, carrying an unsealed message to Congress from Governor George Clinton of New York. Washington opened the dispatch and began reading aloud to his staff: "Last night at 8 o'clock the capitulation whereby General Burgoyne and the whole army surrendered themselves prisoners of war, was signed . . ."

The general's voice faltered and, as one officer said, "broke under the intensity of his feelings . . . he could read no more." Wash-

"A Weak General and Bad Counsellors"

ington passed the sheet to an aide, who finished the reading of the message. The general ordered a day of celebration, a holiday in camp, a firing of salutes, praying of chaplains, and a noisy congregation about the rum barrels.

But as days passed with no confirmation of the report, Washington began to doubt its authenticity and wrote to R. H. Lee that he could not "help complaining most bitterly of General Gates's neglect," for failure to keep him informed. By now his need for reinforcements was again acute. Howe's fleet, which had gone down the Chesapeake and sailed up the Atlantic coast, had ascended the Delaware, only to be blocked below Philadelphia by two rebel forts, river obstructions and gun boats. It was obvious that Howe would soon attack the forts and open his supply route to Philadelphia. Washington wrote Gates, ordering the return of troops he had sent him for the northern campaign.

At Saratoga, Gates had withheld his report until his negotiations with Burgoyne were complete and the captives were safely in his hands. Even then he declined to report to Washington and delayed for several days, as if he had become independent of Congress itself. When Gates sent his dispatches to York at last, he entrusted them to his favorite aide, Major James Wilkinson, without instructions that he hurry on his way. The major had hardly left camp when he became so ill that he "nearly expired under the anguish of a convulsive cholic" and was carried in a wagon to Albany, where he spent a few days recuperating. Wilkinson then jogged southward at such a slow pace that it was October 31 before he appeared before Congress in York with the official battle report and a copy of the convention with Burgoyne. There was also a request from Gates for promotion of the boy adjutant who bore the momentous news: "From the beginning of this war, I have not met with a more promising Military Genius." Congress made the messenger a brigadier general by brevet and ordered a medal struck for Gates.

As an afterthought, Congress forbade Washington to recall more than twenty-five hundred men from Gates, whatever the emergency. One apprehensive delegate proposed an amendment—that Washington might ask for the return of more troops after consulting with Gates—but even this effort to defend the commander in chief against the new hero was shouted down by an overwhelming vote.

Two days after Wilkinson reported to Congress, Washington sent Hamilton north for information, with orders to press both Gates and Putnam to send him every available man. His dispatch to Gates, listing twenty regiments to be "immediately put in march to join this army," was a model of diplomatic reproach to the insubordinate northern commander: "I cannot but regret that a matter of such magnitude . . . should have reached me by report only . . . not . . . by a line under your signature, stating the simple fact."

On the road, Hamilton met the few troops Gates had sent south: Morgan's riflemen, one small brigade of Continentals and a few militia, only a fraction of those Washington had demanded. And when he reached Albany, Hamilton found Gates in an ebullient mood, basking in the praise and flattery that poured upon him from every colony, and determined to hold the rest of his Continentals. "The old midwife" greeted Hamilton disdainfully. He now spoke of the northern and southern armies as equals, as if Washington no longer exercised supreme authority as commander in chief.

Hamilton was so thoroughly intimidated that he wrote to warn Washington that it would be "dangerous" to oppose "a gentleman whose successes have raised him into the highest importance." Hamilton had accurately gauged the mood of Gates, who felt so sure of himself that he openly challenged Washington's authority by reporting directly to Congress on all matters, as an independent commander. No longer did he write with frequent and respectful references to "Your Excellency"; during November, in fact, Gates wrote Washington only three letters, two of those in response to orders or queries from headquarters. He was never to report on Saratoga to Washington. Gates explained his failure to do so in a curt note, saying that since he had asked Congress to pass on copies of his dispatches, he was sure that Washington had "long ago received all the good news from this quarter." Gates was technically within his rights, since Washington had declined even to name a commander of the northern army, but the calculated insult was unmistakable.

"A Weak General and Bad Counsellors"

There were hints that Gates had visions of succeeding Washington as commander in chief. He told Daniel Morgan with a confidential air that there were reports of unrest among Washington's officers, many of whom, Gates said, would resign unless the commander was replaced. But he had misjudged his man. Morgan replied coldly, "I have one favor to ask of you, which is, never to mention that detestable subject to me again; for under no other man than Washington will I ever serve." For this reason, perhaps, Morgan, like Arnold, was unmentioned in the official report of Saratoga.

Only when the first fever of enthusiasm had passed did thoughtful congressmen realize that Gates might have bartered away the fruits of victory by his hasty acceptance of the liberal terms of the Saratoga Convention. There was nothing to prevent the British from using Burgoyne's troops elsewhere, releasing six thousand others for combat. There was some reason to suspect that the British might violate the treaty in any event,* as they had during the Seven Years' War, when George II had repudiated a similar convention as soon as his troops had been returned to him.

It was Burgoyne himself who unwittingly furnished the grounds for congressional repudiation of the convention when he complained of the inhumane treatment of his officers and men in Boston.

The captives were herded like animals from Saratoga to Boston, where Hannah Winthrop watched them pass through the streets. She marveled at the Hessians: ". . . . poor, dirty, emaciated men" trailed by hundreds of ragged, barefooted women, each loaded like a pack mule, "bent double," under heavy baskets of kettles and furniture. From the wagons children peeped through camp griddles, half hidden among piles of utensils. Some women carried infants who had been born on the road. Hannah's most vivid memory was of the stench of the column: "Such effluvia filled the air while they were passing, had they not been smoking all the

---

* Proof of the British plan to violate the convention came to light only in 1932, with publication of some of Henry Clinton's papers. William Howe had ordered Burgoyne to sail his army to New York, rather than London. About half of the troops were to be returned to active duty at once, in retaliation for previous American trickery in an exchange.

time I should have been apprehensive of being contaminated by them."

The captives were cooped up in unheated shanties in Cambridge and Boston and aboard prison ships in the harbor. Snow was sometimes a foot deep in the rooms of officers; ink froze on their quill pens when they tried to write letters home, and their mail from England was withheld, opened and laughed over by guards.

Burgoyne complained to General Heath, saying that through failure to provide adequate quarters for the captives "the public faith is broke." Congress seized upon the offhand phrase as an inference that the helpless Burgoyne did not intend to live up to the agreement, and used it as a pretext to negate the convention: "This charge of a breach of public faith is of a most serious nature, pregnant of alarming consequences." When Howe's transports sailed to Boston in December to take off the prisoners as had been agreed, they were turned away. Congress sparred for more time by suspending the convention, pending its ratification in London, and finally went to the absurd length of demanding the sworn testimony of a reliable witness who had seen George III sign the document.

Even in the misery and squalor of their confinement, the British displayed the dauntless pride of their race. Women camp followers endlessly harassed the guards. When one elderly sentry refused to permit a British doxy to pass his post, she cursed him with such violence that the old man leveled his musket at her. An amused British officer recorded the sequel: "The woman immediately ran up, snatched it from him, knocked him down, and striding over the prostrate hero, profusely besprinkled him . . . nor did she quit her post, till a file of sturdy ragamuffins marched valiantly to his relief."

In the end, Burgoyne's captive troops and their women and children were marched to prisons in Virginia, where they were held throughout the war, many of them hired out to neighboring farmers under conditions little better than slavery. Only Burgoyne and a few of his officers were permitted to return to England.

James Wilkinson, on his unhurried way south to Pennsylvania, discovered that officers of the army were less interested in the victory dispatch from Saratoga than in tales of Thomas Conway's stinging criticism of Washington's failure at Brandywine, outlined in the Irishman's letter to Gates. Wilkinson heard gossip of the letter in Easton, Pennsylvania, from Dr. William Shippen, the director of army hospitals, and from two congressmen at the home of Thomas Mifflin in Reading. It seemed to be common knowledge that Gates had called together a group of his officers and read to them Conway's letter in which Washington had been held up to scorn. Wilkinson visited the headquarters of Lord Stirling in Reading and talked freely of Conway's letter during a drinking bout after dinner. No one else in the party recalled the conversation later, but Stirling's aide, Major William McWilliams, told the general the next morning that Wilkinson claimed to have seen the celebrated letter, and had quoted some of Conway's words: "Heaven has been determined to save your country or a weak general and bad counsellors would have ruined it."

Stirling wrote of this at once to Washington with the comment, "Such wicked duplicity of conduct I shall always think it my duty to detect." Though he was stunned by the discovery that Conway and Gates were confidants, Washington's first thought was that Gates was merely warning him of Conway's hostility. The commander sent Conway a terse note that suggested only his restrained anger, and revealed nothing of his suspicions of a plot against him:

> Sir, A letter, which I received last night, contained the following paragraph.
> In a letter from Genl. Conway to Genl. Gates he says, *"Heaven has been determined to save your country, or a weak General and bad counsellors would have ruined it."*
> I am Sir Yr Hble Servt.

Conway responded immediately with a curious medley of flattery and remonstrance, the whole written with an obvious relish for controversy. He conceded that he had corresponded with Gates, but though he had spoken his mind freely "and found fault with several measures pursued in this Army," he had not written the paragraph quoted by Stirling. "My opinion of you, Sir, without flattery or envy is as follows: You are a brave man, an honest man, a patriot and a man of good sense. Your modesty is such that although your advice is commonly sound and proper you have often been influenced by men who were not equal to you in point of experience, knowledge or judgment."

Conway added archly, "I believe I can assert that the expression *Weak General* has not slipped from my pen"—and if it had, he explained, this was only a reference to Washington's "excess of modesty." He also charged Washington with an "inquisition in letters . . . of which there are few instances in despotic countries," and finally, in what he may have intended as a threat, announced his intention to publish a book on his American campaigns when he returned to France.

Washington made no reply to this letter, but the controversy had only begun. Conway, though he made no mention of Washington's rebuke to Gates, turned wrathfully upon Stirling, and set off a quarrel between Stirling and young Major Wilkinson, who could say only that though he had no clear recollection of what was said between the drinking companions, he had spoken the truth, "I may be indiscreet, My Lord, but be assured I am not dishonorable."

It was three weeks later before Conway showed Washington's note to his friend Thomas Mifflin, who was so shaken that he hurried off a warning to Gates that "an extract from Conway's letter" had reached headquarters, and might make trouble. The alarmed Gates turned to Conway in an effort to discover how much Washington knew: "I entreat you, dear General, to let me know which of the letters were copied off."

Gates then wrote to Washington himself, saying nothing in defense of his correspondence with Conway and attempting no denial of his involvement in a plot against Washington.

Instead, he begged the commander to "give me all the Assistance you can, in tracing out the Author of the Infidelity, which put Extracts from General Conway's Letters to me into your Hands. Those Letters have been stealingly copied . . ." Such exposure of confidential letters between officers, he said, was a threat to the country's security: "Crimes of that magnitude ought not to remain unpunished."

Washington replied that it was Wilkinson who had revealed

Conway's remark, "not in confidence, that I ever understood," and said he had sent a copy to Conway "merely to show that Gentl. that I was not unapprised of his intriguing disposition."

Washington's letter ended:

> I never knew that General Conway (who I viewed in the light of a stranger to you) was a correspondant of yours; much less did I suspect that I was the subject of your confidential Letters. . . . I considered the information as coming from yourself . . . to forewarn . . . me against a secret enemy . . . a dangerous, incendiary; in which character, sooner or later, this country will know Genl. Conway—But, in this, as in other matters of late, I have found myself mistaken.

Washington's attention was now drawn to the final phase of the battle for Philadelphia, an amphibious assault by the Howes against rebel defenses blocking the Delaware below the city, Fort Mifflin on Mud Island near the Pennsylvania shore, and the opposite Fort Mercer at Red Bank, New Jersey. After weeks of laborious effort and at great cost, the stream below and between the little forts had been blocked by menacing iron-tipped wooden beams as tall as ships' masts, embedded in huge wooden crates which were filled with stones and sunk in the channel of the Delaware. Row after row of the sharp spars lay a few feet beneath the water's surface, pointed downstream, so placed that they would rip the hulls of any approaching ships.

Washington had garrisoned the forts with some of his best gunners and engineers but had no control over Pennsylvania's independent navy, which joined the defense with a frigate and a brig, floating gun batteries and several swift little galleys. In the end he could do little more than watch through his telescope from the roof of the Chew House in Germantown as some of the war's most furious fighting erupted. After a two-week bombardment of Fort Mifflin, several large British ships sailed up to the barricade on October 22 and opened a duel with the Pennsylvania sailors, with firing "so incessant that . . . the elements seemed to be in flames." H.M.S. *Augusta,* a big 64-gun ship of the line, was blown up, "a glorious sight," an American officer said, "the flames issuing thro every port she had." The Pennsylvania gunners also blew up the 18-gun *Merlin,* and Admiral Richard Howe withdrew his surviving ships.

On the same day twelve hundred Hessians stormed Fort Mercer from the land side, after ordering Colonel Christopher Greene and his six hundred defenders to surrender or be killed without quarter. Greene withdrew from his outer works, and decimated the ranks of the exultant Germans as they closed in. Washington sent more supplies and ammunition to the forts during the lull of the next few days, but his stocks were pitifully low. Thomas Mifflin, who had not been at headquarters since the army began the Philadelphia campaign, had neglected his work as quartermaster general, and the army's stocks of matériel had virtually disappeared.

The British returned to the attack on November 15 and began pounding at the small blockhouses of Fort Mifflin, a bombardment so intense that an estimated thousand shells fell on the fort every twenty minutes. In the last hours British ships drew so near the island that marines tossed grenades from the rigging into the fort. Each night a fleet of small rebel boats went to the island to carry off casualties and leave replacements for the 300-man garrison, but the cause was hopeless. The ruins of Fort Mifflin were evacuated in the night of November 15–16, and Fort Mercer four nights later. The Delaware became a British river.

The first snows found the rebel army still in its exposed camps near Philadelphia, but there was no further action until Howe emerged on December 5 and probed Washington's strong position at Whitemarsh at 4 A.M., seeking another opening for a flank attack. Morgan's riflemen drove off one redcoat column, Washington quickly shifted reserves to cover his flanks, and after two days the British returned to the city.

The campaign of 1777 had ended, and Howe had fought his last battle. Sir William's failure to press Washington vigorously had led George Germain to scold him in an ironic dispatch obviously calculated to provoke the Howe brothers to resign or wage a more ruthless war. The general submitted his resignation in a brief note protesting "the little attention given to my Recommendations" and the lack of support from London. Admiral Richard Howe was to remain in America for another year, but the era of their leadership was over, a period of almost unbroken, but fruitless, victories. Neither Germain nor Sir William seemed to realize the extent to which the indomitable Washington was responsible for their failure. Despite successive defeats and the almost unrelieved chaos of supply and recruitment, the Virginian had prevailed merely by enduring and holding his army together. He had become a symbol of resistance whose very presence seemed to render the Americans unconquerable.

In any event, William Howe had failed. Henry Clinton was now to become Washington's adversary. This change of command was to prove decisive. The petulant Clinton, though he had found fault with William Howe's tactical and strategic plans, was to become ever more cautious as commander in chief, until finally his indecisiveness immobilized the large British army in the north and invited disaster to the royal cause in America.

16

VALLEY FORGE
"Starve—Dissolve—Or Disperse"

In his search for winter quarters Washington turned first to Wilmington, Del., where soldiers would be comfortable and supplies could be shipped by water. This drew a furious protest from Pennsylvania's legislature, which insisted that the army should not go into winter quarters, but stay in the field to protect the Pennsylvania and New Jersey countryside from British raiders. The Council and Assembly threatened to withdraw their financial support of the army.

Washington responded tartly to the "Remonstrance" of the legislature:

> I can assure these gentlemen, that it is a much easier and less distressing thing to draw remonstrances in a comfortable room by a good fireside, than to occupy a cold, bleak hill, and sleep under frost and snow, without clothes or blankets; however, although they seem to have little feeling for the naked and distressed Soldiers, I feel super-abundantly for them, and, from my Soul, I pity those miseries, which it is neither in my power to relieve or prevent.

Anthony Wayne proposed Valley Forge as a compromise camp, a desolate site in a countryside that had been devastated by both armies. As Baron de Kalb said, "The idea of wintering in this desert can only have been put into the head of the commanding general by an interested speculator . . ."

But the reluctant Washington felt that he had no alternative, and on December 11 the army broke camp on a march through sleet and snow to the bleak hillside that was to become synonymous with its fortitude and misery. The march was a foretaste of what was to come. No one told the story more eloquently than Dr. Albigence Waldo, the twenty-seven-year-old surgeon-diarist from Connecticut:

> December 12 A bridge of wagons laid across the Schuylkill last night, consisting of thirty-six wagons with a bridge of rails between each. Some skirmishing . . . Sun set. We were ordered to march over the river. It snows. I'm sick. Eat nothing. No whiskey. No forage. Lord, Lord, Lord . . . cold and uncomfortable. I am sick, discontented, and out of humor. Poor food. Hard lodging. Cold weather. Fatigue. Nasty clothes. Nasty cookery. Vomit half my time. Smoked out of my senses. The Devil's in it, I can't endure it. Why are we sent here to starve and freeze? What sweet felicities I have left at home, a charming wife, pretty children, good beds, good food, good cookery . . . Here all confusion, smoke and cold, hunger and filthiness. A pox on my bad luck.

The column slowed on the approach to Valley Forge, creeping over the frozen ruts of the uphill road at the speed of a mile an hour. Washington rode up the final slope over the bloody trail of a barefoot regiment and halted its colonel to ask why he had not drawn shoes for his men. He heard a familiar story: "They gave out, Sir, before they got to us." The general moved ahead at the roadside past mute marchers who did not look up as he went by. Some of them heard his muttered groan, "Poor fellows."

The first men saw the campground at twilight, a heavily timbered, wind-swept plateau that rolled to the bluffs of the Schuylkill.

A nearby village of a dozen stone houses clustered about the site of an ancient iron works; otherwise there were only the charred ruins of a sawmill and a few army storage sheds, burned by British raiders some weeks before. Most of the troops lay all night about campfires, too exhausted to pitch tents.

The camp was eighteen miles northwest of Philadelphia, a strong defensive triangle between the south bank of the Schuylkill and Valley Creek. Soldiers were soon complaining that there were no springs on the heights and water must be carried up the hill from a stream half a mile away: "The warter we had to Drink and to mix our flower with was out of a brook that ran along by the Camps, and so many a dippin and washin . . . maid it very Dirty and muddy."

Another congressional proclamation of national thanksgiving was announced the next morning, but the troops were beyond laughter. Lieutenant Colonel Henry Dearborn took note of the holiday in his diary: "Upon the whole I think all we have to be thankful for is that we are alive and not in the grave with many of our friends." Sergeant Joseph Martin celebrated with "half a gill of rice" for dinner, taken with a tablespoon of vinegar to guard against scurvy. Sergeant Ebenezer Wild, who was lucky enough to have a few bites of fresh beef, grumbled that there was no salt.

The men were turned out at once to build huts designed by Louis Duportail, log cabins fourteen by sixteen feet, with a door at one end and a chimney at the other. Thomas Paine, who spent the day in camp, was cheered to see the army at work "like a family of beavers; everyone busy, some carrying logs, others mud, and the rest fastening them together." Axes rang in the woods as trees were felled, chopped into lengths and notched. Hundreds of men hauled mud from the stream banks to chink cracks between the logs; others collected sticks or stones for chimneys. By the end of the second day a crew of a dozen expert woodsmen had completed their hut and claimed the $12 prize offered by Washington.

But it was slow work to build a thousand cabins with no tools other than axes, and the last of the army was not to be under cover until mid-January. Even so, the huts were scarcely better than tents. Most of the roofs were crudely thatched with branches and straw and leaked in the lightest rain or snow. The earthen floors were cold and dank and the fires of green wood filled the huts with blinding smoke.

Washington moved into one of the first completed huts, and

had a dining cabin added to accommodate his staff and visitors, who came even now in an endless stream. When the army was finally housed he was to move to comfortable quarters in the stone house of Mrs. Deborah Hewes. Other ranking officers lived in neighborhood houses and outbuildings, but not always in luxury. Colonel Buysson, a French newcomer, lived in a cave that had served as a farmer's spring house.

The army was to suffer acutely at Valley Forge from shortages of food, clothing and medical care, but there was also to be, at a most crucial time, a crisis of command. Washington discovered that his critics were still active, and seemed to be gaining influence in Congress.

The troops had hardly settled at Valley Forge when the general's suspicions of a conspiracy against him were renewed by a series of warnings from friends in Virginia. Benjamin Harrison wrote that Congressman Richard Henry Lee was working secretly with John and Sam Adams to "divide the command." A few days later Washington heard from Dr. James Craik, who had served with him as surgeon in the French and Indian War, a warning that "Base and Villainous men" were trying to ruin his reputation. Craik urged the general to "have an Eye toward" R. H. Lee, Mifflin and Gates, who were said to be behind the plot.

About the same time—in mid-January—Patrick Henry received an anonymous letter declaring that since Washington's army had degenerated into a mob, the troops could be disciplined only by Gates, Lee or Conway, one of whom could "in a few weeks render them an irresistible body of men." The writer asked Henry to burn the letter, but instead he sent it to Washington, who recognized the handwriting as that of Benjamin Rush, and was particularly offended, since the doctor had been "elaborate and studied in his professions of regard for me." Washington told Henry that he had known of the plot to replace him, but had kept it secret: "My caution to avoid any thing, which could injure the service, prevented me from communicating, but to a very few of my friends, the intrigues of a faction which I know was formed against me . . ."

A final warning came from Henry Laurens, the new president of Congress, who sent Washington a long, anonymous diatribe against him entitled "Thoughts of a Freeman," a document found on the steps of the congressional building in York. The author demanded Washington's immediate removal from office:

> I believe . . . that the proper method of attacking, beating, and conquering the enemy has never as yet been adopted by the Commander-in-Chief . . . that the late success to the northward was owing to a change of commanders; that the southern army would have been alike successful, had a similar change taken place; . . . that it is a very great reproach to America to say there is only one general in it . . . that the people of America have been guilty of idolatry, by making a man their god; and the God of heaven and earth will convince them by woful experience, that he is only a man; that no good may be expected from the standing army, until Baal and his worshippers are banished from the camp.

Washington complained that his enemies had "taken ungenerous advantage of me . . . They know I cannot combat their insinuations . . . without disclosing secrets it is of the utmost moment to conceal." But he urged Laurens to show this attack to Congress and said he would never try "to suppress a free spirit of inquiry" into his conduct: "Why should I expect to be exempt from censure, the unfailing lot of an elevated station? . . . My heart tells me that I have tried to do my best yet I may have been very often mistaken in my judgment . . ."

Though Congress never saw this document officially, and the question of Washington's tenure as commander in chief was not debated, he was at this time convinced that powerful enemies were intriguing to remove him from office.

John Adams, though he vehemently denied taking part in a plot against Washington, now favored an annual change of generals, and declared that more than half the congressmen who had voted for Washington as commander in chief in 1775 had come to regret it. Not only did Adams appear to rue his role in the commissioning of Washington, he now attributed the general's popularity to the terms of his employment:

. . . great as his talents and virtues are, they did not . . . contribute so much to it as his serving without pay, which never fails to turn the heads of the multitude. His ten thousand officers . . . and all his other admirers, might have sounded his fame as much as they would, and they might have justly sounded it very high, and it would not all have produced such ecstasies among the people as this single circumstance. Now, I say, this is all wrong. There should have been no such distinction made between him and the other generals. He should have been paid, as well as they, and the people should have too high a sense of their own dignity ever to suffer any man to serve them for nothing . . . it has been the people themselves who have always created their own despots.

It seemed an age ago that Adams had praised Washington's refusal to "accept a shilling for pay." The volunteer who had once seemed "generous . . . noble and disinterested" had now become an ambitious schemer in the eyes of his creator.

Thomas Conway now appeared at headquarters to announce that the Board of War had promoted him to major general and sent him to take over a new post as inspector general of the army. Washington received the Irishman with icy courtesy, in a manner so humiliating, Conway protested, "as I never met with before from any General during the course of thirty years in a very respectable army." When Washington asked for Conway's plans for his work, the Irishman replied in detail, but was so offended by Washington's obvious hostility that he offered to resign "if my appointment is . . . anyways disagreeable to Your Excellency."

Washington told Conway that though his appointment as inspector general had not caused "the least uneasiness" among officers, his promotion to major general was being protested by brigadier generals who had been passed over. Washington said that his only interest was to see that no "extraordinary promotion" was made without good cause. Conway retreated to lodgings some distance from camp, "greatly disappointed and chagrined" at his rejection, and began to bombard Washington with insulting letters. He denied that his promotion was extraor-

VALLEY FORGE

dinary, and in one particularly sarcastic letter linked Washington with the name of the greatest soldier of the time:

> The . . . merit which you wish every promoted officer might be endowed with is a rare gift. We see but a few men of merit so generally acknowledged. We know but the Great Frederick in Europe and the great Washington in this continent. I certainly was never so rash as to pretend to such a prodigious height. . . . But you, sir, and the great Frederick, know perfectly well that this trade is not learned in a few months. I have served steadily thirty years . . .

Once more Conway offered to resign.

When Washington made no reply, Conway wrote impatiently:

> I cannot believe, Sir . . . that the objection to my appointment originates from any body living but from you . . . Since you will not accept of my services, since you cannot bear the sight of me in your camp, I am very ready to go wherever Congress thinks proper, and even to France . . .

Washington sent his correspondence with Conway to Congress, determined to make it clear that though he felt the Irishman's promotion threatened the stability of the army, he would support him or any other duly appointed officer. He also denied Conway's charge that he had been received disrespectfully at headquarters, but he made no effort to conceal his distaste for the Irishman: "If General Conway means, by cool reception . . . that I did not receive him in the language of a warm and cordial friend, I readily confess the charge . . . My feelings will not permit me to make professions of friendships to the man I deem my enemy, and whose system of conduct forbids it . . ."

Nine of Washington's brigadiers protested to Congress the promotion of Conway, saying that they had detected "no superior act of mind which could entitle him to rise above us." Nathanael Greene wrote in their support with a warning that irregular promotions would ruin the service by encouraging "low intrigue" for commissions. Congress tabled the protests.

Though Washington corresponded no further with Conway, there was now an explanation from Gates, who claimed that

Conway's original letter was "harmless" and did not include the insulting phrases reported to Washington. He added a bumbling defense of his own role but made no offer to produce the offensive letter.

Washington replied that he had "no small difficulty in reconciling the spirit and import of your different Letters, and sometimes of the different parts of the same Letter with each other." Then, probably with the aid of Hamilton, he added caustic challenges: If Conway's letter was harmless, why did it remain secret? Why had the Irishman, who had been one of Washington's "bad counsellors," remained silent while the defense of Philadelphia was being planned and fought? "It is greatly to be lamented that this adept in Military science did not employ his abilities in the progress of the Campaign . . . The United States have lost much from that unseasonable diffidence, which prevented his . . . displaying those rich treasures of knowledge . . . he has since so freely laid open to you . . . I can't help being a little sceptical as to his views."

Conway was heard from once more when his letter to Gates was back in his hands, reporting "with great satisfaction that the paragraph so much spoken of does not exist in said letter, nor any thing like it," but he, too, failed to send Washington a copy of his letter.

Washington learned the partial truth from Henry Laurens, who wrote to confirm Conway's claim: the letter did not mention a "Weak General"—but did include a passage "ten times worse in every view." Laurens quoted from Conway's original: "What a pity there is but one Gates! But the more I see of this army, the less I think it fit for general action under its actual chiefs and actual discipline . . . I wish I could serve under you."

There was a final exchange between Gates and Washington in which Gates apologized and expressed the hope that "no more of that time, so precious to the public, may be lost upon the subject of General Conway's letter." He denied that he had ambitions of replacing Washington: "I solemnly declare that I am of no faction . . ."

Washington ended it with an air of weary resignation: "I am as averse to controversy as any Man and had I not been forced into it, you never would have had occasion to impute to me, even the shadow of a disposition towards it . . ." He hoped to bury the whole affair "in silence and, as far as future events will permit, oblivion."

Washington may have felt that his prompt challenge to possible rivals had saved the army from a fatal controversy, but among his friends he seemed to take a keen personal satisfaction in the confused retreat of the suspected conspirators. The general wrote his aide, John Fitzgerald, "Gates has involved himself in his letters to me, in the most absurd contradictions: Mifflin has involved himself in a scrape he does not know how to get out of . . . In a word, I have a good deal of reason to believe that the Machinations of this Junto will recoil upon their own heads . . ."

The affair echoed noisily for a few weeks. Gates accused Wilkinson of betraying him and provoked the infuriated major into a challenge to a duel, to assert his *"wounded* honor at the point of my sword and ratify my integrity in blood . . . May the God of Justice help you!" Wilkinson hurried to York, where Gates was then stationed, but there was no bloodshed. As Wilkinson told the story: "I found General Gates unarmed and alone, and was received with tenderness, but manifest embarassment; he asked me to walk, turned into a back street . . . he burst into tears, took me by the hand, and asked me, 'how I could think he would wish to injure me? . . . I should as soon think of injuring my own child.' "

Wilkinson returned to Valley Forge to avenge himself on Stirling, but was once more mollified, when Stirling signed a statement declaring that the fateful conversation had "passed in a private company, during a convivial hour," and that the major could not be justly accused of betraying a confidence. Wilkinson's honor was preserved, but he lost a promising position as secretary of the Board of War, and resigned his brevet commission in face of a protest by forty-seven colonels. Wilkinson was to remain out of service for a year, until he returned as clothier general. In his later years Wilkinson was to play a dubious role in American history as a co-conspirator of Aaron Burr in the plot to create a new nation in the Mississippi Valley.

Gates was reassigned to the northern command, Conway was

off on a brief, ill-starred expedition against Canada, and Thomas Mifflin soon resigned from the Board of War, protesting his innocence: "I love and esteem General Washington and know him too well to even wish for a Change . . ."

As Henry Laurens had prophesied, the alarms of the Conway Cabal died away without damage to Washington's reputation. Laurens had long since sought to reassure the anxious Lafayette that the conspiracy against Washington was "little more than tittle tattle," and that the commander was "out of reach of his Enemies, if he has an Enemy." Laurens had also attempted an explanation of the curious political behavior of Americans, who were "sometimes very troublesome in their disputes which are carried to such extremes as seem to threaten a dissolution of all friendships. Nevertheless, danger from a common Enemy will reduce them to good order and as it were by a Charm, instantly establish a coalition."

In the first weeks of the encampment at Valley Forge it seemed that the enemy was the least of the army's worries.

On December 21 men who had worked on their cabins all day made their supper on fire cake, a thin paste of flour and water baked on hot stones. The supply system had collapsed.

A chorus of protest began after dark when a soldier began calling, "No meat! No meat!" and was joined by thousands of others until the countryside echoed with the mournful croaking from the ridge. When these died away, men hooted like owls and shrilled crow calls. Officers quieted the bedlam after an hour or so, but reported the men in a dangerous mood.

Dr. Waldo's diary appraised the diet: "Fire-cake and water for dinner! Fire-cake and water for supper! The Lord send that our Commissary for Purchases may have to live on fire-cake and water till their glutted guts are turned to pasteboard . . ." Washington called commissary officers to headquarters and was dismayed when only one appeared, to confess the "melancholy & alarming truth" that there were no animals in camp to be slaughtered, that the only food on hand was twenty-five barrels of flour, and that no one knew when supplies could be delivered. The general had sent out foragers with the few horses and wagons in camp, but this would not suffice. "Three or four days of bad weather," he wrote, "would prove our destruction."

The next day, when he learned that a British raiding party had marched out of Philadelphia, and called out troops to attack, he was told that none of them could leave camp. The army was immobilized. Washington wrote Congress that the supply problem could no longer be neglected:

> Unless some great and capital change suddenly takes place in that line, this army must inevitably be reduced to one or other of these three things—Starve—dissolve—or disperse, in order to obtain subsistence. . . .

For the first time, he charged Thomas Mifflin with failure to perform his duty, which he had neglected for months, forcing Washington himself to attempt to supply the army:

> Since the month of July we have had no assistance from the quartermaster general. . . . The soap, vinegar, and other articles allowed by Congress, we see none of, nor have we seen them, I believe, since the battle of Brandywine . . .

The army was also almost literally naked. In many huts there was barely enough clothing to outfit two or three men to stand guard duty, while the others remained naked in their bunks. More than one barefoot sentry stood in the snow with his feet in his hat. Colonel Allen McLane, the cavalry raider, sometimes poured rum into his boots to keep his feet from freezing.

Lafayette saw that the naked men could not long survive: "Their feet and legs froze until they became black and it was often necessary to amputate them."

Washington summed up the army's plight on the last day of the year: "Our sick naked, our well naked, our unfortunate men in captivity naked!"

Disease spread rapidly through the camp. To combat typhus, doctors advised men to burn spoonfuls of sulfur and gunpowder in the huts, which were made almost uninhabitable by the acrid fumes. Men weakened by dysentery, who refused to walk through the snow to latrines, often defecated on the floors. Anthony Wayne said he would rather go into battle than make a tour of inspection.

Disease was also thought to have spread from the rotting carcasses of hundreds of horses, buried in shallow graves after they had died of starvation, exposed after each rain despite the efforts of fatigue parties to keep them covered. The fate of the army's horses, Washington said, was "still more lamentable than that of the men."

Sick soldiers besieged the army's few doctors. Dr. Waldo left a glimpse of a patient who was typical of hundreds:

> . . . his bare feet are seen thro' his worn-out shoes, his legs nearly naked from the tattered remains of an only pair of stockings, his Breeches not sufficient to cover his nakedness, his Shirt hanging in Strings, his hair dishevell'd, his face meagre . . . He comes and crys with an air of wretchedness & despair, I am Sick, my feet lame, my legs are sore, my body covered with this tormenting Itch . . .

Sergeant Joseph Martin, whose body was so covered with raw sores of camp itch—scabies—that he could hardly lift his hands overhead, treated himself with sulfur and melted tallow. Martin and his friends made a jug of hot whiskey toddy and lay before a blazing fire, plying "each other's outsides with brimstone and tallow and the insides with hot whiskey sling," a remedy so effective that Martin "lay out naked all night. Somehow, got to bunks, most of them . . ."

At least twenty-five hundred men were to die of disease, a quarter of those who had entered the camp before Christmas. Many of these were treated in a hospital at nearby Yellow Springs, surrounded by rows of graves so shallow that droves of hogs dug up the corpses, but hundreds of others were carried to makeshift hospitals in other towns of the region: abandoned houses, barns, sheds and tents that were already overrun by sick and wounded from Brandywine and Germantown. Soldiers from Valley Forge suffering from smallpox and typhus, "in rags swarming with vermin," were laid beside the convalescent wounded on filthy, blood-stained layers of straw that were used over and over, unchanged until four or five patients had died upon them.

Doctors and nurses succumbed to the epidemics. Two doctors who were attempting to care for two hundred and fifty patients in the village of Lititz came down with typhus, and five hundred of the fifteen hundred men carried there from Valley Forge died within a few weeks. In Bethlehem every nurse and orderly fell ill, and few surgeons escaped. Only three of forty patients from John Marshall's Virginia regiment lived through hospital treatment.

It now appeared that the hapless army would soon be left without officers, since those of every rank were leaving for home. As one officer was to report, he was handed letters every day by veterans who stood with tears in their eyes as he read the pathetic pleas of their wives: "am without bread, and cannot get any, the committee will not supply me, my children will starve, or if they do not, they must freeze, we have no wood, neither can we get any. Pray come home."

At the urging of Washington, Nathanael Greene agreed to serve as quartermaster general in an effort to save the army—reluctantly, despite the enticement of riches promised by congressmen: he was to receive a commission of one percent of supplies purchased. Greene complained to Washington that "nobody ever heard of a Quarter Master in history," and to Henry Knox; "His Excellency presses it upon me exceedingly. I hate the place, but hardly know what to do." The Quaker finally accepted, with the understanding that he was to regain his troop command, and though it was to be several weeks before his new title became official, Greene set to work with his customary vigor. He sent four thousand raiders into Chester and Bucks counties with orders to "forage the country naked," seizing or destroying everything of value to the enemy. Greene reported to Washington from the field: "The inhabitants cry out and beset me from all quarters, but like Pharoah I harden my heart." His victims resisted, despite threats of floggings and confiscation of property. Some farmers sent their horses into other states; others burned their wagons or smashed their wheels, and refused to thresh their grain, even though it was seized and paid for merely as straw in the inflated Continental currency. Despite all opposition, Greene's men returned to camp on February 26 with a caravan of wagons loaded with meat, vegetables, honey, salt, hay and grain. On the same day Anthony Wayne's men drove in an enormous herd of cattle, pigs and sheep from a raid into New Jersey. The famine was over.

Washington named Colonel Jeremiah Wadsworth as commissary general to succeed Joseph Trumbull, who was seriously ill in Connecticut. Within a few weeks the army was being adequately supplied for the first time. Greene and Wadsworth established a network of agents from Virginia to New England. Greene alone had three thousand quartermasters, auditors, clerks, forage and wagon masters, with more than a hundred express riders to carry his orders through the country. Greene persuaded states to exempt teamsters from army service, and impressed teams and wagons wherever they could be found. Scandal was to follow in his wake, but Greene did not allow the army to suffer for lack of supplies during his three years in office.

The volume of Greene's purchases grew rapidly. Within two months he had spent four million Continental dollars, and said "this was but a breakfast" for his needy department.

With the passing of February some soldiers began to suspect they might survive the winter. One of them wrote: "I am very Happy in having my Health at this present time. And More so A Stedfast Resolution to Remain a Strong Libertine As long As my much Ronged Country May Call for Soldiers sword and Ball."

Greene and his quartermasters now provided decent daily rations, a pound and a half of bread, a pound of beef or fish or pork and beans, and a gill of whiskey or rum for each man. This was supplemented in March by a feast of fresh shad, caught by the thousands in their annual spawning run up the Schuylkill and brought to camp in wagons, to be baked by the fires, or salted down in brine barrels to feed the army in the months ahead.

Though Washington's hospitality at headquarters continued to attract guests, it was much reduced in scale. Food and drink were no longer lavishly served—even the rum was diluted with water into an unpalatable punch known as "grum." Washington complained that the servant who waited on his table was "indecently and most shamefully naked."

Mrs. Washington had arrived in February and the army's ranking officers and their wives spent almost every evening at headquarters. The young Frenchman, Pierre Duponceau, was impressed by the simple dignity of Martha, who reminded him of "the Roman matrons of whom I had read so much"; but he found the evenings long at the Deborah Hewes House. There was conversation over tea or coffee, and no dancing, and "no amusements of any kind, except singing. Every Gentleman or lady who could sing was called upon in turn for a song." There were compensations. The Frenchman admired Lord Stirling's wife, her daughter Lady Kitty Alexander, and young Kitty's friend Nancy Brown, "a distinguished belle." Some of the women were attractive indeed, especially Mrs. Greene, who was not only "handsome, elegant and accomplished," but was also flirtatious and spoke French so well as to be "well versed in French literature." Kitty Greene spent so much time in animated conversation with Lafayette and some of his countrymen that her husband complained of it to his friend Jeremiah Wadsworth.* Lafayette wrote to his wife of his fondness for Mrs. Greene—and Lucy Knox noted that "all was not well with Greene and his lady."

The first public celebration of Washington's birthday was enlivened by a serenade by the band of the 4th Continental Artillery, which pleased the general so much that he distributed a tip of 15 shillings, an expense he charged to the government, as he did all tips to headquarters servants. (Washington also charged Congress for expenses of Martha's visits to headquar-

---

* Long afterward, when Greene was dead, Kitty confessed to Wadsworth, with whom she had an affair: "I believe I forgot to mention my noble lover to you. The Marquis of —— I forgot what, but he had very serious propositions."

ters, on the ground that, unlike other officers, he never took a leave of absence during the war.)

As the weather improved, the army had infrequent glimpses of Washington exercising with his officers. One camp diarist reported:

"This day His Excellency dined with G Nox and after dinner did us the honor to play at wickets with us." The general may also have played "base" with younger officers, a game similar to the old English "rounders." The French officer Barbé-Maurois noted not long afterward that Washington "sometimes throws and catches a ball for whole hours with his aides-de-camp."

The daily life of the army changed markedly—and permanently—in February with the coming of a German drillmaster, Baron von Steuben, who had landed in America a few days earlier. Washington welcomed him gratefully.

The baron arrived in a new sleigh with an Italian greyhound at his side, trailed by a carriage and riders, five grooms and drivers, a military secretary, two French aides and three servants. Only one of his party spoke English. Steuben emerged from fur robes, a short, powerful man of forty-seven with a seamed and grizzled face, immaculate in a scarlet and blue uniform, his breast ablaze with decorations.

The Prussian, Friedrich Wilhelm Ludolf Gerhard Augustin, Baron von Steuben, impressed Washington as forthright, modest and genial. Through Hamilton and John Laurens as interpreters, he said that his only wish was to drill troops. He would not seek a field command, so as to avoid offending senior officers. He brought letters from Franklin and Deane in Paris recommending him as an expert in troop training and a former lieutenant general under Frederick the Great. Congress had already gratefully accepted him as a volunteer who sought neither rank nor pay.

The baron was dismayed by his first glimpse of the army's "literally naked" men and their weapons, muskets "in a horrible condition, covered with rust" and bayonets used only for roasting meat over campfires. Hundreds of soldiers had gone home for the winter. Many colonels had no muster rolls of their troops, and others, though they reported their regiments at from two hundred and fifty to three hundred men each, sometimes had as few as thirty men. One company had dwindled from a strength of one hundred to a single man.

Steuben marveled that the army still existed. As he said later, "My determination must have been very firm that I did not abandon my design when I saw the troops." But he realized that despite their comic efforts on the drill ground, these ragged, undisciplined men were resolute survivors of untold hardships who could be made into soldiers. No European army, he told Washington, would have clung together for so long under such conditions. He set out at once to transform Washington's starvelings into disciplined troops before spring brought fighting weather.

Steuben began as drill sergeant to a company of one hundred veterans, first teaching a squad of ten "the position of the soldier" through pantomime, nodding approval or correcting faults until the squad could dress its line, march, halt and about-face in unison. Steuben's drills became the army's favorite entertainment, where thousands learned by example. Within a few days his model company marched flawlessly, even over rough terrain, without the aid of fifes and drums. The Prussian gave the troops their first real instruction in bayonet fighting, so that within a few weeks men who had feared to face the British steel were eager to meet the enemy. He also devised a brief drill manual based on Prussian methods, and with the aid of scores of volunteer copyists, circulated it through the army. His French, translated by his aide, Pierre Duponceau, was polished by Hamilton and John Laurens, and Steuben, who could not understand a word of the English version, memorized the commands and barked them at his company. His audience roared with laughter at the baron's attempts at multilingual swearing. He once burst out to his translators, "My dear Walker—Duponceau—come swear for me. These fellows won't do what I tell them! *Sacre Goddam! Die gaucheries of dese badouts. Je ne puis.* I can curse them no more."

Within a month Steuben's instruction battalions had the whole army drilling by regiments and brigades, so that for the first time the troops could march "in compact masses with steadiness and without losing distance." No longer would Washington be obliged to maneuver the army in single file, which had prevented his rapid concentration in battle.

The baron found that he must frequently justify his commands to the rebels. As he wrote a European friend, "The genius of this nation is not in the least to be compared with that of the Prussians, Austrians or French. You say to your soldier, 'Do this' and he doeth it; but I am obliged to say, 'This is the reason you ought to do that'; and he does it."

Washington soon learned that Steuben was a fraud, with the most tenuous claim to the title of baron, and was actually a penniless soldier of fortune, a country parson's son who had risen no higher than the rank of major in the Prussian army. Even the trappings of his entourage—servants, carriage, sleigh and horses—were not his own, but had been provided by John Hancock, and unfortunately, as he confessed to Washington, Steuben could not afford to serve without pay. But Washington reacted to the discovery as Franklin had: whatever his rank, Steuben was an ideal drillmaster who had transformed the army, and the value of his service could hardly be overestimated. At Washington's urging, Congress appointed him inspector general with the rank of major general.

The letter of an anonymous officer paid tribute to Steuben's work:

> The Army grows stronger every day . . . and there is a spirit of discipline among the troops that is better than numbers . . . You would be charmed to see the regularity and exactness with which they march and perform their maneuvers . . . Last year . . . it was almost impossible to advance or retire in the presence of the enemy without disordering the line and falling into confusion. The misfortune, I believe, will seldom happen again . . .

Most important of all was the confidence the men gained from their skills—"a new morale, never more to be extinguished, soon pervaded the ranks of the Continental Army."

In the midst of the army's transformation Charles Lee returned after more than a year of imprisonment, and was given a hero's welcome by Washington, as if the Englishman's insubordination had been forgotten. The commander had persisted until the British agreed to Lee's exchange for the recently captured Major General Robert Prescott. Washington led an entourage out the road to Philadelphia to greet Charles Lee, a reunion watched with disapproval by Elias Boudinot, the commissary of prisons: "Gen. Washington dismounted and rec'd Gen. Lee as if he had been his brother."

Lee rode to camp with Washington through files of waiting troops, was greeted at headquarters by Mrs. Washington and settled in a room adjoining her parlor. The Washingtons entertained in Lee's honor that night, "an Elegant Dinner" with "the Music playing the whole time."

Lee lay abed late the next morning, and breakfast at headquarters was delayed for him. The thin-shanked Englishman finally emerged from his room, as Boudinot remembered it, "as dirty as if he had been in the street all night." Lee had not returned alone: "He had brought a miserable dirty hussy with him from Philadelphia (a British Sergeant's wife) and had actually taken her into his Room by a Back Door and she had slept with him that night."

If Washington took note of Lee's companion he gave no sign of disapproval. His pleasure at Lee's return was obvious, as if he had been uneasy at the prospect of opening another campaign without him. Months earlier, when he had sent Boudinot through the lines to New York to investigate British treatment of rebel prisoners, Washington had made it clear that his most pressing assignment was to arrange the exchange of Lee.

Boudinot found Lee living in luxury, quartered with some of Howe's staff officers, well supplied with wine and food and free to move about the city as he wished, furnished with horses by the British and with money by Congress. Lee had complained bitterly to Boudinot that Congress had not sent delegates to visit him: "Sir, I had discovered the whole British summer's campaign. I would have told the committee all—for Mr. Boudinot, it is in vain for Congress to expect to withstand British troops in the field."

"They have been withstood, General. With all their strength, the enemy gained nothing in the campaign."

"Starve—Dissolve—or Disperse"

Lee scoffed at hopes of an American victory under "such an ignorant Commander in Chief," and outlined to Boudinot a fantastic strategic scheme for Washington's conduct of the war. Further American resistance in battle was useless, Lee said. The rebels should retreat and build a strong fortress at Pittsburgh, where old men, women and children, and the country's treasure could be sent. If the British followed, Congress could escape down the Ohio into Spanish territory. The American army should be reorganized as a guerrilla force. Boudinot said he would carry no such absurd message to Congress and advised Lee to forget his scheme.

But Lee had not forgotten. A few days after his arrival at Valley Forge he told Boudinot that his proposed strategic retreat to the west was the only hope for the Americans. The army was in much worse condition than he had expected. He was unimpressed by the work of Steuben, and further, he told Boudinot, "Washington is not fit to command a Sergeant's Guard."

Lee spent a few days in York lecturing congressmen on the importance of guerrilla warfare, but Henry Laurens was so disgusted with his proposals that he refused to report them on the floor. Lee returned to Valley Forge, and as soon as his exchange became official, he was given command of the army's 1st Division. Thanks to Lee, Washington knew that he would face a new antagonist in the summer's fighting, for the Englishman brought definite word of Howe's resignation. Lee saw Sir William as the victim of inept London officials: "He shut his eyes, fought his battles, drank his bottle, had his little whore, advis'd with his Counselors, received his orders from North and Germain, one more absurd than the other . . . shut his eyes, fought again, and is now I suppose to be called to Account for acting according to instructions . . ."

Lee failed to tell Washington that only two weeks after rejoining the army at Valley Forge, he had written Henry Clinton to congratulate him on his promotion.

The Steuben-trained troops gave their first public performance on May 6, when civilians thronged to Valley Forge to help the army celebrate the thrilling news of the French alliance.

VALLEY FORGE

The news had come haphazardly to Washington through gossip from camp visitors and in unofficial letters, and he shrewdly assessed its importance: Great Britain was in "a greater ferment" than she had known since her own revolution, and "all Europe is getting into a flame." He spoke for the country as well as the army: "I believe no event was ever received with a more heartfelt joy." The news was better than Washington realized. Not only had France recognized the United States and offered military aid in case England declared war on her; a fleet of sixteen ships had already sailed for America under command of the Count d'Estaing. When Washington asked Congress for official confirmation of the treaty so that he could notify the troops, there was no reply. He read its details in *The Pennsylvania Gazette* and ordered a celebration in phrases so ecstatic as to be almost incomprehensible to the troops:

> It having pleased the Almighty Ruler of the Universe propitiously to defend the cause of the United American States, and finally, by raising us up a powerful friend among the Princes of the Earth, to establish our Liberty and Independence upon a lasting foundation; it becomes us to set apart a day for gratefully acknowledging the Divine Goodness . . .

Prisoners were set free "that they might taste the Pleasur of the Day" and there was an extra issue of rum. Banquet tables were set up beneath an enormous awning pieced together from the tent flies of officers. Quartermasters had ransacked the army's larders to spread the tables with "a cold collation" that seemed a Lucullan feast to most officers, though Baron de Kalb dismissed it as "a profusion of fat meat, strong wine and other liquors."

The troops were paraded at nine o'clock, each "with a nosegay in his hat," to hear chaplains read news of the alliance from *The Gazette* and offer long prayers. After Washington spoke briefly, "a most eloquent, very touching" tribute to Louis XVI, Steuben put the army through its paces, its files swinging past Washington and his generals in line of battle, a professional display executed "with admirable rapidity and precision," and after an artillery salute, the army's thousands of muskets blazed in a running fire. Soldiers and civilians joined in mass cheers for the King of France, "The Friendly European Powers" and "The American States," and salutes of cannon and the army's running fire were repeated. The uproar was heard by the mystified British in Philadelphia.

When the troops had gone back to their huts for rum, their officers formed, thirteen abreast, and marched with linked arms to the banquet tent, where they were greeted by the general and Mrs. Washington. The crowd lingered over the tables for innumerable toasts. One officer said he had never seen "such unfeigned and perfect joy," and John Laurens said that Washington "received such proofs of the love and attachment of his officers as must have given him the most exquisite feelings."

Not the least of the day's wonders to his troops was the smile that never faded from Washington's face, "a countenance of uncommon delight and complacence." The crowd burst into spontaneous applause when the general left the banquet, "a universal clap, with loud huzzas" that followed him until he had ridden a quarter of a mile, where he paused to wave his hat overhead and return the cheer, a gesture that precipitated a final spectacle— "a thousand hats were tossed in the air."

A British spy who was caught watching the drill and celebration parade was set free by an American officer: "The news of this army today will be more painful to them than the loss of a spy. Be sure that he is free to report all he has seen."

Benedict Arnold appeared in camp near the end of May, a shocking caricature of the veteran Washington had admired as one of the army's most aggressive combat officers. Four soldiers helped Arnold from his carriage to his quarters, since he could not yet hobble on his wounded leg, which was now two inches shorter than the other. The thirty-seven-year-old general had aged suddenly, his swarthy face drawn with pain and his pale gray eyes grown dull.

Since Arnold's wound would keep him from active service for many months, Washington made plans to leave him in command of Philadelphia when the British evacuated the city. Already there were signs that the enemy was preparing to abandon the capital that William Howe had won at such great cost and effort in eight months of campaigning. For weeks the reports of "deserters, townsmen, women of different qualities, spies" had been unanimous: the British were leaving the city. Though their destination was unknown, and Washington feared the enemy might take the offensive, he guessed that they were likely to retreat, across the New Jersey countryside, to New York. He prepared for this more than a month in advance, by sending Philemon Dickinson and William Maxwell with their New Jersey troops to burn bridges and fell trees across roads on the most direct route to New York.

17

MONMOUTH,
JUNE 28, 1778

"I Expect My Orders to Be Obeyed!"

Sir Henry Clinton arrived in Philadelphia early in May, a reluctant successor to Howe as commander in chief in America. A paunchy, hook-nosed, near-sighted little man of forty-eight, neurotic and contentious, Clinton was given to quarrels and frequent resignations over imaginary slights. Though generally regarded as a capable officer, he was often indecisive and tormented by self-doubts. "I'm a shy bitch," he once said. Some of his subordinates found Clinton incompetent—General James Robertson, for one: "He has not the understanding necessary for a corporal. He is as inconstant as a weathercock, and knows nothing." Sir Henry had recently taken a mistress, Mrs. Mary Baddeley, the wife of a soldier whom Clinton had promoted to captain. Mary was to remain with Clinton throughout his life and bear him several children. Already, the general confessed, she had saved him from ruin by her management of his teeming headquarters in New York, where she directed a staff of thirty servants, prepared receptions and meals for hundreds of guests and coped with the general's staggering expenses of £7,000 per year.

For all his criticism of William Howe, Clinton was loath to see his chief leave America. He had come to lean on him, and felt that the Howes together were "irresistible." Only the brothers, Clinton said, could succeed in America. "I therefore cannot suppose

it possible that this command should fall upon my shoulders."
Now that it had done so, Clinton was filled with misgivings. "No
officer who had the least regard for his professional career," he
had said, would seek a command "so hopeless as this." His government had been equally reluctant to give him the post, which
had been refused by other, more promising candidates. Soon
after his arrival he was directed from London to take the army
back to New York. He complained of these orders: "I cannot mis-
understand them, nor dare I disobey them. I am directed to
evacuate Philadelphia. My fate is hard; forced to an apparent
retreat with such an army is mortifying."

As Clinton prepared to carry out these distasteful orders,
young officers of the army bade a bizarre farewell to William
Howe in a day-long spectacle known as a Meschianza, a Baby-
lonian extravaganza conceived and directed by Captain John
André, an amateur dramatist. Hundreds of Philadelphia Tories
and British sympathizers received invitations designed by
André, cards bearing Howe's crest and a setting sun, with a
Latin inscription to the effect that the sun would rise again,
more dazzling than ever.

The fete opened with a regatta as a fleet of decorated barges
swept down the river to Walnut Grove, the country estate of
Thomas Wharton, to the accompaniment of massed bands and
broadsides from warships. A mock tournament between the
Knights of the Blended Rose and Burning Mountain was staged
on a four-acre lawn flanked by pavilions filled with Tory girls
who wore gowns of gold, scarlet and blue, designed by André.
Senior sergeants dressed in red and white silk served as pages,
and the fleet's marines, in blackface and wearing the broad silver collars of Nubian slaves, knelt to the ground as William Howe
appeared. The tournament was followed by a banquet in a room
two hundred and ten feet long. A fireworks display featured
a blazing tableau that depicted Fame saluting Howe with a blast
from her trumpet, "Thy laurels shall never fade."

The officers and young women danced in the banquet hall until
dawn.

Not even this extravagant tribute to the departing chief
impressed the gruff old Hessian General Leopold von Heister,

who was gratified when Howe sailed for home on May 23: "He is as valiant as my sword, but no more of a general than my arse."

A few days later the British fleet sailed down the Delaware, loaded with three thousand Loyalists who fled the wrath of the incoming rebels, and with two regiments of mutinous Hessians Clinton feared to trust on the march.

Three British commissioners arrived in Philadelphia on June 6, empowered to offer the rebels virtually every reform they had sought in 1775: repeal of taxes, the right to elect their own Congress and state officials, and to become an autonomous dominion within the empire. The commission also had secret instructions to entertain even a rebel demand for complete independence, which was to be referred to London for consideration. But there were to be no negotiations.

The commissioners were stunned to find Clinton preparing to retreat. The Earl of Carlisle, who headed the mission, saw that his cause was futile: "So long as we had the army to back us, we had hopes of success; but this turning our backs upon Mr. Washington will certainly make them reject offers."

He was right. Congress refused to consider any peace offer short of the King's "explicit acknowledgement of the independence of these states, or the withdrawing his fleets and armies."

The frustrated commissioners left with Clinton's army for New York, where they were to spend several weeks in vain attempts to bribe American leaders, and then sailed for England, after threatening the rebels with war to the death.

The son of a Philadelphia laundress brought indisputable evidence that the British were ready to depart on June 16: the peace commissioners had called for their linen, ready or not. Cannon disappeared from British earthworks about the city during the night.

A final council of war at Valley Forge the next day found Washington's generals all but unanimous in their advice to follow Clinton's army through New Jersey—two voted for a full-scale attack, six for harassment of the enemy column with small parties. Charles Lee urged that the British be allowed to march unmolested to New York.

MONMOUTH, JUNE 28, 1778

Clinton crossed the Delaware and set off through New Jersey on June 18, and Washington moved his twelve thousand troops at once, crossing higher up the Delaware, confident for the first time that he had an opportunity to destroy an enemy army. Benedict Arnold was left behind to govern Philadelphia until civilian authority could be restored. Arnold declared martial law at once, closed all shops and stores and ordered goods held for congressional identification of Loyalist property, which was to be confiscated.

Four days after his arrival Arnold signed a secret agreement with James Mease, the army's clothier general, and his deputy William West: the three would sell all surplus army goods for their own benefit and divide profits equally.

Returning patriots found the city incredibly dirty. Lucy and Henry Knox came but did not tarry: "It stunk so abominably that it was impossible to stay there." Congress was forced to use College Hall, because the State House was in a "filthy and sordid" condition. Some houses had been used as stables and the manure dumped into the cellars through holes cut in parlor floors. One civilian, at least, was surprised that the heart of the city had been so little damaged by the enemy, but unlike the buildings, he said, "the morals of the inhabitants have suffered greatly." The young women of the city suffered from "scarlet fever," had adopted outlandish London fashions, and hundreds of them were pregnant: "Many people do not hesitate in supposing that most of the young ladies who were in the city with the enemy and wear the present fashionable dresses have purchased them at the expense of their virtue. It is agreed on all hands that the British officers played the devil with the girls. The privates, I suppose, were satisfied with the common prostitutes . . ."

Two columns of the British army snaked into the New Jersey pinelands under a broiling sun, the men sweating in heavy woolen uniforms, struggling beneath packs that weighed from fifty to eighty pounds, beset by clouds of mosquitoes during the frequent halts while bridges were replaced and felled trees were cleared

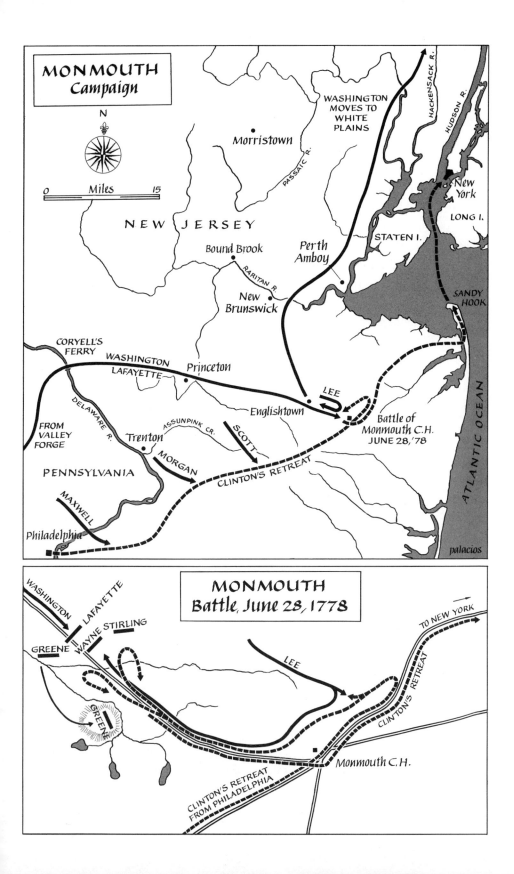

MONMOUTH
Campaign

N

0 — Miles — 15

WASHINGTON
MOVES TO
WHITE
PLAINS

HACKENSACK R.

HUDSON R.

Morristown

PASSAIC R.

New
York

NEW JERSEY

LONG I.

Bound Brook

Perth
Amboy

STATEN I.

RARITAN R.

New
Brunswick

SANDY
HOOK

CORYELL'S
FERRY

WASHINGTON
LAFAYETTE   Princeton

DELAWARE R.

Englishtown

LEE

ATLANTIC OCEAN

FROM
VALLEY
FORGE

ASSUNPINK CR.

Trenton

SCOTT

Battle of
Monmouth C.H.
JUNE 28, '78

MORGAN

PENNSYLVANIA

CLINTON'S RETREAT

MAXWELL

Philadelphia

palacios

MONMOUTH
Battle, June 28, 1778

WASHINGTON

LAFAYETTE

WAYNE STIRLING

TO NEW YORK

GREENE

LEE

CLINTON'S RETREAT

GREENE

Monmouth C.H.

CLINTON'S RETREAT
FROM PHILADELPHIA

from the roads. There was no water. Sunstroke felled several men in the ranks.

Fifteen hundred wagons lumbered along in the rear, a train twelve miles long, "wantonly enormous" as Henry Clinton said, loaded with food, equipment and loot from Philadelphia, and encumbered with carriages, extra horses, blacksmith's forges, baker's ovens, boats and bridges, "mistresses and every other kind of useless stuff."

The general had ordered most of the women sent to New York by ship, and limited the troops to two women per company, but camp followers, drawn by the prospect of plunder, had eluded the guards and trailed in the rear by the hundreds.

For several days the temperature was near 100 degrees, and though the army was swept by occasional rainstorms, the broiling sun soon reappeared over the steaming countryside. It was June 23, six days out of Philadelphia, before the British reached the village of Allentown, N.J., a distance of little more than thirty miles. Clinton was now forced to reveal his route to Washington, who had been marching more swiftly over a course to the northwest and was nearing Hopewell, some twenty miles away. The lightly laden rebels could win a race to the crossing of the Raritan at Brunswick, or catch the British at a disadvantage in the swamps along the direct road to New York, and Gates might be moving down from the north to reinforce Washington. Clinton chose to turn eastward over a single road that led through Monmouth Courthouse to Sandy Hook, though he would be forced to abandon his compact formation on parallel roads and string out his column along the narrow track through the barrens. The baggage train was now placed in the center for protection, with Knyphausen leading the way, and the best of Clinton's troops, under Cornwallis, in the rear.

Washington learned of Clinton's move on June 24, and during the morning, while an eclipse darkened the sun, held another council of war to ask advice on how he should strike the tempting target. Charles Lee dominated the discussion. It would be foolhardy—even "criminal"—for the army to attack an almost equal force of British troops, so clearly superior in discipline and equipment. Washington had only to wait for the French alliance to bring victory. Rather than risk an assault on Clinton, the Americans should be willing to "build a bridge of gold" to help him on his way to New York.

Others disagreed: the British should be struck on the move, while they were most vulnerable. But Lee was eloquent and insistent, Steuben and Duportail were unable to express themselves clearly in English, and by a narrow margin the council disapproved a general attack. Instead, the army should strengthen the force already hanging on the British flanks and rear, harassing the enemy at every opportunity. Only Wayne refused to sign the recommendation, but others openly challenged the decision which, Hamilton said, "would have done honor to the most honorable body of midwives and to them only." Lafayette said he wished the council had never been called, and both Wayne and Greene urged a heavier assault. Greene felt that the army should try to "make a serious impression," since "people expect something from us and our strength demands it . . . we . . . have come to our grief repeatedly—marching until we get near the enemy and then our courage fails and we halt."

As usual, Washington was hesitant to overrule the council, but he was eager to attack Clinton and, swayed by Greene and Wayne, ordered his vanguard strengthened. He moved the army nearer Monmouth Courthouse, sent Wayne's troops to join the advance, and since that force had now grown to four thousand men, he offered the post to Lee, as the senior officer. An odd conflict of wills ensued. Lee declined to take over. Such a minor operation, he said, was more worthy of "a young volunteering general than that of the second in command of the army." Washington turned to Lafayette, who left for the front at once. Lee then advised Washington that he would take command, after all. The detachment was larger than he had thought, and his friends urged him to lead it, since giving it up would have "an odd appearance." During several hours of discussion Lee changed his mind frequently and, as Hamilton said, behaved so childishly that Washington wearied of his "fickle behavior," but when the Englishman finally insisted that his honor was at stake, the patient commander acquiesced and ordered him to the front. The striking force of the army passed into the hands of the man who was so adamantly opposed to an attack.

Washington's fondness for Lee and his respect for his military reputation had never been more clearly demonstrated than in this strange passage. Not only had he treated Lee with the utmost deference, he had, as one historian pointed out, committed "the fundamental error of the campaign. It is . . . a military axiom that the execution of any intended operation should never be committed to an officer that disapproves of the plan. 'That', says Jomini in his Art of War, 'is to employ but one-third of the man; his heart and his head are against you; you have command only of his hands. . . . An unwilling commander is half beaten before the battle begins.' "

Lee went forward with reinforcements, increasing his command to more than five thousand men—six thousand four hundred, if Philemon Dickinson's New Jersey militia and Daniel Morgan's riflemen on the British rear and flanks were included. On June 27 Washington called Lee to headquarters, and in the presence of Lafayette, Wayne, William Maxwell and Charles Scott, ordered him to attack the British rear as soon as the enemy moved from Monmouth the next morning. The rest of the army would be brought up to support him.

Lee held a conference of his own, but gave his officers no plan of battle, since the ground had not been scouted and the exact strength and location of the enemy were unknown. He said rather vaguely that each unit should act according to circumstances. Lee made no attempt to secure information during the night.

At 4:30 A.M. on June 28 Philemon Dickinson saw the British beginning to move from the courthouse and sent couriers to Lee and Washington. Lee ordered an advance half an hour later, but his troops did not get under way until 7 A.M. The Sunday morning dawned clear, hot and windless. The battlefield was like an oven. Heat waves shimmered over the pine forest and by midmorning the temperature was 97 degrees in the shade. Civilians in nearby towns collapsed in their houses from heat exhaustion.

There was confusion from the start. Since Lee's field officers were strangers to him and he marched without a thorough knowledge of his command, units were mingled and misplaced in his column, which wound toward Monmouth Courthouse across three marshy ravines, each of them spanned by long narrow causeways. Lee halted for half an hour after eight o'clock when Steuben reported that the British had not moved—the Prussian had seen the rear guard of Cornwallis still in camp—but Dickinson had seen other troops moving eastward, led by Clinton.

At this time Colonel Richard Kidder Meade arrived from headquarters with orders for Lee: he was to attack the enemy as soon as possible, "unless some very powerful circumstances forbid it." If the attack was not made soon it would be too late; the hills of Middletown were only twelve miles away, and once there Clinton's baggage train would be safe. Lee told Meade he would try to obey Washington's orders but that he was baffled by conflicting information. Lee called Wayne from his own troops and sent him to take command near the courthouse. Lee rode after him, listening to a light spattering of musket fire from the village, where Dickinson's New Jerseymen and Colonel William Grayson's Virginians had been pushed back by dragoons and infantry pickets.

Within a few moments the advance of Lee's force was scattered and uncoordinated, its units irregularly posted at varying distances from the enemy and moving under orders from field officers as well as from Lee, Wayne and others, marching and countermarching, skirmishing tentatively with the enemy, then breaking off. Lee soon met Philemon Dickinson, who reported that the British were now flanking the advance troops near the courthouse. Lee shouted in anger: "You're a native. You're recommended to me for reliable information—how is it you bring me such uncertain reports?"

Dickinson retorted that he had sent news of every move of the enemy, some of whom were still near the courthouse: "General Lee, you may believe it or not, but if you cross that ravine, your whole force will be in danger."

Lee halted once more while William Maxwell's men, who had moved into a byroad through mistaken orders, were turned back and rejoined the column. Lee had lost an hour and a half on the road, and still short of the third ravine, could not yet see the open fields around the courthouse.

Farmers from the neighborhood brought more conflicting stories of British movements, until Lee stormed at one of them, "Go about your business, and bring me no more reports!" But he sent no scouts forward.

Lee had moved his troops back and forth in the narrow road so frequently to conform with each fresh report from the front that he was now fuming, "teased, mortified and chagrined by these little marches and counter-marches, from one hill to another, over the ravine . . . it gave an awkward appearance to our first manoeuvres!"

Lafayette, who came up about this time, found the distraught Lee countermanding his orders so often that he sent word back to Washington, urging that he come up and take command— the message was not delivered. Lee told Lafayette he was going forward despite the alarms, and as he neared the courthouse the sight of the enemy seemed to steady him. He saw only a small party of infantry, three or four cannon and a few troops of dragoons; in fact, the rear-guard troops Lee scouted were the two thousand of Cornwallis; Clinton, who was returning to the courthouse with four thousand more men, had not yet appeared.

Officers who saw Lee at this time thought he seemed cool and self-possessed. He sent troops circling forward to flank the British at the courthouse and told Lafayette with sudden elation, "My dear Marquis, I think those people are ours." When Colonel Grayson reported for orders, Lee said, "By God, I will take them all!"

When Dr. James McHenry came up from Washington to ask for information, Lee told him that he had "great certainty" of cutting off the rear guard of the enemy.

By now, however, about ten o'clock, Clinton had arrived with his fresh troops and the British fired a few rounds of cannon and advanced on Wayne's front. The artillery fire damaged Lee's one small battery of guns, commanded by Colonel Eleazer Oswald, but the cannon ceased after Wayne's infantry drove some charging British cavalrymen back with a bayonet charge.

Nearby officers noted that Lee's mood changed once more when British reinforcements appeared in the village, and as the redcoats advanced, he became irritable and erratic. When General Forman offered to guide him into the enemy rear, Lee snapped,

"I know my business!" Lafayette volunteered to lead a counterattack, but Lee at first refused, "Sir, you do not know British soldiers. We cannot stand against them. We shall certainly be driven back . . ."

The Frenchman retorted, "It may be so, General, but British soldiers have been beaten and they may be again. At any rate, I'm disposed to try." Lee then sent Lafayette with about eight hundred of Wayne's men to strike the enemy flank, but when he was within six hundred yards of the British, the marquis saw some of Lee's troops hurrying toward the rear, and began falling back himself. Generals Scott and Maxwell and Colonels Grayson and Jackson followed him, leaving only Butler's small 9th Pennsylvania on that part of the front, until Butler saw that he was unsupported and joined the retreat. Lee issued no orders during these movements, but seemed increasingly excited. He cried out at the sight of a body of his troops in motion, "Where is that damned blue regiment going?" When Colonel Stewart of Pennsylvania asked where Lafayette's retreating troops should be placed, Lee pointed to an orchard, "Take them any place to save their lives," he said. He shouted to another officer who was riding to the rear, "By God, sir, I will have you know that I am your general and you had no business to leave the field without my orders!"

When Richard Meade returned and asked for news to take to Washington, Lee said he had nothing to report, and added bitterly, "They are all in confusion. They are all in confusion." To John Laurens, who came up later on the same mission, Lee muttered, "I don't know what to say."

Lee's subordinates were disgusted by his inaction. The French engineer Captain Pierre Charles L'Enfant (the future designer of the city of Washington) asked why troops were not hurried forward, and Lee shouted, "I have orders from Congress and the Commander in Chief not to engage."

Lee halted Colonel Oswald, who was retreating with his artillerymen, but when Oswald explained that he had lost one gun and several men and horses, and was moving back to his ammunition wagon, Lee said no more. He sent no infantry support to Oswald.

When Lee saw British infantry pouring into a woodland abandoned by General Charles Scott, he said indignantly that Scott had been in no danger, and that he had been on the point of going to that flank to take command himself. "Disobedience to my orders," he said, "will ruin the day." But though he did not know where Scott's men had gone, Lee made no attempt to find them. William Maxwell's troops followed Scott in retreat and the fields near the courthouse were left to the enemy. It was near noon.

Lee had turned rearward himself, riding through the disorganized regiments, urging men to hurry, when he met Henry Knox, who asked why the troops were retreating. "I can't tell," Lee said. "I never saw such disorder, for everyone takes it upon himself to give orders without my knowledge." The Englishman now appeared to have given up, as if the failure of his mission had been a foregone conclusion and that his judgment had been vindicated.

Lee halted for about twenty minutes with a body of troops at William Kerr's house, two and a half miles from the courthouse, but issued no orders to form a defensive line. Officers who saw him at this stage of the retreat had varying impressions of his mood. Some recalled nothing unusual in his behavior, but John Fitzgerald found him "serious and thoughtful," and to John Laurens, Lee seemed embarrassed and his speech indistinct; Hamilton thought he issued orders hurriedly.

As the column swarmed back along the narrow road to the middle ravine, Lee began to seek a place to make a stand, but rejected each position shown to him. Duportail pointed out a nearby hillside, but Lee said that was "an execrable position." Captain Peter Wikoff, who lived in the neighborhood, suggested another ridge in the rear, but Lee said that was too far away.

The only defense made by Lee was hardly more than a gesture: a brief stand by a few troops supporting a couple of Oswald's guns, which fired briskly to cover units in the rear. When these guns were pulled back, Lee's vanguard was in full retreat.

Washington had spent the whole morning moving toward Monmouth Courthouse with the main army, which was now only slightly larger than Lee's force. Men had left their blanket rolls behind and most of them were stripped to the waist, but by ten o'clock scores of them had been prostrated by heat and were rolled into thickets at the roadside, where a number of them died. Washington halted for a late breakfast in the village of Englishtown six miles from the courthouse, and from there, at eleven-thirty, reported to Congress that Lee had advanced to attack the British rear "if possible."

James McHenry returned soon afterward with word that Lee expected to cut off Clinton's rear guard, and Washington rode forward with growing confidence until he met a doctor from the neighborhood who told him Lee was retreating. The general was incredulous, and when the doctor said he got the story from a fifer, a man in civilian clothes who was then hurrying past to the rear, Washington put a guard over the frightened musician and threatened to have him whipped if he spread more such rumors.

Harrison and Fitzgerald were sent ahead to investigate, but they had hardly disappeared when Washington heard more tales of retreat, most of them from men out of uniform. The general felt that hysterical stragglers and camp followers were spreading false alarms, until he met a disorderly company whose men said they didn't know why they were retreating. Regiments appeared, all streaming rearward as fast as the weary men could move.

Washington hailed the first officer he recognized in the column, the enormously fat Israel Shreve of the 2nd New Jersey, "What's the meaning of this retreat, Colonel?"

Shreve gave him an enigmatic smile. "I don't know, sir. But I retreated by order."

At that moment Lee and his staff appeared at the head of a larger column. Washington galloped to them, shouting, "What's the meaning of this?"

Lee stammered, "Sir? Sir?"

"Why all this confusion and retreat?"

Lee's thin voice rose in indignation. The only confusion, he said, had been caused by conflicting intelligence, disobedience of his orders, and the "impertinence and presumption" of his officers, especially General Scott, who had abandoned a strong position. Lee later said he was bewildered by Washington's attack and was "incapable of making any coherent answers to questions so abrupt." He now protested that false reports from officers had exposed his troops on "the most extensive plain in America," where they were helpless before British cavalry.

"My information is that it was only a strong covering party of the enemy," Washington said.

"Perhaps, but they were much stronger than I was, and I felt it was unwise to risk so much. Besides, this whole action was undertaken against my own opinion."

Washington roared: "Whatever your opinions, sir, I expect my orders to be obeyed! If you did not believe in the attack, you ought not to have undertaken it." Lee protested once more that his plan of attack had been foiled by disobedient subordinates.

Others were to recall that Washington cursed Lee in a fury. General Scott cherished a long memory that Washington "swore till the leaves shook on the trees. Charming! Delightful! Never have I enjoyed such swearing . . . he swore like an angel from Heaven!" Lafayette, who was not nearby at the moment, said later that Washington called Lee "a damned poltroon." Whatever he said, the commander halted the retreat and began hurrying men into lines of defense.

When Washington turned away, Lee was already protesting his innocence to nearby officers with an air of offended virtue. He was a soldier, he said, ready to obey orders, but he had consistently opposed full-scale battle with British veterans and had spoken against it in every council of war.

Washington had ridden only a few yards from Lee when Robert Harrison reported that the British were no more than fifteen minutes away. There was little time to herd scattered regiments into a strong defensive line; the army might be destroyed on this broiling landscape. Tench Tilghman saw that Washington was distraught: "He seemed at a loss, as he was on a piece of ground entirely strange to him."

The general recovered swiftly. With the aid of Lieutenant Colonel David Rhea of the 4th New Jersey, who knew the terrain, Washington began moving men into position behind a hedgerow, facing the enemy. He ordered an issue of rum in the hope of steadying the troops.

Lafayette and Hamilton watched admiringly as the general rode back and forth on a tall white horse, a gift from Governor William Livingston of New Jersey. Lafayette wrote: "General Washington seemed to arrest fortune with one glance. . . . His graceful bearing on horseback, his calm and deportment which still retained a trace of displeasure. . . . were all calculated to inspire the highest degree of enthusiasm. . . . I had never beheld so superb a man." Hamilton agreed: "I never saw the General to such an advantage. His coolness and firmness were admirable. He instantly took measures for checking the enemy's advance, and giving time for the Army, which was very near, to form and make a proper disposition." Washington rallied Lee's troops until the white horse fell beneath him, dead of a sunstroke, and Billy Lee brought up his old favorite, a long-tailed English chestnut mare.

Washington crossed the causeway over the ravine at a gallop and met two regiments falling back in good order, Colonel Walter Stewart's 13th Pennsylvania, and Lieutenant Colonel Nathaniel Ramsay's 3rd Maryland. He put them into line, shook Ramsay's hand and said he depended on these regiments to slow the enemy, who were now only two hundred yards away.

"We'll check them," Ramsay said.

Washington then recrossed the ravine and was forming a second line of five regiments under Wayne when British cavalry charged the troops of Stewart and Ramsay. Stewart was badly wounded and carried off the field and Ramsay, the last man to withdraw as his Marylanders were pushed back, was wounded and captured in a hand-to-hand fight with a dragoon.

During this action, while men were still retreating across his front, Washington began forming his main line on the slope behind Wayne just as the fresh divisions of Greene and Stirling arrived to settle on his right and left flanks. Lafayette, with still another line, formed in the rear. It was a formidable defense, quickly organized by Washington and the field officers, to whom the troops responded readily, without question. Hamilton was convinced that the defense would have disintegrated into a rout under any other commander, but he also gave credit to Steuben, who appeared on the left as fugitives were passing through Stirling's lines. The Prussian shouted in the harsh accents that had become so familiar on the drill fields of Valley Forge, and the stragglers halted and "wheeled into line with as much precision as on an ordinary parade." Hamilton said he had never appreciated the value of military discipline until that moment.

Washington met Lee once more on Stirling's front and asked him to take command of troops covering the last of the retreat. Lee retorted that he had already been given that command, but when Washington said mildly that one of them must halt the enemy there, Lee said he would do everything in his power. "You may rely on it," he said impulsively, "I'll be one of the last men off the field." But as Washington rode away, Lee turned abruptly to Alexander Hamilton: "Do I appear to be out of my senses?"

The British now struck Wayne's front in waves, impetuous attacks by their most veteran troops, the 17th Light Dragoons, the Grenadiers, the Black Watch and the 45th Foot, who were known as the Sherwood Foresters. Henry Clinton led one reckless charge of the dragoons. Heavy volleys from the Pennsylvanians broke three of these assaults as Wayne called to his men: "Steady, Steady! wait for the word, then pick out the king-birds." Lieutenant Colonel Henry Monckton of the Sherwood Foresters was killed in the third attack, and the Americans took his body and the regimental flag into their lines. The British infantry fell back and rested for an hour while the cannonade continued to roar, the longest and heaviest of the war. When a fourth and extended British assault outflanked Wayne, the Pennsylvanians clambered up the hill to join the main line.

Charles Lee led the last of these men onto the slope, where he met Washington for the third time, and asked where he should take his scattered vanguard. Washington ordered him to re-form at Englishtown, where Steuben saw the Englishman later in the afternoon, a birdlike figure perched stock-still in his saddle, staring incredulously toward the roar of the distant battlefield where the Americans were repulsing Clinton's assaults.

The British finally struck at the American flanks, first Stirling's and then Greene's, but were halted by massed musketry and cannon fire. The American artillery had never been so deadly. Its guns were well mounted on knolls from which they could enfilade Clinton's ranks; one round of solid shot that swept along a redcoat platoon knocked the musket from the hands of each man. The severe fighting raged for hours without a pause.

A legendary heroine, Mary Ludwig Hayes, helped her husband serve a cannon during this action. This Pennsylvania Dutch girl, an illiterate army veteran who smoked, chewed tobacco and "swore like a trooper," was seen at work by Sergeant Joseph Martin:

> While in the act of reaching a cartridge and having one of her feet as far before the other as she could step, a cannot shot from the enemy passed directly between her legs, without doing any other damage than carrying away all the lower part of her petticoat. Looking at it with apparent unconcern, she observed that it was lucky it did not pass a little higher, for in that case it might have carried away something else, and continued her occupation.

When she was not helping to load and fire, Mary Hayes carried water for the artillerymen and won a nickname that was to endure, "Molly Pitcher."

Washington ordered a counterattack in the gathering dusk, but it was too late. Men of both armies were exhausted. A battalion of British grenadiers who had charged to the top of a hill collapsed in their tracks; several of them died there and the others were unable to defend themselves. If the rebels had charged "they might have . . . had us an easy prey." Clinton said that he "was near going raving mad with heat" by the end of the battle.

The British withdrew about 6 P.M. and had disappeared by morning. The armies had fought the longest battle of the war, and the last major one in the northern theater. It was also to be Henry Clinton's only engagement as commander in chief, expertly fought against tenacious rebel opposition such as William Howe had never faced.

Though Monmouth was at best a drawn battle and though Washington made no claim of victory, he reported that the troops had fought as well as men could fight, once they recovered from the shock and confusion of the early retreat. Congress sent a profuse resolution of praise, and Henry Laurens wrote as if Washington had been on the field alone: "Love and respect for your Excellency is impressed on the heart of every American and your name will be revered by posterity."

Clinton had lost at least twelve hundred men, about four times the rebel casualties, and Benedict Arnold reported that almost six hundred deserters turned up in Philadelphia, most of them Hessians.

The aftermath of the battle was to be almost as bitterly fought as the final blazing hour of Monmouth.

Though other officers talked of Charles Lee's strange behavior at the opening of the battle, Washington apparently said nothing, and made no plans to discipline him. Lee was named as major general of the day in general orders as if nothing were amiss. The commander was thus astonished to receive a letter of angry outrage from the Englishman the day after Monmouth.

Lee had worked himself into a fury. He insisted vehemently that his withdrawal had saved the army by giving it time to prepare a defense, and he was outraged as he recalled the commander's harsh challenge on the field. He wrote a defiant letter that Washington read with mounting anger:

> Sir: From the knowledge I have of your Excellency's character, I must conclude that nothing but the misinformation of some very stupid, or mis-representation of some very wicked person could have occasioned your making use of such very singular expressions as you did on my coming up to the ground where you had taken post: they implied that I was guilty either of disobedience of orders, of want of conduct, or want of courage. Your Excellency will, therefore, infinitely oblige me by letting me know on which of these three articles you ground your charge, that I may prepare for my justification, which I have the happiness to be confident I can do, to the Army, to the Congress, to America, and to the world in general . . .

Since Washington and his aides had not been in the front, Lee wrote, they could not judge "the merits or demerits of our maneuvers." The Englishman insisted that he alone had won "the success of the day" and accused Washington of "cruel injustice," but said he could not believe that the commander had spoken his own mind on the battlefield. Washington's angry remarks, he thought, had been "instigated by some of those dirty earwigs who will forever insinuate themselves near persons in high office."

Washington accepted the challenge at once:

Sir: I received your letter . . . expressed as I conceive, in terms highly improper. I am not conscious of having made use of any very singular expressions at the time of my meeting you, as you intimate. What I recollect to have said was dictated by my duty and warranted by the occasion. As soon as circumstances will permit, you shall have an opportunity, either of justifying yourself to the army, to Congress, to America, and to the world in general or of convincing them that you were guilty of a breach of orders and of misbehavior before the enemy on the 28th instant, in not attacking them as you had been directed and in making an unnecessary, disorderly and shameful retreat. I am, etc.

Lee wrote once more to request a court-martial, rather than a court of inquiry, deliberately risking a severe sentence, perhaps even death. Washington did not hesitate. He placed Lee under arrest and outlined charges on which he would be tried, repeating the two of his earlier letter: First, "Disobedience of orders in not attacking the enemy on the 28th of June, agreeable to repeated instructions." Second, "Misbehaviour before the enemy on the same day by making an unnecessary, disorderly and shameful retreat." Washington added a third charge, "disrespect to the Commander in Chief in two letters."

The army moved northward to the Hudson, trailing Clinton's move into New York, too busy to leave officers behind for Lee's court-martial. The trial was conducted on the march, with Stirling as president, and four brigadiers and seven colonels as members of the court. Lee conducted his own defense, effectively, volubly and at great length.

The day before the trial opened, Lee wrote to his friends in Philadelphia that he had been betrayed. He told Robert Morris: "Not content with robbing me and the brave men under my command of the honor due to us—a most hellish plan has been formed . . . to destroy for ever my honour and my reputation . . ." He had now convinced himself that he had single-handedly won a victory at Monmouth. "If I had been let alone, I should with patience suffered 'em to pick up the laurels which I had shaken down and lay'd at their feet . . . Washington had scarcely any more to do in it than to strip the dead."

His role in the battle, he wrote Dr. Rush, had been the salvation of an incompetent commander: ". . . be assur'd of this—that G. Washington saw, knew, and was almost as little concern'd in the affair of the 28th as he was in the battle of Philippi." The sympathetic Rush, who saw Lee as another victim of Washington's vanity, wrote John Adams: "General Conway, who was the *nerves*; Mifflin, who was the *Spirit*; & Lee, who was the *Soul* of our army, have all been banished from Head-Quarters . . ."

The perambulating court sat from July 4 until August 9 with Wayne, Scott and Washington's aides as chief witnesses for the prosecution and Lee's aides as defense witnesses. Though the case for conviction was weak, except for the charge of disrespect to the commander in chief, Lee was found guilty of all three charges and suspended from the army for a year. The court came to an odd compromise in the second charge, eliminating Washington's adjective "shameful" as applied to the retreat and describing Lee's withdrawal as disorderly only "in some few instances." The striking discrepancy between the serious charges and the relative lightness of the sentence was not a mystery to the army: Lee's real crime had been his disrespect for Washington.

Laurens and Hamilton may have strengthened Washington's resolve to punish Lee, since both suspected him of treason at Monmouth, despite the lack of evidence that he had retreated deliberately to aid the British. Hamilton attacked Lee as "either a driveler in the business of soldiership or something much worse . . . his conduct was monstrous and unpardonable."

Washington himself felt that the army's failure to win complete victory at Monmouth was due to "a capital blunder or something else somewhere."

The army's most dependable officers were by no means unanimous in condemnation of Lee. Henry Knox, Benjamin Lincoln, Alexander McDougall, Samuel H. Parsons, and the artillery officers, Eleazer Oswald and Samuel Shaw, all felt that the judgment of the court was too harsh, and some of them insisted that Lee

appeared for a brief welcome and then retired. After breakfast Washington crossed the river to West Point in a small boat and landed at the foot of the cliff crowned by the fortifications which were the key to highland defenses. Seen from the river, the works where troops had been laboring for three years were imposing—a cluster of works connected by a maze of turf, stone and log walls.

The post was strangely quiet. There was no salute from the heights, and no one appeared to welcome Washington at the waterside. Except for a few sentries the post was almost deserted. Colonel John Lamb, an artilleryman, greeted Washington with surprise. Arnold was not there, and Lamb had not seen him during the morning. Washington began a tour of the defenses, expecting to find Arnold at one of the scattered construction sites. He was appalled by what he saw. The stronghold that had frowned so formidably from the heights was falling into ruins. One bastion called Fort Arnold was an incomplete log work that looked as if it would burst into flames from the first enemy shell. The eastern wall of nearby Fort Putnam had caved in, and both works were dominated by Rocky Hill, which was crowned by a small and vulnerable outpost. A few carpenters and masons worked amid piles of logs and stone rubble. Only a handful of the 1,800-man garrison of the post were in sight. The neglected fortress, virtually worthless as a river barrier, could be restored only by months of labor. It was obvious that Arnold had found it in a state of disrepair and had done little or nothing to improve it.

Arnold was nowhere to be found. Washington felt a vague uneasiness. He knew that only the most pressing emergency could have prevented the post commander from greeting him on his announced tour of inspection. But, though this unexplained absence "struck me very forcibly," the general said later, "I had not the least idea of the real cause."

It was late afternoon when Washington returned to Arnold's house. Hamilton entered his bedroom almost at once, bringing a thick sheaf of papers forwarded by Lieutenant Colonel John Jameson, a cavalry officer who was stationed a few miles away. Jameson had written to explain that these documents had been taken by pickets from a man calling himself John Anderson who had carried the papers concealed in his stockings.

Washington read them with increasing apprehension: a pass through the lines for John Anderson; a copy of "Remarks on Works at Wt. Point . . . to be transmitted to his Excell'y General Washington"; a summary of the strength of the army and the West Point garrison; a return of the ordnance of West Point, including gun locations; and a copy of the minutes of Washington's most recent council of war. Two of the confidential documents were in Arnold's handwriting; he had also signed Anderson's pass.

A second message from the cavalry outpost confirmed the general's fears, for it contained a letter to Washington from the prisoner, a confession of his true identity: "The person in your possession is Major John André, adjutant general to the British army." André confessed that he had come up the river on the enemy sloop *Vulture* and gone ashore in uniform to meet "a person who was to give me intelligence," but insisted that he couldn't be considered a spy because he had come under a flag of truce and had unwittingly entered the American lines, where he was forced to change into civilian clothes and flee overland toward New York. "Thus . . . was I betrayed into the vile condition of an enemy in disguise within your lines." The major's chief concern seemed to be to convince Washington that he had not "assumed a mean character for treacherous purposes or self interest . . ." It was obvious that Arnold must have passed the secret documents to André.

Lafayette first learned of the treason when James McHenry burst into the room where he was dressing for dinner, snatched up his pistols and left without a word. The Frenchman hurried to Washington's room and found the general standing with the sheaf of papers in his hand, blinking tears from his eyes. Washington's voice was unsteady. "Arnold is a traitor . . . Whom can we trust now?"

Otherwise, his officers noted no sign of the general's distress. He described the papers to Hamilton and Robert Harrison, and from them learned that Arnold had fled. During breakfast, so James McHenry said, Arnold had received a message that so upset him that he had left the table, gone to his wife's room and hurried from the house.

No one could say how extensive the plot had been. Other messages may have been passed, a British attack force might be under way. Varick and Frank or other Americans might be involved, and other posts endangered. But Washington's first thought was of Arnold. He sent Hamilton and McHenry downstream in pursuit, hoping that the traitor might be halted at King's Ferry, where there was a small fort at the riverside.

A piercing scream from Peggy Arnold's bedroom echoed through the upper hall: "There's a hot iron on my head! No one else can take it off!" Colonel Varick descended to ask Washington to talk with the distraught young woman. She had been "raving mad" all day, racing half naked through the house, sobbing and babbling incoherently. She now demanded to see the general. Washington followed the colonel into Peggy's room. She was now as Varick had described her, "hair dishevelled and flowing about her neck," wearing only a thin gown, too nearly nude to be seen "even by Gentlemen of the family, much less by . . . strangers." Her face was contorted and tear-stained. Varick told her that General Washington had come. "No, it's not General Washington," she moaned. ". . . not General Washington. That's the man that was a-going to help Colonel Varick kill my child." She refused to be quieted. Her husband could no longer protect her, she cried. "General Arnold will never return. He's gone, he's gone forever!" She pointed frantically to the ceiling. "There, there, there. The spirits have carried him up there. They have put hot irons in his head." She flounced in and out of bed, and strode about the room with her child in her arms in a display of uncontrollable despair. Washington left the room, convinced that she was in a state of shock, and innocent of treason.

The general dined with his officers without a mention of Arnold's disappearance, and Varick, at least, was impressed by his composure, "affability and politeness." To Lafayette the meal seemed interminable: "Never was there a more melancholy dinner. The general was silent and reserved, and none of us spoke of what we were thinking about . . . Gloom and distress seemed to pervade every mind." The table was loaded with food but the men ate little.

Washington rose at last and asked Varick to walk outside, where he told him of Arnold's treachery. The general said he had no reason to suspect either of them, but that Varick and Frank must consider themselves under arrest, Varick said he understood, and then told the general "the little all" he knew. The aides had puzzled over Arnold's frequent meetings with Joshua Hett Smith, whom they suspected as a spy, but knew nothing of their plans. Varick and Frank turned over the keys to chests at headquarters, their own as well as Arnold's.

Hamilton reported in the early evening: Arnold was already beyond reach, safely aboard the *Vulture,* from which the traitor had sent a letter to Washington. The general was visibly shaken as he began to read:

> The heart which is conscious of its own rectitude cannot attempt to palliate a step which the world may censure as wrong. I have ever acted from a principle of love to my country . . . The same principle of love to my country actuates my present conduct, however it may appear inconsistent to the world . . .

Arnold asked protection for his wife, ". . . she is good and innocent as an angel, and is incapable of doing wrong." He asked Washington to send her to Philadelphia, or through the lines to join him, as she chose, and enclosed a letter to her. Arnold added that Varick and Frank and Joshua Hett Smith knew nothing of the plot. He also asked Washington to send his clothes to him—he would pay for them if necessary.

There was no longer doubt of Arnold's attempted treason, and it might already be too late to save West Point, since a strong wind, blowing upriver, could bring British ships before dawn. Washington recalled parties of the West Point garrison that Arnold had scattered through the region, and changed commanders of several nearby posts as a precaution against Arnold's having placed collaborators there. Washington also ordered André brought to headquarters and sent a search party for Joshua Hett Smith. He warned Jameson that his prisoner must be "most closely and narrowly watched . . . André must not escape." By 2 A.M., when West Point was finally on the alert and prepared to meet an attack, the wind had changed and blew downriver with such force that enemy ships could not have approached. Washington ordered Greene to rush troops to West Point from the main army, and Wayne's Pennsylvanians, who got the summons at 1 A.M., were on the march by two o'clock and moved sixteen miles over a dark road in four hours. They reached the fort at sunrise, as Wayne reported proudly, "without a single halt or a man left behind."

Washington's emergency moves to protect the post were made in vain. Ironically enough, Clinton had not launched an attack against West Point, because he did not yet know that Arnold had passed the plans of the post to André.

Arnold's confession only bolstered Washington's belief in Peggy's innocence, and the twenty-three-year-old Hamilton, who took the unopened letter from her husband to her room, was overcome by her histrionic performance. Hamilton was so deeply touched that he saw in her "all the sweetness of beauty, all the loveliness of innocence, all the tenderness of a wife, and all the fondness of a mother . . . we have every reason to believe she was entirely unacquainted with the plan."

Peggy was more composed the next day, and said she could recall nothing that had happened on the twenty-fifth. But when Washington, Hamilton and Lafayette returned to her bedroom, they found her so apprehensive of public reaction against her that she refused to be consoled. Hamilton was taken in completely: "Could I forgive Arnold for sacrificing his honor, reputation and duty, I could not forgive him for acting a part that must have forfeited the esteem of so fine a woman."

Washington sent Mrs. Arnold to Philadelphia the next day under the escort of Major Frank, and Lafayette wrote Luzerne, urging that he help her: "It would be exceedingly painful to General Washington if she were not treated with the greatest kindness."

André had arrived at headquarters at dawn under escort of a hundred dragoons, after a six-hour ride through a rainstorm. The prisoner was halted briefly at the house, a bedraggled figure in a sodden purple coat and an old beaver hat, but with fine underclothing and army boots. Washington sent André to nearby Tappan under heavy guard and declined to see him then or later.

Colonel Jameson and Major Benjamin Tallmadge told the general the story of the capture: André had been taken near Tarrytown by three young militiamen, John Paulding, Isaac Van Wart and David Williams, who halted him about 9 P.M. Since he mistook them for Tories, he had shown no pass, had talked a great deal, and tried to bribe them after the discovery of his papers.

André had been taken to the nearest post, at North Castle, where his documents were inspected by Colonel Jameson—and, more important, by Major Tallmadge, who was secretly Washington's chief of intelligence. Jameson was convinced that the captured papers were forgeries designed to discredit Arnold, wrote an explanation of the arrest to the traitor, and started André to West Point under guard. Tallmadge protested so vehemently that Jameson recalled André and sent the documents to Washington, but the colonel had insisted upon sending news of the capture to Arnold, and the traitor, thus warned, had fled.

Joshua Hett Smith was brought to headquarters about 8 A.M., and told his story under intensive questioning by Washington. Young Smith said that he had been aiding the American cause by handling correspondence with spies and other agents reporting to West Point, and had thus been unsuspecting when Arnold had sent him to the British sloop *Vulture* in the Hudson. He had met a John Anderson on the boat and guided him ashore "on important army business." Anderson and Arnold had met in Smith's house, where they had talked privately for several hours. After this secret conference, on the night of September 22, Smith had taken Anderson across the ferry at Stony Point and started him on his way to White Plains. Smith insisted that he had thought he was helping Arnold obtain valuable information.

Why had André been out of uniform when he was captured? Arnold, so Smith said, had explained that John Anderson was a civilian who had borrowed an army coat to create the idea he was an important personage, but was forced to abandon the disguise when he passed through the lines. The prisoner had worn one of Smith's old coats.

When Washington asked why André had gone by land rather than aboard the *Vulture*, Smith said that he himself had come down with a violent fever and was unable to arrange for the boat. When asked how he had managed to escort André over dark roads toward White Plains with such a fever, Smith made no reply.

Washington and his officers examined Arnold's papers, which

contained confidential information on West Point and other defenses, but no incriminating evidence against other officers. The letters in Arnold's files cast suspicion only upon Smith. The traitor had apparently acted without other accomplices and his treason had been discovered by chance—by "a miraculous chain of accidents and circumstances," Lafayette said. Washington gave credit to "a most providential interposition" for the failure of Arnold's attempted betrayal. As for the traitor himself: "There are no terms that can describe the baseness of his heart."

Though it was by no means certain that the loss of West Point would have snuffed out the rebellion—unless Washington, Knox and Lafayette had been captured—news of Arnold's attempted treason caused a sensation. Greene's orders to the main army expressed the shock that spread swiftly through the country:

> Treason of the blackest dye was yesterday discovered! General Arnold, who commanded at West Point, lost to every sentiment of honor . . . was about to deliver up that important post . . . such an event must have given the American cause a deadly wound, if not a fatal stab. Happily, the treason has been timely discovered . . .

And Alexander Scammell wrote:

> Treason! Treason! Treason! black as h-ll! . . . Heaven and earth! We were all astonishment, each peeping at his next neighbor to see if any treason were hanging about him. Nay, we even descended to a critical examination of ourselves.

When Washington was satisfied that West Point had been sufficiently reinforced, he rejoined the main army, moved his headquarters to Tappan, in the small house of John de Windt, and dealt with André, who was imprisoned in a nearby stone building, Maybie's Tavern. Clinton and Arnold wrote to plead for the major's life, on the ground that he could not be considered a spy because he was under Arnold's flag of truce—an argument Washington rejected as an absurdity. He called a court of inquiry, fourteen general officers with Greene as president; its verdict was swift and the sentence inevitable. André made a full confession and conceded that he could not claim protection under Arnold's flag of truce. As Baron von Steuben said, "It is not possible to save him. He put us to no proof, but in an open, manly manner, confessed every thing but a premeditated design to deceive. Would to God the wretch who drew him to death could have suffered in his place!"

In this case Washington did not ask the approval of Congress. He set André's execution for the next day, October 1. The major's courage failed him for a moment when he was read the sentence by his guard, Captain Ebenezer Smith: "The agony of his mind as he walked the room was most distressing, and it seemed to me that the very flesh crawled upon his bones." André quickly mastered his fear. He wrote Washington, saying that though he was "above the terror of death," he dreaded the thought of dying on a gibbet. He begged that he not be hanged, but shot like "a man of honor."

Washington made no reply.

By now André had become a hero in the American camp. Stories of his frank, courageous testimony before the court spread through the ranks and won sympathy for him. Benjamin Tallmadge, who was at the major's side almost constantly, said his affections had never been "so fully absorbed in any man." Alexander Scammell said the prisoner was "perhaps the most accomplished officer of the age." And Richard K. Meade said "his conduct was such as did honor to the human race."

The handsome twenty-nine-year-old André had also captivated Hamilton, who pled with Washington to grant the prisoner's wish and have him shot. It was in vain. As Washington explained to Congress, "The practice, and usage of war . . . were against the indulgence." He was careful to add that his treatment of the major was not "guided by passion or resentment." André was a spy, and should be hanged, or he was merely a prisoner of war and should not die at all. Any mitigation would suggest that he had been unjustly condemned. Hamilton was not convinced: "Some people are only sensible to motives of policy, and sometimes from a narrow disposition, mistake it. When André's tale comes to be told . . . the refusing him the privilege of choosing the manner of his death will be branded with too much obstinacy."

Washington felt that he had taken the only course open to him. Not even the critical Hamilton suggested that Washington was sadistic, or even cruel, but like several of their contemporaries, he noted that the commander was inflexible in handling serious problems of discipline and military protocol, as if he feared that a relaxation of control would invite ruin.

In his cell, André passed his time greeting visitors, American officers who left in sorrow, completely won over by the major's insouciance. André wrote farewell letters to his family and to Clinton, and impressed his guards by drawing a self-portrait without the aid of a mirror.

At 1 P.M. on October 1, four hours before André was to die, Washington had another message from Clinton, a protest that the court had acted without full knowledge of the facts. To explain the case more fully he was sending Lieutenant General James Robertson up the Hudson with two civilian officials, Lieutenant Governor Andrew Elliott and Chief Justice William Smith. Washington sent Greene to meet Robertson on an unofficial basis, under orders to make no concessions; the civilians were not to be permitted to come ashore. Robertson repeated Clinton's earlier arguments and ended by asking that Washington spare André as a personal favor to Clinton. Washington refused. The execution was set for noon the next day. A gibbet fashioned of two forked poles with a crossbar was erected on a knoll within half a mile of Washington's headquarters.

Men who were in the prisoner's room when the new hour of execution was announced noted that André's expression was unchanged. When a servant burst into tears the major said sharply, "Leave me until you can behave like a man."

Breakfast came to him from Washington's table, as usual, and he ate everything that was put before him. He rested for a time, then shaved and dressed himself in the uniform Washington had permitted sent through the lines, a scarlet coat with green facing, bright buff breeches and waistcoat. At last he said, "I'm ready, gentlemen," and a small party moved out from the tavern, first a wagon in which a few officers rode with a crude black-painted coffin, trailed by a few fifers and drummers. André followed the musicians, his arms linked with an officer on each side. About a thousand soldiers and civilians waited on the hilltop, including all the general officers except Washington, who was at work in the de Windt House.

André walked steadily, betraying no fear, looking ahead with "a complacent smile." He exchanged nods with senior officers he had met in the courtroom. A small girl slipped into his hand a peach, which he held until he was out of her sight. The fifers played "The Blue Bird" and André called to compliment them.

As the party mounted the slope the major looked up and saw the gallows. He flushed and paused, put his hands on his hips, bowed his head and looked upward once more, biting his underlip and shaking his head slightly. "I've borne everything," he said, "but this is too degrading." He spoke rapidly to one of the officers. The manner of his death mattered little to him, he said, but his mother and sisters would be mortified.

There was a wait while the wagon was placed beneath the scaffold. The executioner approached, a Tory prisoner named Strickland, who wore a disguise of tarred grease over his face and hands; he was to receive his freedom for his work.

André waited nervously as the wagon moved back and forth until Strickland was content. The prisoner rolled a small stone to and fro beneath his boot, and choked several times in vain efforts to swallow. When all was ready André placed his hands on the wagon to vault into its bed but faltered and clambered up on one knee. He walked rapidly back and forth in the narrow space of the wagon bed, looking beyond the crowd.

Strickland stepped forward with the noose, but André said, "Take your black hands off me," and put the rope about his own neck, making the knot snug under one ear. He took two handkerchiefs from his pocket, bound one about his eyes and handed the other to a guard, who tied his arms behind him.

Alexander Scammell, the commanding officer, asked André if he had any last words, and the major lifted the handkerchief from his eyes. "Only bear witness that I died like a brave man."

Scammell lifted his sword, then slashed it downward and Strickland led the horse forward. The wagon lurched away. André's body made "a most tremendous swing back and forth," but when he had hung only a few seconds Scammell sent a soldier to press down on his shoulders. André died at once. A watching private remembered the end of it for years: "In a few minutes he hung entirely still . . . he remained . . . I think from 20 to 30 minutes, and during that time the chambers of death were never stiller than the multitude by which he was surrounded."

Within an hour after the execution more letters arrived from the British, another protest that André had come under protection of a flag of truce, and a threat from Arnold that if André died, Clinton would hang forty South Carolinians captured at Charleston, ". . . if this warning should be disregarded . . . I call Heaven and earth to witness that your Excellency will be justly answerable for the torrent of blood that may be spilt in consequence."

Henry Clinton was almost inconsolable when he learned of André's death. He shut himself in his room for three days and refused to permit publication of news of the hanging. He wrote to his sisters in England, "Washington has committed premeditated murder." The American army also mourned the brave major. Even the stern Washington wrote, "He was more unfortunate than criminal."

Within a month, in response to a public clamor, the Pennsylvania Council banished Peggy Arnold from the state, and she was soon living with Arnold, next door to Clinton's headquarters. An anonymous observer in New York noted that all was not well with the new British brigadier:

General Arnold is a very unpopular character in the British army, nor can all the patronage he meets with from the CiC procure him respectability . . . The subaltern officers have conceived such an aversion to him, that they unanimously refuse to serve under his command.

Lafayette had predicted that Arnold would be so overcome with shame that he would blow his brains out when he reached New York, but Washington was convinced that the traitor was utterly without conscience and "so hackneyed in villainy and so lost to all sense of honor and shame that . . . there will be no . . . remorse." The commander was an accurate prophet. A few days after André's death, while Clinton was still grieving for his favorite aide, Arnold tried to persuade Sir Henry to pay him the full £10,000 he had originally demanded for surrender of West Point.

Arnold wrote an address to "The Inhabitants of America," denouncing congressional tyranny, saying that France was too feeble to help, and called on officers and men who were "determined to be no longer the tools and dupes of Congress or of France" to join a corps he was forming. He suggested ways of increasing defections to Clinton and Germain, and said they should offer land as an inducement, adding, "Money will go further than arms in America."*

Washington entertained a formidable visitor for a few days during November, the Chevalier de Chastellux, a celebrated philosopher and leader of the French Academy who was gathering material for a book on America. The sophisticated Parisian was surprised by the unmistakable signs of discipline and alertness at army headquarters, and to find that Washington's officers were not only polite but displayed "a great deal of ability." Chastellux was struck by Washington's presence, but though his appearance was "mild and agreeable," it was such as to make it "impossible to speak particularly of any one of his features, so that, on leaving him, you have only the recollection of a fine face. He has neither a grave nor a familiar air, his brow is sometimes marked with thought, but never with worry."

The philosopher also discovered that Washington and his staff, at least, were not threatened by starvation. He was astonished by the dining regimen at headquarters. Washington seemed to spend half of each day at the table. In midafternoon the general and his staff and visitors had dinner "in the English fashion," with eight or ten enormous dishes of meat and poultry, numerous

---

* Arnold probably made more money out of the war than any other American officer. He got £6,315 for his unsuccessful attempt to deliver West Point, plus a colonel's pay for the rest of the war and half pay for life, a life pension of £500 for Peggy, £100 pensions for each of her five children, and half pay for life for his older sons (Benedict and Richard were commissioned at twelve and Henry at the age of nine.) All told, the Arnold family in London had an income of about £1,200, roughly the equivalent of $72,000 to $88,000 in U.S. currency in 1975.)

vegetables and pies and puddings. A young aide kept wine bottles in circulation and rose on command to propose toasts for the
officers. When the dishes were empty, waiters whisked off the
tablecloth and brought bowls of apples and cracked hickory nuts.

Washington sat and picked over the nuts for two hours, "eating, toasting and conversing all the time." When the party left
the table three and a half hours later, servants immediately laid
the table for supper. Within an hour Washington and the staff
were eating once more, and when Chastellux protested that he
was not hungry the general said mildly, "I'm accustomed to take
something in the evening." At 11 P.M., after consuming three or
four "light dishes," more mounds of fruit and hickory nuts, and
emptying several bottles of claret and Madeira, the officers finally
left the table for the day.

Washington himself took a candle and led Chastellux upstairs
to his bedroom, a gesture of unstudied hospitality that the
Frenchman found "neither embarrassing or excessive."

It was late in November before Washington settled the army
into winter quarters; he was forced to scatter the troops for lack
of wagons to haul supplies to a central camp—they were now
based at Albany and West Point, and at Pompton and Morristown, N.J., the latter post held by Anthony Wayne's Pennsylvania Line. The general himself made headquarters in "a dreary
station" at New Windsor, N.Y.

Lafayette, who now pinned all hopes on the French, sent dozens
of appeals to his relatives, friends and officials in Paris, urging
"the absolute necessity" of contributing money for a final offensive in America. The Americans, he said, "show a fortitude in
misery which is unknown in European armies," but could endure
little longer without massive aid—hard cash, ten thousand more
troops, and most important, French command of the sea. He
wrote to Benjamin Franklin: "We are nack'd, shockingly nack'd,
and worse off in that respect than we have ever been. For God's
sake, my dear friend, let us have any how fifteen or twenty
thousand compleat suits . . ."

Many of these messages crossed the Atlantic with young
Rochambeau, who committed them to memory, as a precaution

against capture by a British warship. A few weeks later, when Congress sent John Laurens as a special emissary to Paris, Lafayette provided him with letters to many of the most influential people in Paris, and urged one old friend to convince the court that Laurens was on an emergency mission of the last resort: "See that he is well received, especially by the Queen."

There was encouraging news for Washington from the south late in the month, the report of a remarkable victory at King's Mountain, S.C., by a band of militiamen from the mountains of Tennessee, North Carolina and Virginia who had destroyed a 1,000-man army of Tories led by Major Patrick Ferguson. The entire enemy force had been killed, wounded or captured by the little army of backwoodsmen, who dispersed as rapidly as they had gathered, and returned to their homes in the Appalachian wilderness. Cornwallis withdrew from his new base at Charlotte, N.C., to Winnsboro in the South Carolina uplands, but his main army was still intact, and as winter approached there were further signs that the British were shifting forces to the south, planning to consolidate their hold of the Carolinas and Georgia. Washington had warned Congress of the danger in early October, and spies now reported from New York that three thousand more redcoats were to be shipped to Charles Cornwallis in South Carolina.

Henry Clinton, in sending these crack troops from his New York garrison, was responding to orders from George III, who followed the course of the war with the enthusiasm of an ardent amateur soldier. The King had been assured by his advisers that the southern colonies, torn by civil war between marauding bands of Whigs and Tories, were basically loyal in sentiment. Now that British bases dominated the South Carolina and Georgia coasts, the King felt that the whole vast and thinly populated plantation country from the Potomac to Florida could be controlled. The lively tobacco trade, the "principle resource for the support of their foreign credit," would be cut off, and as George Germain told Clinton, "it might not be too much to expect that all America . . . south of the Susquehanna would return their allegiance and . . . the northern provinces might be left to their own feelings and distress to bring them back to their duty."

In brief, the King's plan was to make "backdoor warfare against Washington's army" by striking northward from the Carolinas to the Chesapeake, since North Carolina was merely "the road to Virginia." The new strategy was to hold Henry Clinton immobile in New York, maintaining a threat to the armies of Washington and Rochambeau simply by his presence, while British land and sea power were applied to force a decision in the south.

Washington recommended to Congress that Nathanael Greene be sent to revive the army of Gates in North Carolina and defend the south, but he was none too hopeful, "I think I am giving you a General; but what can a General do, without men, without arms, without clothing, without stores, without provisions?" The Quaker was soon on his way, followed by the few troops Washington could spare, the little cavalry bands of Lighthorse Harry Lee and William Washington.

21

MUTINY

"The American Army Can Furnish But One Arnold"

Anthony Wayne celebrated his thirty-sixth birthday on January 1, 1781, at Morristown, where he dined in his quarters with two of his colonels, Walter Stewart and Richard Butler. He had declined an invitation from civilian friends who lived nearby, pleading the press of army business. The Blacksnake was afraid to leave his troops tonight.

Six regiments of the Pennsylvania Line, some two thousand men, were camped about him in the old huts of Mount Kemble. Most of them had not been paid for a year, even in paper dollars. The enlistments of almost all the companies had expired during the day, but since they had signed in for three years or the duration of the war, the Pennsylvania Council insisted on holding them for the duration.

Few general officers were closer to their men than Wayne. He and his colonels frequently worked with the troops, helping to build or repair huts in the freezing weather, and sometimes shared their meals of bread and water. For months he had pled for help, first from Congress and then from the Pennsylvania Council. After the states had taken over support of their own troops, Wayne had begged his friends in the legislature to send cash, clothing, food, blankets, even needles for mending the rags of the men. All had been in vain until three days earlier when

"The American Army Can Furnish But One Arnold"

Brigadier General James Potter of the Pennsylvania militia arrived from Philadelphia with a bag of coins—every coin that could be had by public contribution, for the state treasury was empty. There was a bewildering variety of foreign mintage, English guineas, half-carolines, French louis d'or, Spanish pistoles and dollars, moidores, ducats, half-Johanneses, many of them old pieces that had circulated for generations through a country with no coinage of its own and no gold or silver mines.

It was not enough. Only a few of the men could be paid from Potter's hoard, and the troops then discovered that they had been cheated in August, when a lieutenant had been sent from the capital with $14,000 Continental for their pay, money that never reached camp. The officer insisted that he had spent the whole sum on the road for food, drink and lodging. The outraged veterans also learned that Pennsylvania's new six-month recruits had been paid in gold.

One of Wayne's last warnings to Congress had been a forecast of disaster: ". . . I very much dread the ides of January . . . it is not the prowess of the enemy I dread, but their taking advantage of our necessitous situation and internal disunion . . . Exert every power . . . at all events find means to clothe the soldiers who belong to this state by the first of January."

The men had drawn an extra issue of rum for New Year's Day, and some had found more in the countryside. Wayne, Stewart and Butler were playing cards about 9 P.M. when they heard men moving on the parade ground, speaking in undertones.

A musket roared.

Wayne and the colonels ran to the parade ground, where a few sergeants were forming men into ranks. Officers rushed out and herded soldiers into their huts, but they reappeared immediately, protesting that they had been mustered to meet the approaching enemy. A captain led a few men of his regiment in a bayonet charge against the men in the growing ranks, but his soldiers fell away behind him in the darkness, leaving three officers in the charge.

Wayne drew and cocked his pistols, but he was instantly surrounded by men who thrust bayonets within inches of his body. A sergeant said, "General, we love and respect you. But you command us no longer. I warn you—if you fire, you're a dead man. If you try to enforce any commands, we'll kill you."

Wayne began to plead with them, but the surrounding men listened in silence unmoved. A rocket burst overhead. There were scuffles on the frozen field. Captain Adam Bettin died of a musket wound in his abdomen. Two or three officers were slashed with bayonets. Colonel Butler, who began shouting to his men, was driven into his hut. When Wayne once more made an appeal to the troops, a volley was fired over his head. Wayne pulled open his coat. "If you mean to kill me, shoot me at once. Here, in the breast." A soldier assured him that the mutineers did not intend to harm their officers, and that they would not desert to the enemy. They were only demanding fair treatment, and were determined to make a settlement in which they could meet with officers on equal terms. They would march to neutral ground so that their grievances could be heard.

Within half an hour about two-thirds of the troops had formed into a column and moved southward out of camp, with six cannon rolling behind. The mutineers were under command of half a dozen sergeants, one of them a British deserter.

Wayne's horse had been stolen but he found another, and galloped past the moving files to the first fork of the road. The right led toward Princeton, and the left toward Chatham and Elizabethtown, the approach to British lines in New York and on Staten Island. Wayne, Stewart and Butler stood their horses in the left-hand road, determined to block the way or die, but the troops passed to the right without hesitation, on the road leading to Princeton and Philadelphia. Two or three sergeants paused to reassure the general—the mutineers wanted to be mustered out when their enlistments were up. They demanded food, clothing and pay. They would not go to the enemy, and would "hang any man who would attempt it." If the British appeared, they would fight as they had always fought. The relieved Wayne was still uncertain of what his men might do, but he planned to follow them and try to lead them to Philadelphia, where they could negotiate with state officials and Congress.

Wayne hurried back to camp, and in hopes of placating the desperate men, loaded a few wagons with all the provisions that could be found and sent them after the mutineers. At 4 A.M. Wayne began writing a report to Washington, a long and melodramatic narrative that he withheld, and substituted a briefer version:

> The most general and unhappy mutiny took place about 9 o'clock last night. It yet subsists; a great proportion of the troops, with some artillery, are marching toward Philadelphia. Every exertion has been made by the officers to divide them in their determination to revolt; it has succeeded in a temporary manner with near one half; how long it will last, God knows . . .

Wayne gave the brief message to Major Benjamin Fishbourne, who carried it toward Washington's headquarters at New Windsor, N.Y., fifty-five miles to the north. With Stewart and Butler, Wayne then followed the mutineers, who had halted in Princeton.

Wayne's report reached Washington at noon on January 3. He sent officers through his own camps to observe the mood of the troops, ordered reinforcements to West Point and sent messengers south, urging Wayne not to use force but to meet with the mutineers, talk over their grievances and prevent them from going to the enemy. When he heard that two Pennsylvania officers had gone to warn Congress to leave Philadelphia, Washington insisted that the delegates must not retreat, since the mutineers might "wreak their vengeance upon the . . . citizens." The general at first planned to go to Philadelphia himself, but his officers reported that the main army was in too dangerous a state for him to leave. Washington ordered a detachment of a thousand reliable men held ready to march against the Pennsylvanians in case of an emergency. Now he could only wait.

Wayne found the mutineers lodged in Nassau Hall, whose ruined upper floors were vacant and cold, left as they had been stripped by the enemy.

A committee of sergeants, led by one William Bouzar, presented Wayne their demands:

1. Immediate discharge of those who had enlisted for three years or the duration of the war.

2. Those who remained in service would be paid the enlistment

bounties given to new troops, and were to be paid in coin, and not in Continental paper.

3. Back pay and clothing were to be distributed at once.

Lafayette, Arthur St. Clair and John Laurens rode into town, were allowed to pass the pickets, and were courteously received by the sergeants, who firmly repeated their demands. The three officers were then ordered to leave Princeton.

Joseph Reed and a committee of congressmen left Philadelphia with a cavalry escort as soon as they heard news of the mutiny, ready to negotiate with the Pennsylvanians.

Although news of the mutiny reached Henry Clinton in New York almost at once, he moved cautiously, for fear of alienating Wayne's men. Instead of attacking, he sent an agent to Princeton to urge the mutineers to put themselves under British protection. Clinton offered full pardons, food, clothing and all their back pay. His messenger, John Mason, a recently freed convict, picked up a young guide on the road, one Benjamin Ogden, and the pair arrived in Princeton while Reed's party was still on the road. When Mason delivered Clinton's message, the sergeants were so incensed that they seized him and Ogden and turned them over to Wayne in his tavern quarters at 4 A.M., "to show him that the American army can furnish but one Arnold."

By the time Reed began negotiations during the day, the sergeants had moderated their demands: men who had served since 1777 would be paid in full and discharged, and though they would not accept worthless Continental paper, they offered to take certificates issued by the state.

Reed and the sergeants signed an agreement after a long session, but this was amended at Wayne's insistence—there was to be no punishment of the mutineers. The men were furloughed for forty days; two-thirds of them reenlisted and served throughout the war. As early as January 17 General William Irvine reported to Washington that many mutineers in Trenton "are now pestering us to re-enlist them."

Clinton's two messengers, Mason and Ogden, were tried by a court-martial headed by Wayne, found guilty at once, and hanged outside Trenton. Their bodies swung from a roadside tree for a week.

There was a final matter to be settled: Wayne had offered a reward of fifty guineas to each of the two sergeants who had brought in Clinton's agents. Reed squirmed—Congress had no gold, he said, and the rewards were excessive. The sergeants put Reed at ease; they had delivered the spies not for money, but for their country. They expected no reward.

When the terms of the settlement reached headquarters, Washington felt that though Reed had done his best under the circumstances, his leniency toward the mutineers would have "a very pernicious influence on the whole Army," but his pride in the troops was obvious when he wrote Rochambeau of the mutiny: "It is somewhat extraordinary that these men, however lost to a sense of duty, had so far retained that of honor, as to reject the most advantageous propositions from the enemy." He marveled that the entire army had not revolted long since: "The rest of our Army (the Jersey troops excepted) being chiefly composed of natives, I would flatter myself, will continue to struggle under the same difficulties . . . which I cannot help remarking seem to reach the bounds of human patience."

Disturbing news of a second mutiny reached the general from Trenton the next day. Two hundred men of the New Jersey Line, most of them drunk, had defied their officers and were marching on the state capital. This time the commander acted without hesitation. He sent the reliable North Carolinian, General Robert Howe, with a detachment of six hundred men from West Point, under orders to compel unconditional submission of the mutinous men, and to grant them no terms so long as they were armed.

On January 25 the impatient Washington rode south from West Point toward Trenton through the drifts of fresh snow. At the village of Ringwood, N.J., he learned that New Jersey civilian authorities had attempted to deal with the mutineers, had refused them the terms won by the Pennsylvanians, and that the men had returned to their camp eight miles from Ringwood in a riotous mood.

General Howe marched on the camp at midnight and by dawn had surrounded the Jerseymen, with artillerymen and infantry ready to fire. The Jerseymen shouted defiantly at first, but when Howe gave them five minutes to assemble in the open without arms, the mutineers emerged and stood in ranks, waiting. Howe demanded the names of the ringleaders of the group, marched three of them to the front, condemned them quickly by a field court-martial, and had them shot by a firing squad of a dozen of their companions. The doomed men were forced to kneel, and the weeping men of the firing squad shot them down one by one.

Robert Howe—who was no relation to the departed British leaders—lectured the survivors on "the heinousness of their guilt, as well as the folly of it," and reported confidently to Washington, "they showed the fullest sense of their guilt, and such strong marks of contrition, that I think I may pledge myself for their future good conduct."

Washington returned to his New Windsor headquarters, and when the mutinies seemed to have been suppressed, exhorted the army in his orders:

> The General is deeply sensible of the sufferings of the Army. He leaves no expedient unessayed to relieve them . . . Congress and the several states are doing everything in their power for the same purpose. But while we look to the public for the fulfillment of its engagements we should do it with an allowance for the embarrassments of public affairs. We began a contest for liberty . . . ill provided with the means of war . . . we expected to encounter many wants and distresses . . . it is our duty to bear present evils with fortitude, looking forward to the period when our country will have it more in its power to reward our services . . . I hope this will completely extinguish the spirit of mutiny . . . The General . . . flatters himself no similar instance will hereafter disgrace our military history.

Washington realized that the army was not yet out of danger. In the first week of January there was not "a single farthing in the military chest," and though he had urged upon John Laurens "the absolute necessity of an immediate, ample" supply of gold and silver, it was obvious that further aid from Paris could not arrive soon. The one source of hope, since it appeared that the French and American armies would never join, was a newly arrived French admiral, the Chevalier Charles Destouches, who had replaced the unaggressive Ternay.

22

THUNDER IN THE SOUTH

"These English Are Mad"

By one of the ironies of war it was Benedict Arnold who, in the opening days of 1781, drew Washington's attention to the Chesapeake Bay country of eastern Virginia, the vast complex of estuaries, tidal rivers and ranked peninsulas that was to become the theater of the decisive campaign of the Revolution. Already, in an evolving pattern of seemingly unrelated events, land and naval forces had begun moving into positions from which they would converge upon the inland sea which had been familiar to Washington since his boyhood. The men, ships and guns that would be drawn together in the final major battle of the war were in posts as far distant as the crowded Channel bases of the French navy, British harbors in the West Indies, the village camp of Charles Cornwallis in the South Carolina backwoods, Rochambeau's barracks in Rhode Island, and scattered hutments of Washington's army along the Hudson.

Henry Clinton had sent Arnold on a raid through eastern Virginia with a force of sixteen hundred men, and the new British brigadier moved up the James River to burn Richmond, a nearby foundry and military stores. He met little opposition, for despite Washington's warnings to Governor Thomas Jefferson the state had few troops in the field. Arnold thus moved about at will in early January, ranged through the most thickly populated counties to prevent the raising of militia to reinforce Greene's army in North Carolina, and within a few days settled near Norfolk in the town of Portsmouth, where he began to fortify his position. Washington was tantalized by the prospect of capturing Arnold.

A freak storm that struck the northeastern coast in late January seemed to offer an ideal opportunity to bring the traitor to justice. Fierce gales scattered and damaged the British fleet in Gardiner's Bay, near the tip of Long Island, but left the ships of Destouches unharmed in their anchorage at Newport. From his headquarters on the Hudson, Washington hurried a plea to Rochambeau, urging that the French fleet sail at once for the Chesapeake to trap Arnold. Slow mails between the allied camps delayed a reply, and it was mid-February before Washington received an ambiguous response from Rochambeau: "I am going this moment aboard of the Admiral to know whether he intends going out with all his ships, or at least send a detachment of some of them to Chesapeake Bay . . . I think that two men-of-war and two frigates will destroy all the expedition of Arnold's in Chesapeake Bay, and that . . . we have a fair chance for the accomplishing of that plan." Rochambeau also explained that the narrow entrance to the Chesapeake made it dangerous to send the entire French fleet.

Though uncertain as to whether the French had sent only a few ships or the entire fleet, Washington responded vigorously. He asked Rochambeau to send all available ships to Virginia, and to put a thousand infantry aboard. To help ensure success, he offered to send Lafayette overland with twelve hundred American troops to aid Destouches in a joint attack. In the midst of these long-distance negotiations, with his headquarters staff reduced by transfers and illness and tempers frayed by stress, Washington lost his most talented aide.

Alexander Hamilton had become increasingly restless, resentful of his "personal dependence" on Washington and eager for a change of post. Hamilton had sought the position of adjutant general, but lost it to Edward Hand; he had been eager to go on the mission to Paris, for which John Laurens was chosen; the new position of finance officer to Congress, to which he aspired, had gone to Robert Morris. The relationship between Washington and his young protégé had grown so cool that Hamilton made one of his proposals in writing "to avoid the embarrassment of a personal explanation."

Hamilton had come to feel that the general was consumed with "self-love," and he intended to break with him at the first opportunity. "For three years past," Hamilton said, "I have felt no friendship for him and have professed none. The truth is, our dispositions are the opposite of each other." Though the only full account of the breach between the two was left by Hamilton, his testimony made it clear that Washington also found their relationship difficult.

On February 16, during a particularly hectic day at headquarters, Washington and Hamilton passed on the stairs. The general asked the aide to come into his office and Hamilton said he would do so as soon as he delivered some papers to Tench Tilghman.

Hamilton was delayed by Lafayette, who held him in conversation for some time—two minutes, by Hamilton's reckoning—before he returned to Washington.

He found the general outside his office in a stern mood. "Colonel Hamilton, you have kept me waiting at the head of the stairs ten minutes." His voice rose, "I tell you, sir, you treat me with disrespect."

"I'm not conscious of it, sir. But since you've thought it necessary to tell me so, we part."

"Very well, sir, if that's your choice."

Washington recovered a few moments later, but though he sent Tilghman to offer his apologies and ask that they talk over their differences, Hamilton was adamant. The breach was final. He would report if the general insisted but a conversation could produce only "mutually disagreeable" explanations. Hamilton offered to remain at his post, but only until he could be replaced.

Though he had asked that Washington treat the matter confidentially, Hamilton sent word of it to several correspondents. He wrote James McHenry: "The Great man and I have come to an open rupture . . . He shall for once at least repent of his ill-humour..."

And to his father-in-law, Philip Schuyler, Hamilton revealed his growing irritation at serving the proud Virginian, "to whom all the world is offering incense." The young aide made the revealing admission that though the general had frequently sought to establish a closer personal relationship, he had rebuffed him. Obviously, as even Hamilton said, Washington sought persistently to patch up their differences.

Even now, the self-centered youth saw Washington as the indispensable leader of the revolution: "The general is a very honest man. His competitors have slender ability, and less integrity. His popularity has often been essential to the safety of America, and is still of great importance to it . . . I think it is necessary he should be supported . . ."

The astute Schuyler urged his son-in-law to be more tolerant of Washington: "It falls to the lot of few men to pass through life without one of those moments which wound the feelings of a friend . . . Make the sacrifice . . . Your services are wanted." It was in vain.

Hamilton continued to implore Washington for a field command and returned his commission when he was refused. The patient general sent it back, urging him to remain in the army a few weeks longer, until a suitable command could be found. Hamilton agreed reluctantly, but he was near the end of his service at headquarters. Within a few weeks he would be with troops in the field.

Washington sent Lafayette to Virginia after Arnold with eight hundred New Englanders, three hundred of Harry Lee's Virginia cavalrymen, a few riflemen and four small cannon. He gave the Frenchman stern orders as to Benedict Arnold: ". . . if he should fall into your hands, you will execute him in the most summary way," and even if Destouches did not appear with his fleet, Lafayette was to make every effort to trap the traitor, with the aid of other small American forces in Virginia. The marquis took his troops off on February 19, on such short notice that most of them were penniless, and officers had to send back for their baggage. "It's a funny thing to see us making a journey," Lafayette wrote. "We haven't a sou, a horse, a wagon, a whisp of hay."

Lafayette's column had hardly disappeared to the southward when Washington had the discouraging news that Destouches had taken only one line of battle ship and two frigates to the Chesapeake, a force too small to be effective against Arnold. This was followed by a dispatch from Rochambeau, explaining that the admiral had sailed before the arrival of Washington's request for the full fleet and an infantry detachment.

A few days later, on March 1, the news from the French camp took a surprising turn. Destouches had returned from his brief raid into the Chesapeake with five hundred prisoners, after capturing a British frigate and burning four troop transports—so encouraged that he was willing to "risk everything" to trap Arnold. The admiral was returning to the Chesapeake with his entire fleet, carrying eleven hundred of Rochambeau's veteran infantry. Not only was there the promise of capturing the traitor; the large allied force in Virginia might be able to relieve Nathanael Greene, who was hard-pressed in his campaign against Cornwallis in North Carolina.

The prospects stirred Washington to action. Within a few hours after receiving this news from Rochambeau, he left his New Windsor headquarters on a long-postponed visit to Newport, to confer with the French on details of the expedition and urge them to speed. Nothing must be left to chance.

While the general was on his 200-mile ride to Rhode Island, on March 2, 1781, the first tentative form of the government of the United States became official in Philadelphia. The thirteen states had approved the Articles of Confederation after five years of bickering. As a delegate said, "The child Congress has been big with . . . is at last brought forth . . . you will think it a monster." This was an event of which most Americans took scant notice— a feeble union of independent republics without an executive or a judiciary, and without powers to enforce its laws. Still, it was a step towards a central government, one that Washington had been urging since the start of the war. Final passage had come only when Virginia had relinquished claims to the vast lands west of the Ohio that ranged into the future states of Wisconsin and Minnesota. Upon this concession by Virginians, Maryland had signed the articles and the confederation became operative.

Washington held titles to vast tracts in the ceded territory, and the validity of his claims was now uncertain. In any event he had been unable to give them a thought during the war and feared that his western interests would dissolve into "absolute ruin before I am at liberty to look after them." The future control of these lands was yet very much in doubt, though Major George Rogers Clark, a former Virginian, had driven the British from most of the territory in an invasion by a handful of Kentucky riflemen. It now remained for the allies to destroy British power on the eastern seaboard.

The French received the general with great ceremony in Newport, but the fleet did not sail until two days after he arrived and Washington grew impatient; every hour was precious, since all hopes of catching Arnold depended upon Destouches gaining a long lead toward the Chesapeake before the British learned of his departure. The big French vessels lay at anchor throughout March 7, in readiness to sail, so far as Washington could see, but idle despite a wind favorable to them and unfavorable to the British fleet. It was near sunset of March 8 before Destouches finally put to sea, after delays incomprehensible to Washington, who knew little of the problems of shiploading.

Three days later the commander learned that the British ships had left Gardiner's Bay early on March 10, sailing southward as confidently as if they knew the details of the allied plan. Destouches had a narrow lead in the run for Virginia. Washington's hopes of capturing Arnold now hung upon the outcome of the race for the Chesapeake.

The commander returned to New Windsor to find a mortifying letter from Benjamin Harrison, who was now Speaker of the Virginia House of Delegates: the House was considering a pension for Washington's seventy-four-year-old mother, who had complained that she was destitute.

The querulous, penurious Mary Ball Washington had long been

365

"These English Are Mad"

resentful of George's attention to affairs other than her own. She had been so scornful of his army career that many Virginians considered her a Tory. The old woman had made the long journey from Virginia to Washington's headquarters in New York State earlier in the war to insist that he find a reliable overseer for her farm.

Harrison had blocked the proposed pension to avoid embarrassment to Washington, but assured him that the House would provide funds if he approved. The lifelong strain of his relationship with his mother was evident in Washington's reply: he explained that he had set her up in a house in Fredericksburg at her request, "to make her latter days comfortable and free from care," had always responded to her requests for money, and that her children "would divide the last sixpence to relieve her from *real* distress."

He added with obvious humiliation: "This she has been repeatedly assured by me, and all of us, I am certain, would feel much hurt, at having our mother a pensioner while we had the means of supporting her; but in fact she has an ample income of her own." The general urged that the House pass no bill for his mother's relief.

It was the end of March before news of final failure of the expedition against Arnold reached Washington in New Windsor. The French and British fleets had clashed in battle off the Chesapeake entrance after racing southward along the coast, and though Destouches had damaged the enemy in a brief engagement of an hour, he had been turned back to Rhode Island to make repairs to his own fleet. Arnold was safe to continue his raids, and Lafayette, left without reinforcements, began the long return northward to Washington's headquarters. The marquis had joined Baron von Steuben and a few Virginia militiamen in a reconnaissance of Arnold's base at Portsmouth, but was forced to turn away because of a lack of men and naval support.

This was not Washington's only concern. In his exasperation over the lost opportunity to destroy Arnold, he had complained to several correspondents that though he had done his best to defend Virginia, he had been foiled by French delays. Each of his letters of criticism was marked "private," but one of them, to Lund Washington, was to cause him acute embarrassment. He had written his nephew: "It was unfortunate—but this I mention in confidence—that the French fleet detachment did not undertake the enterprize . . . when I first proposed it to them —The destruction of Arnold's Corps would have been inevitable . . ."

After this letter was captured by the British and published in New York, Rochambeau wrote Washington with a restraint that intensified the Virginian's embarrassment. The Frenchman pointed out that Destouches had sailed on his first expedition before Washington had appealed for support in the Chesapeake. Rochambeau added an assurance of loyalty: "I only state these facts to call to your mind these dates . . . that you may be entirely persuaded that there will never be the least delay . . . in the execution of your orders, as soon as I shall receive them."

Washington's reply, though apologetic, made only the most oblique confession of guilt. "The enemy have fabricated whole letters for me . . . and it is not improbable that they may have given a different turn to some of my expressions in the present instance. It would however be disingenuous in me not to acknowledge, that I believe the general import to be true . . ." In any case, he asked Rochambeau to consider that the letter had been personal, with no intent of publication. The possibility of an allied quarrel evaporated with Rochambeau's final comment: "I did what I thought was the most consistent with a sincere heart . . . I wrote only to have the means of smothering that trifle at its birth."

Nathanael Greene's bitter struggle to hold the Carolinas had by now become an epic retreat northward through the rugged North Carolina interior. Closely pursued by Cornwallis, the Quaker fell back skillfully from one rain-swollen stream to another, drawing the British farther from their coastal bases each day, taking a steady toll of redcoat strength.

Greene had arrived in Charlotte, N. C., in December to find only eight hundred survivors of the old army of Gates fit for duty, ". . . a few ragged, half-starving troops in the wilderness,

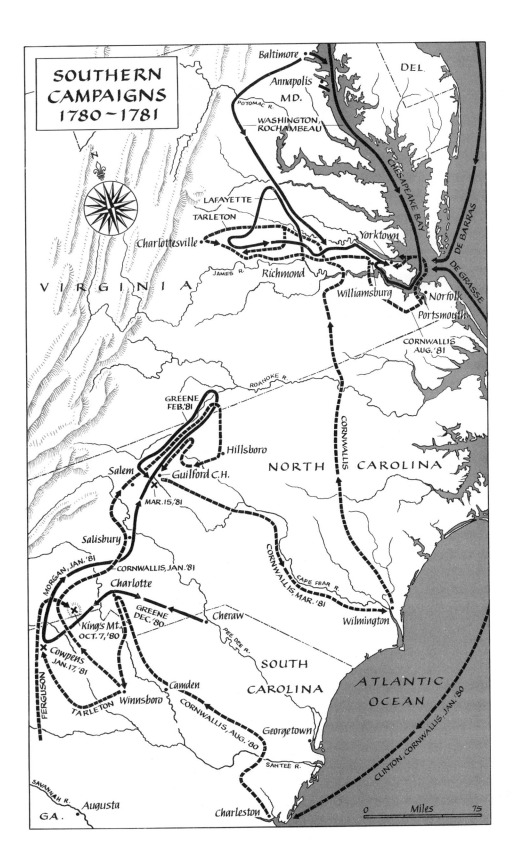

SOUTHERN
CAMPAIGNS
1780~1781

Baltimore
DEL.
Annapolis
MD.
POTOMAC R.
WASHINGTON
ROCHAMBEAU
CHESAPEAKE BAY
DE BARRAS
LAFAYETTE
TARLETON
Yorktown
DE GRASSE
Charlottesville
JAMES R.   Richmond
VIRGINIA
Williamsburg   Norfolk
Portsmouth
CORNWALLIS
AUG. '81
ROANOKE R.
GREENE
FEB. '81
Hillsboro
CORNWALLIS
Salem   NORTH   CAROLINA
Guilford C.H.
MAR. 15/81
Salisbury
MORGAN, JAN. '81   CORNWALLIS, JAN. '81
Charlotte
CORNWALLIS, MAR. '81
CAPE FEAR R.
GREENE
DEC. '80   Cheraw
King's Mt.
OCT. 7, '80   Wilmington
PEE DEE R.
Cowpens
JAN. 17, '81
Camden
SOUTH
FERGUSON
TARLETON   Winnsboro
CAROLINA
ATLANTIC
OCEAN
CORNWALLIS, AUG. '80
Georgetown
SANTEE R.
CLINTON, CORNWALLIS, JAN. '80
SAVANNAH R.   Augusta
GA.   Charleston   0   Miles   75

destitute of everything . . . the country is almost laid waste and the inhabitants plunder one another with little less than savage fury. We live from hand to mouth." Undaunted, the Quaker had divided this outnumbered band into two wings and sent one of them into western South Carolina under command of Daniel Morgan, who gathered a few militiamen as he went, and moved rapidly into the backwoods.

Tempted by the exposed rebel band, Cornwallis detached a wing of his army under his cavalry commander, Banastre Tarleton, with orders to attack. Tarleton found Morgan in a remote South Carolina clearing known as the Cowpens, and advanced with eleven hundred men in a dawn assault on January 17, with all the confidence of British veterans facing green militia. Carolina and Georgia riflemen picked off Tarleton's charging cavalrymen and many infantry officers, and Morgan's Delaware and Maryland Continentals led a final charge that routed the redcoats. Tarleton escaped with only fifty of his troopers.

Morgan gathered his wounded and herded the prisoners northward within two hours, closely followed by Cornwallis and his main army. Morgan rejoined Greene's troops a few days later and together they fell back before the British. To speed the chase, Cornwallis burned most of his baggage wagons, but his column was slowed by thousands of slaves and women camp followers.

Guerrilla bands harried the redcoats, food became scarcer, wagons broke down, and officers became more apprehensive as Cornwallis moved farther from his base in Charleston, S.C.; Benedict Arnold was still too far away to help. No soldier could leave the column in safety: "It is with great concern that Lord Cornwallis hears every day reports of the soldiers being taken by the enemy in consequence of their straggling out of camp in search of whiskey . . ."

Greene's men suffered as severely as they had in northern campaigns, "The miserable situation of the troops for want of clothing has rendered the march the most painful imaginable, with hundreds tracking the ground with bloody feet . . . Myself and my aides are almost worn out with fatigue . . . The army is in good spirits notwithstanding its suffering." But Greene's skilled retreat saved supplies he had collected for his troops and gave time for Virginia militia to gather before his arrival in that state. Washington praised the withdrawal as if the Quaker had won a rousing victory.

Greene moved across the North Carolina border into Virginia, halted to gather recruits and horses, and when his ranks had increased to about forty-five hundred men, turned back southward and challenged Cornwallis in open battle.

The armies met on March 15 at Guilford Courthouse, N. C., where British and German veterans broke Greene's militia lines, but were fought to a standstill by Delaware and Maryland veterans in one of the most savage engagements of the war. Greene's regulars were driven from the field only when Cornwallis ordered his gunners to fire grapeshot through the ranks of his own men to halt a rebel advance, causing most of his casualties. The earl had lost about a fourth of his army.

Cornwallis claimed victory at Guilford, but was soon in retreat to the sea at Wilmington, N. C. Greene followed him closely, then returned to South Carolina, where he began a campaign against exposed British outposts in the interior. When news of Guilford Courthouse reached London, Charles Fox said, "Another such victory would be the ruin of the British army."

Cornwallis reported to Clinton from Wilmington that he now planned an invasion of Virginia: "Until Virginia is in a manner subdued, our hold of the Carolinas must be difficult, if not precarious. The Rivers in Virginia are advantageous to an invading army; but North Carolina is of all the provinces the most difficult to attack."

Clinton was distressed to learn that Cornwallis had lost North Carolina, was leaving South Carolina open to Greene, and was moving to the Chesapeake: "I shall dread what may be the consequences . . . Had it been possible for Your Lordship . . . to have intimated your intention . . . I should certainly have endeavored to have stopped you—as I did then, as well as now, consider such a move as likely to be dangerous to our interest in the Southern Colonies."

Clinton had felt from the first that he must defer to Cornwallis, who was his social superior and an influential figure in London, but his indignation had become unbearable when Cornwallis ignored him during the southern campaign and wrote directly to London for advice and orders. Clinton now wrote caustically to the earl, "As Your Lordship is now so near, it will be unnecessary for you to send your dispatches to the Minister; you will therefore be good enough to send them to me in the future."

Within a few weeks Cornwallis was in eastern Virginia, looting and burning tobacco and other stores as Arnold and Phillips had done before him, raids that aroused the wonder of Lafayette: "These English are mad. They march through a country and think they have conquered it."

At his distance in New York, Henry Clinton was similarly puzzled, but lacked the firmness to assert authority over his lieutenant: "My wonder at this move of Lord Cornwallis will never cease. But he has made it, and we shall say no more but make the best of it." The basis of Clinton's concern was that a large French fleet might arrive in the Chesapeake, where loss of control of the sea, even for two days, "may catch us in very critical movements."

23

LAFAYETTE IN VIRGINIA, SUMMER, 1781

Matters of Very Great Importance

Lafayette arrived in the upper Chesapeake on April 8 on his way northward after the futile campaign against Arnold. It had been an exhausting journey, for the marquis had circled far to the west to visit Mount Vernon and Fredericksburg before rejoining his troops in Annapolis. The detour had been irresistible, he wrote Washington, because of "an ardent desire I had long ago of seeing your relatives and above all your mother." The French boy had made long night rides to recover the lost time.

Lafayette was distressed by an order from Washington that awaited him on the Chesapeake: he was to turn back southward and march his troops to the aid of Greene in North Carolina, some five hundred miles away. The Frenchman prepared to move, though he foresaw trouble with his troops.

"Our officers and men are none too happy about it," Lafayette wrote Washington, but "though we have neither money, nor clothes, nor shoes, nor shirts and in a few days shall be reduced to green peaches . . . all that will not prevent us from marching."

His men had left New York expecting to be gone a few days, but they had been away almost two months, and now that they had started back home they would be reluctant to return southward. The hot season was approaching, and New Englanders feared that the southern air was unhealthy, the cause of agues and fevers "which would certainly kill as the smallpox." Some of Lafayette's officers told him that since he was growing bald and wore no wig, the Virginia sun would kill him. Despite all protests and hardships, Lafayette assured Washington, "they will certainly obey, but they will be unhappy, and some will desert."

Desertions began on April 10, when Lafayette faced his men about and moved toward Virginia. Thirty of his best men disappeared in the first two days. When he arrived at the Susquehanna River two days later, the marquis had another message from Washington. Greene no longer needed his aid, since Cornwallis had been forced to retreat. Lafayette was to command in Virginia and campaign against Arnold once more. The little army halted for three days at the river, waiting for rough water to subside. Lafayette hanged a captured spy and announced to his sullen troops that they were free to return home, but that he was going to Virginia if he must go alone. "To throw a kind of infamy upon desertion" he said he would take with him only the bravest men. Somehow, the boy general persuaded them. Two or three volunteers stepped forward and a sick sergeant burst into tears, begging to be carried with the army on a cart. Few of the troops asked for passes back home.

When eight deserters returned to camp and asked to be taken back into service, Lafayette hanged one of them, honorably discharged another and dismissed the rest. After his barges crossed the Susquehanna, Lafayette's force was still nearly one thousand.

As the army passed through Baltimore, Lafayette borrowed money from merchants on his promise to repay within two years, when he came into his inheritance, and bought shoes, hats and linen to be made into uniforms. When women of the city gave a ball for his officers, Lafayette persuaded them to make linen shirts for his troops. He wrote officials on the route ahead, including Governor Jefferson, who warned that he could expect little support in Virginia, a state with "mild laws and a people not used to prompt obedience." Lafayette made an advance apology for "the necessity of disturbing" Virginians, but said he must confiscate what he needed for the troops: "Uncommon dangers require uncommon remedies." Jefferson approved.

The marquis learned that Benedict Arnold had been joined by the British general William Phillips, an artilleryman whose guns had killed Lafayette's father at the battle of Minden, many years before. The news inspired the Frenchman to an ingenious method of speeding his march: half of his troops rode on wagons while the other half walked, and by changing at regular intervals, Lafayette kept them fresh and moved the column toward Richmond at a pace that astounded the British. Lafayette reached the Virginia capital on April 29, too late to halt the destruction of tobacco warehouses south of the James by Phillips and Arnold. Lafayette learned that Cornwallis had entered the state, and wrote Washington: "It now appears that I have business with two armies, and this is rather too much. Each is more than double, superior to me." For a time Lafayette's dispatches to Washington became more somber, "I am not strong enough even to get beaten. Government in this state has no energy and laws have no force . . . our expenses are enormous, yet we can get nothing . . ."

Inflation was even more ruinous than in the north. The Virginia Assembly had fixed the price of a cavalry horse at $150,000, and there were none to be had even at that price.

Lafayette also complained of his lack of strength: "I am wavering between two inconveniences. Was I to fight a battle, I'll be cut to pieces, the militia dispersed, and the arms lost. Was I to decline fighting, the country would think herself given up. I am therefore determined to skarmish, but not too far . . ."

Washington promised the marquis that Anthony Wayne and his Pennsylvanians would soon join him, but the reinforcements were slow in coming. Lafayette was first joined by a few militiamen led by Baron von Steuben, who brought dissension in his wake. Steuben had provoked bitter quarrels by denouncing Governor Jefferson for failure to raise enough men to drive off Arnold's small force. The Prussian had been called to a country courthouse to take command of a promised force of five hundred volunteers and found only five men, three of whom deserted at once. Jefferson denied responsibility: the people disregarded the laws out of "obstinacy of spirit," he said.

Steuben fumed: "I am not less tired of this State than they are of me . . . I shall always regret that circumstances induced me to undertake the defense of a country where Caesar and Hannibal would have lost their reputation, and where every farmer is a general, but where nobody wishes to be a soldier."

Cornwallis marched swiftly up the James and entered the capital without opposition. Governor Jefferson and the Assembly fled to Charlottesville, where Banastre Tarleton's cavalrymen captured seven delegates, and narrowly missed taking Jefferson at Monticello. Steuben, who had retreated westward up the James to defend an army supply depot, fled at the approach of a few enemy cavalrymen. The indignant Lafayette hinted that Steuben's cowardice was to blame: ". . . The militia left him. His new levies deserted. All Virginia was in an uproar against him. The enemy laughed at him, and I cannot describe to you what my surprise has been."

Lafayette himself fell back before the British advance toward Fredericksburg, but maneuvered so skillfully that Cornwallis declined to risk battle in the unfamiliar countryside. He turned eastward to take a position on the Chesapeake from which he could easily rejoin Henry Clinton's army in New York, for Clinton's half-formed plan for the year's campaign was to occupy Philadelphia once more. Cornwallis thus began a leisurely march through central Virginia toward the sea. No one yet perceived that the British were moving into terrain that abounded in vulnerable positions, small ports in which they might be cut off by both sea and land.

Lafayette followed the British column closely, hoping to create an impression that he was driving Cornwallis before him, "I try to give his movements the appearance of a retreat. God grant that there may be an opportunity to give them the appearance of a defeat."

Almost five hundred miles to the north, at his New Windsor headquarters, Washington resumed the diary he had habitually kept for so many years, only to give it up on the day he became commander of the army in June 1775. "I lament not having attempted it from the commencement of the War, in aid of my memory," he wrote, and on May 1 made his first new entry. It was an appraisal of affairs almost as cheerless as any he had made during the war:

> Instead of having Magazines filled with provisions, we have a scanty pittance . . . Instead of having our Arsenals well supplied with Military Stores, they are poorly provided, and the Workmen all leaving them . . . we are daily and hourly oppressing the people —souring their tempers—and alienating their affections. Instead of having the Regiments compleated . . . scarce any State in the Union has, at this hour, an eighth part of its quota in the field . . . In a word—instead of having everything in readiness to take the Field, we have nothing and instead of having the prospect of a glorious offensive campaign before us, we have a bewildered and gloomy defensive one. . . .

Less than two weeks later there was news from the French that changed the prospect beyond Washington's power of imagination. The Viscount de Rochambeau, son of the general, had returned from Paris with a report that the French navy was to make a new effort. Destouches had been replaced by a newly arrived admiral, the Count de Barras, and Rochambeau asked for an immediate conference with Washington on a new campaign. Washington arranged to meet the Frenchman in Wethersfield, Conn., on May 21.

The Virginian knew more of the plans of his allies than Rochambeau realized, for Chastellux, who had become his liaison with the French in the absence of Lafayette, had written him confidentially of details Rochambeau had withheld: more help was on the way from France, and Rochambeau was ready to propose that his troops move down from Rhode Island to join the rebels.

The generals met in Hartford on the twenty-first and began their talks in Wethersfield the next day, with Chastellux as interpreter. De Barras had not come because of threatening moves by the British fleet.

Rochambeau began by giving Washington details of the news Chastellux had revealed in his secret letter to Washington: a powerful new French fleet under Admiral de Grasse was already on the way to the West Indies, carrying infantrymen, six hundred of whom would be sent to Newport. The French troops were now ready to take the field. Where did Washington suggest they should attack?

Of the two obvious objectives, New York or Virginia, Washington preferred New York, to avoid the punishing 450-mile march to the Chesapeake. The most effective defense of Virginia, Washington felt, would be a blow at New York, which would force Clinton to recall Cornwallis. Rochambeau, on the other hand, felt that New York was too strong to be stormed by the allied force. The veteran saw much greater promise of a victory in the Chesapeake, where there was room for maneuver, and where seizure of control of the sea by De Grasse could be decisive.

There was a lack of candor throughout the debate, since only Rochambeau realized that De Grasse had been ordered to join the armies in a combined offensive in the late summer. Rochambeau concealed this from Washington—and from Chastellux—on the ground that the information had come to him from Paris in confidence.

This conference ended with mutual assurances of friendly cooperation, but Chastellux was outraged by Rochambeau's rudeness to Washington. "Papa" had treated his ally with "all the ungraciousness and all the unpleasantness possible," treatment that must have left the Virginian with "a sad and disagreeable feeling in his heart." Some of Rochambeau's hostility may have stemmed from an awareness that his ignorance of American affairs had been held up to scorn by Chastellux, who was considered by other staff officers as *trop américain*.

Washington seemed to take no offense at Rochambeau's manner, perhaps because he suspected that the Frenchman was still nettled by the recent exposure of Washington's critical letter. Washington was unaware that Rochambeau was also smarting under a barrage of criticism from his own officers, who had written home of the growing difficulty of serving under him. Count Fersen noted that Rochambeau had come to distrust even his senior officers, and treated them in a "disagreeable and indeed insulting manner."

Rochambeau was not only a harsh disciplinarian who displayed no feeling of warmth for his officers and men; he seemed to be increasingly irritated by his assignment in this strange country. The chief commissary officer, Claude Blanchard, found Papa's mood trying: "M. de Rochambeau . . . mistrusts everyone and always believes that he sees himself surrounded by rogues and idiots. This character, combined with manners far from courteous, makes him disagreeable to everybody."

The real source of Washington's frustration at the end of the conference was Rochambeau's evasiveness about the role of De Grasse's fleet. He wrote Luzerne in exasperation, "It is not for me to know in what manner the fleet of His Most Christian Majesty is to be employed . . . or to enquire at what epoch it is to be expected on this coast."

Rochambeau and Washington signed an agreement on a plan of campaign before they parted: if De Grasse came to the coast, an attack on New York by the combined allied forces was to be the first objective, and was preferable to a move southward. But after signing the document, Rochambeau wrote secretly to De Grasse, first giving his assessment of the unpromising military situation:

> These people here are at the end of their resources. Washington has not half the troops he counted on; I believe, though he is hiding it, that he has not 6000 men. M. de la Fayette has not 1000 regulars with the militia to defend Virginia. . . . This is the state of affairs and the great crisis at which America finds itself. . . .

Only the grand fleet, Rochambeau said, could save the revolution. His final plea to the admiral put an end to Washington's hopes of attacking New York. Ignoring his agreement with Washington, he urged De Grasse to bring five thousand troops and all the money he could raise to join in a southern campaign:

> The southwesterly winds and the distressed state of Virginia will probably lead you to prefer Chesapeake Bay, and it is there that we think you can render the greatest services . . .

Rochambeau continued to press Washington to consider a move to Virginia, where Cornwallis was still moving toward the Chesapeake, closely followed by Lafayette. On May 26 Washington had a message from John Laurens in Paris: De Grasse had been ordered to North America, and the King had sent six million livres to help supply American troops. It was Washington's first inkling that De Grasse might actually cooperate in the campaign by coming to North America. Even now, when they discussed the coming of De Grasse, Rochambeau continued his deception of Washington. The Frenchman explained disingenuously that he had told De Grasse of Washington's plan to attack New York, but had taken the liberty of suggesting that the fleet might make a raid into the Chesapeake on its way northward.

Washington's reply revealed that he had not closed his mind to a campaign in Virginia. He stressed to Rochambeau the importance of flexibility in their plans: "Your Excellency will be pleased to recollect that New York was looked upon by us as the only practicable object under present circumstances; but should we be able to secure a naval superiority, we may perhaps find others more practicable and equally advisable."

The Virginia summer had already begun when Anthony Wayne, with eight hundred Pennsylvania regulars, joined Lafayette a few miles north of Richmond. The little army of the marquis had now grown to five thousand men, exclusive of Steuben's Virginians, and Lafayette's confidence returned. Cornwallis was now his only antagonist, for General Phillips had died of fever and Benedict Arnold had returned to New York. Lafayette followed the outnumbered Cornwallis more closely as he trailed into Tidewater Virginia.

It was only on June 26, when the armies collided in a brief skirmish of pickets outside Williamsburg, that Cornwallis realized that Lafayette had been following closely on his hundred-mile retreat. The earl reported to Henry Clinton that he planned to turn on the young Frenchman, "if I can get a favorable opportunity of striking a blow at him without loss of time."

Cornwallis ambushed Lafayette's vanguard on July 6, at Greenspring on the James, near Williamsburg. With his baggage sent across the river, Cornwallis waited until the impetuous Anthony Wayne led the head of the American column into the trap and opened fire with masked cannon. Wayne withdrew his troops, and Cornwallis crossed the river unmolested the next day. It had been a costly lesson for Lafayette, who lost a hundred and forty men and had two horses shot from under him in the brisk skirmish, but he praised the bravery of his men, and encouraged the impression that he had forced Cornwallis to cross the James. Dr. McHenry and his staff credited Lafayette with "sorcery and magic." Washington wrote from his headquarters outside New York about this time:

> The command of the troops in that state cannot be in better hands than the Marquis's. He possesses uncommon military talents, is of quick and sound judgment, persevering, and enterprizing without rashness, and besides these, he is of a very conciliating temper and perfectly sober, which are qualities that rarely combine in the same person.

Cornwallis had hardly reached the south bank of the James when he had an urgent dispatch from Clinton, calling on him for reinforcements to strengthen the New York garrison in the face of threatening moves by Washington and Rochambeau. Cornwallis complied, but warned that a reduction of his strength would invite disaster. His army, he predicted, would be penned up in "some Acres of an unhealthy swamp . . . forever liable to become a prey to a foreign Enemy, with temporary superiority at Sea."

By now Cornwallis had a new servant in his headquarters tent, an obliging black man named James Armistead, who had joined the army during the river crossing. James was a spy for Lafayette. He sent frequent reports as the British marched to Portsmouth, but the marquis could learn nothing of the future plans of Cornwallis: "His Lordship is so shy of his papers that my honest friend says he cannot come at them."

Despite every effort by Armistead, and his almost daily reports of activity in the British camp, Lafayette fretted that he must "guess at every possible whim of an enemy that flies with the wind and is not within the reach of spies or reconnoiterers."

The earl loaded his troops on transports at the end of July, but they lay near Portsmouth day after day, as if Cornwallis could not decide upon their destination.

Lafayette was awaiting the enemy's move when a rider from the north brought a cryptic message from Washington: "I shall shortly have occasion to communicate matters of very great importance to you." Lafayette realized instinctively what plans were being made in the north, and that the Chesapeake was to become the scene of action. He responded to Washington, "Should a French fleet now come in Hampton road, the British army would, I think, be ours." To Luzerne in Philadelphia he wrote impetuously, "Mon Dieu, why haven't we a fleet here? . . . If the French army could fall from the clouds into Virginia and be supported by a squadron we should do some very good things."

On August 1 Lafayette's scouts reported that Cornwallis was unloading his troops at Yorktown, a village tobacco port on the south bank of the broad York River, a few miles inland from the Chesapeake. Lafayette passed the news to Washington immediately. He assured the commander that he would do his best to hold Cornwallis in place, watching him closely without risking battle: "His Lordship plays so well that no blunder can be hoped from him to recover a bad step of ours."

Lafayette had been told by now that De Grasse was on his way, and sent lookouts to the capes of the Chesapeake entrance. The marquis settled near Yorktown, a few miles to the west, to await events, and wrote Washington:

I hope you will find we have taken the best precautions to lessen his Lordship's chances to escape. He has a few left but so very precarious that I hardly believe he will make the attempt. If he does he must give up Ships, Artillery, Baggage, part of the Horses, all the Negroes. He must be certain to loose the third of his Army and run the greatest risk to loose the whole . . .

The village in which Cornwallis had settled lay along a bluff that rose eighty feet above the York River, its wharves at the water's edge, with some thirty or forty houses strung along sandy streets atop the bluff. South of the town, some fifteen miles away, lay the James River, and to the westward stretched the narrow peninsula that lay between the York and the James.

Cornwallis had been reluctant to settle here, as he wrote General Charles O'Hara, his second in command: "the position is bad, and of course we want more troops." But the village was, as Cornwallis reported to Clinton, ". . . the only harbour in which we can hope to give effectual protection to line-of-battle ships." It had not yet occurred to Charles Cornwallis that the next ships he saw approaching from the Chesapeake might be French.

24

HOODWINKING
HENRY CLINTON

"The Mask Is Being Raised!"

Rochambeau's army moved down from Rhode Island in early July to join the Americans on the Hudson with admirable speed despite the heat—two hundred and twenty miles in eleven days. The troops marched smartly at a quick, mincing step, under firm discipline but as carefree as a carnival band. A shortage of horses forced them to travel light, and many young officers, lately courtiers at Versailles, set an example by marching with their men. In the rear were hundreds of wagons piled with baggage, servants leading horses, and a throng of American women. The four French regiments were forty-eight hundred strong, about the strength of the American detachment Washington was leading south.

Heat felled a few of the French, and some deserters from the Soissonais regiment dropped out to return to their mistresses, but most of the troops made the forced marches cheerfully, in relief at their escape from Newport. The troops were preyed on by New England farmers who hawked produce in the camps, extorting high prices. An occasional straggler was murdered by civilian marauders. The army settled at last near the rebels. The Americans camped on a line from Dobbs Ferry on the Hudson to the Sawmill River, and the French to the east, across the Bronx River to White Plains.

"The Mask Is Being Raised!"

The armies were not long in becoming well acquainted. Like most Americans, Washington's troops thought of the French as effeminate fops who lived on frogs and coarse vegetables, "light, brittle, queer-shaped mechanisms, busy frizzling their hair and painting their faces." The Chevalier du Pontgibaud encountered a typical American bias against Frenchmen when he stopped at a New England farmhouse and was warmly greeted by the farmer, "I'm very glad to have a Frenchman in my house—my barber lives far away, you can shave me."

Pontgibaud protested that he could not even shave himself without the aid of a servant. "That's strange," the farmer said, "I was told that all Frenchmen were barbers and fiddlers."

But now the unkempt American troops who swarmed Rochambeau's camps were lost in admiration. Five bands played exotic airs, and pairs of men danced between the tents. The Americans joined. A French diarist recorded, "Officers, Soldiers and the Americans mix and dance together. It is the feast of Equality, the first fruits of the Alliance."

The rebels were dazzled by the French uniforms. The infantry wore white broadcloth coats, long waistcoats and gaiters, with regimental colors on their collars and silk lapels—pink, yellow, sky blue, green, rose or crimson. Most spectacular of all was the Lauzun Legion, mustachioed hussars in tall fur hats who used saddlecloths of tiger skin and carried lances and curved sabers. Many of these men were soldiers of fortune, Irish, Germans and Poles.

The troops were commanded by a variety of noblemen, barons, counts and viscounts and one prince, De Broglie, the son of a marshal of France. There were Chastellux and Fersen; Count Guillaume Deux-Ponts, whose German-speaking troops came from the Saar; there was Lafayette's brother-in-law, the Viscount de Noailles, from whose regiment Napoleon was to rise; young Captain Louis Berthier, who would become Napoleon's chief of staff; the engineer officer, Count Mathieu Charlus, son of the Minister of Marine; and Count Mathieu Dumas, who was to become a hero at Waterloo. Among many who were to die in the Terror of the French Revolution was the Duke de Lauzun, a lover of Marie Antoinette, who would one day say calmly to his executioner at the guillotine, "we are both Frenchmen; we shall do our duty."

The rebels were not long in learning that the French were much like themselves: accomplished pillagers, sly conspirators against their officers, men resolved to fight as little but as fiercely as possible. A skeptical Virginia officer acknowledged, "Finer Troops I never saw."

The French troops were unsatiably curious about their unlikely allies, who by European standards were not soldiers at all, most of them without uniforms, barefoot, lank-haired and lousy, men who carried no baggage and slept in the open, or on branches covered with filthy blankets, four men to each odorous tent. Hundreds of old men and boys of twelve or thirteen were mingled in the ranks. Their movements on the road or drill field could not be called marching, but there was a spirit of confidence on the lean faces, the muskets were clean, and the Americans seemed indifferent to the stifling heat. The Count du Bourg wrote: "I cannot insist too strongly how I was surprised by the American army. It is truly incredible that troops almost naked, poorly paid, and composed of old men and children and Negroes should behave so well on the march and under fire."

Some French officers, like Deux-Ponts, were dismayed to discover that Washington commanded only a handful of men: "They told us at Newport that the American army had 10,000 men. It has 2500 or 2000 men, and that is not much of a lie for the Americans." Others, including the Abbé Claude Robin, a French chaplain, concluded that Washington, an American Gideon, was shrewdly concealing his numbers: "Now with a few soldiers he forms a Spacious Camp and spreads a large number of tents. Then again with a large number of men he reduces his tentage and his force and almost vanishes."

Rochambeau's officers openly admired Washington, but found him an enigma: his modesty was "very astonishing, especially to a Frenchman." The Virginian had not only refused to accept pay for his services, but he spoke of the war he directed as if he were no more than an interested spectator. Washington's unassuming manner impressed the courtiers, one of whom said, "I have never seen anyone who was more naturally and spontaneously polite. . . . He asks few questions, listens attentively, and answers in low tones and with few words."

The Prince de Broglie attempted an explanation for his countrymen: ". . . he preserves that polite and attentive good breeding which satisfies everybody, and that dignified reserve which offends no one. He is a foe to ostentation and to vainglory . . . He does not seem to estimate himself at his true worth."

Count Mathieu Dumas, who had ridden through Providence with the general one night, saw that he had captivated the American people. The count was deeply moved to see men, women and children press around Washington, carrying torches in his honor, content merely with a sight of him, overjoyed to touch his boots or his horse. The crowd had once halted the officers in the street. Washington turned to Dumas: "We may be beaten by the English; that is the chance of war; but here is the army that they will never conquer."

The Abbé Robin, who saw Washington followed by such processions through many towns, said, "The Americans, that cool and sedate people . . . are roused, animated, and inflamed at the very mention of his name, and the first songs that sentiment or gratitude has dictated, have been to celebrate General Washington."

The armies lay outside New York in the July heat while Washington and Rochambeau prowled along the river, inspecting the formidable British position. They once crossed the Harlem to Manhattan itself, but found the enemy alert everywhere. The commanders reconnoitered from Throg's Neck, and looking from the New Jersey side of the Hudson, Washington found New York sadly changed under British occupation: "the island is totally stripped of Trees, and wood of every kind . . ." Forests that had covered the hillsides of Harlem Heights had disappeared, and only thickets grew there. British and German outposts covered every sector of the river front. An assault across the Hudson would be hazardous indeed.

In mid-July Rochambeau pressed Washington for a definite plan of campaign, but even now did not reveal his scheme to meet De Grasse in Virginia. Though Washington was reluctant to give up hope of attacking Henry Clinton, and urged that they wait for De Grasse, who might appear off New York, he was thinking of a move to Virginia. He wrote in his diary on August 1: "I could scarce see a ground upon which to continue my preparations against New York . . . and therefore turned my views more seriously than I had before done to an operation to the southward."

It was August 14 before Washington realized that Rochambeau had been deceiving him from the start. The Virginian learned that De Grasse had already left the West Indies for the Chesapeake to cooperate in an attack on Cornwallis. The allied armies must hurry southward at once to take advantage of the movement. Washington was infuriated by the discovery of Rochambeau's deception.

Timothy Pickering and Robert Morris, who reached headquarters at this moment, discovered Washington in a rage, "striding to an fro in such a state of uncontrolled excitement" that he took no notice of the visitors. "Resentment, indignation and despair had burst upon him," Pickering said. "His hopes were blasted, and he felt that the cause was lost and his country ruined." Morris and Pickering left quietly, and returned within half an hour to find Washington composed and smiling. "I must apologize for my extraordinary appearance when you came in," the general said. "I had been hoping for so many months to carry out our plans with the French—only to have them thwarted." Even now, Pickering thought, Washington was "tossing like a volcano within." In a final outburst the commander growled, "I wish to the Lord the French would not raise our expectations of a cooperation, or fulfil them."

Pickering, who was unaware of the complexities of Washington's negotiations with the French, may have exaggerated the importance of the scene, but did not misjudge the depths of Washington's anguish when he realized at last that Rochambeau and De Grasse had never intended to storm New York. The commander's diary entry for the night reflected his lingering resentment:

Matters having now come to a crisis and a decisive plan to be determined on, I was obliged, from the shortness of Count de Grasse's promised stay on this Coast, the apparent disinclination in their Naval Officers to force the harbour of New York and the feeble compliance of the States to my requisitions for Men . . . to give up all idea of attacking New York; and instead thereof to remove the French Troops and a detachment from the American Army . . . to Virginia.

For all his protests, Washington had made contingency plans for a secret move southward. Wagons had been assembled and the artillery prepared to move. Plans were completed with almost incredible speed, and within five days after Washington learned of De Grasse's approach, the troops had begun the move. Supplies were waiting on the road for many marches ahead. Duportail was on his way to advise De Grasse of the approach of the armies, Admiral de Barras had been asked to sail from Newport to reinforce De Grasse in the Chesapeake, and William Heath had been left with a force of four thousand New England troops to guard the Hudson. Lafayette had been alerted: ". . . I hope you will be enabled to maintain that superiority which you seem to be gaining over Lord Cornwallis. . . ."

A band of alert British spies passed freely through the allied camps, but though they sent frequent warnings that Washington planned a march to Virginia, Henry Clinton did nothing to prevent the move. Still haunted by the fear of an assault on New York, Clinton busied himself daily, riding out to watch troops dig fresh trenches, build new forts, demolish houses and chop down orchards to give his artillerymen broader fields of fire. He ordered a canal dug across the peninsula as an additional barrier.

Life at headquarters was an endless round of bickering. The navy was hostile and uncooperative. Admiral Thomas Graves had moved his headquarters to South Brooklyn, far from Clinton's quarters on the future site of 52nd Street. Dispatches were frequently delayed.

It was August 16, only two days after the allied decision became final, that a woman spy sent Henry Clinton the first positive evidence of the enemy movement: the French had struck tents and marched. The rebels would cross the Hudson the next morning. For hours during the river crossing, Clinton's spies heard rebel soldiers gossiping as to their destination, Philadelphia, Baltimore or Virginia. Another spy sent word that the Viscount de Rochambeau, the general's son, had sent his mistress ahead by horseback to Trenton, N. J., an infallible sign of the route of the allied march. Still the passive Clinton did nothing, though by launching an attack from New York he could almost certainly have halted the southward march of Washington and Rochambeau. Sir Henry seemed to be paralyzed by the dilemma facing him.

Each day one of Clinton's spies, Marquand, reported new enemy campsites on the roads leading south, but Sir Henry made no move beyond shifting troops within the city and on Staten Island. On August 22 he had a message in cipher from a spy who was known as Squib: "General Washington with about six thousand, including French, are on their march for this neighborhood. It is said they will go against New York, but some Circumstances induce me to believe they will go to the Chesapeake. Yet for God's sake be prepared at all points. . . ." One important message was missing for three days during this decisive period. Clinton's staff urged immediate offensive action. Benedict Arnold was especially insistent that the allied camps should be attacked.

As the days slipped away Clinton surrendered to his frustrations. He developed a paralyzing fear of French seapower, "If the Enemy remain only a few Weeks superior at Sea, our situation will become very critical." He suffered two attacks of temporary blindness, and when he recovered, spent hours composing petulant letters to Lord Cornwallis, demanding reinforcements. Judge William Smith found Clinton taken by "gusts of passion." He wrote, "I despair of Clinton . . . He will make the apprehension of a French fleet an excuse for inactivity."

In mid-August, when Sir Henry heard more positive word of a French fleet in American waters, he wrote skeptically to Admiral Graves, "I cannot say I credit the reports of the French fleet being upon the coast."

Clinton's delusion as to allied intentions dated from June 4, when a scout had brought him a captured rebel mail pouch including dispatches from Washington and Rochambeau to Congress and Lafayette. There were reports on the Wethersfield conference and plans for the campaign: the allies would attack New York or, as an alternative, march to Virginia. As a headquarters aide noted, "The capture of this Mail is extremely consequential, and gives the Commander in Chief the most perfect knowledge of the designs of the Enemy." Clinton was so alarmed that he was to remain convinced for many weeks that he, and not Cornwallis, was in peril. Clinton ordered Cornwallis to halt his march of conquest through Virginia and settle in a fortified post near the sea, and called for reinforcements to be sent to New York. It was a conviction to which Sir Henry clung despite arguments that the announced plan was merely a ruse, since Washington had broadcast it to rebel governors. Clinton failed to realize that Washington's objective might have been to neutralize British pressure in Virginia.

Sir Henry marshaled persuasive evidence that the captured dispatches were genuine, since they included a message to Benjamin Tallmadge about his spies in New York, a warning to Lund Washington that British raiders might burn Mount Vernon, and even an order to Washington's dentist for wire and scrapers to repair his false teeth.

The distractions of the dissolute and corrupt life at British headquarters may also have dulled Clinton's perception during this crucial period. His mistress, Mary Baddeley, was soon to bear him a child; the round of drinking bouts and musical concerts continued without interruption at Clinton's colonial court; he maintained four houses and a farm, and moved endlessly from one to another with his entourage of guests in tow. He conducted a feud with the senile General James Robertson, whom he despised as "Smelling after every giddy girl that will let him come nigh her, and retailing amongst his female acquaintances the measures of headquarters . . ." Robertson, "an accomplished thief," and his partner, Oliver Delancey, extorted profits from civilians by abolishing courts, seizing control of all trade to and from the city, confiscating estates and diverting public funds to their own use. The profits of these two, gossips said, were "lavished away, and squandered upon favourites, upon little misses, upon strumpets, panderers and hangers-on;

in balls, dances, in rents, and feasts, in making walls, laying walks, illuminating trees, building music galleries and in every other kind of dissipation that two old souls could imagine."

Clinton, when faced with complaints and investigations of his command, said coolly: "That the expense is enormous is certain . . . that commissioners and contractors make fortunes—true. But in what war have they not done so?"

Washington resorted to elaborate ruses in hopes of deluding the enemy. On August 19 his advance troops had burned barricades on the road to New York as if he planned to attack the city. He sent Colonel Moses Hazen's Canadian regiment to feign an assault on Staten Island, and a few days later sent his rear guard, Colonel Philip Van Cortlandt's New York regiment, in the same direction. Van Cortlandt's men hauled boats, pontoons and entrenching tools, and moved with their bands playing, wagoners shouting and cracking whips over plodding oxen, to draw the attention of every bystander. As this regiment left the Hudson, Washington took Van Cortlandt by the arm and led him down an empty road, where he gave him verbal orders in a low voice and passed him a written copy.

Washington revealed an unexpected relish for the attempted deception of his own men as well as enemy spies in the final hours before the army moved. He swore the staff to absolute secrecy: "If we do not deceive our own men, we will never deceive the enemy." Even Henry Knox wrote his wife that he could not tell her Washington's destination: "We don't know it ourselves." Count Deux-Ponts grumbled as he led his men from camp at Phillipsburg on Washington's guarded orders: "We do not know the object of our march, and are in perfect ignorance whether we are going against New York or . . . to Virginia . . ."

Jonathan Trumbull, Jr., the general's new secretary, made numerous copies of a letter to state governors, which Washington ordered held to the last moment, in order to preserve secrecy. Even the staff was baffled by the general's closely kept plans, but Trumbull was delighted: "No movement perhaps was ever attended with more conjectures . . . some were indeed laughable, but not one I believe penetrated the real design."

"The Mask Is Being Raised!"

Washington had outlined his strategy for the governors and hinted at his hopes. ". . . should the time for the fleet's arrival prove favorable, and should the enemy under Cornwallis hold their present position in Virginia . . . we will have the fairest opportunity to reduce the whole British force in the south."

Dr. James Thacher was excited by the secret:

> Our situation reminds me of some theatrical exhibition, where the interest and expectations of the spectators are constantly increasing, and where curiosity is wrought to the highest point. . . . Bets have run high on one side, that we were to occupy the ground marked out on the Jersey shore, to aid in the siege of New York, and on the other, that we are stealing a march on the enemy, and are actually destined to Virginia.

The armies began the long march southward at last on August 25, in three columns, through the villages of Paramus and Springfield, Pompton, Suffern, Parsippany and Chatham. Even as they left, Washington's troops looked apprehensively rearward toward New York, but the enemy was strangely indolent. Count Deux-Ponts was incredulous: "An enemy of any boldness or any skill would have seized an opportunity so favorable for him and so embarrassing for us. . . . I do not understand the indifference with which General Clinton considers our movements."

When Rochambeau's troops reached Pompton, N.J., Count Deux-Ponts was still puzzled: "I cannot make up my mind as to the object of our march. I am inclined to believe that the Americans will attack one of the two points which they are threatening . . ." A day later, at Whippany, Deux-Ponts wrote, "I learned, under the strictest secrecy . . . that all the maneuvers by which we threaten New York are only a feint, that Lord Cornwallis is the real object of our marches . . ."

Baron Ludwig von Closen, riding with the French column, realized that Washington's goal was not New York, but Virginia. "The mask is being raised!" he wrote.

Washington continued his elaborate ruses for several days, even after the infantry had passed through Brunswick. Small units were turned into byroads to mislead the British, whose pickets were often within sight. Frenchmen worked in the open, under the pretext of building ovens at Chatham, as if for a winter encampment. Officers prowled about the waterfront, asking for small boats. Washington himself questioned a farmer closely about roads to Staten Island. A typical order to an artillery unit would have revealed little even to the enemy: "You will march through the Scotch Plain, Quibble Town, and Bound Brook. On the 30th to Princeton, 31st to Trenton, where you will meet me and further orders. You will keep these orders a perfect secret." False dispatches were sent by several couriers, in the hope that they would fall into enemy hands. It was years later before Washington offered an explanation:

> . . . much trouble was taken, and finesse used, to misguide and bewilder Sir Henry Clinton . . . by fictitious communications as well as by making a deceptive provision of ovens, forage, and boats, in his neighborhood . . . Nor, was less pains taken to deceive our own army; for, I had always conceived, when the imposition does not completely take place at home, it would never sufficiently succeed abroad.

Washington's mood of expectancy was tempered with the old anxieties almost to the last. He wrote Maryland's governor, Thomas Sims Lee, "the moment is critical, the opportunity precious, the prospects most happily favorable." But on the same day, as he rode among grim-faced men in camps around Chatham, he feared that they might break into mutiny when they finally realized that they were bound for Virginia. He wrote urgently to Robert Morris, begging him to raise one month's pay for the army, ". . . part of these troops have not been paid anything for a long time past, and have on several occasions shown marks of great discontent. The service they are going on is disagreeable to the northern regiments; but I make no doubt that a *douceur* of a little hard money would put them in proper temper."

As the troops passed through Morristown, hurrying southward toward Trenton, Washington had an alarming message from General David Forman, who had an outpost near Sandy Hook: eighteen large British ships had arrived during the day, enough to swell the total to twenty-nine and challenge De Grasse. It was two days later before Forman reported that the enemy fleet was only twenty-two strong, still inferior to the French.

Once the main force of Americans was nearing Princeton, Washington abandoned his efforts at deception and invited Rochambeau to join him in the college town for dinner the next day. Soldiers tossed their packs on wagons and the columns increased their speed. Von Closen took boyish delight in confirmation of the news when it reached French headquarters. "How happy I was when the General told me to accompany him to Philadelphia! The disguise is gradually going to be removed from our campaign." Dr. Thacher also rejoiced: ". . . the deception has proved completely successful . . . the menacing aspect of an attack on New York will be continued till time and circumstance shall remove the delusive veil from the eyes of Sir Henry Clinton, when it will probably be too late . . ."

Rochambeau and Washington spent the night of August 29 in Trenton, left at daybreak the next morning and crossed the Delaware into Pennsylvania. Washington noted in his diary for the day only that "I set myself out for Philadelphia to arrange matters there."

Clinton's bewilderment persisted in the face of mounting evidence from his spies. On August 27 he wrote Cornwallis: "I cannot well ascertain Mr. Washington's real intentions . . ." He surmised that the rebels were going into winter quarters at Morristown. Two days later he had a positive report from "Squib": "The Chesapeake is the Object. All in motion." But the next day Clinton advised Cornwallis that Washington was still near Chatham, "and I do not hear that he has yet detached to the southward." Washington was entering Philadelphia as Clinton sent off this message.

On September 1, at last, the British fleet left New York. Twenty-four hours later Clinton grasped for the first time the design of the allied campaign. He wrote Cornwallis:

New York, Sept. 2, 1781
Mr. Washington is moving an army to the southward, with an appearance of haste; and gives out that he expects the cooperation

of a considerable French armament. Your Lordship, however, may be assured that if this should be the case, I shall endeavor to reinforce your command by all means within the compass of my power; or, make every possible diversion in your favor. . . .

Years later Henry Clinton offered a remarkable explanation of his fateful indecisiveness as Washington and Rochambeau slipped away from him: "I will not pay Mr. Washington's understanding so bad a compliment as to suppose he thought it necessary to deceive me . . . for he too well knew I was in no capacity to intercept his March to the Southward, whenever he pleased to make it. . . ."

25

CONCENTRATION IN THE CHESAPEAKE

"Keep Lord Cornwallis Safe"

Philadelphia greeted the general as a conquering hero, as if the campaign and the war were already won. A troop of militia horsemen met Washington in the country and escorted him to City Tavern, past crowds of civilians who were obviously reassured at the sight of the Virginian. Chastellux had noted that all Americans seemed to find something comforting in the presence of the tall, expressionless rider who sat his saddle with an ease born of a lifetime of fox hunting, "He has not the imposing pomp of a *Maréchal de France* who gives *the order*. A hero in a republic, he excites another sort of respect." Every civilian who glimpsed Washington, Chastellux observed, felt that his own safety and the future of his family depended solely on the resolute general who had won so few victories.

Today, as usual, Washington's horsemanship drew attention. As Chastellux had noted, the general rode at a gallop whenever possible, even when there was no hurry: "He is a very excellent and bold horseman, leaping the highest fences and going extremely quick without standing upon his stirrups, bearing on the bridle, or letting his horse run wild."

The militia company was pressed to keep pace with the general until he dismounted at City Tavern, where he shook hands with congressmen, city officials and "all the notables," and went inside briefly to drink rum punch. He rode to the home of Robert Morris, where he was to stay, a mansion oddly empty, since the Morris family was away for the summer and had left little furniture behind. The only spare bed was for Washington himself. His aides were forced to sleep on the floor.

In the afternoon the general went to the State House and delivered a brief speech to Congress, remarks that were not recorded. It was more than six years since he had accepted command of the army in this crowded room—a day, as he had emotionally told Patrick Henry, that marked "the ruin of my reputation." The general evidently said nothing publicly of shortages of money, food and clothing for his grumbling troops, nor of the uncertainties of the campaign.

Morris entertained a brilliant company of officers and congressmen at dinner. Among the guests were Washington and Rochambeau, Chastellux, President Thomas McKean of Congress, and Generals Knox, Sullivan and Moultrie. The diners were served "all the foreign wines possible," and toasted the Kings of France and Spain, the United States, the allied armies, and the speedy arrival of Admiral de Grasse. Thomas McKean toasted an inevitable French victory over the British: "Where lilies flourish, roses fade," he said. The city celebrated during the meal with bonfires, crowds surged through the streets bearing torches, and cannon fired salutes from the waterfront.

Afterward, Washington walked through the city, followed by a mob "eagerly pressing to see their beloved general." But even here were some Loyalists who did not join the cheers. One Tory onlooker wrote bitterly,

> I saw this man, great as an instrument of destruction and devastation to the property, morals and principles of the people . . . walking the street, attended by a concourse of men, women and boys who huzzaed him and broke some of my father's windows and others near us.

The people of Philadelphia crowded the walks to watch the American troops pass through on September 1, a hot Sunday afternoon. The column was almost two miles long—grim-faced men in rags, many of them barefoot, veterans who had not been paid in months, made mutinous by the sight of Philadelphia's prosperous, carefree civilians. "Great symptoms of discontent . . . appeared on their passage through the city," an officer said. But though the civilians were shocked by the appearance of Washington's soldiers, a Frenchman felt that they were more formidable than they looked. Many of them wore filthy rags, but their muskets were in good order and they seemed to be ready for a fight: "The plainly dressed American army lost no credit in the steadiness of their march and their fitness for battle."

Dr. Thacher found the march through the city streets unpleasant: "We raised a dust like a smothering snow-storm; this was not a little mortifying as the ladies were viewing us from the open windows of every house we passed."

Washington had sobering news during the morning, a report from New York that a fleet of twenty British warships had put to sea. The general feared that the enemy might intercept De Barras coming down from Newport and bar the French from the Chesapeake; it was now almost a month since De Grasse had been heard from, announcing that he was leaving the West Indies. In this uncertainty Washington had no choice but to hurry the army southward, in the hope that he might still close the trap about Cornwallis by land and sea.

The next day, after halting outside Philadelphia to change into fresh uniforms, the French troops followed their bands through the city, sturdy men in white broadcloth whose silk lapels gleamed with regimental colors. Officers wore pink and white plumes on their caps. A French chaplain thought the passing column gave these civilians a new appreciation of their allies: "All Philadelphia was astonished to see people who had endured the fatigues of a long journey, so ruddy and handsome, and even wondered that there could possibly be Frenchmen of so genteel an appearance." Washington and Rochambeau stood with a few congressmen at the State House to review the French, who passed in single file, saluting in turn. The civilians, uncertain of military etiquette, asked a French officer for advice and were told that the King always returned salutes. The officer was amused by the result—Thomas McKean, the president of Congress, doffed his broad-brimmed black Quaker hat to each soldier, bowing so low that he seemed in danger of toppling forward on his head. He was imitated by the others with a great flopping of hats: "The thirteen members took off their thirteen hats at each salute."

The next day more than twenty thousand people flocked to the French camp in a meadow beside the Schuylkill to watch a regiment in formal drill. The civilians admired the colorful files as they marched and wheeled in precision—particularly a messenger whom they mistook for the commander, a boy who carried a huge silver-headed cane and strode haughtily about in rose-colored shoes and a coat embroidered in silver. Philadelphians were unaware that these troops were also mutinous, and were being driven southward only by the will of the watchful Rochambeau. Count Fersen confessed: "Our army, unfortunately, is as little disciplined as the French army always is . . . Our chiefs are very strict, and not a day passes that there are not some two or three officers placed under arrest." More than once, Fersen had seen these unruly troops defy their officers in "some lamentable scenes where a whole corps of men ought to have been cashiered, but as we only number five thousand we cannot afford to lose a man . . ."

Rochambeau doubled the guard around the camp that night to prevent his men from deserting, for many of them had been visited by relatives who had migrated to America and were now living in Pennsylvania.

A fresh round of parties followed the review, opening with a dinner for a hundred and eighty guests at the home of the French minister, the Chevalier de La Luzerne, who borrowed thirty cooks from Rochambeau's army for the occasion. Joseph Reed, who was now president of the Pennsylvania Congress, entertained officers with a "sumptuous, spectacular" banquet whose main dish, a ninety-pound turtle, was admired by French epicures: "The soup was served in an immense shell, and the fat, seasoned and peppered, had the taste of consomme."

The restless Washington was eager to be off. He wrote ahead to civilian officials in Maryland and Virginia, urging them to gather supplies and boats for the armies, and to fill mudholes and ruts in roads his wagons and guns must travel.

Lafayette had reported that Cornwallis, who had occupied the

"Keep Lord Cornwallis Safe"

village of Yorktown on August 1, had settled there and had not yet taken alarm; the British were not even fortifying the place. Washington responded in a long letter, promising to hurry arms, food and clothing to the young Frenchman's worn troops. The general could not conceal his apprehension:

> But, my dear Marquis, I am distressed beyond expression to know what has become of the Count de Grasse, and for fear that the English fleet, by occupying the Chesapeake . . . may frustrate all our flattering prospects . . . Should the retreat of Lord Cornwallis by water be cut off, I am persuaded you will do all in your power to prevent his escape by land. . . .
>
> You see how critically important the present moment is . . . adieu, my dear Marquis. If you get any thing new from any quarter, send it I pray you, on the spur of speed for I am almost all impatience and anxiety . . .

Washington was forced to deal with other problems as he prepared to leave Philadelphia. Henry Knox, whose gunners had come south with only twelve wagons of ammunition, fumed at officials of "the vile and water-gruel" state governments, who did not seem to realize that the crisis of the war was at hand. The exasperated Robert Morris warned that the states would be to blame if the campaign against Cornwallis failed, "If they will not exert themselves upon the present occasion, they never will." Washington agreed, "Certainly, certainly, the people have lost their ardor in attempting to secure their Liberty and Happiness." Knox besieged the Board of War, but it was helpless to fill his needs: 300,000 cartridges, 20,000 flints, 1,000 powder horns, and much more. Morris, who had been ordered to gather small boats to ferry seven thousand troops down the Chesapeake, had found enough for no more than two thousand.

John Laurens, who had just returned from a mission to Paris, met Washington in the city with news that a shipment of French money was on its way, a treasure of six million livres, recently landed in Boston and on the way overland in heavily guarded wagons. But this silver horde was weeks away. The army must continue its march southward, and Lincoln's troops threatened to halt unless they were paid.

Washington urged Morris to find money immediately, and the

banker turned to the French, who refused him. Rochambeau had only $40,000 in his chests, he said—too little to pay his own troops. But the persistent Morris rode south with the French to follow Rochambeau's treasurer. "We must have money for the men," he said, "or it's all over with us." The French were his last hope. He had exhausted other resources in the city and had already endangered his substantial private fortune: "The late movements of the army have so entirely drained me of money that I have been obliged to pledge my personal credit very deeply . . . besides borrowing money from my friends and advancing every shilling of my own."

On September 5 the army's mood of frustration and uncertainty was abruptly changed by electrifying news from Virginia. As Washington rode through the village of Chester, a few miles south of Philadelphia, a dispatch rider brought a message from De Grasse: the French fleet had sailed into the Chesapeake. Cornwallis was cut off by sea. If Lafayette could hold the enemy in place at Yorktown until Washington and Rochambeau joined him, the British army was doomed.

Count Deux-Ponts, who had seen Washington self-possessed and unsmiling in his "naturally cold" manner only a moment before, now saw him transformed: ". . . his features, his expression, his whole carriage were changed in an instant . . . like a child whose every wish had been gratified. I have never seen a man more overcome with great and sincere joy."

For once Washington's reserve had vanished, melted by the prospect that this campaign would bring victory at last. The general wheeled his horse to take the news to Rochambeau, waving his hat in one hand and a handkerchief in the other, shouting like an excited boy. Rochambeau was astonished to be clasped in a fierce embrace by the big Virginian.

Washington wrote a reply to De Grasse, promising that he would arrive in Virginia almost as soon as his letter reached the fleet. He also issued a triumphant order to the troops, hinting at "glorious events" that lay ahead and urging officers and men to "exert their utmost abilities in the cause of their country, to share with him . . . the difficulties, dangers, and glory of the enterprise."

"Keep Lord Cornwallis Safe"

Washington's men had other cause for celebration. The French treasurer succumbed to the news from De Grasse, and Robert Morris took money to Chester, 144,000 livres in kegs, most of it in half crowns, a silver rain of French treasure that officers poured upon the ground before the eyes of the cheering troops.

Major William Popham of New York wrote, "This day will be famous in the annals of history for being the first in which the Troops of the United States received one month's pay in specie." Von Closen said that the glimpse of the silver coins "raised spirits to the required level," and there was no longer talk of mutiny in the American camp.

This transaction by Morris was a bit of legerdemain—his only hope of retiring the loan was to offer Rochambeau some of the French silver en route from the north, so that Washington's allies were to be repaid with their own money. (Apparently this loan was never repaid.)

Washington watched as French infantry and artillerymen embarked from the Elk River on the upper Chesapeake—men, guns and horses loaded aboard tiny civilian craft, oyster boats, scows, grain-hauling sloops and schooners. The raffish little fleet moved off on September 8, beating its way down the bay under a stiff breeze, many of the overburdened vessels awash almost to the gunwales. The rest of the army marched overland toward Virginia.

By now, the trap fashioned by Rochambeau was closing about Cornwallis in Yorktown. Admiral de Grasse had sailed northward from San Domingo on August 5 with an armada of thirty-nine ships, a fleet piloted by twenty-five Americans who were familiar with Chesapeake waters.

Like all other fighting ships of the day, the French vessels wallowing toward Virginia were little more than clumsy gun platforms, broad-beamed, difficult to maneuver and top-heavy under a vast weight of canvas that towered as much as two hundred feet above the waterline. The primitive smooth-bore cannon, elevated by guesswork without locks or sights, hurled more than a half-ton of metal in each broadside. In battle, crewmen were penned—often locked—with the guns in cramped cribs between decks, where they were often slaughtered by enemy broadsides that plunged through the fragile wooden hulls in a hail of iron and splintered oak.

The French fleet carried the infantry demanded by Rochambeau, three regiments under the Marquis Claude Henri de Saint-Simon, reinforced by cavalrymen and artillerymen. There were also chests of money and jewels raised in Havana, whose Spanish citizens had responded with wild enthusiasm to the admiral's appeal, and donated 1,200,000 livres within six hours; women of the city had contributed their diamonds to aid the American cause.

As he swept northward, capturing stray vessels in his path to preserve secrecy, De Grasse saw nothing of the British fleet posted in the Indies under Admiral Samuel Hood. The way to the Chesapeake was open.

François Joseph Paul de Grasse-Tilly, the most veteran French admiral, had fought the British since his youth. Though he tended to corpulence, De Grasse was said to be one of the handsomest Frenchmen of his day. The admiral was six feet two inches tall, but as his sailors said, he stood six feet six on days of battle, an enormous grim-faced and haughty nobleman from Provence whose severity cowed his captains.

The French fleet came to anchor inside the Chesapeake capes on September 1, and within a few hours forty small boats were carrying Saint-Simon's four thousand troops up the James River to join Lafayette. On September 4 the reinforced Virginia army of eighty-five hundred was led into Williamsburg by the young marquis, who wrote Washington to congratulate him upon the arrival of the French fleet, adding, "Thanks to you, my dear General, I am in a very charming situation and find myself at the head of a Beautiful body of Troops."

The boy general grasped the importance of holding Cornwallis in place until Washington arrived with the main army. He was confident of his own security:

> Williamsburg and its strong buildings are in our front . . .
> There is a line of armed Ships along James River, and a small
> reserve of militia . . . Should Lord Cornwallis come out against

such a position as we have everybody thinks that he cannot but repent of it.

On September 8 Washington left Lincoln in command of the troops on the upper Chesapeake and continued southward with Rochambeau and Chastellux, riding so rapidly that he soon outdistanced the Frenchmen. Accompanied only by Billy Lee, the general rode into Baltimore at nightfall, to a welcome from city militia and salutes by artillery. An admiring crowd gathered before his lodgings at the Fountain Inn, a local official read an address of welcome and Washington responded briefly. The city was illuminated by candles in windows and torches borne through the streets.

The general was off once more before dawn. Accompanied only by his secretary, David Humphreys, and Billy Lee, he completed an exhausting sixty-mile ride to Mount Vernon after sunset. It was his first sight of home in almost six and a half years. Among the crowd that greeted him were four of Martha's new grandchildren born during the war, children of Jacky Custis. The general wrote several dispatches before he retired, and in the morning worked with his farm manager. Rochambeau, Chastellux and the staffs arrived during the day, and Mount Vernon's neighbors were invited to dine with the officers. Chastellux thought Washington's manor house "simple," but John Trumbull, making his first visit to the South, had only praise for plantation life: "A numerous family now present. All accommodated. An elegant seat and situation, great appearance of opulence and real exhibitions of hospitality and princely entertainment."

After two days the anxious commander prepared to leave, but he had first to deal with Jacky Custis, who begged to go to Yorktown. The general reluctantly agreed to take his stepson along. The indolent, weak-chinned Jacky was not a favorite with the general, who felt that the boy had been spoiled by his mother. Jacky's schoolmaster had said of him, "I never did in my life know a youth so exceedingly indolent or so surprisingly voluptuous: one would suppose Nature had intended him for some Asiatic Prince." The boy already exhibited traits of the eccentric Custis clan—he had taught his tiny daughter, Elizabeth Parke, to sing obscene verses to parties of his drinking companions and household servants, who roared with laughter at the antics of the innocent child. To the protest of his wife, Jacky replied, "I've been given no son, and little Bet must make fun for me until I have one."

Riders from Mount Vernon took Washington's orders to militia officers and pleas to governors of nearby states, urging that they send food and clothing and crews to repair roads and river landings.

He advised Lafayette that he was on the way and added, "I hope you will keep Lord Cornwallis safe, without provisions or Forage until we arrive."

Washington was on the road through northern Virginia, near the village of Dumfries, when a courier brought disturbing news: the French fleet had left the Chesapeake, fought the British at sea, and disappeared. The outcome of the battle was unknown. The general seemed shaken by this news. "Much agitated," John Trumbull wrote in his diary.

The vigil of the French fleet came to an end on the early morning of September 5, when De Grasse's lookouts sighted the British fleet—twenty warships under Admiral Graves bearing for the capes under full sail. Though eight ships were off on other errands, and two thousand seamen were ashore to find water and firewood, De Grasse ordered his fleet to the attack.

The twenty-four remaining French ships began to emerge from the Chesapeake at noon, when the tide turned outward, led by swift vessels of Commodore Louis Antoine de Bougainville, a veteran already renowned for his voyages of discovery in the Pacific. The British might have fallen upon these isolated ships, but Graves dallied and hesitated, wasting hours in maneuvering. Though his leading ships were separated from the fleet, and the British had the advantage of wind and tide, Bougainville closed with the enemy at close range.

The French gunners, as was their habit, fired into the rigging, and when masts crashed and sails flopped to the decks, immobilizing the British ships, Bougainville's crews blasted the hulls, killing and maiming men below and wreaking havoc with the *Shrewsbury.* This leading British ship lost her captain, first lieutenant and thirteen seamen in the opening broadsides, and soon lost fifty more men. The ship dropped out of the battle, and the next in line, *The Intrepid,* was riddled as she came forward to shield the cripple, and was also put out of action.

French casualties were also serious, and the *Réfléchi* and *Diadème* also dropped out of the battle. Bougainville continued to press the enemy and, amid rolling broadsides, drove his flagship almost into the wounded British *Terrible.*

There was a lull after an hour of fierce fighting when the central divisions of the fleets dueled at longer range with few hits. It was all over, in about two hours, when Graves hauled down his signal flag for attack and the fleets drifted seaward in parallel lines. The night passed with the ships within sight of one another, and gunners standing by with ready matches. Carpenters began repairs in both fleets.

Graves found that three of his ships could no longer keep up, a fourth was in danger of losing her main topmast, and two others, *Terrible* and *Ajax,* were leaking badly, struggling to stay afloat with all pumps at work. The French now had a numerical advantage of ten or eleven ships. Graves had lost 90 men killed and about 250 wounded; total French casualties were 209.

The fleets drifted for four days, until they lost sight of each other off the North Carolina coast near Cape Hatteras. Neither commander dared to attack, and the British admirals had spent their time in squabbling. Samuel Hood accused Graves of failure to seize an opportunity to destroy the French fleet at a time when it was vulnerable, and denounced his commander for his "great dilatoriness" and "shyness."

On September 11 the *Terrible* was burned, in sinking condition, and the British turned back to the Chesapeake capes. When Graves saw that De Grasse had already returned and blocked the entrance, he turned back toward New York in defeat.

When Washington reached Williamsburg, Lafayette was abed with fever, depressed and exhausted after four months of campaigning against Cornwallis and struggling to compel Virginians to supply his army. Only two days earlier the young Frenchman had written Thomas Nelson, Jr., the new governor who had replaced Thomas Jefferson during the British cavalry raid on Monticello and Charlottesville:

> I could wish to sleep tonight but I fear it will be impossible with the prospect which is before us tomorrow. There is not one grain of flour in camp either for the American or French army. What we are to do I know not . . . Has your Excellency any hopes for tomorrow? I am distressed in the extreme, in a thousand ways and without the power of offering either myself or the soldiers the smallest relief.

But at the moment Washington arrived Lafayette was miraculously cured, and the war in Virginia was transformed. The commander had appeared with Rochambeau at the edge of the village when Lafayette galloped toward them along the sandy street, reined abruptly and threw himself into Washington's arms. The Virginia Major St. George Tucker never forgot the French boy's emotional welcome of Washington: "He . . . opened both his arms as wide as he could reach, and caught the General round his body, hugged him as close as it was possible, and absolutely kissed him from ear to ear once or twice."

Williamsburg was familiar to Washington as a second home. He reviewed French troops on the grounds of the College of William and Mary, where he had won his surveyor's license as a boy of seventeen. The central building of the school, almost a century old, now wore a forlorn look. French troops were quartered and hospitalized there, and a huge three-story privy of rough scaffolding was raised across the front. An American physician, Dr. James Tilton, was amazed by this addition: "Doors opened upon each floor of the hospital; and all manner of filth and excrementitious matters were dropped and thrown down this common sewer, into the pit below. This sink of nastiness perfumed the whole house . . . and all the air within the wards."

The general passed Bruton Parish Church, in whose box pews he had so often sat, one of the last times in 1774 when he had gone with other Virginia leaders to join in a day of fasting and prayer as a protest against British closure of the port of Boston. Half a mile to the east, down Duke of Gloucester Street, he saw the capitol where he had served as a burgess for twenty years, and beyond Palace Green, the governor's palace, abandoned after Governor Jefferson moved the capital to Richmond, but little changed since the general had first seen it more than thirty years before. Washington halted on Palace Green, to make headquarters in the brick house adjoining Bruton Church—the home of George Wythe, Jefferson's old law professor, who had been a signer of the Declaration of Independence. Rochambeau settled in a white house facing Market Square, the home of the widow, Mrs. Peyton Randolph, whose husband had been the first president of Congress.

Still anxious over lack of news from De Grasse, Washington went with Rochambeau and other officers to the quarters of Saint-Simon, where a band played operatic airs in tribute to the American general, and the officers of Lafayette's band filed past to be introduced and shake hands with Rochambeau and Washington. In the evening Saint-Simon's stewards served a lavish supper, with fine French wines.

Reassuring news from De Grasse arrived during the banquet: he was back at his anchorage after having fought off the British. Hardly less important, Admiral de Barras and his fleet had arrived from the north, bringing heavy siege artillery, provisions and barges to speed the movement of allied troops down the Chesapeake. Washington did not yet appreciate the decisiveness of the brief battle at sea, which he spoke of as "a partial engagement," but it was clear that the last major route of escape was closed to Cornwallis. The arrival of De Grasse all but completed the complex strategic plan over which Washington and Rochambeau had wrangled in the spring. But even now, when victory over Cornwallis seemed certain, Washington was not content. He reported De Grasse's victory over the British fleet to Congress, but warned that his army's supplies were so short as to hamper his planned march against Yorktown: "How far I shall succeed in my endeavors time must discover."

To hold Cornwallis in position, Washington placed a line of picket boats in the York River and sent a force of Virginia militia under Brigadier General George Weedon to keep watch on the British outpost at Gloucester Point. He ordered more troops from the north as reinforcements, begged Virginia officials to send uniforms to their ragged militia, and negotiated with Virginia farmers who refused to sell grain to the army unless they were paid in French gold or silver.

The general wrote urgently to General Lincoln in Maryland: "Every day we now lose is comparatively an age. As soon as it is in our power with safety, we ought to take our position near the enemy. Hurry on, then, my dear Sir, with your troops on the wings of speed." In Yorktown, a dozen miles east of Williamsburg, Cornwallis was steadily improving his defenses, and every day's delay meant the cost of more allied lives.

Washington's uneasiness was increased by another dispatch from De Grasse, delivered after midnight of September 14, an imperious letter announcing that the admiral was "annoyed" by the slow progress of the army, and that he must soon sail to avoid autumnal storms. "The season is approaching when, against my will, I shall be obliged to forsake the allies for whom I have done my very best and more than could be expected." Washington was stunned.

On September 17 he left the army in Williamsburg to visit De Grasse, determined to convince the admiral that he must remain in the Chesapeake until Cornwallis surrendered, or all was lost. Washington, Rochambeau, Knox, John Trumbull and several aides sailed down the James and across the open Chesapeake in a small captured British cutter, the *Queen Charlotte*. In Lynnhaven Bay they approached the huge thirty-six line of battle ships of the combined French fleet, an impressive array of sea power such as the American officers had never seen. The party boarded the towering triple-decker flagship *Ville de Paris*, which was said to be the largest warship afloat, and on her deck amused American officers watched as the admiral clasped Washington in an impetuous greeting that was to become part of the army's stock of Washington legends. De Grasse, enormously fat and an inch or so shorter than Washington, clasped the Virginian, kissed him on the cheeks and cried, *"Mon cher petit General!"*

The admiral's geniality survived a conference on strategy con-

ducted through interpreters. Washington pointed out that Yorktown could be taken by storm within a few days, but at the cost
of heavy casualties. If the fleet remained until the end of October,
there would be time for an orthodox siege, which would save
allied lives. De Grasse agreed; he had orders to leave the American coast by October 15, but he would remain two weeks longer
on his own responsibility. He also offered two thousand sailors
to join an attack on the village if that became necessary. When
Washington asked that French ships sail up York River above
Yorktown, to close the noose more tightly about Cornwallis, De
Grasse said the waters were dangerous but he agreed to recon-
noiter and consider the move.

Washington was satisfied. The armies had almost six weeks to
force the surrender of Cornwallis. The general was anxious to
return to Williamsburg, but there were interminable delays. De
Grasse entertained the Americans at dinner, conducted a tour of
the flagship, and invited the captains of the fleet to meet Washington. It was near sunset when the guests escaped to the *Queen
Charlotte* and sailed westward, saluted by the fleet's broadsides
and cheered by thousands of French sailors who had clambered
into the rigging to fire their muskets. The cutter was first buf-
feted by strong headwinds, then becalmed, and finally grounded
on a sandbar, where Washington and his party were forced to
spend the night. The party transferred to a frigate the next day,
then returned to the *Queen Charlotte* when she was refloated, but
the small craft was forced to anchor near shore to ride out a
storm.

Washington spent September 21 in misery aboard the anchored
craft. At his insistence, the cutter's captain tried to sail upriver,
but choppy waters forced him to turn back toward shore. The
cutter rocked at this anchorage overnight, until Washington and
his party left her at last, to be rowed up the James in an open
boat, hugging shore to escape the full force of the wind. It was
noon of September 22 before the general rode back into Williamsburg. Six hours aboard De Grasse's flagship had kept him from
headquarters for almost five days. He was relieved to find that
the village had been filling with troops during the week and that
the British remained quietly in Yorktown. Big guns, ammunition

and supplies were piling up at landings along the James. "Happy circumstance," Trumbull wrote.

Washington's spirits lifted: "Lord Cornwallis is incessantly at work on his fortifications, and is probably preparing to defend himself to the last extremity; a little time will probably decide his fate; with the blessing of Heaven, I feel it will be favorable to the interests of America."

A dispatch from the north brought word of British naval reinforcements in New York, but since these were vaguely reported at from three to ten more enemy ships, Washington was not alarmed, since the French still held clear superiority. Still, he sent word to De Grasse by Baron von Closen, who found that the news "alarmed and disquieted these excitable gentlemen of the navy, who think only of cruises and battles, and do not like to oblige or to cooperate with land troops." Urged by his officers, the mercurial De Grasse wrote Washington that he must leave the Chesapeake on the first favorable wind. Since the enemy in American waters was now nearly his equal in strength, the admiral said, he would cruise in the open sea, ready to fight. He warned that contrary winds might prevent his return.

Washington protested immediately:

> I am unable to describe the painful anxiety under which I have labored since the reception of your letter . . . the attempt upon York under the protection of your shipping, is as certain of success, as a superior force . . . can render any military operation . . . the capture of the British army is so important in itself . . . that it must greatly tend to bring an end to the war . . . If you quit the Bay . . . The consequence will be the disgrace of abandoning a design on which are founded the fairest hopes of the allied forces, after a prodigious expense, fatigue, and exertions . . . your leaving the Bay ruins the cause to all intents and purposes. Consider the good of the common cause. . . .

The general entrusted this message to Lafayette, and urged him to beg the admiral to hold his position.

Washington opened a reply from De Grasse on September 27, an exasperatingly casual report of a council of war in which the admiral was overruled by his officers, ". . . The plans I had suggested for getting underway, while the most brilliant and glorious, did not appear to fulfill the aims we had in view." The fleet would remain in the bay. Cornwallis was still blocked by sea. With that the admiral subsided, but Washington remained watchful. He conceded that De Grasse was brave, but was impetuous. Rochambeau agreed: "By the vivacity of his head, he always did take violent parts."

Omens of the approaching crisis multiplied in Yorktown after Cornwallis learned of the arrival of De Grasse. Labor parties toiled day and night. Corporal Stephan Popp of the German Bayreuth regiment protested, "We hardly had time for eating. Often we had to eat raw meat." Other German troops worked in the harbor, stripping cannon from warships and moving them into the trenches on the land side, where the allies must attack. The earl's secretaries busily made copies of dispatches bearing the chilling news in cipher, some of them written on Continental bank notes, coded numbers bearing the message: "An enemy's fleet within the Capes, between thirty and forty ships of war, mostly large." These messages were sent up the coast in small dispatch boats, whaleboats and galleys, rowed by crews of eight to a dozen men, up the long route of the Virginia, Maryland, Delaware and New Jersey coasts, into New York. Five days after leaving Yorktown, the news reached Henry Clinton.

Men began dying of fever, and a few soldiers deserted to the allies. One of these, a Private Froelich, was caught and made to run the gauntlet twenty-six times in two days, forced to scamper for his life as three hundred of his companions flailed at him with clubs and musket butts. The punishment continued until Froelich could no longer crawl.

The roll of cannon from seaward on September 5 caused no alarm in Yorktown; Cornwallis learned only three days later that Admiral Graves had come, and the sea action was dismissed as "some slight skirmish" from which the British had withdrawn. The earl reported cheerfully to Clinton, "I am now working very hard at the redoubts of the place. The Army is not very sickly. Provisions for six weeks. I will be very careful of it." But the Hessian Private Johann Doehla noted in his diary on September 11, "we get terrible provision now, putrid ships meat and wormy biscuits that have spoiled on the ships."

CONCENTRATION IN THE CHESAPEAKE

British staff officers in Yorktown were alarmed by the indolence of Cornwallis. Colonel Banastre Tarleton argued that Clinton could not send a relief force, and that the garrison should attack the allies before they gathered in full strength. Tarleton's brother dramatized the futility of defending the town against a siege by jumping over the earthworks. Cornwallis responded languidly, "In that case, the blame will fall on Clinton, and not on us."

Even so, the Tarletons had persuaded Cornwallis to attack Lafayette's force in Williamsburg, and the movement was under way when it was halted by the arrival of two dispatches from Clinton: ". . . it would seem that Mr. Washington is moving an army to the Southward . . . Your Lordship . . . may be assured that . . . I shall . . . reinforce the army under your command." The second dispatch estimated Washington's force at six thousand, and promised a British reinforcement of four thousand men, who were already embarked on ships in New York harbor. To Tarleton's dismay, Cornwallis canceled the planned attack on Williamsburg, almost at the time Washington arrived in the colonial capital.

Lanterns now burned all night as troops and Negroes worked on the Yorktown defenses. Houses were pulled down, trees were cut and ground was leveled to give gunners clear fields of fire. Log palisades rose before the trenches. Lieutenant Bartholomew James, a navy gunner, was cheered by the burst of activity. "Preparations on all sides going on with great expectation and life, and full of the hopes . . . of a relief by the arrival of a British fleet."

The allied troops struck their first blow on September 24, when a small rebel party crept from thickets, captured a German picket post, and vanished into the night.

The diarist Corporal Stephan Popp had not given up hope that the army could hold out until Clinton's relief fleet arrived from New York: "Day and night we are at work strengthening our lines—have little time to eat and little food, but we are getting ready to make a stout defense."

He added a somber afterthought, "There are reports we are in a very bad situation."

26

THE SIEGE OF YORKTOWN

*"The Liberties of America
Are in Our Hands"*

The army left Williamsburg at dawn of September 28 on the twelve-mile march to Yorktown, the last move of the campaign. So that they would not be shamed by the French, Washington's troops had been issued flour to powder their hair, and ordered to "look as neat and respectable as possible . . . take care to be well shaven."

The army was more impressive once it had taken to the road. The Pennsylvania lieutenant William Feltman, who overestimated American regulars at fifteen thousand, confessed that he could make no count of the militia swarms. A French engineer appraised the marching rebels:

> Six regiments of regulars, disciplined, hardened, and in condition to fight in the line . . . twenty-five hundred militiamen of the country; and five hundred riflemen or mountaineers . . . these last two troops are not in uniform, they wear baggy breeches with or without shoes . . . good marksmen for skirmishing in the woods, but not for fighting in the line . . .

The column threaded a sandy track through tangled growths of pine, holly and bayberry, occasionally splashing through tidal creeks that drained the marshes of the York River. The sun blazed down upon a quiet countryside during the noon halt, when the French and Americans divided into two columns, with the French taking the more direct road. There was no sign of the enemy until midafternoon, when leading French troops climbed onto a rolling sandy plain and saw the earthworks of Yorktown. Crescent lines of trenches and redoubts shielded the village from the land side, with their flanks anchored on the river, below and above the town. The key to the position was the broad plain of the center, whose approaches were commanded by British batteries.

When Washington rode out to study the familiar landscape through his glass, his troops were still filing into line across the fields. He had visited the town occasionally in his youth to gamble on cockfights and had sailed from its docks on his only foreign trip, to visit his dying brother Lawrence in Barbados. The village lay on land once owned by his first American ancestor, the Huguenot Nicholas Martiau (who was also to become a forebear of Elizabeth II of England).

Washington rode the front for several hours, studying enemy positions until they were lost in the dusk. He saw seven redoubts in the enemy's inner line and a crescent of sand embankments that guarded the outer works, all screened by barriers of sharpened logs and piles of brush. He saw British ships anchored offshore, and beyond, eastward, the dim lights of two or three French ships at anchor in the Chesapeake. He realized that it might be weeks before he could open a heavy bombardment of the village. Already a few of his cannon were moving up, dragged through the sand by long lines of men who toiled at ropes. The general was anxious for the arrival of the huge French mortars, most of them brought down by the fleet of De Barras.

The allied armies settled noisily into improvised encampments. Several dozen British and German deserters came out from Yorktown and were put under guard. Axes rang all night as trees were felled to build huts, and bridges to span marshy ravines. Men and officers alike slept in the open. Since his baggage had not come up, Washington slept under an old mulberry tree, probably disturbed by troops who hunted stray pigs most of the night. The woods behind the line were soon filled with the smell of roasting pork. The men also searched vainly for pure drinking water. Sergeant Martin, the explosives expert, took his buckets into a stagnant pond where horses were being watered, and returned to his campfire with water "thick with mud and filth . . . and full of frogs." Despite hardships, the army was in an optimistic mood. There was talk of an early victory at headquarters, and Dr. Thacher sensed "unbounded confidence in our . . . commanders" among the troops.

The American wing shifted position under British cannon fire the next day, but only one soldier was hit, a boy who screamed in agony for half an hour as Dr. Thacher amputated his mangled leg and tried to stanch the flow of blood. Washington rode the front once more under a blazing sun, exposing himself to enemy fire as he was to do throughout the siege. New tales of his coolness under fire soon became part of army folklore. As he rode in the open with his staff, British gunners fired on his party, which scattered as the shot flew overhead—except for Washington, who continued to sit his horse, studying the enemy line through his glass. The British did not fire again, though he remained in the spot for some time.

A few days later, as he led a group of officers along the front under fire, a cannonball fell nearby and showered a chaplain's hat with sand. The frightened minister held out his hat to Washington. "Mr. Evans," the general said, "you'd better carry that home, and show it to your wife and children."

During a brief daytime foray against the British lines when Washington stood in the open with Lincoln and Knox, he was urged by Colonel David Cobb of his staff to take cover: "Sir, you're too much exposed here. Hadn't you better step back a little?"

Washington replied tersely, "Colonel Cobb, if you are afraid, you have the liberty to step back." The group remained in the open.

Allied troops awoke to a surprise on the second day of the siege: Cornwallis had abandoned the outer line of his works. Washington was puzzled by the move but took immediate advantage of it. As he wrote John McKean, the president of Congress, "We are in possession of very advantageous grounds, which command their line of works." Troops moved quickly into the vacated line and American work parties began digging to extend the line.

Colonel Richard Butler of Pennsylvania realized that the army had much to learn, ". . . our works go on slow, the heavy artillery hard to get up; not one piece of cannon yet fired at them; indeed I discover very plainly that we are young soldiers in a siege; however, we are determined to benefit ourselves by experience; one virtue we possess, that is perseverance."

Washington realized that Cornwallis might escape over the York River by night, free to march through the undefended Virginia countryside to the north. When he reminded De Grasse that French ships should be sent into the York to aid in the siege, the admiral sent a curt reply:

> I am impatient as your Excellency can be that the Wind will not permit vessels . . . to ascend the York River. The Sea is not like the Land . . . and we have not yet found out a method of sailing against the Wind. But I assure your Excellency that the moment it can be done it shall be done, be it by day or night if the pilots will undertake it.

The French fleet was to remain at the Chesapeake capes, barring the entrance to the bay. The armies prepared for the siege without a blockade of the York River. Washington continued to find De Grasse difficult. Soon afterward, when Washington asked for a few pounds of artillery candles, the admiral replied testily, "Damn it! You have stretched the blanket too tight." He sent an immediate apology through Rochambeau, "I am a Provençal, and a sailor, which is enough to entitle me to a quick temper and I acknowledge my fault and trust in your friendship."

Washington's tents had now been pitched near the center of his line, the same canvas shelters he had bought in Philadelphia and carried to Cambridge so long ago. The gray tents were now worn by more than five years of campaigning. The general slept as usual on a hard cot in the inner chamber of the smaller tent, a few yards away from the coming and going of officers in the dining tent, where headquarters business was conducted by day and night. Headquarters were patrolled as usual by picked men of Washington's Life Guard, who screened every unrecognized visitor. Among the first orders issued from the tents at Yorktown was an exhortation to a final effort to end the war:

> The General . . . expects and requires the officers and soldiers to pursue the duties of their respective departments . . . with the most unabating ardour. The present moment . . . will decide American independence . . . the passive conduct of the enemy argues his weakness . . . the liberties of America and the honour of the Allied Arms are in our hands.

There was also a charge that the British were resorting to desperate measures:

> Our ungenerous enemy having, as usual, propagated the small-pox in this part of the country, the Commander-in-chief forbids . . . any communication, with the houses or inhabitants in the neighborhood, or borrowing any utensils from them.

The plight of the British in Yorktown had become obvious by October 1. A drove of starving horses shambled out from the village at dawn, and during the morning, officers in the American line saw six or seven hundred swollen carcasses floating in the York. From his post in the trenches the Hessian Corporal Popp had begun to realize that the army would not escape: "October 1. The enemy began to fortify heavily to really block us up. They threw no shots against us, because they had no cannon yet. But we fired steadily upon them and destroyed much of their labor again. We . . . had no rest day or night. . . ."

Near midnight British sentries caught a Negro deserter who tried to smuggle through the lines a message from a Yorktown merchant, a letter revealing the "state of the garrison's distress." The merchant was arrested at once. Cornwallis had received a dispatch from New York promising that Henry Clinton would soon sail with a force of five thousand men, and the earl replied with assurance, "I . . . have no doubt if relief arrives in any reasonable time, York and Gloucester will be both in possession of his majesty's troops."

But only two days later, on October 4, Cornwallis sent off a ciphered message to Clinton, acknowledging that he was surrounded and that his lines were constricted by new enemy fortifications:

> I expect they will go on with their Work this night. From the time that the Enemy have given us, and the uncommon exertion of the Troops our works are in a better state of defence than we had reason to hope.
>
> I can see no means of forming a junction with me but by York river, and I do not think that any diversion would be of use to us . . .

By now virtually all of Washington's troops were at work. Each morning a third of the army was marched into the woods to chop saplings and bind them into bundles for use in making earthworks. Huge mounds of fascines and gabions—wicker baskets woven from saplings—grew by the roadsides. Washington's anxiety to open fire on the enemy was expressed in an order to the army: ". . . it is of the utmost importance that the Heavy Artillery should be brought up without a moment's loss of time." He and other officers sent their own horses and wagons to the rear to help move guns and ammunition.

The general made his first offensive move on the night of October 6, in the midst of a cold rainstorm. Soon after dark a column of forty-three hundred men moved out from the American line and halted in the darkness only eight hundred yards from the British trenches, where fifteen hundred of them began digging. Within an hour or so the party had opened a new trench some two thousand yards long, running from the head of Yorktown Creek near the center of the enemy position in a long arc to the right, ending on the bluff overlooking the York. Joseph Martin, who had gone out with engineers the night before to stake out the line, saw Washington begin the work, striking a few quick blows with a pickaxe—a ceremonial gesture, the cynical Martin thought, so that it could be said that the general "with his own hands first broke ground at the siege of Yorktown."

The work went swiftly in the moist sandy soil. Hundreds of gabions were dragged into line and filled with earth, so that within an hour the ditch was already two or three feet deep,

"The Liberties of America Are in Our Hands"

shielded by the mound of freshly dug earth. There were no
interruptions from the enemy, and the line was almost complete
by dawn when British sentries saw the new trench, almost within
musket range. American troops occupied the line during the day.

British gunners fired a few rounds, and a huge white English
bulldog sprinted into the open and leaped over the new trench
in chase of cannonballs. Officers ordered American soldiers to
catch the dog so that they could send a message into Yorktown.

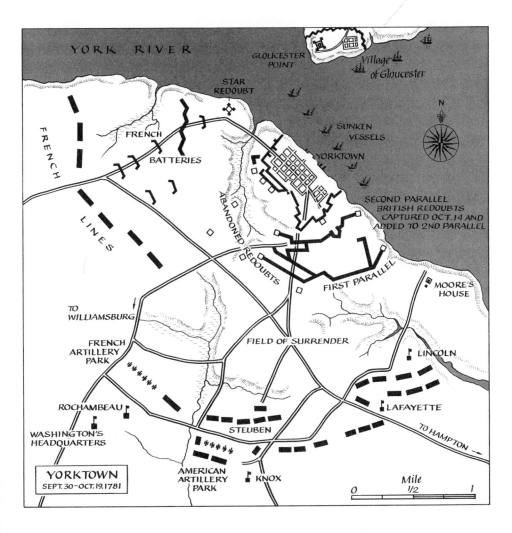

THE SIEGE OF YORKTOWN

The troops were mutinous: "He looked too formidable for any of us to encounter," Joseph Martin said.

Work parties swarmed about the new line for two days, building gun platforms and dragging artillery into position. The newly arrived French mortars were mounted on platforms, designed by Henry Knox, so that the enormous tubs could lob shells into the town. Sporadic British gunfire hampered the work, but could not halt it. The sight of new batteries in the front seemed to demoralize the enemy. Colonel Butler wrote: "The enemy seem embarrassed, confused and indeterminate . . . although we have not as yet fired one shot from a piece of artillery, they are as cautious as if the heaviest fire was kept up."

Washington was satisfied at last on October 9, when all French and American guns were in line. A deserter came out from Yorktown during the morning with a report that Cornwallis had assured his troops that they had nothing to fear, since the Americans had brought no heavy guns and the French fleet, which had entered the Chesapeake in search of tobacco, was afraid to attack. Henry Knox and his gunners enjoyed the story: the American front was actually dominated by huge guns, half a dozen heavy mortars, two eight-inch howitzers and six other siege guns, three of them twenty-four pounders.

French guns opened first, without ceremony, and at 5 P.M., when Washington appeared in the American trenches, a flag was run up and troops cheered. Joseph Martin was moved: "I felt a secret pride swell my heart when I saw 'The Star Spangled Banner' waving majestically in the faces of our implacable adversaries; it appeared like an omen of success." Washington then touched off an American cannon, firing a shot that crashed into a house in Yorktown. The ball, it was said, plunged into a headquarters dining room and killed a British officer.

That night's diary entry by Lieutenant William James of the royal navy confirmed the accuracy of Washington's shot: "I could hear the ball strike from house to house, and I was afterwards informed that it went through the one where many of the officers were at dinner, and over the tables, discomposing the dishes and either killed or wounded the one at the head of the table. . . ."

"The Liberties of America Are in Our Hands"

There was a lull in the bombardment on October 10, when a white flag waved from the British works and an old man hobbled toward the American line led by servants—he was old Thomas Nelson, uncle of Virginia's Governor Thomas Nelson, sent to safety after allied shells had demolished his house. Nelson brought news from British headquarters, which had now been driven into a cave in the marl bluff at the riverside: a British relief fleet was expected; the shelling had battered the town to pieces; thousands of horses had been slaughtered; casualties among troops and Negro camp followers were rising, and the British were "a good deal dispirited."

Cornwallis sank a dozen or more of his own vessels in York-town harbor during the day, and after dark, French gunners heated red-hot shot and fired into the remaining fleet. One shot plunged into the British 40-gun warship *Charon* and set other vessels afire. Dr. Thacher described the blaze:

> The ships were enwrapped in a torrent of fire, which spread with vivid brightness among the combustible rigging, and running with amazing rapidity to the tops of the several masts, while all around was thunder and lightning from our numerous cannon and mortars . . . one of the most sublime and magnificent spectacles which can be imagined. Some of our shells, overreaching the town, are seen to fall in the river, and bursting, throw up columns of water like the spouting of the monsters of the deep.

More than thirty-six hundred shots fell on the harbor and town within twenty-four hours of this display, and the bombardment of the village itself was lethal. Johann Doehla, a Hessian private who was on the beach, said the shelling "felt like the shocks of an earthquake":

> One saw men lying everywhere who were mortally wounded and whose heads, arms and legs had been shot off . . . enemy cannon balls of 24 and more pounds flew over our whole line and city into the river, where they often struck through 1 and 2 ships.

American troops opened a second parallel line during the darkness of October 11–12, once more working all night undisturbed. British fire continued to fall on the old line to the rear, as

if Cornwallis did not suspect that a new parallel was being dug.
By daylight the new work was almost complete, four hundred
yards nearer to the British lines. Washington puzzled over the
enemy's indifference: "Lord Cornwallis' conduct has hitherto
been passive beyond conception; he either has not the means of
defence, or he intends to reserve his strength until we approach
very near him."

The second parallel did not satisfy Washington's engineers,
since it could not be completed to the riverbank unless the Americans stormed two large British redoubts that blocked the way.
The commander agreed that the two small forts must be
assaulted, and on October 14 turned all his guns on the two
works. At 2 P.M., when he saw that the shells had blasted the
approaches, defensive guns and parapets, the general issued
orders for night attacks. Two parties of four hundred men each
were picked from French and American troops. The Americans,
under Lafayette, were assigned to take the Rock Redoubt, nearest the river. The French, led by Alexander Hamilton, were to
storm the formidable work beside the road, near the Moore
House, a post defended by German veterans of the Bose regiment.

The two small columns gathered near the front at dusk, and
Washington went out to the American party and delivered a
brief, simple speech, urging the men to be brave in this all-
important attack. An officer wrote, "I thought then that His
Excellency's knees rather shook, but I have since doubted
whether it was not mine."

Captain Stephen Olney, a Rhode Island veteran who feared
some of his company would quail, said a few words when Washington had left, "I know you'll be brave men. If you lose your
weapons, don't fall back—take one from the first man killed."

Rochambeau spoke to the Frenchmen just before the attack,
calling in a low voice to men of the regiment he had commanded
in his youth: "My children, I have great need of you tonight. I
trust you will not forget that we have served together in the
brave Regiment of the Auvergne—*Auvergne sans tache*, the
spotless." An excited young soldier replied from the darkness,
"We will fight like lions . . . until the last man is killed."

Axes were passed out among the American assault troops, and

the watchword for the night was given: "Rochambeau." Men were ordered to empty their muskets for fear of alerting the enemy with accidental firing. The leading files were armed with long poles tipped with bayonets so that they could stab British and German defenders in the towering works.

Count Deux-Ponts, who led the French party toward the enemy, was besieged by last-minute volunteers, most of them young officers who refused to be left behind. It was seven o'clock when the two lines disappeared into the fog. Gunners diverted the enemy with a few rounds of fire.

The Americans halted when they had crept halfway to their goal, and the column was divided. Twenty men led by Lieutenant John Mansfield of the 4th Connecticut, "the forlorn hope," were chosen to climb first over the enemy wall, and another band, under John Laurens, circled to the rear, to cut off retreat from the redoubt.

Sergeant Joe Martin, who was with the American advance, stumbled among the sharp tree limbs of the defenses and found them only slightly damaged by artillery fire. He and his companions began chopping with axes, and were fired on from above. The Americans broke into a spontaneous cheer, and Mansfield's suicide squad rushed past the sappers and miners, struggled through the barrier and across a ditch, and scrambled up the parapet. Sergeant Martin, who saw men falling rapidly on every side, thought British fire was decimating the column until he realized that they were falling into huge holes torn by shell fire, clambering out and rushing forward, only to stumble again. Mansfield, one of the first men in the fort, was stabbed by a bayonet, but his men rushed past him and grappled with the enemy. Captain Olney, wounded in the abdomen and thigh by bayonets, was saved by some of his men who had loaded their muskets in violation of orders, and now drove back the British with a volley.

The diminutive Hamilton, who was too short to reach the top of the wall, ordered a soldier to kneel, stood on his back, and vaulted into the fort. As a brief clangor of bayonets cleared the redoubt, Sergeant Martin saw figures leaping to the ground and fleeing toward Yorktown—one of them plunged thirty or forty feet over the bluff to the riverside. The remnant of the redcoat garrison surrendered, and John Laurens soon appeared with a file of prisoners, among them Major Campbell, commander of the redoubt.

The Americans had lost nine dead and twenty-five wounded in the assault, and one of the wounded, Sergeant William Brown of the 1st Connecticut, was decorated with the Purple Heart, the first American military award for valor in action without regard to rank.

The fort had hardly been cleared when Lafayette sent a taunting message to the French column, "I am in my redoubt. Where are you?" Baron Viomenil, who was then lying under fire, waiting for his troops to clear the British barricade, replied, "Tell the Marquis I am not in mine, but will be in five minutes."

The French advance lost heavily under Hessian fire aimed down at them at point-blank range, until Count Deux-Ponts lost patience with his flailing axmen and led the way into the barrier: "We threw ourselves into the ditch . . . and each one sought to break through the fraises and to mount the parapet." The first officer up, the young Chevalier de Lameth, was shot through both knees, and the veteran Baron l'Estrade, who followed closely, was dragged backward into the ditch by a soldier who tugged at his coattails. The baron struggled on the sand for a moment, trampled by rushing men, and cursed them steadily. The German defenders charged the French, were driven back by a volley and huddled behind a row of barrels in their fort. As Frenchman fired on them from the high parapet the Germans dropped their muskets and raised hands in surrender. Just as the French shouted in triumph, the British line near Yorktown erupted with a volley, an almost unbroken seam of orange fire more than a mile long. Deux-Ponts said, "I never saw a sight more beautiful or more majestic."

Hamilton's Frenchmen, though they were late in breaking the outer defenses of their redoubt, had taken the post within in seven minutes of fighting at close range and had killed 18 Hessians and taken 50 prisoners. Deux-Ponts lost 15 men dead and 77 wounded.

Heavy French casualties were blamed on Count Custine,

whose command was to have covered the attack with heavy volleys, but did not open fire until fifteen minutes after the redoubt had fallen. Rochambeau arrested Custine, who was said to have been drunk, and kept him under guard for twenty-four hours.

Working parties opened new trenches, linking the forts to the second parallel. British gunners fired steadily for an hour or more, and though their shot flew high overhead on the American sector, the French lost heavily; one exploding shell felled more than a hundred men, killing twenty-seven of them. More than five hundred wounded were taken rearward to Claude Blanchard's field hospital before dawn. By sunrise, the new line was virtually complete, a trench that ran to the bluff overlooking the York. Washington, who had watched the attacks from close range, wrote President McKean, "The works we have carried are of vast importance to us. From them we shall enfilade the enemy's whole line."

The assaults on the redoubts frightened German veterans in the inner defense line. One Hessian noted in his diary that at least three thousand men had attacked. "They made such a terrible yell . . . that one believed nothing but that the whole 'Wild Hunt' had broken out . . . The alarm was sounded throughout our entire camp." Several German and British soldiers who escaped from the redoubts were killed by their own men. Corporal Popp looked on helplessly, "Some of them were even shot by us with grapeshot . . . A Hessian was found in three pieces." Desertions among the Germans increased during the night. The next morning, October 15, Cornwallis confessed for the first time that his plight was hopeless. He sent off a dispatch to Henry Clinton:

> My situation now becomes very critical. We dare not show a gun to their old batteries, and I expect their new ones will open To-Morrow Morning . . . we shall soon be exposed to an assault in ruined Works, in a bad position and with weakened Numbers.
> I cannot recommend that the Fleet and Army should run great risque in endeavouring to save us.

After nightfall, as if driven beyond endurance by rage and frustration, Cornwallis launched a desperate attack against the allied line, a foray by three hundred and fifty men who crept among sleepy French and American troops, killed or wounded about twenty men and spiked half a dozen of Washington's cannon. The British were driven off after a few minutes, with a loss of about a dozen men. The spiked French cannon were soon repaired and joined a renewed bombardment of the village.

It was only on October 16, after this attack had failed, that Cornwallis succumbed to pleas of his officers and attempted an escape across the York River—"the last resource," as Banastre Tarleton said. Just before midnight, in cold, cloudy weather, a thousand British regulars filed out of the trenches and were ferried over the river in small boats. Cornwallis was to follow with other troops when he had completed a letter to Washington, asking mercy for the remnant of the garrison he planned to abandon. Boats had hardly nosed into the river with the second wave of troops when a savage squall swept down the York, scattering boats and marooning the men on the north bank.

Guns fired slowly from the village trenches, without response from the allies. A few British troops returned from the beach, but most of the men from the north shore were not brought back until noon of the next day. Cornwallis abandoned the attempt to break away. In Tarleton's words, "Thus expired the last hope of the British army."

The allied guns then opened on Yorktown once more, nearer than ever. Johann Doehla, who was in the strongest redoubt at sunrise, now understood the enemy's nightlong silence: "Toward morning they brought a trench and a strong battery of 14 guns so close to our hornwork that one could nearly throw stones into it."

The increased French and American fire stunned the defenders, who had not imagined that the cannonading could become more intense. One young Hessian said: ". . . with the dawn the enemy began to fire heavily, as he had not done before . . . so fiercely as though the heavens should split . . . this afternoon the enemy firing was almost unendurable. Now we saw what was to happen to us."

Yorktown's remaining civilians fled with their household treasures to the riverbank and dug caves in the bluff to hide from the barrage, an almost endless fire of 100-pound and 200-pound shells that burst over the village and the littered beach. German soldiers reported heavy casualties among these townspeople, ". . . many were badly injured and mortally wounded by the fragments of bombs which exploded partly in the air and partly on the ground, their arms and legs severed or themselves struck dead . . . everywhere were mortally wounded . . . whose heads, arms and legs had been shot off." The cannon also rained fire among British ships, and an occasional shell burst across the river on the Gloucester shore.

Cornwallis made his decision to surrender on the morning of October 17. His battered works, he saw, "were in many places assailable in the forenoon." He could no longer fire even one large gun. About half of his force were wounded or ill, and the remaining troops were near exhaustion. The earl expected the French fleet to appear in the York and join the bombardment. "Under all these circumstances, I thought it would have been wanton and inhuman to . . . sacrifice the lives of this small body of gallant soldiers."

Meanwhile, in New York, British hopes for a rescue of Cornwallis were frittered away: admirals and generals squabbled over the feasibility of entering the Chesapeake, indolent ships' carpenters caused agonizing delays, and Clinton and his officers bickered through thirteen inconclusive councils of war in little more than a month. Somehow, there was always time for gay parties at headquarters in the evenings.

Old General Robertson, now scorned because he betrayed symptoms of senility, urged Clinton to rush troop transports to the Chesapeake under convoy of a single warship—a desperate scheme, but as Robertson insisted, the alternative was to lose Cornwallis and his army. When Clinton rejected the plan, Robertson took consolation in nights "abandoned to Frivolity . . . Parties of Girls in the Fort Garden, in the midst of his own Fears, and the Anxieties of this Hour."

Naval officers dallied while carpenters went leisurely about the task of refitting the fleet; sailors jumped ship and went into hiding, but were dragged out by posses of loyal civilians. New York businessmen raised money to hire volunteer sailors, and still the admirals squabbled with Clinton over trifles. Admiral Graves refused to attend one of Clinton's councils because it conflicted with a meeting of his own. The belligerent Admiral Samuel Hood felt that Graves was deliberately delaying the fleet's departure. "I think very meanly of the ability of our present commanding officer," Hood said. "I know he is a cunning man, he may be a good theoretical man, but he is certainly a bad practical one."

When the fleet was ready at last, a storm damaged several ships. The wind failed and prevented sailing for one more day, during which another council of war approved a revised landing plan. The fleet left New York on October 19, with Clinton and Graves both aboard the flagship *London.*

Before departure the general wrote friends in England to explain that though the expedition was risky, it was essential if British America was to be saved. Clinton left a copy of his will with his mistress, Mrs. Baddeley, and sent another to England.

At the hour the last of the big ships disappeared from Sandy Hook, the troops of Cornwallis were marching from Yorktown's battered trenches to surrender their arms.

27

VICTORY

"The World Turned Upside Down"

At nine o'clock in the morning, when the sun was already high over the Yorktown bluffs, a redcoat drummer appeared on a parapet and pounded away with his sticks for several minutes, unheard in the bombardment. Washington's infantrymen saw him first, and then the artillerymen. The guns fell silent one by one. The Pennsylvania ensign Ebenezer Denny saw the British boy at once. "He might have beat away till Doomsday if he had not been sighted by men in the front lines . . ." Denny felt the exultation that swept through allied ranks: "I thought I had never heard a drum equal to it—the most delightful music to us all."

A British officer emerged, holding aloft a white handkerchief, and moved toward the American lines with the drummer at his side, the drum still rolling furiously, beating a call for a parley. An American officer crossed the shell-torn field, blindfolded the Englishman and led him into a house behind the allied line. Among the thousands of American soldiers who watched from the trenches were many who recalled that this was the fourth anniversary of the victory of Saratoga.

At headquarters Washington opened the message from Cornwallis:

VICTORY

Sir, I propose a cessation of hostilities for twenty-four hours, and that two officers may be appointed by each side, to meet at Mr. Moore's house, to settle terms for the surrender of the posts at York and Gloucester.

But though these words meant a victory at last, clear-cut and complete, his first since Trenton and Princeton, the Virginian did not seem to realize even now the possible significance of York-town—that the long campaigns might have come to an end, and that his war was virtually won. It was now almost six and a half years since the June morning in Philadelphia when he had accepted command of the army, but the general was not in a reflective mood today, and if officers at headquarters sensed that American independence had been won on this field, they left no record of it.

The capitulation had come much sooner than Washington had expected, only twenty days after the opening of the siege. Noisy celebrations swept the allied line, but Washington was hesitant. It was almost three hours later, near noon, when he replied to Cornwallis, refusing to lift the siege for a day. He offered a delay of two hours, until the earl could put his proposals into writing. Washington was so confident of the outcome, however, that he invited De Grasse to come ashore for the surrender which would "shortly take place." Under the noon sun, while men of the opposing armies watched from atop the works, the British officer reappeared and walked across the open with Washington's message. American guns resumed firing the moment the redcoat disappeared into his line.

Cornwallis read Washington's reply: "An Ardent Desire to spare the further Effusion of Blood, will readily incline me to listen to such Terms for the Surrender of your Posts. . . ."

A British messenger emerged once more and was escorted to Washington's tent.

Cornwallis attempted a belated bargain. His second message blandly proposed that his entire army be set free under an exchange of prisoners, after a ceremony of surrender:

. . . the time limited for sending my answer will not admit of entering into . . . detail . . . but the basis of my proposals will be . . . that the British shall be sent to Britain and the Germans to Germany . . . not to serve against France, America or their allies until released or regularly exchanged. . . .

The Virginian responded tersely, agreeing only to halt the bombardment for a day to negotiate surrender terms. In the quiet that fell on the field, messengers bearing white flags crossed and recrossed between the lines during the late afternoon.

Washington and Rochambeau and other officers discussed terms to be offered the British until late in the night, and it was the morning of October 18 before John Trumbull's draft of the allied proposal was ready for delivery to Cornwallis:

> Head Quarters before York, October 18, 1781.
> MY LORD: To avoid unnecessary Discussions and Delays, I shall at Once . . . declare the general Basis upon which a Definitive Treaty and Capitulation must take place. The Garrisons of York and Gloucester, including the Seamen . . . will be received Prisoners of War. The Condition annexed, of sending the British and German troops . . . to Europe . . . is inadmissible. Instead of this, they will be marched to such parts of the Country as can most conveniently provide for their Subsistence . . . the same Honors will be granted to the Surrendering Army as were granted to the Garrison of Charles Town . . .
>
> The Artillery, Arms, Accoutrements, Military Chest and Public Stores of every denomination, shall be delivered unimpaired. . . .

Washington requested that two British officers be chosen to discuss surrender terms. Once more he allowed Cornwallis only two hours to reply.

The commander agreed to allow a small shipload of British and German officers and Loyalist civilians to sail for New York without inspection, but he refused to grant immunity for most of the Tories and American deserters in Yorktown. The Virginian insisted on dealing with turncoats as he saw fit—in his eyes these men were traitors, and he was resolved that some of them should hang. Washington agreed to permit British and German troops to keep their personal property.

Flag bearers moved almost constantly between the lines during the day, bearing messages between the headquarters. When

Cornwallis agreed to send two officers to the nearby Moore House to negotiate a formal surrender, Washington chose John Laurens as the American commissioner. Rochambeau named the Viscount de Noailles, Lafayette's brother-in-law. A few moments after allied guns halted for the day, at 5 P.M., British sailors and civilians went aboard ships in the harbor; merchants removed stores and piled them ashore, and naval crews scuttled the *Guadeloupe* and *Fowey* at the water's edge. The village was noisy throughout the night as troops destroyed stores and equipment. When a powder magazine exploded in the early morning, killing more than a dozen men, the German soldier Doehla saw the victims, "blown to bits . . . flying in pieces into the air."

Major St. George Tucker of the Virginia militia was roused the next morning by serenading bagpipers from the British works, whose shrill tunes were echoed by the band of the Deux-Ponts regiment. British, German, American and French troops crowded atop the parapets to listen, along lines barely two hundred yards apart. Tucker saw old Thomas Nelson's house in the early light, with shell holes gaping in the roof and its towering brick walls on the point of collapse. Men still swarmed about the waterfront and the harbor, where signs of British defeat were unmistakable:

> On the Beach of York . . . hundreds of busy people might be seen moving to and fro—At a small distance from the Shore were seen ships sunk down to the Waters Edge—further out in the Channel the Masts, Yards and even the top gallant Masts of some might be seen. . . .

Two French ships emerged from the misty distance of the Chesapeake, and by noon had dropped anchor among the British hulks in the harbor. By now the negotiators were at work in the white frame Moore House, on the river bluff half a mile to the rear of the first American parallel. Laurens and Noailles had a long wait before the British joined them, Lieutenant Colonel Thomas Dundas and Major Alexander Ross, both professional soldiers.

Expecting an immediate agreement, Washington sent forward detachments of French and American troops, ready to occupy enemy trenches, but these men, who waited in columns until midafternoon and then until nightfall, were sent back to their posts.

Within the Moore House the four officers squabbled over terms, point by point. Ross and Laurens argued angrily over the fate of American deserters who now wore British uniforms, and though the article protecting these Loyalists was added to the agreement at the insistence of the Englishmen, Laurens warned that it would be deleted by Washington.

Once they had agreed to the unconditional surrender of the garrison, the British fought over trifles. It was only after bitter debate that they consented that their army would march out with furled flags, playing one of their own tunes, rather than "Yankee Doodle" or some other derisive rebel music, as was customary. Laurens threatened to leave the house if the British did not agree to this article, and reminded the protesting Ross that this indignity had been forced upon Americans who surrendered at Charleston, S.C.

The four men also wrangled over the money chest of Cornwallis, which contained £1,800 sterling. The Viscount Noailles, who belonged to one of Europe's wealthiest families, scorned the amount as too insignificant to be included in the settlement, but when Laurens protested that "in our new country, with its poor currency, this means a great deal indeed," the money was awarded to the Americans.

It was near midnight when the weary allied commissioners brought a draft of the surrender agreement to headquarters, where Washington read it slowly and made marginal notes in his careful hand. He wrote "granted" after ten of the fourteen articles, but as Laurens had foreseen, he refused to grant immunity to Tory civilians, army deserters and merchants who had followed the British. The general also insisted that Cornwallis care for his own sick and wounded, since his own hospital was overcrowded. He then had the document copied and sent it to Cornwallis, noting without further comment the changes he had made. He asked that the British sign and return the agreement by 11 A.M. The Yorktown garrison would march out to surrender its arms at 2 P.M.

Washington, Rochambeau and staff officers rode to the Rock Redoubt, where they were joined by Admiral de Barras, as a representative of De Grasse, who was confined to his cabin with an attack of asthma. When the surrender document was returned from Yorktown to the small fort, the general saw that Cornwallis and Captain Thomas Symonds, the ranking British naval officer, had signed. Without hesitation he scrawled a hurried signature: "G. Washington," and Rochambeau and De Barras signed for the French. Washington asked Trumbull to add a line: "Done in the trenches before Yorktown in Virginia, October 19, 1781." The ceremony was over before the troops were aware that it had begun. Almost at once the commander sent Cornwallis an invitation to dinner after the surrender ceremony.

At noon American and French soldiers filed into the vacated enemy trenches, where they took over stores and ammunition dumps. Work parties with picks and shovels began leveling trenches at road crossings.

Two departing German soldiers, at least, felt only relief that the end had come. Private Johann Doehla was profoundly grateful: "I . . . had indeed just cause to thank my God . . . who had so graciously preserved my life throughout the siege . . . Oh! how many thousand cannon balls I have escaped, with danger of my life hanging before my eyes!"

Corporal Popp, the Anspacher, wrote: "We were heartily glad . . . we were not harmed in the least . . . we were treated with justice and military usage. We had no complaints to make."

A smoldering rivalry among allied officers provoked the only incident during allied occupation of the trenches. Ensign Ebenezer Denny, the youngest of Colonel Richard Butler's Pennsylvania officers, scrambled up the enemy parapet with his regimental colors, only to lose them to Baron von Steuben, who snatched the staff and drove it into the sandy soil. French and American cheers rolled across the field at sight of the flag, but the angry Butler cursed the Prussian and sent him an insulting message; and only the intervention of Washington and Rochambeau prevented a duel.

As the hour of surrender approached, the allied armies marched toward an enormous field southwest of Yorktown, where they formed in parallel files to await the passage of the British army between them. The French and American columns faced each other a few yards apart; the Americans stood in two files, Continentals to the front and militia in the rear. Washington's tattered troops had prepared for the ceremony only by washing their hands and faces and combing their lank hair, but the French, spruce in white linen and pastel regimental silks, looked at their allies admiringly, as Baron von Closen did: ". . . most of these unfortunate persons were clad in small jackets of white cloth, dirty and ragged, and a number of them were almost bare foot . . . What does it matter! . . . These people are much more praise-worthy to fight as they do, when they are so poorly supplied with everything." In the field beyond the waiting infantry, where arms were to be stacked, French hussars formed a circle, a splendidly uniformed band of mustachioed riders sitting restless horses whose freshly curried coats gleamed in the sunlight. On every side of the waiting troops, now beginning to press into the field, were thousands of civilians, drawn by rumors of the surrender—people of the countryside, who had been gathering for two days, families in carriages, carts and wagons, men and women on horseback, all surrounded by throngs of Negroes. Hundreds of boys and young men had climbed trees about the field and clung to the branches, peering expectantly toward the village.

Axel Fersen, the Swede in Rochambeau's column, thought the Virginia planters were much like aristocrats the world over; "The only wonder is how they were ever induced to accept a government founded on a perfect equality of rights." Fersen was fascinated by the courtly native families of the Tidewater counties:

> It really seems as if the Virginians belonged to a totally different race of people . . . No white man ever labors, but all the work is done by black slaves, guarded by white men who in their turn are under an overseer . . . Business men, of course, are considered quite an inferior order of being by the lordly planters who not looking on them as gentlemen, preclude them from their society.

At last, not long before 3 P.M., the British emerged from the village with a somber roll of drums, the column led by a guard

carrying cased colors and a band playing a dirge-like march,
"The World Turned Upside Down":

> If ponies rode men and if grass ate cows,
> And cats should be chased into holes by the mouse . . .
> If summer were spring and the other way round,
> Then all the world would be upside down.

Men in Washington's ranks saw that the redcoats were not so
formidable at close range, and felt a vague sense of loss, as if
they had been defrauded in the moment of victory. The enemy
had been issued new uniforms, but though the ranks gleamed in
scarlet and white, they moved awkwardly. Ensign Denny thought
the drummers were beating "as if they didn't care how." Dr.
Thacher saw that the file shambled past, "disorderly and unsol-
dierly . . . their step irregular, and their ranks frequently
broken." Lieutenant Feltman said, "The British prisoners all
appeared to be much in liquor." Another American officer noted
that "their knees seemed to tremble," and a New Jersey soldier
thought the British officers behaved like schoolboys who had
been whipped: "Some bit their lips; some pouted, others cried."

As they drew nearer, the enemy files seemed shorter; about
thirty-five hundred men had marched from the village, and
almost as many more awaited within, most of those sick and
wounded.

Soldiers in the German ranks were even more distraught than
the British. Several men of Johann Doehla's regiment sobbed as
they marched, and tears flowed down their colonel's cheeks when
he ordered them to lay down their arms. One indignant German
officer thought that these unlikely victors—a pack of farmers
and shopkeepers—could never fathom the depths of grief and
rage felt by professional soldiers forced to surrender in this place.

Men in the German ranks were astonished by the size of the
allied army. Corporal Popp said, "we . . . were staggered by the
multitude of those who had besieged us. We were just a guard
mounting in comparison with them, and they could have eaten
us up with their power." Popp was enraged by the scornful
laughter of the French officers, but he admired Rochambeau's
common soldiers: "They were mostly fine young men and looked

"The World Turned Upside Down"

very good. Their generals were in front and had aides who were beautifully attired in silver."

Colonel Lighthorse Harry Lee had the feeling that the onlookers—soldiers and civilians—were in the grip of powerful emotions, "an awful sense of the vicissitudes of human life, mingled with commiseration for the unhappy."

Washington, trailed by a party of generals and staff officers, had walked his horse between the allied files for half a mile and halted near the junction of sandy roads that led south and west toward the villages of Warwick and Hampton. Rochambeau and his staff took their places across the road, in front of the French column. The generals were there when the sound of the British bands reached them.

As the head of the redcoat files came into sight, allied officers stood slightly in their stirrups, craning their necks to look for Cornwallis. The earl did not appear. The British were led by Brigadier General Charles O'Hara, a handsome Irishman in old-fashioned military dress whose curls hung like tiny sausages about his "black and ruddy" face. American bystanders noted that he was remarkably erect and well-groomed. O'Hara flashed a broad smile toward the French staff, and when Count Mathieu Dumas rode forward to act as guide, O'Hara called, "Where is General Rochambeau?" The Frenchman pointed to his commander, but when he saw that O'Hara intended to surrender to Rochambeau, and refuse to recognize the Americans, Dumas blocked the road with his horse.

O'Hara drew his sword and extended it to Rochambeau, but the old general pointed across the road to Washington: "We are subordinate to the Americans. General Washington will give you orders."

Still smiling, O'Hara reined his horse before the Virginian, apologized for his mistake and once more offered his sword with a courtly gesture.

Washington's face was expressionless. "Never from such a good hand," he said quietly.

O'Hara identified himself and explained that Cornwallis was ill. Washington introduced the Irishman to Benjamin Lincoln, who, as field commander, would direct the surrender. Lincoln explained that each regiment in turn would deposit arms in the field where the French hussars were waiting, and then retrace their steps into Yorktown. The field was now so quiet that the bootfalls of the British and Germans could be heard in the deep sand of the road.

The solemnity of the scene was marred by Admiral De Barras, an inexperienced but resolute horseman, who had vowed that he would sit in the saddle for two days, if need be, to witness the surrender. But now, in the midst of the ceremony, De Barras shouted in alarm as his mount stretched to relieve himself. "Bon dieu! I believe my horse is sinking!"

As the approaching column passed between the allied files, British officers barked commands and heads snapped to the right, ignoring the Americans and acknowledging only the French as victors. Lafayette responded to the insult by motioning to his musicians, who played a few bars of "Yankee Doodle"; but when the redcoats turned curious stares on the Frenchman and his command, the music ceased.

The reluctant column came at last to the field where muskets were to be surrendered, and there, encircled by the French horsemen, the British sullenly grounded arms and hurled their weapons onto the pile with such violence that many guns were broken; the resentful troops were halted by a brusque order from General Lincoln.

Washington had probably left the field when the dramatic scene of the surrendered arms had scarcely begun. He returned to his tent and worked over the details of handling the prisoners and occupying Yorktown; he was anxious for news of the simultaneous surrender of the British garrison across the river at Gloucester Point; and among the bustle of officers and civilians coming and going, the headquarters cooks and steward were busy with preparing dinner, to which General O'Hara had been invited.

The impromptu banquet was surprisingly free of tension. The ebullient O'Hara charmed his hosts by his poise, and there was a laughing camaraderie among the officers, especially between the British and French. John Trumbull found the occasion "very social and easy," as if the war were in the distant past, and its passions had already cooled. Other American officers, with memories of British atrocities fresh in mind, were enraged by the new spirit of brotherhood between enemies.

During the evening Washington turned aside to say goodbye to his stepson, Jacky Custis, who was sent westward by carriage. Jacky had insisted upon watching the surrender despite his illness with "camp fever," and soon afterward had been sent homeward by Dr. Craik, who told Washington that Jacky's condition was critical.

It was not until late in the night—almost as if it were an afterthought—that Washington turned his attention to composing a victory message to Congress, his first from a battlefield in almost five years. Trumbull wrote the first draft, which was copied by David Humphreys and slightly revised by the general—a brief message that made no claim of final victory:

> Sir: I have the Honor to inform Congress, that a Reduction of the British Army under the Command of Lord Cornwallis, is most happily effected. The unremitting Ardour which actuated every Officer and Soldier in the combined Army in this Occasion, has principally led to this Important Event, at an earlier period than my most sanguine Hope had induced me to expect. . . .

A few additional lines praised officers who had played major roles in the campaign.

The general sent the dispatch northward by Tench Tilghman, the Marylander who had served so long on the staff without pay, and had only recently won a commission as lieutenant colonel. Tilghman left at once aboard a sailboat manned by a Chesapeake waterman. The small craft scudded down the York and turned up the bay under a steady breeze, but "by the stupidity of the skipper," as the impatient Tilghman said, ran aground near Tangier Island. There was worse to come next day, when the boat made only twenty miles under a light breeze, and was then becalmed thirty miles south of Annapolis. Tilghman fumed with anxiety. He knew that Admiral De Grasse had sent a dispatch to Philadelphia on October 18, before the final surrender, and that delay in confirmation from Washington would raise doubts in Congress, so often misled by false tidings.

Tilghman suffered a recurrence of an "intermittent fever" he had contracted in camp as the boat drifted for hours under a glaring sun, but at last the skipper landed him at the village of Rock Hall, on Maryland's eastern shore. The colonel galloped northward on relays of borrowed horses, now and then shouting to an astonished farmer, "Cornwallis is taken! A horse for the Congress!"

The feverish Tilghman reached Philadelphia after midnight of October 23, and it was only with the aid of an old German night watchman that he delivered the victory message to the home of Thomas McKean, the president of Congress. The State House bell soon began to ring, and did not cease until dawn; the night watchman cried the news of the British surrender on his rounds. Tilghman went to bed to recover from his fever, and since he had made the journey without a penny in his pocket, was forced to ask Congress for a loan. McKean reported that the treasury was empty, but congressmen contributed one dollar each to pay for the colonel's room and board. It was several days before Tilghman could return to Yorktown.

Philadelphia celebrated with an illumination of the city on the evening of October 24, and a noisy mob surged through the streets, attacking houses whose windows were not lighted with candles. Elizabeth Drinker, the wife of a Quaker shipowner, reported:

> Scarcely one Friend's house escaped. We had nearly 70 panes of glass broken . . . the door crashed and violently burst open; when they did not enter . . . some houses, after breaking the door, they entered and destroyed the furniture. Many women and children were frightened into fits.

Congress bickered over terms of the surrender; some members called for the execution of Cornwallis, in revenge for atrocities committed by his troops in the Carolinas. It was by a narrow majority that the body defeated a resolution calling for the earl to be hanged. Congress sent a vote of thanks to the allied army at Yorktown, awarded two cannon to Rochambeau and some captured British flags to Washington, and voted Tilghman a horse, saddle and sword.

The Yorktown victory was celebrated in cities and villages, from Georgia to the Maine border, with oxroasts, bonfires, fireworks, displays, dances and militia drills. Gunpowder burned in salutes would have seen the army through a major battle. In Newburgh, N. Y., William Heath's troops burned an effigy of Benedict Arnold. As the stuffed figure was hauled toward the flames a soldier protested that one of the legs should not be burned, since Arnold had been wounded while fighting bravely for his country. The leg was removed and "laid safely by."

Washington deplored the country's jubilant mood, and feared that the victory would "produce such a relaxation" as to prolong the war. The British could launch a new offensive at any time, for at least thirty thousand redcoats remained in America, in garrisons scattered from Canada to Charleston, almost half of them under Henry Clinton's command in New York.

PEACE AT LAST

"An Affectionate Farewell"

Allied troops found the village of Yorktown a landscape of horrors. Dr. Thacher noted that most of its houses were ruined, "shot through in a thousand places and honey-combed, ready to crumble to pieces. Rich furniture and books were scattered over the ground, and the carcasses of men and horses half-covered the earth." Ensign Denny was sickened by the sight of hundreds of Negroes, who lay about the streets and yards, sick and dying "in every stage of the small pox." Baron von Closen wrote: "One could not take three steps without running into some great holes made by bombs . . . half-covered trenches, with scattered white or Negro arms or legs."

Yorktown's apprehensive villagers tried in vain to guard their remaining stores from American troops. Von Closen estimated that soldiers stole at least half of the civilian supplies left in the town. They also seized hoards of food inexplicably denied to the garrison by Cornwallis: 100,000 pounds of salt meat, 150,000 pounds of bread and flour, 20,000 pounds of butter, and great stores of chocolate, coffee, oatmeal, rice and peas.

Despite the earl's doleful reports that his stocks were depleted, the allies found 144 cannon and mortars, 1,500 round shot, 500 shells, thousands of cartridges for big guns, 600 hand grenades, 120 barrels of powder, 3,400 flints, 266,000 musket cartridges,

and more than 2,000 swords and sabers. American ordnance officers were astounded by the supplies of other equipment: tools and
leather, fuses, powder horns, carts and harness, nails, sheet iron,
and all the apparatus of a large artillery park.

Almost a hundred stands of colors were captured, including
eighteen German and six British regimental flags.

Casualties during the siege seemed trifling: Cornwallis had lost
156 men killed and 326 wounded, and allied casualties were even
lighter, 20 dead and 56 wounded for the Americans and 52 dead
and 134 wounded for the French. Total British and German losses
at Yorktown, including those surrendered, were 7,247 soldiers and
840 seamen.

A round of dinners and receptions continued the friendly
exchange between the victors and the defeated army which had
begun on the day of surrender. Allied officers paid homage to
their British guests as if their roles had been reversed.

The French were especially impressed by the "reflective, mild,
and noble bearing" of Cornwallis. Baron von Closen, who accompanied Rochambeau to British headquarters the day after the surrender, was struck by the earl's composure, "His appearance gave
the impression of nobility of soul, magnanimity, and strength of
character." Cornwallis did not seem to reproach himself for the
loss of his army. The earl talked candidly of the hardships of the
siege, and once produced his maps to explain his attempted
escape across the York River to Lafayette, who responded by
showing him how the allies had planned to cut off his retreat in
case he had crossed the river.

Cornwallis finally emerged from Yorktown on November 2 to
attend a dinner given by Rochambeau. He also visited Lafayette's
headquarters, where he was surprised to find James Armistead,
who had served so faithfully at his headquarters; only then did
he realize that Armistead had been a spy for the marquis.

The entertainments embarrassed Baron von Steuben, who was
now a pauper. He had drawn $220,000 for his services, but had
spent much more to replace the three horses he had lost in the
Virginia campaign. "We are constantly feasted by the French
without giving them a bit of bratwurst," he said. "I will give
one grand dinner, should I eat my soup with a wooden spoon

forever after." Steuben sold his favorite horse and a set of silver spoons he had brought to America, and gave a dinner for allied officers that Commissary Blanchard remembered gratefully for years.

When the penniless Prussian prepared to leave Yorktown, he swallowed his pride and borrowed twenty guineas from Washington. The commander could give Steuben no promise that the government would ever give him his back pay or a pension. The baron left for the north in early November, hoping to persuade Congress to settle his accounts. He left his carriage for an aide who was ill and set off on horseback with a single gold coin in his pocket, all that remained of Washington's loan.

On the second day after the surrender the commander started more than six thousand prisoners off to the west, toward camps in Winchester, Va., and Frederick, Md., beyond reach of enemy raiders. Guarded by Virginia militia, the British and Germans marched under the command of one hundred and eighty unfortunate junior officers assigned to this duty, unable to sail for home on parole like other officers of the defeated army. Claude Blanchard, who visited the prisoners at their first campsite, resented the haughty air of the British toward their captors: "There was no call for this; they had not even made a handsome defense, and, at this very moment, were beaten and disarmed by peasants who were almost naked, whom they pretended to despise."

The British sloop *Bonetta* left the village on October 23, under the terms of surrender, without having been inspected by allied officers. Colonel Richard Butler correctly suspected that the enemy had violated the treaty by taking aboard an "iniquitous cargo of deserters, stolen Negroes and public stores"; Cornwallis had sent some two hundred and fifty American army deserters and Loyalists to safety aboard the small vessel, a riotous band so troublesome that the skipper risked the loss of his ship to set them ashore in New York during a howling storm.

The British rescue fleet, on its fifth day out of New York, neared the Chesapeake entrance in the gale-swept night of October 24, and by four o'clock the next morning the flagship

London took aboard three refugees who had fled Yorktown in a sloop. Stunned by the news of the surrender of Cornwallis, Admiral Graves sailed back and forth just outside the capes, watching the French fleet lying inside the bay. Henry Clinton and Admiral Samuel Hood urged that Graves fight his way in past the French and attempt to reach Yorktown, but after tacking ineffectually for two days, the admiral turned back to New York and sent the small ship *Rattlesnake* to London with word of the surrender of Cornwallis, "the most melancholy news Great Britain ever received," as Hood said. Hood complained indignantly of his superior's refusal to attack, ". . . a most heartbreaking business, and the more so to my mind, as I shall ever think His Lordship ought to have been succoured or bought off . . . which Mr. Graves had in his power to effect at his pleasure . . . my mind is too greatly depressed with the sense I have of my country's calamities to dwell longer upon the painful subject."

Washington realized that America could not be adequately defended without the aid of French sea power, and urged De Grasse to join Greene in an assault on the British garrison in Charleston, S.C. The Frenchman refused, since he was committed to return to the West Indies and help defend French possessions against a large British fleet operating there. Within a few weeks De Grasse was to lose all his ships in battle in the Indies and become a British prisoner.

Within a few days after De Grasse left the Chesapeake the Americans moved northward on the return to New York, sailing up the bay in a flotilla of small boats, bound for camps along the Hudson, to keep watch on Henry Clinton's New York garrison. Cornwallis and his staff left for England, and only the French remained near the site of the siege. Rochambeau's army settled into winter quarters in Yorktown, Williamsburg and Hampton.

After the British fleet returned to New York on November 7, there was official pretense that the navy would turn about and open a new campaign in the Chesapeake, but at headquarters there was an oppressive air of gloom. Henry Clinton now spent his days in bitter denunciation of others for the defeat at Yorktown, an incessant protest that the blame was not his. Clinton insisted that Germain, who had never adequately supported him from London, was "the falsest man alive. If I could have ended the war in half an hour, he would have prevented it." Sir Henry also opened a controversy with Cornwallis that was to drag on for years, a fruitless bickering over the responsibilities for the disaster at Yorktown.

Judge William Smith grew weary of Sir Henry's monologue, "a desultory justification of his own conduct and censure of everybody else . . . He is a distressed man, looking for friends and suspicious of all mankind, and complains of the number of his enemies . . . the man is wild . . . I pity him in his disgrace."

The news of Yorktown reached London three weeks after Clinton's return to New York, and was sent to Lord North's office in Downing Street. The King's Minister took it "as he would have taken a ball in his breast . . . opened his arms, exclaiming wildly, as he paced up and down . . . 'O! God! it is all over!'—words which he repeated many times . . ."

George III, by contrast, remained optimistic and resolute: "I have no doubt that when men are a little recovered of the shock felt by the bad news . . . that they will then find the necessity of carrying on the war . . ." The King did not ignore the capture of Cornwallis and his troops: "I particularly lament it on account of the consequences connected with it and the difficulties which it may produce in carrying on the public business . . . But I trust that neither Lord George Germain nor any member of the Cabinet will suppose that it makes the smallest alteration in those principles of my conduct which have directed me in past time and which will always continue to animate me under every event in the prosecution of the present contest."

But within three months, when the significance of Yorktown had become more apparent, the King was so depressed that he drafted a message of abdication:

March 1782
. . . His Majesty is convinced that the sudden change of Sentiments of one Branch of the Legislature has totally incapacitated him from either conducting the War with effect, or from obtaining any Peace but on conditions which would prove destructive to the Commerce as well as essential Rights of the British Nation.
His Majesty therefore with much sorrow finds He can be of no

"An Affectionate Farewell"

further Utility to His Native Country which drives Him to the painful step of quitting it for ever.

In consequence of which Intention His Majesty resigns the Crown of Great Britain and the Dominions appertaining thereto to His Dearly Beloved Son and lawful Successor, George Prince of Wales, whose endeavours for the Prosperity of the British Empire He hopes may prove more Successful.

Though this draft message was never sent to Parliament and George III reigned until his death in 1820, it reflected grim political realities as viewed from London in 1782, and undoubtedly influenced the terms of the Treaty of Paris as finally signed a year later.

Washington left Yorktown on November 5, and after halting in Williamsburg to visit sick and wounded soldiers hospitalized in the governor's palace, rode westward to Eltham, the plantation house of his brother-in-law, Burwell Bassett, near the head of the York River. The general arrived to find Jacky Custis dying. Washington remained with his grieving wife for a few days to arrange for the funeral, and then rode on toward Mount Vernon, halting in Fredericksburg at the home of his mother, and hurrying homeward when he found that she was away on a visit.

A few weeks later the general received a letter from Mary Washington, a quaint message that made no mention of the war, nor of his victory at Yorktown: "MY DEAR GEORG   I was truly unesy by Not being at hom when you went thru fredirecksburg it was a onlucky thing for me now I am afraid I Never Shall have that pleasure agin I am soe very unwell . . . I gott the 2 five ginnes you was soe kind to send me i am greatly obliged to you for it . . ." She was no longer content with the handsome small house he had provided for her and asked that he build her another on his land west of the Blue Ridge, "some little hous of my one if it is only twelve foot squar." She sent her love to Martha and added, but then struck through, these words: "I would have wrote to her but my reason has jis left me." Washington made no reply; he had not written to his mother during the war.

After only a week at Mount Vernon the general and Mrs.

Washington left for Philadelphia, where he reported to Congress, continued to fret over the intentions of the enemy, and held daily sessions with the first high-level administrative officers of the government—Robert Morris, the Superintendent of Finance; Benjamin Lincoln, the Secretary of War; and Robert R. Livingston, the Minister of Foreign Affairs. He persuaded Congress to call on the states for fresh troops for the campaign of 1782, but agreed to retire a number of generals he felt were no longer needed.

Clinton remained quietly in New York, except for a brief raid on New Brunswick, N. J., in January 1782, but Washington still nursed his fears that he would be defeated in the wake of the victory at Yorktown, since he no longer had the aid of the French fleet. "Without a decisive naval force," he said, "we can do nothing definitive."

Washington spent almost three months in the city before he became restive, then joined the army on the Hudson, with headquarters at Newburgh, N. Y.

A month later, in early May, the war reached another turning point. Henry Clinton was recalled to England after five years of fumbling and largely ineffectual command. His replacement was Sir Guy Carleton, the former British commander in Canada, who had been chosen to supervise the withdrawal of English forces from America.

In August, Carleton wrote Washington of a peace conference under way in Paris, and hinted that the generals should open negotiations of their own. Washington suspected British trickery to delude Americans while a new offensive was being prepared, and repeated his invariable theme of preparedness in orders to his army: "The readiest way to procure a lasting and honorable peace is to be fully prepared vigorously to prosecute war."

In the fall, without explanation, Rochambeau marched his army northward from Virginia, and after a joyous reunion of the allied troops on the Hudson, around Verplanck's Point, the French infantry, too, made preparations to leave. Rochambeau's troops were needed in the continuing struggle for control of the West Indies, and Paris had concluded that they were no longer needed in America. By December the French troops were gone.

"An Affectionate Farewell"

Carleton wrote Washington once again to urge an armistice between the armies, saying that he had already suspended "all hostilities." Washington refused to treat with him, and once more responded warily, "I can have no conception of a suspension of hostilities but that which extends to naval as well as land operations."

But the British were obviously leaving America. The redcoat garrison evacuated Savannah in July and Charleston in December. There were rumors that Carleton's troops would soon leave New York, but Washington had visions of a threat more ominous than enemy troops. For months he had foreseen trouble, perhaps even a violent uprising led by officers who had been unable to collect their back pay and pensions from the bankrupt Congress:

> I cannot help fearing the result . . . when I see such a number of men . . . about to be turned into the world, soured by penury and what they call the ingratitude of the public, involved in debts without one farthing of money to carry them home, after having spent the flower of their days, and many of them their patrimonies, in establishing the freedom and independence of their country . . . the patience and long sufferance of this army are almost exhausted . . .

A committee of officers went to Philadelphia in January 1783 to plead their case before Congress, which was still powerless to provide money, since the states denied it the power to tax. When delegates declined to consider the issuance of federal notes for future payment to impoverished officers, the frustrated veterans warned that their companions might rush "blindly into extremities."

As the spring of 1783 drew on, and the feeble government struggled as vainly as ever to cope with problems of finance, the general began to fear the unpaid army would plunge the country into violence before the last enemy soldier left America. He wrote Alexander Hamilton: "The sufferings of a complaining Army on one hand, and the inability of Congress and the tardiness of the States on the other, are the forebodings of evil . . ."

The threat of violence was so serious that Hamilton, who was now a congressman, wrote Washington, urging him to influence officers to remain "within the bonds of moderation," but Hamilton felt that the power of the army should be exerted to establish a system of federal taxation, which was the only hope for "justice to the creditors of the United States." In any event, Hamilton insisted, Washington should lead the officers in their quest for justice, rather than try to suppress their demands.

This was not the first suggestion that only Washington could save the country from anarchy. Some six months earlier Colonel Lewis Nicola had proposed to the commander that since the war had demonstrated "the weakness of republics," a monarchy should be established with Washington as king. The general replied, "Be assured, sir, no occurrence in the course of the war has given me more sensations . . ." He said he had read the suggestion that he become America's George I "with abhorrence . . . I am much at a loss to conceive what part of my conduct could have given encouragement to an address which seems to me big with the greatest mischiefs that can befall my country. If I am not deceived in the knowledge of myself, you could not have found a person to whom your schemes are more disagreeable."

Washington was so alarmed by Nicola's suggestion that he went so far as to have his aides certify in writing that his reply had been sealed and mailed to the colonel.

The general ignored Hamilton's advice that he sponsor the demands of his officers, but the movement did not subside. Major John Armstrong, an aide to Gates, wrote and distributed an anonymous broadside urging officers to be bold in their demands and to "suspect the man who would advise to more moderation and longer forbearance."

Washington saw this as a step toward military dictatorship, and issued an order forbidding a clandestine meeting called by Armstrong. Instead he proposed a regular meeting of officers on March 15 in which they could discuss their grievances. When Armstrong circulated a second anonymous letter on the eve of this meeting, declaring that Washington had "sanctified" the claims of officers, the commander felt that he was obliged to appear before the group. The meeting was held in a huge hall known as The Temple, a barnlike wooden structure built by soldiers that served as both chapel and dance hall. The general read a prepared speech from the rostrum before a throng of officers that packed the hall. Men in the audience watched him as if he were a stranger, with skeptical, almost hostile expressions.

Washington began with an apology for his presence, but said that he felt an obligation to speak in the interest of the army because of the wide circulation of the anonymous, and dangerous, proposals.

Washington paraphrased Armstrong's appeal to the officers: "If war continues, remove into the unsettled country . . . and leave an ungrateful country to defend itself. But who are they to defend? Our wives, our children, our farms which we leave behind us?"

The second proposal of the unknown agitator, Washington said, was equally disturbing, "If peace takes place, never sheath your swords, says he, until you have obtained full and ample justice. This dreadful alternative, of either deserting our country . . . or turning our arms against it . . . has something so shocking in it that humanity revolts at the idea. My God! What can this writer have in view . . . Can he be a friend to the army? Can he be a friend to this country?"

The faces of the audience remained expressionless.

The general's voice rose, "And let me conjure you, in the name of our common country . . . to express your utmost horror and detestation of the man who wishes . . . to overthrow the liberties of our country, and . . . open the flood gates of civil discord and deluge our rising empire in blood . . .

"Let me entreat you gentlemen . . . not to take measures which . . . will lessen the dignity and sully the glory you have hitherto maintained . . . rely on the plighted faith of your country and place a full confidence in the purity of the intentions of Congress . . ."

This was the end of his prepared speech. Washington sensed that he had not convinced his officers, who continued to regard him coldly. He drew from his pocket a letter from the Virginia congressman Joseph Jones and read a few lines, then halted to pull out a new pair of spectacles, which most of the officers had never seen him wear. "Gentlemen," he said, "I have grown gray in your service, and now I am going blind." Major Samuel Shaw was profoundly impressed: "There was something so natural, so unaffected in this appeal . . . It forced its way into the heart . . ." Shaw noted that most of the men about him were blinking back tears, that the general had won them merely by putting on his glasses, and that his simple remark had reminded them of all they had suffered together in a way that no oration could have matched.

The general read from Jones's letter an explanation of the burdens facing Congress, and then a firm promise that officers of the army would be paid as soon as possible. With that, he folded the letter, nodded to his officers and turned from the podium.

Washington left the hall, Horatio Gates took over as presiding officer, and the officers promptly rejected the anonymous proposals and asked that Washington act in their behalf. Most of the army felt that he had averted the threat of a military coup. Samuel Shaw expressed the admiration of officers: "On other occasions Washington had been supported by the . . . Army . . . but in this he stood single and alone . . . He appeared, not at the head of his troops, but, as it were in opposition to them; and for a dreadful moment the interests of the Army and its General seemed to be in competition; He spoke—every doubt was dispelled, and the tide of patriotism rolled again in its wonted course."

Washington was relieved by the reaction to his speech, but his fears were not allayed. He wrote Joseph Jones that Congress should not depend on his influence to "dispel other clouds."

British, French and American peace commissioners had been meeting in Paris for months, debating terms of treaties between the three nations, but it was late in March 1783 before Washington had official word of an Anglo-American treaty signed four months earlier, a preliminary document that guaranteed American independence, ended the fighting and provided for exchange of prisoners. Since the treaty would become final only when England and France had concluded an agreement, Washington accepted the news as "very inconclusive" and warned that the army might be forced "to worry through another campaign." It was only a week later, however, when even his fears were laid to rest. The Treaty of Paris had been signed on January 20 and the long struggle was over at last. Washington wrote from New-burgh to Nathanael Greene, "It remains only for the States to be wise, and to establish their independence on the basis of inviolable, efficacious union . . . which may prevent their being made the sport of European policy; may Heaven give them the wisdom to adopt the measures still necessary for this important purpose."

On April 19 the "cessation of hostilities between the United States of America and the King of Great Britain" was announced to the army from the door of the hall where Washington had addressed the officers. It was eight years to the day since the first volley of musket fire had rolled across Lexington Green.

In June the general wrote another of his "Circulars to the States," through which he had so frequently appealed for men, supplies and money during the war. This challenge to the thirteen states was to be known as Washington's Legacy:

> . . . This is the moment when the eyes of the world are turned upon them, this is the moment to establish or ruin their national character forever . . . For, according, to the system of Policy the States shall adopt at this moment, they will stand or fall . . . it is yet to be decided, whether the Revolution must ultimately be considered as a blessing or a curse . . . not to the present age alone, for with our fate will the destiny of unborn millions be involved.

Washington added:

> There are four things which I humbly conceive are essential to the well being, I may even venture to say, to the existence of the United States as an independent power:
> 1st. An indissoluble Union of the States under one Federal Head.
> 2dly. A sacred regard to public justice.
> 3dly. The adoption of a proper peace establishment, and
> 4thly. The prevalence of that friendly and pacific disposition among the people of the United States which will induce them to forget their local prejudices and policies, to make . . . mutual concessions . . . to the general prosperity, and in some instances, to sacrifice, their individual advantages to the interest of the community . . .

Prospects of "a proper peace establishment" were not bright. Most of his troops were unceremoniously mustered out in mid-June, straggling away homeward from their camps without pay, and even without promised requisitions to their state governments for three months' pay. The credit of Congress had sunk so low that Robert Morris failed to persuade manufacturers to provide paper for printing these requisitions. For a time it appeared that men left in service would plunge the country into bloodshed.

Later in the month a band of disgruntled Pennsylvania soldiers, most of them new recruits, mutinied in Lancaster and marched to Philadelphia, where they were joined by troops stationed in the city's barracks. Five hundred strong, these men seized the public arsenal, surrounded the State House where both Congress and the Pennsylvania Executive Council were meeting, and threatened to storm the building if they were not given a hearing. The men finally returned to barracks, but Congress requested protection from Washington, who marched fifteen hundred troops to the capital at once, with orders to put down "the infamous and outrageous" mutiny.

Fearful of more disorders, Congress moved to Princeton and remained there, though the mutiny was over by July 4, the seventh anniversary of the Declaration of Independence.

In mid-November Carleton notified Washington that he would evacuate New York on the twenty-third, but there was a delay and the commander did not enter the city until November 25, a few hours after the last British soldiers had left. Mounted on a handsome gray horse, Washington led a few of his officers down from Harlem, through the fields over which his panic-stricken troops had fled from the British landing at Kips Bay more than seven years earlier. The riders passed into the city and halted at the Tea Water Pump near the corner of Chatham and Pearl streets, where a few civilian officials joined them and formed a procession.

The party halted there for an hour or more, until the American flag could be raised atop Fort George on the Battery. The departing British had removed the halyard and cleats and greased the pole, and the new flag rose only after several sailors had failed to clamber up the slippery pole and an enterprising young man found a few cleats in a nearby ironmonger's shop. The anonymous hero tied a halyard about his waist and mounted slowly, driving in the new cleats one by one. Cannon fired when the flag fluttered up and Washington's procession began clattering down Broadway, past eight hundred troops who stood at attention as an honor guard. These were Massachusetts and New York veterans who were well turned out by the army's standards, but a young woman among the crowd of cheering civilians on the walk saw the soldiers through tears, remembering the smartly dressed British troops who had occupied the city throughout the war, ". . . the troops that marched in, on the contrary, were ill-clad and weather beaten, and made a forlorn appearance; but then they were *our* troops, and as I looked at them and thought upon all they had done and suffered for us, my heart and my eyes were full, and I admired and gloried in them the more . . ."

After a greeting from state and city leaders, a few troops were posted about the streets, Washington dined at Cape's Tavern, and the occupation was complete. For a week the general endured a succession of banquets, receptions and official ceremonies, until, at noon on December 4, he attended a farewell dinner with a few of his officers at Fraunces Tavern. A barge was waiting for him at the waterfront, to carry him over the Hudson to Paulus Hook, on his way to Philadelphia, where he was to settle his accounts. He would then ride to Annapolis, where he would resign his commission to Congress before returning home. Steuben was to ride with him as far as Philadelphia, and three aides would accompany him to Mount Vernon, to begin work on the mass of headquarters papers collected during the war, among them voluminous records of his expenses.

Washington joined a small crowd of his veterans in the tavern dining room at Fraunces. Many ranking officers were missing. Only four of the seventy-three general officers who had been commissioned to serve under him were present: Major Generals Knox, Steuben and McDougall and Brigadier General George

Clinton, the governor of New York. The only colonel present was Henry Jackson of the 4th Massachusetts. Benjamin Tallmadge saw the commander enter, in the grip of "emotion too strong to be concealed," and the tension endured throughout the brief meal until Washington rose and proposed a toast. As Tallmadge remembered it, the general said, "With a heart full of love and gratitude, I now take leave of you. I most devoutly wish that your latter days may be as prosperous and happy as your former ones have been glorious and honorable."

When the wine glasses had been emptied, Washington said, "I can't come to each of you, but shall feel obliged if each of you will come and take me by the hand."

Knox, who was at his side, turned to shake hands. Washington was speechless, his eyes filled as he embraced his artilleryman. The other officers moved up in turn to kiss the commander. Tallmadge said he had never heard so much weeping, but there was no other sound to break "the solemn silence . . . or to interrupt the tenderness of the . . . scene."

The general walked through the group of tearful officers, waved his hand and emerged into the street, where he passed between files of infantry to the dock without speaking, clambered into a waiting barge with Steuben and the three aides and Billy Lee, and moved off into the river, watched by "a prodigious crowd." As the oarsmen pulled him toward the Jersey shore there was a faint shrilling of bosun's pipes from British transports in the outer harbor, and the last of them made sail.

Philadelphia greeted Washington's little party with a tolling of church bells and salutes from cannon. Crowds surged through the streets after the general wherever he appeared. He was welcomed by the Pennsylvania Council, addressed the General Assembly, received numerous delegations, and attended state dinners each night.

The general made a final settlement of his expense accounts during the visit. On July 1, 1783, Washington had submitted his bill to the Treasury for more than $414,000 in "lawful money," most of which was paid him. This amounted to about eight and a half times the $48,000 he would have been due if he had

"An Affectionate Farewell"

accepted only a salary, as other general officers had done—but he was, in fact, the one army officer who was forced to bear the expenses of a large headquarters establishment.

Of his total expenses, about $88,000 was for "household" expenses, the care and feeding of his staff and the endless swarm of visitors, congressmen, diplomats, state and other civilian officials, and army officers, both French and American—expenses incurred during the turbulent years when his headquarters served as a mobile court of sorts, usually the only visible seat of effective governmental power in the country. Among items included were food, drink, servants, barbers, tailors and tips. Washington felt that his bargain with Congress, made at a time when American independence seemed an impossible dream, assured him reimbursement for expenses he would normally incur as commander in chief. He had included the obvious costs of maintaining field headquarters in the style of his accustomed life at Mount Vernon.

Military expenses were in addition to his household costs. These ran to $55,000 for "secret intelligence"; almost $39,000 for reconnoitering the enemy and travel (usually with a cavalry escort); and miscellaneous charges of nearly $77,000. In addition, some $160,000 of the total had been included as an adjustment to compensate for depreciation of the currency, on a scale approved by Congress.

Most items were substantiated by vouchers and bills. Some entries however, were notably vague and unspecific. For example, the general accounted for costs incurred during a long period when he had lacked a bookkeeper at headquarters in this fashion:

1781—September 6
To Household Expences from the close of Major Gibbs's acct Nov. 21, 1780 till the commencement of them by Lt. Colfax the 6 of Sept. 1781—amounts from the best accounts & Estimates that can be had & from recollection (exclusive of what was obtained by bartering a little salt wch was put into the hands of the Housekeeper for that purpose) to at least* $20,800

---

* This business during the above Interval was in such a variety of hands for want of a proper Steward (wch in vain by myself & others endeav-

Even the large total of $414,000, as Washington had discovered in the July settlement, failed to cover advances he had made from his pocket over the seven-year period since his first settlement with the government. Washington explained that there were items "I have omitted to charge," largely due to "hurry, I suppose, and the perplexity of business (for I know not how else to account for the deficiency)." It was only now that the general decided to add the cost of Martha's six winter visits to headquarters. He explained that he had not intended to include his wife's expenses because they were personal, but since "the embarrassed nature of our public affairs" had prevented his planned annual visits to Mount Vernon and he had submitted to the "self-denial" of remaining in camp, he felt that the charge was just.

Since Congress had already made payments on his accounts, he was now due a balance of about $50,000 in "lawful" currency, which was paid without question. No one, then or later, challenged the propriety of paying Washington's large headquarters expenses at a time when Congress was unable to fund the back pay and pension costs of the army's officers.

Whatever the appropriateness of the general's charges, his accounts had been kept with such meticulous care that auditors later found the grand total of charges, $449,261.51, in error by less than a dollar.

Baron von Steuben was not so fortunate in his dealings with the Treasury. Though an audit showed that the Prussian was due $8,500 in lawful money, he was paid only $1,700, plus a 6 percent Treasury certificate for $6,800. He later tried in vain to sell the note for ten cents on the dollar.

---

oured to obtain)—and the accounts were not only irregularly kept, but many of them were lost or mislaid, & some of them so defaced as not to be legible, that it is impossible for me to make out a statement of them; But as it comprehended that space of time in which the French & American armies formed one camp at Philipsburgh & our Expences were at the highest; and as this sum corrisponds as nearly as can be expected with the average Expenditures per Month as will appear by Lieut. Colfaxs accts since—The above sum is charged under these Circumstances, upon the principle which seems most equitable to do justice to the public, and no injustice to myself—

"An Affectionate Farewell"

Washington left Philadelphia after a week, on December 15, and now traveling only with Humphreys and Walker, Billy Lee and two or three other servants, rode toward home.

The party set off rounds of celebration in towns along the route, and was delayed for balls, receptions and banquets in Wilmington, Delaware, and Baltimore. It was December 20 before Washington reached Annapolis, where Congress was sitting after moving from Princeton. Only seven states were now represented in the diminished body, but Washington notified Thomas Mifflin, the newly elected president of Congress, that he was anxious to present his resignation as commander in chief and asked for instructions. Mifflin invited him to appear in Maryland's State House on December 23, but in the interim the general was honored at dinner parties given by Mifflin and Congress, made two public addresses, and enjoyed a ball given in his honor by the Maryland General Assembly. One delegate noted that Washington danced every set so that "all the ladies might have the pleasure of dancing with him, or, as it has since been handsomely expressed, *get a touch of him.*"

Despite the hectic pace of his social life in Annapolis, Washington found time to write and revise a brief speech of resignation. In the first version he bid Congress "an affectionate and final farewell," and took "ultimate leave" of public service, but in his revision struck out the words "and final" and "ultimate," as if he already glimpsed the future. David Humphreys made a fair copy of the address to be left with Congress, and at noon on December 23, as Billy Lee waited at the door with the saddled horses, Washington was escorted into the chamber of the Maryland State House where about twenty congressmen sat, wearing their hats. The commander took a chair beside Mifflin, with Humphreys and Walker standing on either side of him. Civilians and a few army officers filed in and filled the empty seats and gallery and jostled into place around the walls. Silence fell as Mifflin rose and spoke to Washington, "Sir, the United States in Congress assembled are prepared to receive your communications."

Washington stood and bowed to the delegates, who doffed their hats briefly. The general held a sheet of paper in a trembling hand. "Mr. President: The great events on which my resignation depended having at length taken place, I have now the honor of offering my sincere congratulations to Congress and . . . to surrender into their hands the trust committed to me and to claim the indulgence of retiring from the service of my country . . . I resign with satisfaction the appointment I accepted with diffidence—a diffidence in my abilities to accomplish so arduous a task, which however was superseded by a confidence in the rectitude of our Cause, the support of the supreme power of the Union and the patronage of Heaven . . ."

He spoke of his debt to the army and of "the peculiar services and distinguished merits" of his staff. The general seized the paper with both hands, but still it trembled: "It was impossible the choice of confidential officers . . . could have been more fortunate. . . ."

For a moment the general could not go on. His voice faltered, and "the whole house felt his agitation." Like many another in the audience, Dr. James McHenry saw Washington only dimly, through tears. The commander recovered and hurried to the end: "I consider it an indispensable duty to close this last solemn act of my official life by commending the interests of our dearest Country to the protection of Almighty God. . . . Having now finished the work assigned to me, I retire from the great theater of action, and bidding an affectionate farewell to this august body under whose orders I have so long acted, I here offer my commission and take my leave of all the employments of public life." He had spoken for three minutes.

Washington drew his commission from his pocket, folded the copy of his address and handed the papers to Mifflin, who responded briefly and passed a copy of his own remarks to Washington. The general took the paper and bowed once more to Mifflin and the delegates, who gravely removed and then replaced their hats. The general left the room, but returned when the spectators had gone and Congress had adjourned, to shake the hand of each delegate. He did not linger, but went out to his horse, where Billy Lee, Humphreys and Walker were waiting. He was off for Mount Vernon, just in time for Christmas.

Selected Bibliography

Adams, Charles Francis, ed., *Familiar Letters of John Adams and His Wife Abigail* . . . New York, 1876.

Adams, John, *Letters Addressed to His Wife* . . . 2 vols. New York, 1876.

Alden, John R., *General Charles Lee, Traitor or Patriot?* Baton Rouge, La., 1951.

Alden, John R., *General Gage in America*, Baton Rouge, La., 1948.

Anderson, Enoch, "Personal Recollections . . ." *Papers of the Hist. Soc. of Del.*, XVI, Wilmington, Del., 1896.

André, John, *Major André's Journal* . . . Tarrytown, N.Y., 1930.

Bakeless, John, *Turncoats, Traitors and Heroes*, Philadelphia, 1959.

Baker, William S., *Itinerary of George Washington*, Philadelphia, 1892.

Barker, John, *The British in Boston* . . . Cambridge, Mass., 1924.

Benedict, E. C., *The Battle of Harlem Heights* . . . New York, 1880.

Bill, Alfred H., *Valley Forge*, New York, 1952.

Blanchard, Claude, *Journal*, Albany, N.Y., 1876.

Bolton, Charles K., *The Private Soldier under Washington*, New York, 1902.

Boudinot, Elias, *Journal or Historical Recollections* . . . Philadelphia, 1894.

Bowen, Catherine Drinker, *John Adams and the American Revolution*, Boston, 1950.

Burnett, Edmund C., ed., *Letters of Members of the Continental Congress*, 8 vols., Washington, 1921–26.

Butler, Richard, "Journal of the Siege of Yorktown," *Historical Magazine*, VIII, 1864, 102–112.

Butcher, H. B., *The Battle of Trenton* . . . Princeton, N.J., 1934.

Carrington, H. B., *Battles of the American Revolution*, New York, 1888.

Chastellux, Marquis de, *Travels in North America* . . . Trans. and ed., H. C. Rice, Jr., 2 vols., Chapel Hill, N.C., 1963.

Chinard, Gilbert, *Lafayette in Virginia*, Baltimore, 1928.

Clinton, Sir Henry, *The American Rebellion*, ed., William B. Willcox, New Haven, Conn., 1954.

Closen, Baron Ludwig von, *Revolutionary Journal* . . . Chapel Hill, N.C., 1958.

Commager, Henry S., and Richard B. Morris, *The Spirit of '76*, 2 vols. Indianapolis, Ind., 1958.

Cresswell, Nicholas, *Journal, 1774–1777*, New York, 1924.

Custis, George Washington Parke, *Recollections of Washington*, New York, 1860.

SELECTED BIBLIOGRAPHY

Dearborn, Henry, *Journals, 1776–1783*, Cambridge, Mass., 1887.

Duer, William A., *The Life of William Alexander, Earl Of Stirling*, New York, 1847.

Deux-Ponts, Guillaume, Comte de, ed., S. A. Greene, *My Campaigns in America*, Boston, 1868.

Dumas, Mathieu, *Memoirs of His Own Time*, Philadelphia, 1839.

Eelking, Max von, *The German Allied Troops in the North American War*, Albany, N.Y., 1893.

Field, Thomas W., "The Battle of Long Island, *Long Island Hist. Soc. Memoirs*, Vol. II, Brooklyn, N.Y., 1869.

Fitzpatrick, John C., ed., *The Writings of George Washington*, 39 vols., Washington, 1931–44.

Flexner, James T., *George Washington in the American Revolution*, Boston, 1967.

Force, Peter, ed., *American Archives*, 4th and 5th series, 6 vols. and 3 vols. Washington, 1837–46, 1848–53.

Fortescue, Sir John W., *A History of the British Army*, 13 vols., London, 1899–1930.

Freeman, D. S., *George Washington*, Vols. III, IV, V, New York, 1951–52.

French, Allen, *The First Year of the American Revolution*, Boston, 1934.

———, *General Gage's Informers*, Ann Arbor, Mich., 1932.

Frothingham, Richard, *History of the Siege of Boston*, Boston, 1851.

Fuller, J. F. C., *Decisive Battles of the U.S.A.*, New York, 1942.

Garden, Alexander, *Anecdotes of the American Revolution*, 3 vols., Brooklyn, N.Y., 1865.

Gordon, William, *The History . . . of the United States of America*, 4 vols., London, 1788.

Gottschalk, Louis, *Lafayette Comes to America*, Chicago, 1935.

———, *Lafayette Joins the American Army*, Chicago, 1937.

———, *Lafayette and the Close of the American Revolution*, Chicago, 1942.

Graydon, Alexander, *Memoirs of His Own Time*, Philadelphia, 1846.

Greene, George W., *The Life of Nathanael Greene*, 3 vols., New York, 1867–1871.

Gruber, Ira, *The Howe Brothers and the American Revolution*, New York, 1972.

Heath, William, *Memoirs . . .* New York, 1901.

Huddleston, F. J., *Gentleman Johnny Burgoyne*, Indianapolis, Ind., 1927.

Hughes, Rupert, *George Washington*, 3 vols., New York, 1926–1930.

Huntington, Ebenezer, *Letters Written During the American Revolution*, New York, 1914.

Irving, Washington, *Life of George Washington*, 5 vols., New York, 1855–1859.

James, W. M., *The British Navy in Adversity*, London, 1926.

Johnson, Victor L., *The Administration of the American Commissariat During the Revolutionary War*, Philadelphia, 1941.

Johnston, Henry P., "The Campaign of 1776 around New York and Brooklyn." *Long Island Hist. Soc. Memoirs*, Vol. III, Brooklyn, N.Y., 1878.

Jones, Thomas, *History of New York During the Revolutionary War . . .* 2 vols., New York, 1879.

Kapp, Friedrich, *The Life of John Kalb*, New York, 1884.

———, *Life of Friedrich Wilhelm von Steuben*, New York, 1859.

Kitman, Marvin, *George Washington's Expense Account*, New York, 1970.

Knollenberg, Bernhard, *Washington and the Revolution*, New York, 1940.

SELECTED BIBLIOGRAPHY

Lafayette, Marquis de, *Memoirs, Correspondence and Manuscripts*, 3 vols., London, 1837.

Lee, Henry, *Memoirs of the War in the Southern Department* . . . New York, 1869.

Lossing, Benson John, *The Pictorial Field Book of the American Revolution*, 2 vols., New York, 1852.

Lowell, E. J., *The Hessians . . . in the Revolutionary War*, New York, 1884.

MacElree, Wilmer W., *Along the Western Brandywine*, Westchester, Pa., 1909.

Mackenzie, Frederick, *Diary*, 2 vols., Cambridge, Mass., 1930.

Mahan, Alfred T., *The Major Operations of the Navies in the War of American Independence*, Boston, 1913.

Martin, Joseph P., *A Narrative of Some of the Adventures, Dangers, and Sufferings of a Revolutionary Soldier*, New York, 1962.

Martyn, Charles, *The Life of Artemas Ward*, New York, 1921.

Montgomery, Mrs. Richard, *Biographical Notes Concerning General Richard Montgomery*, Louise L. Hunt, ed., Poughkeepsie, N.Y., 1876.

Moore, Frank, *Diary of the American Revolution*, 2 vols., New York, 1863.

Reed, William B., *Life and Correspondence of Joseph Reed*, 2 vols., Philadelphia, 1847.

Morison, Samuel E., *The Young Man Washington*, Cambridge, Mass., 1932.

Muhlenberg, Henry A., *The Life of Major-General Peter Muhlenberg*, Philadelpha, 1849.

Pickering, Octavius, and C. W. Upham, *The Life of Timothy Pickering*, 4 vols., Boston, 1867–73.

Popp, Stephan, "Journal," 1777–1783, 26 *Pennsylvania Magazine of History and Biography*, pp. 25 ff.

Rochambeau, Comte de, *Memoirs . . . relative to the War of Independence*, 2 vols., Paris, 1838.

Rossman, Kenneth R., *Thomas Mifflin*, Chapel Hill, N.C., 1952.

Rush, Benjamin, *Autobiography*, ed., G. W. Corner, Princeton, N.J., 1948.

Scheer, George F., and Hugh F. Rankin, *Rebels and Redcoats*, Cleveland, Ohio, 1957.

Schenck, David, *North Carolina, 1780–81*, Raleigh, N.C., 1889.

Sellers, Charles C., *Charles Willson Peale*, New York, 1969.

Serle, Ambrose, *The American Journal of Ambrose Serle*, San Marino, Calif., 1940.

Smith, Page, *John Adams*, 2 vols., New York, 1962.

Sparks, Jared, ed., *Writings of Washington*, 12 vols., Boston, 1834–37.

Stedman, Charles, *The History . . . of the American War*, 2 vols., London, 1794.

Stevens, B. F., ed., *The Campaign in Virginia, 1781*, 2 vols., London, 1888.

———, *The Clinton-Cornwallis Controversy*, London, 1888.

Stillé, C. J., *Major General Anthony Wayne* . . . Philadelphia, 1893.

Stryker, W. S., *The Battle of Monmouth*, Princeton, N.J., 1927.

Stryker, W. S., *The Battles of Trenton and Princeton*, Boston, 1898.

Tallmadge, Col. Benjamin, *Memoir of . . .*, Boston, 1876.

Thacher, James, *Military Journal of the American Revolution* . . . Hartford, Conn., 1862.

Thayer, Theodore, *Nathanael Greene, Strategist of the American Revolution*, New York, 1960.

Tucker, Glenn, *Anthony Wayne and the New Nation*, Harrisburg, Pa., 1974.

Van Doren, Carl, *Secret History of the American Revolution*, New York, 1941.

———, *Mutiny in January*, New York, 1943.

SELECTED BIBLIOGRAPHY

Waldo, Albigence, "Diary, Valley Forge, 1777–1778," *Pennsylvania Magazine of History and Biography*, XXI, 1897, 299–323.

Ward, Christopher, *The War of the Revolution*, 2 vols., New York, 1952.

Washington, George, *Account of Expenses while Commander-in-Chief*, with annotations by John C. Fitzpatrick, Boston, 1917.

———, *Diaries*, ed., John C. Fitzpatrick, 4 vols., Boston and New York, 1925.

———, *Writings*, ed., W. C. Ford, 14 vols., New York, 1889–1893.

———, *Writings*, ed., John C. Fitzpatrick, 39 vols., Washington, 1931–44.

Wilkinson, James, *Memoirs of My Own Times*, 3 vols., Philadelphia, 1816.

Willcox, William B., *Portrait of a General: Sir Henry Clinton*, New York, 1964.

Notes

Note: Complete bibliographic data for major sources are given on pages 461–464. "G.W." refers to *The Writings of George Washington,* edited by JOHN C. FITZPATRICK.

1 Commander in Chief

The brief description of Philadelphia in the opening pages is drawn from *The History of Philadelphia,* Vol. I, by J. Thomas Scharff and Thompson Westcott (Phila., 1884); *Philadelphia, A History . . . ,* Vol. I, by Ellis P. Oberholtzer (Phila., 1912); *Early Philadelphia,* Horace Lippincott, pp. 125–26 (Phila., 1917); *Revolutionary Doctor: Benjamin Rush,* Carl Binger, p. 72 (New York, 1966). Weather conditions, recorded in files of the American Philosophical Society, were supplied by William T. Hodge, chief of Climatic Information Section, National Weather Records Center, Asheville, N.C.

The work of Congress during this week is detailed in E. C. Burnett's *Letters of Members of the Continental Congress,* Vol. I, especially pp. 92 ff.; in *Journals of the Continental Congress,* Vol. II, pp. 80 ff.; and in *The Papers of the Continental Congress,* Vol. CLII, Part 1, pp. 1 ff. (Manuscripts Division, Library of Congress). Appropriate quotations from these sources are presented in narrative form by Allen French in *The First Year of The American Revolution,* pp. 276 ff.

Despite the rich background revealed in these official sources, virtually all we know of the actual selection of Washington as commander in chief is based on the recollections of John Adams twenty-seven years later—a description found in Vol. II of *The Life and Works of John Adams* (Charles F. Adams, ed.), pp. 417 ff.

Additional details were left by Washington himself in his *Diaries,* Vol. II, pp. 196 ff., in two surviving letters to his wife (June 18 and 23), and in *The Autobiography of Benjamin Rush,* p. 113.

The major documents involved—the letters to Martha, Washington's offer to serve without pay, and his acceptance speech—are found in *G.W.,* III, 292–95, 301.

The sketch of Washington's appearance and character at this time is based on a description by his friend George Mercer, at the end of the French and Indian War, and on the valuable summary by Douglas S. Freeman in his exhaustive biography of Washington, Vol. II, pp. 369 ff.

The sketch of Charles Lee is drawn largely from John R. Alden's definitive biography, whose major source was the four-volume *Lee Papers,* published by the New York Historical Society. The portrait of Thomas Mifflin is drawn from Kenneth Rossman's biography, that of Schuyler from Bayard Tuckerman's biography, and that of Reed from *The Dictionary of American Biography.* John Adams is sketched from Catherine Drinker Bowen's *John Adams and the American Revolution,* especially pp. 552 and 633–34.

2 The General Meets His Army

Due largely to the industry of W. S. Baker, who published in his detailed *Itinerary of General Washington* (1892) every recorded wartime movement of the new commander, it is possible to trace with some confidence the general's journey from Philadelphia to Cambridge. His departure was noted by the *Pennsylvania Evening*

Post and documented by the first item of his expense account, the purchase of five horses.

It was apparently Washington Irving who created the tradition of Washington's stirring response to the news of Bunker Hill. This embellishment of a circumstantial account by John Adams is in Volume I of Irving's life of Washington, p. 488, and is instructive as to the nature of the growth of the Washington legend.

"The Rules of Civility," copied so laboriously by Washington in his youth, seem to have originated with French Jesuit priests in the sixteenth century. In light of Washington's deep reserve, his lifelong self-discipline and his rather rigid views of social behavior, it is tempting to seek in this amusing little copybook some of the formative influences of his life.

Charles Willson Peale's revealing anecdote of Washington and his first portrait is found in C.C. Sellers, *Charles Willson Peale*, Vol. I, p. 121.

The rendition of Washington's personality in these pages owes much to Samuel Eliot Morison's *The Young Man Washington*, which remains after forty-odd years the most penetrating analysis of the general. Washington's comment that "it is easy to make acquaintances . . . ," one of the most illuminating of his remarks, is found in *G.W.*, XXVI, 39.

The glimpse of the wild inhabitants of the American frontier in this period is from Charles Woodmason's *Journal of the Carolina Backcountry on the Eve of the Revolution* (6 vols., New York, 1922), p. 153.

Washington's later recollection of his prospects of victory as the revolution opened is in *G.W.*, XXX, 297.

The doleful prewar prophecies of British leaders are cited by J. W. Fortescue in his *History of the British Army*, Vol. III, pp. 169–71.

Contemporary accounts of Washington's passage through New York have been assembled by J.N. Stokes in his *Iconography of Manhattan Island*, Vol. V, pp. 894–95. The eyewitnesses cited include Mrs. Richard Montgomery, William Smith and Judge Thomas Jones. Official note of the visit is taken in *The Journals of the Provincial Congress*, Vol. I, pp. 54 ff.

Washington's assurance to the New York Congress that he would shun the role of military dictator, opening with the words "When we assumed the soldier," is in Force's *American Archives*, (4th series) Vol. II, p. 1321. Early versions published elsewhere were bowdlerized.

The quixotic response of Charles Lee to greetings from the Massachusetts Provincial Congress in Watertown is found in the *Lee Papers* (New York Historical Society) Vol. I, pp. 186–87.

Private John Kettel's comment on the uneventful day of Washington's arrival in Cambridge is cited by Charles Martyn in his *Life of Artemas Ward*, p. 153n; Martyn also recounted the tale of Putnam's deception of the irascible British officer.

Washington described American defensive lines and the British position in Boston in *G.W.*, III, 320–331.

The tradition of the drinking party in General Ward's quarters, cited by Rupert Hughes from T.C. Amory, *Old Cambridge and New*, p. 23, should be regarded as traditional.

The Rev. William Emerson's graphic description of the army's camp is in the Bancroft Transcripts, *American Papers*, Vol. II, pp. 447 ff., New York Public Library.

Washington's outburst, describing the "exceedingly dirty and nasty people" of the New England army, is in a private letter to Lund Washington, his farm manager at Mount Vernon, August 20, 1775, Emmett Collection, 7738, New York Public Library. The general's reprimand to the lieutenant who degraded himself by performing the duties of a sergeant is in *General Orders*, October 3, 1776, cited by Rupert Hughes, Vol. II, p. 283.

Washington's optimistic estimate that the raw materials of his army could be transformed into "good stuff" is in *G.W.*, III, 374.

NOTES

3   Boston Besieged

Washington noted the purchase of his identifying ribbon in his account book, July 10, 1775. His appearance at this time was recorded by Dr. Thacher in his *Journal*, p. 30, and by Abigail Adams (*Familiar Letters of John Adams and His Wife . . .* , C.F. Adams, ed., p. 78).

The early version of "Yankee Doodle" is given in *The Library of American Literature* (11 vols., New York, 1891), by Edmund C. Stedman and E. M. Hutchinson, Vol. III, p. 338.

The anecdote concerning Greene and his wig is from Mabel Lorenz Ives's *Washington's Headquarters* (Upper Montclair, N.J., 1932), p. 38.

The clumsy bit of British propaganda attacking Washington as a seducer of young women, published in *The Gentleman's Magazine*, London, was exposed as a forgery only after the war, when Harrison's original letter, preserved in the British Public Record office, was found to contain no mention of the pliant Sukey. This forgery is examined by John C. Fitzpatrick in "The Washington Scandals," *Scribner's Magazine*, April 1927.

The plaint of John Adams about greedy, rank-conscious officers appears in C.F. Adams, *Familiar Letters . . .* , p. 276.

Returns of the army's strength at Cambridge in July 1775 are given (none too accurately) in *G.W.*, III, 319.

The description of conditions in occupied Boston is drawn from French's *The First Year of the War*, pp. 320 ff., and from Frothingham's *The Siege of Boston*, pp. 290 ff.

Nathanael Greene's reassurance that New England had no plans for subjugating the southern colonies is cited by Frothingham, p. 266.

The anecdote about Washington's role as peacemaker between his battling troops, which should be accepted as traditional, is cited in T.C. Amory's *Military Services and Public Life of Major General John Sullivan* (Boston, 1868), p. 69.

Washington's stunned silence when he learned of his powder shortage was reported by Sullivan to the New Hampshire Committee of Safety (*New Hampshire State Papers*, 7:572).

Washington's eagerness to attack the Boston garrison contrary to the advice of his generals is detailed in *G.W.*, III, 483–84, 485n, 511; and in *G.W.*, IV, 243.

Early examples of Washington's doleful forecasts to Congress of the army's dissolution appear in Washington's *Writings* edited by Ford, Vol. III, pp. 146, 191, 195, 214.

Details of headquarters expenses at Cambridge, especially those dealing with Washington's domestic staff, appear in his account books, pp. 6–7, 11, 35–36; and his wine consumption on pp. 14–15, 18–19.

A facsimile of the American propaganda broadside contrasting life in the opposing armies appears in Bolton's *The Private Soldier under Washington*, p. 90.

General Gage's reports from Boston are found in *The Gage Papers*, William L. Clements Library, University of Michigan. His letter to Barrington on the effects of Bunker Hill was dated June 26, 1775.

Washington's efforts to create a navy of his own are detailed in Force, *American Archives*, (4th series), Vol. III, pp. 683–84, 688.

Charles Lee's criticism of Congress for failure to fortify New York is in a letter to Robert Morris, January 3, 1776 (*Lee Papers*, New York Historical Society, I, 233).

Washington's final outburst to Reed described in this chapter appears in Washington's *Writings*, edited by Ford, Vol. III, p. 247.

4   A Surprise for William Howe

The jubilant British reaction to the sight of the strange new American flag was reported in Dodsley's *Annual Register* (London, 1775), pp. 269 ffff. Washington's jocular reaction is in *G.W.*, IV, 211.

The disorderly departure of Washington's troops from his Cambridge camp was reported in David Ramsay's *History of the American Revolution* (London, 1793), p. 261.

Washington's protest over his difficulties ("How it will end," etc.), is in *G.W.*, IV, 211–12; his plea for Reed's return is in *ibid.*, p. 269; and his report of his midnight prowls along the front is in *ibid.*, p. 240.

Howe's careless reconnaissance of the Dorchester position was reported in Howe–Dartmouth, as cited in Force (5th series) Vol. IV, p. 458; and the order by Howe of February 14 is quoted by Archibald Robertson in his *Diaries and Sketches in America* (New York, 1930), p. 72.

This narrative of Washington's decisive occupation of Dorchester is drawn from French's *First Year*; Frothingham's *Siege*; *Ward*, I, 52 ff.; Carrington's *Battles*, pp. 150 ff.; and the *Correspondence and Journals of Samuel B. Webb*, Vol. I, p. 133.

The panic in Boston as the British evacuation progressed is described in J. Williamson's *Memorial History of Boston*, Vol. III, p. 164; and Lorenzo Sabine's *Loyalists of the American Revolution* (Boston, 1864), Vol. I, pp. 509 ff.

5 Can New York Be Defended?

Charles Lee's excoriation of his men is to be found in *Connecticut Historical Society Collections*, Vol. VII, p. 129; details of his board and wine bill are given by Jones in *History of New York During the Revolutionary War*, Vol. I, p. 82.

Washington's exchange with the Massachusetts Assembly is from *Force*, Vol. V, (4th series), pp. 539–40; and from Ford's *Writings*, III, pp. 497–500.

The story of the whores in New York is drawn from the *Journal* of Isaac Bangs (Arno Press, N.Y., 1969), pp. 29–31; and from the *Col. Laommi Baldwin Papers* (Harvard Library), p. 29.

Washington's brusque letter to Colonel Gridley is in *G.W.*, IV, 451; and his estimate of Charles Lee is in *ibid.*, p. 451.

News of the arrival of the Hessian troops is drawn from Francis Wheaton's *The Revolutionary Diplomatic Correspondence of the U. S.*, Vol. II, pp. 71 ff.

The congressional attitude toward the Canadian expedition is set forth in Josiah Bartlett–John Langdon, May 19, 1776, cited in Force, *American Archives* (4th series), Vol. VI, pp. 10–21.

Washington's comment on the need for a constitution was in a letter to his brother John Augustine; Washington's *Writings*, edited by Ford, Vol. IV, p. 107.

Putnam's prowess as a tippler is mentioned in Moore's *Diary of the American Revolution*, Vol. I, p. 254.

This version of the Hickey Plot on Washington's life is drawn from Force (4th series), Vol. VI, pp. 1084 ff.; Jones, *History of New York . . .*, pp. 416 ff.; Caleb Clapp's "Diary," in *Hist. Magazine* (3rd series), Vol. III; *Correspondence of Samuel B. Webb*, Vol. II, p. 148; Washington's moral drawn from the tragedy is in Ford, *Writings*, Vol. IV, p. 188n.

The account of the alarm in the American camp at the arrival of the British fleet is based on *G.W.*, V, p. 192; *Webb*, Vol. I, p. 150, Force, *American Archives* (5th series), Vol. I, p. 967.

Lord Rawdon's observations on the penchant of British soldiers for rapine are found in the *Hastings Manuscripts*, Vol. III, pp. 179–80, *Great Britain Historical Manuscript Commission*.

An account of the destruction of the statue of George III is in *Long Island Historical Society Memoirs*, Vol. III, p. 93n; and in Isaac Bangs, *Journal . . .*, Cambridge, Mass., 1890, p. 57.

6 Long Island, August 27, 1776

Ambrose Serle's comment on the Declaration of Independence is found in his *American Journal*, pp. 28–30.

The controversy over Lord Howe's letter to Washington is outlined in *G.W.*, V,

NOTES

273–74, 297; Serle's *Journal* 32–33; and W.B. Reed's *Life and Correspondence of Joseph Reed*, Vol. I, p. 204, 204n.

The huge British fleet is described in C.H. Van Tyne's *War of Independence* (Boston, 1929), p. 246; Carrington's *Battles of the American Revolution*, pp. 192 ff.; and Pearson's *Those Damned Rebels*, p. 159.

Washington's opinion of John Sullivan is in *G.W.*, V, 152–53.

The chief source for the American account of the battle of Long Island is *The Long Island Historical Society Memoirs*, Vols. II and III, which contain detailed introductory narratives by T. W. Field and Henry P. Johnston, as well as numerous accounts by participants and pertinent official documents. Important British sources are Sir Henry Clinton's account in his *The American Rebellion*; the journals and diaries of Ambrose Serle, Henry Duncan, Frederick Mackenzie, Stephen Kemble, John Montresor and Carl Baurmeister.

The exchange between Lord Stirling and James Grant is drawn from W. A. Duer's *Life of William Alexander*, p. 162n.

Von Heeringen's description of the slaughter of Sullivan's men is in *Memoirs of Long Island Historical Society*, Vol. II, p. 453, and the comment of the anonymous British officer is from Force, *American Archives* (5th series), Vol I, pp. 1259–60.

The capture of rebel fugitives by women camp followers is detailed in Charles Francis Adams' *Studies Military and Diplomatic* (New York, 1911), p. 34.

Washington's warning to cowards and skulkers was reported by Hezekial Munsell, as quoted by T. W. Field in Vol. II of the *Memoirs of Long Island Historical Society*, pp. 502–3.

The hours of waiting in the cold, wet American trenches at Brooklyn are described in Alexander Graydon's *Memoirs of His Own Time*, p. 145. Other phases of the withdrawal of the army from Brooklyn to New York are based on *G.W.*, V, 496, and upon the memoirs of Mifflin, Israel Hand, Joseph Reed and Benjamin Tallmadge; the confusion in orders to the rear guard is described by T.W. Field in "The Battle of Long Island," pp. 281–87.

The final quotation in the chapter, "even the biscuits . . ." is from G.O., Trevelyan, *The American Revolution* (4 vols., New York, 1899–1907), Vol. I, p. 290.

7   The Loss of New York

The opening quotation on the squalid American camp is from Nicholas Cresswell's *Journal*, pp. 157–59.

Washington's report to Congress ("the extreme fatigue . . . ,") is from Washington's *Writings*, edited by Ford, Vol. IV, pp. 373–76; his explanation of his abandonment by the militia is in *G.W.*, VI, 32.

The barbed comment on John Sullivan, made by John Adams to Dr. Benjamin Rush, is from Rush's *Autobiography*, p. 140.

Israel Putnam's surprise at the British failure to follow up the victory at Long Island is in Jones's *History of New York . . .* , p. 119n.

Nathanael Greene's insistence that Washington burn New York is from Force, *American Archives* (5th series) Vol. II, pp. 182–83.

Haslet's early criticism of Washington's leadership and praise of Charles Lee is found in Willard M. Wallace's *Appeal to Arms* (New York, 1951), p. 239 (citing C. Rodney, p. 112).

The futile meeting between Lord Howe and the congressional committee on September 11 was described fully by both Franklin and Adams; the peacemaking effort is described in Michael Pearson's *Those Damned Rebels* (New York, 1972), pp. 178–79; (Adams, *Works*, Vol. III, p. 79; Franklin, *Writings*, Vol. VII, p. 55); a dependable summary is in Carl Van Doren's *Franklin* (New York, 1938), pp. 559 ff.; the British view is drawn from the notes of Howe's secretary Henry Strachey, in *Misc. Papers of Richard Howe*, New York Public Library.

The account of the American loss of Manhattan Island is based on numerous references in *G.W.*, VI, especially pp. 18–30 and 49–55; in Henry P. Johnston's "The Campaign of 1776 around New York and Brooklyn"; and in the memoirs of Heath

NOTES

and Reed and the account of Joseph Plumb Martin. The British side is based largely on Henry Clinton's *American Rebellion* and the diaries of Frederick Mackenzie and Stephen Kemble.

Testimony on Washington's angry assault upon his fleeting troops is somewhat confused, some of it offered by men who were not eyewitnesses. The versions of Heath and Weedon (Weedon–John Page, September 20, 1776, Chicago Historical Society) as the most reliable, are accepted here. Others were likely repeating army gossip of the day.

8 Harlem Heights and White Plains

Washington's report from the position of Harlem Heights is in *G.W.*, VI, 59; details of the skirmish of September 16 are found in Vol. III of the *Memoirs of Long Island Historical Society*, pp. 246–47, but there are also valuable accounts by Reed (in Vol. I of *Life and Correspondence of Joseph Reed*, pp. 237 ff.), Samuel Richards (*Diary*, Phila., 1909, p. 39); and in a letter from Weedon to John Page, September 20, 1776, Chicago Historical Society. The most complete and reliable work on the affair is Henry P. Johnston's *The Battle of Harlem Heights . . .* (New York, 1897).

Washington's doleful comments to John Augustine and Lund Washington are in letters of September 22 and 30, 1776 (*G.W.*, VI, 116, 138).

Among the numerous accounts of the burning of New York, the most valuable is by the Rev. E.G. Shewkirk in a letter of December 2, 1776 (13 *Pennsylvania Magazine of History and Biography*, pp. 377 ff.). Other narratives are in Force, *American Archives* (5th series) Vol. II, pp. 462 ff.; Moore, *Diary of the American Revolution*, Vol. I, p. 311; and Jones, *History of New York . . .* , pp. 611 ff.

Henry P. Johnston, in a privately printed biography of Nathan Hale, said the spy was hanged at what is now First Avenue and 55th Street (cited by Hughes, *George Washington*, Vol. II, p. 505). Hale's purported last words, "I only regret that I have but one life to live for my country," were first reported many years after the event in the memoirs of Capt. William Hull of Connecticut (Mrs. Maria Hull Campbell, *Revolutionary Services . . . of Gen. William Hull*, New York, 1848, pp. 37–38). The lone recorded eyewitness who left an account, Lt. Frederick Mackenzie, said only that Hale died with "great composure and resolution," without mention of the memorable phrase so long embedded in American folklore (Mackenzie, *Diary*, I, 61–62). Hale's arrest and betrayal by his cousin are detailed in Onderdonk's *Revolutionary Incidents of Suffolk and Kings Counties* (New York, 1849), pp. 48–50, citing a letter of Stephen Hempstead.

Charles Lee's triumphal return to the army was noted by William Malcolm, writing on September 6, 1776, Force, *American Archives* (5th series), Vol. II, p. 197; Lee's scornful comment on congressional strategy is found in *Lee Papers*, (published by the New York Historical Society), Vol. II, pp. 261–62.

The movement to White Plains is made clear in detail from original documents in Force, *American Archives* (5th series), Vol. II, pp. 908 and *passim*; vol. 3, pp. 471 ff. The recollections of Heath and Haslet (Vol. IV of Sparks' *Writings of Washington*, p. 528) are especially important. The British version rests largely on Clinton's account in *Rebellion*, and on the diaries of Kemble (Vol. I, pp. 94 ff.) and Mackenzie (Vol. I, pp. 88 ff.).

The fall of Fort Washington is described by H. P. Johnston, "The Campaign of 1776 . . . ," pp. 229–31; the journal of John Reuber in Johnston's *Battle of Harlem Heights*, pp. 229–31, and other Hessian accounts are especially important to an understanding of British moves. The American version is recounted at length in Force, *American Archives* (5th series), Vol. III, especially pp. 169 ff., and in *G.W.*, VI, 257–58, and *G.W.*, XVI, 150–52.

Charles Lee's scolding of Washington after the loss of the fort is in the *Lee Papers*, Vol. II, p. 288.

NOTES

The graphic description of rebel prisoners being herded into New York is from Graydon, *Memoirs of His Own Time*, p. 201, and Mackenzie's *Diary*, Vol. I, pp. 97–98, 111–12.

9 *The Flight Through New Jersey*

An anonymous British officer's description of abandoned Fort Lee is found in Moore, *Diary*, Vol. I, p. 350.

The exchange between Reed and Charles Lee, significant as the first evidence of the so-called cabal against Washington, is documented in *New York Historical Society Collection*, Vol. V, pp. 293–94, 305–6, in letters of the principals.

John Honeyman's role as Washington's spy is recounted in Stryker, *Battles of Trenton and Princeton*, pp. 87 ff.; John Bakeless, *Turncoats, Traitors and Heroes*, p. 167; and is documented by Honeyman's grandson, John Van Dyke, in an article in *Our Home* (Somerville, N.J., 1873), p. 455, and in Minutes of the N.J. Council of Safety, December 5 and December 20, 1777. The story is well summarized by Leonard Falkner in "A Spy for Washington" in *American Heritage*, August 1957, pp. 58 ff.

Washington's orders to Charles Lee, asking that he join the main army with his troops, are in *G.W.*, VI, 263 ff. The progressively more insistent orders appear chronologically in this source to the time of Lee's capture on December 13.

The story of Washington's plan to retreat beyond the mountains and conduct guerrilla warfare is found in Gordon's *History*, Vol. II, p. 127, and should be regarded as traditional.

British atrocities during this phase of the campaign are cited in Force, *American Archives* (5th series), Vol. III, p. 1376; numerous affidavits were published, allegedly by congressional order in the *Pennsylvania Evening Post*, April 24 and 29, May 1, 3 and 10, 1777.

Thomas Paine's appraisal of Washington in adversity is quoted in Force, *American Archives* (5th series), Vol. III, p. 1292. *The American Crisis*, which appeared at this time under difficult circumstances, was apparently published with the aid of Charles Willson Peale.

Peale's arrival in Washington's camp and his meeting with his brother James are recounted in J. T. Flexner's *America's Old Masters* (New York, 1939), pp. 195–96.

The story of the capture of Charles Lee is told in admirable fashion in Alden's *General Charles Lee*, pp. 151 ff.

The development of Washington's daring plan for crossing the Delaware to attack Trenton is fully told, with citation of pertinent documents in Vol. IV of Freeman's *Washington*, pp. 291 ff. The Thompson-Neely House, where Washington and his council completed their plan, is still standing and is now open to the public. The house stands in Washington Crossing State Park, Bucks County, Pa.

Benjamin Rush described his visit to Washington's camp on the eve of Trenton in his *Autobiography*, p. 124. The conjectural date is supplied by George Croner, the editor.

10 *Trenton, December 26, 1776*

This account of the battle of Trenton and its preliminaries, like all others of recent date, is based on the definitive work of Stryker's *Battles of Trenton and Princeton*. Lifelong familiarity with the terrain, an encyclopedic knowledge of traditions and exhaustive studies of American and German sources contributed to this model study. Few supporting references are necessary to an understanding of the battle.

The disappearance of Horatio Gates just before the Delaware crossing is from Wilkinson's *Memoirs*, pp. 127–28.

The glimpse of the red-nosed Washington during the crossing is by David Anderson, as cited in Henry Cabot Lodge's *Washington* (1889), Vol. II, p. 387.

NOTES

It is possible that the attempted lower crossings of the Delaware by American troops were intended as feints, and that Washington's plan was a complete success. Documentary evidence on the point is inconclusive.

11   Princeton, January 3, 1777

Stryker's *Battles of Trenton and Princeton* is also the basis of subsequent narratives, and was so thorough that few additional citations have been made in this version. One additional source of some value is George Weedon's letter to John Page, January 6, 1777, describing the twin victories. The letter is in the collection of the Chicago Historical Society.

The opening description of Washington by Lieutenant Wiederholt is from *Tagebuch das Leutnant Wiederholt*, p. 32, as cited in *Hughes*, Vol. III, p. 8.

Washington's pleas to his troops, described in Freeman's *Washington*, Vol. IV, pp. 332–33, is based on an account by a "Sergeant R." in the Wellsborough (Pa.) *Phenix* of March 24, 1832, as reprinted in *Penn. Magazine*, Vol. XX, p. 515, a late account whose details should be accepted as traditional. A similar appeal by Mifflin is documented in E.M. Stone's *Life and Recollections of John Howland* (Providence, R.I., 1857), p. 71, and in the "Diary" of Stephen Olney, cited in Mrs. Catherine Williams' *Biography of Revolutionary Heroes* (Providence, R.I., 1839), p. 192.

Despite the reliability of Cadwalader as a witness, the revealing map of British positions in Princeton by his anonymous spy has not been generally accepted by historians as the inspiration for Washington's surprise attack. Freeman is inclined to credit Joseph Reed for the move, because of his familiarity with the roads of the region.

The disappearance (and intoxication) of General Fermoy was reported in Wilkinson's *Memoirs*, p. 135n, and in W.B. Reed's biography of Joseph Reed, p. 286. The almost simultaneous capture of Colonel Hausegger is described in Graydon's *Memoirs*, p. 218.

In the absence of testimony as to Cornwallis's state of mind the night before Trenton, it is difficult to say whether the stealthy night march of the Americans should have been anticipated. It is noteworthy that some rebel officers were taken by surprise, and that the council of war was not unanimous in expectations of success. The sparse narratives of the march by Stryker and Freeman rest largely on the diaries of Thomas Rodney and Stephen Olney, Weedon's letter to John Page, and on Wilkinson's *Memoirs*. In his report of the action at Trenton, Washington gave only a few vague details.

Many details of the fighting at Princeton, including the death of General Mercer, are drawn from the account of the unknown "Sergeant R."

The exchange between the British and Capt. John Fleming of the 1st Virginia was reported in the *Virginia Gazette*, January 14, 1777.

Major Fitzgerald's dramatic account of Washington's narrow escape from a British volley, rejected by Freeman, is from G. W. P. Custis's *Recollections of Washington* (New York, 1860), pp. 191–92. Though the source is none too reliable in general, this story seems an accurate reflection of Washington's penchant for exposing himself to enemy fire. Washington's cry, "A fine fox chase . . . !" is given by Wilkinson, who had it from a rifleman, Capt. David Harris.

The commander's angry reaction at the sight of an American body-robber was reported in the *Penna Packet*, January 22, 1777.

Nicholas Cresswell's comment on Washington's rise to glory is in his *Journal*, pp. 180–81.

Von Bülöw's praise is in Heinrich Dietrich von Bülöw's *Militärische und vermischte Schriften* (Leipzig, 1853), p. 52.

NOTES

12 Fox Hunter on the Run

The American retreat to Morristown, as seen by Charles Willson Peale, is from C.C. Seller's *Peale*, pp. 135 ff.

Washington's problems with his troops at Morristown are revealed in *G.W.*, VII, 322, 354; desertion and the resultant floggings are described in Hughes's *Washington*, Vol. III, pp. 72–74, 82, 84.

The protest of John Adams that Washington had become an idol is cited in Burnett's *Letters of Members of the Continental Congress*, Vol. II, p. 263.

The description of Washington's secretarial staff, though it owes much to the rather prejudiced observers, Pickering and Hamilton, is thought to be substantially accurate. Washington himself left no comments of value.

The imprisonment of Charles Lee is detailed in Alden's *Lee*, pp. 164 ff.

The movements of Howe during these weeks are described from contemporary records in Gruber's *The Howe Brothers . . .* , pp. 194, 224 and *passim*; the narrative of the complex maneuvers follows Ward's *The War of the Revolution*, Vol. I, pp. 326 ff., and *Freeman*, Vol. IV, pp. 446 ff.

13 Brandywine, September 11, 1777

The brief sketch of Burgoyne's campaign is based on accounts by Christopher Ward in his *The War of the Revolution*, Lynn Montross in *Rag, Tag, and Bobtail* (New York, 1952), Pearson in *Those Damned Rebels* and C.H. Jones in *The History of the Campaign for the Conquest of Canada . . .* , (Phila., 1882). Important original sources are the letters of Burgoyne and Arnold, the *Memoirs* of James Wilkinson and Burgoyne's *Orderly Book, State of the Expedition (and Supplement)*.

The intricate campaign of maneuver and delay played out by Washington and Howe during the summer is narrated fully in Freeman's *Washington*, Vol. IV, pp. 443 ff., and more succinctly in Ward, I, pp. 325 ff.

The guide to Lafayette's early relations with Washington is Gottschalk's *Lafayette Joins the American Army*; the subsequent wartime career of the young Frenchman is admirably told in the final volume of this series, *Lafayette and the Close of the American Revolution*.

Howe's trying voyage from New York to the upper Chesapeake is documented in reports by Howe and Von Knyphausen and several journals of participants, including John André, Ambrose Serle, Stephen Kemble, John Montresor and von Baurmeister. The loss of a hundred and fifty horses from overeating was reported by Capt. Walter Stewart, U.S.A., in *Gates Papers*, New York Historical Society, Box VII, #107.

Washington's efforts to improve the appearance of his army on its march through Philadelphia are detailed in *G.W.*, IX, especially pp. 17 and 127. The observations of John Adams on this passage are found in C.F. Adams, *Familiar Letters*, p. 298.

The brief account of the battle of Brandywine owes much to the narratives of Hughes, Ward and Freeman, but even these extensively researched versions are incomplete, and Washington's reports (in *G.W.*, IX, 203 ff.) add little to an understanding of the sequence of events. The inescapable conclusion is that Howe's wide flanking movement deceived Washington, and that the Virginian was lax in reconnoitering the ground and in pressing for prompt reports from his right flank in the early hours of the action. The confusing literature on Washington's faulty intelligence effort is summarized in Ward, p. 352*n*, and expanded in Freeman, Vol. IV, notes, pp. 475 ff. Freeman dismisses as merely traditional the stories concerning Thomas Cheyney and Joseph Brown, but the consensus of writers is that, in general, both incidents have been accurately reported, despite their belated publication.

NOTES

14   Germantown, October 4, 1777

Sources for a narrative of Germantown, as Christopher Ward noted (Vol. I, pp. 469–70), are so numerous and scattered as to make conventional annotation impractical. Among the most valuable aids are *G.W.*, IX, *passim*, for Washington's orders and reports; Hughes, Vol. III, pp. 187 ff.; Carrington, pp. 382 ff.; Ward, Vol. I, pp. 363 ff. Nathanael Greene's key role is based on G. W. Greene, *Life of Nathanael Greene*, Vol. I, pp. 474 ff., and F.V. Greene, *The Revolutionary War* . . . (New York, 1911), pp. 91–92. Freeman, Vol. IV, pp. 490 ff., offers the most complete account, but its burden of documentation deprives it of clarity at some points.

John Adams' despair of Washington's leadership is from *Familiar Letters*, edited by C.F. Adams, p. 303; De Kalb's observation is in Friedrich Kapp's *Life of John Kalb* (New York, 1884), p. 127; Benjamin Rush's criticisms are in his *Autobiography*, pp. 132–33.

Congressman Burke's bitter exchange with Sullivan is found in *Burnett, Letters*, Vol. II, p. 519; Heth's attack on Maxwell is in a letter of October 2, 1777, to Daniel Morgan (*Winchester, Va., Historical Society Papers*, pp. 31, 33). Washington's defense of his officers is in Washington's *Writings*, edited by Ford, Vol. VI, p. 72.

Washington's battle plan is ably discussed in Freeman, Vol. IV, pp. 501 ff.; the probable causes of his defeat are examined on pp. 510 ff.

Hugh McDonald's comments, and the incident of Washington's exchange with the inebriated Private John Brantly, are found in McDonald's *Diary*, published in part by Dr. E. W. Caruthers, c. 1840, from the original in the University of North Carolina Library, Chapel Hill, N.C. The diary is now lost; its known portions appeared in *Amer. Hist. Illus.* (Harrisburg, Pa.) #1, Vols. I and II.

Revealing details of the British side of the action are found in the Journal of Lt. Sir Martin Hunter in *Historical Magazine*, Vol. IV, pp. 346–47.

Pickering's narrative is in Pickering's *Life*, Vol. I, pp. 166–70.

Benjamin Chew, the owner of Cliveden, who had been Washington's friend, was at this time a prisoner en route to Fredericksburg with a group of Quakers who had supported the British in the campaign.

William Heth's account of the action is in his letter of John Lamb, October 12, 1777 (*Lamb Papers*, New York Historical Society, Box I, #217).

15   The Conway Cabal

The opening sketch of Jacob Duché is based on Scharff and Westcott, *History of Philadelphia*, Vol. I, p. 291n; Duché's letter appears in Sparks' *Correspondence of the American Revolution . . . Letters . . . to Washington*, Vol. I, p. 458.

The debate over the existence of a "Conway cabal" has endured from 1777 to this day. Though Washington, Hamilton and others near the commander were positive that a plot to remove the general was afoot, many able men within and without the army disagreed, among them Timothy Pickering, Henry Laurens and Richard Peters of the Board of War.

Supporting documents are numerous and familiar. Washington's version of the affair is made clear in *G.W.*, X, *passim*, and in Sparks, Vol. V, *passim*; a few important items, notably Conway's letter of January 10, 1778, are in *Papers* of G.W., Library of Congress (this particular letter: Box 65, item 35). Other important sources are Mifflin's letters and papers, well interpreted in Rossman's *Mifflin*; *The Gates Papers*, New York Historical Society; and Wilkinson's *Memoirs*.

Conway's early denigration of Washington ("No man is more of a gentleman," etc.) is quoted in Graydon, pp. 299–302.

Washington's plaint to Richard Henry Lee ("I have been a slave," etc.) is in *G.W.*, IX, p. 397; Lafayette's warning to Washington about Conway is quoted by Charlemagne Tower in Vol. I of his *Marquis de La Fayette in the American Revolution*, (2 vols., Phila., 1895), p. 262; De Kalb's praise of Lafayette ("No one deserves

NOTES

more than he," etc.) is cited by Gottschalk in *Lafayette Joins* . . . , p. 53; Washington's recommendation of Lafayette as a troop commander ("he is sensible, discreet," etc.) is in *Journ. Cong.*, IX, 870.

The emotional reaction of Washington as he read early news of victory at Saratoga is from Pickering and Upham, *Life of Timothy Pickering*, Vol. II, p. 109.

James Wilkinson's narrative of his journey with the victory dispatch from Saratoga is in his *Memoirs*, Vol. I, p. 323.

Hamilton's reception by Gates at Saratoga is detailed in his *Works* (Henry Cabot Lodge, ed., 12 vols., 1904), Vol. IX, pp. 106 ff.; the comment of Morgan to Gates ("I have one favor to ask of you," etc.) is reported in Henry Lee's *Memoirs* . . . , p. 582.

The description of the Saratoga prisoners by Hannah Winthrop is in *The Warren-Adams Letters*, Vol. II, pp. 451–52 (copyright Massachusetts Historical Society, 1917, 1925).

The dishonorable affair of the Saratoga prisoners dragged on after William Howe's departure. When George III ordered his successor, Clinton, to advise the Americans that he had ratified the convention, Congress retorted that they had seen no evidence of the King's action, that Clinton's request might be a forgery, and thus refused to give up the prisoners until "a responsible witness" swore that he had seen the King sign the order—otherwise, "they would not believe a word that he [Clinton] advanced."

Conway's insulting explanation of his private letter to Gates concerning Washington ("I believe I can assert," etc.) is in 60 *Papers* of G.W., 7, Library of Congress; Gates' subsequent explanation is in *Gates Papers*, New York Historical Society; Washington's response to Gates is in Washington's *Writings*, Vol. VI, p. 278.

William Howe's resignation is in *Germain Papers*, Wm. L. Clements Library, University of Michigan.

16   Valley Forge

Washington's letter of reply to the "remonstrance" of the Pennsylvania legislature is in Washington's *Writings*, edited by Ford, Vol. VI, pp. 257–62.

Albigence Waldo's description of the march to Valley Forge, and life in the camp, is in his "Diary . . . ," *Pennsylvania Magazine of History and Biography* (1897), XXI, pp. 305 ff.

Warnings of a plot against him by Washington's friends came from Benjamin Harrison, cited in Hughes, Vol. III, p. 252 (*Rosenbach Collection*, p. 42); Dr. James Craik, *I, Papers of George Washington*, p. 317, Library of Congress; Patrick Henry in W. W. Henry's *Patrick Henry* (1891), Vol. I, p. 546; and Henry Laurens, who transmitted the anonymous tract reprinted in Burnett's *Letters* . . . , Vol. III, p. 56.

Washington's response to Laurens is in Washington's *Writings*, edited by Ford, Vol. VI, p. 354.

The conclusion of John Adams that Washington should not have been allowed to serve without pay is in Adams' *Works* (1850–56), Vol. IX, p. 542.

The complex story of Greene's career as quartermaster general is narrated in G. W. Greene's biography, Vol. II. The financial arrangements with his assistants, the sources of subsequent charges of profiteering, are detailed in *Reed Papers* (New York Historical Society), edited by Charles Pettit-Joseph Reed, March 5, 1778.

Pierre Duponceau's version of the lively life at headquarters, Valley Forge, is cited from his manuscript in Kapp's *Steuben*, p. 121.

Kitty Greene's alleged affair with Lafayette is based on Knox–wife, December 7, 1777, *Knox Papers*, Maine Historical Society: Greene–McDougall, February 5, 1778, *McDougall Papers*, New York Historical Society; and on Howard Swiggett's *The Forgotten Leaders of the Revolution*, pp. 49–51.

Th sketch of Steuben at Valley Forge is largely drawn from John M. Palmer's *General von Steuben* (New Haven, Conn., 1937), pp. 31 ff., 124 ff.

NOTES

Charles Lee's return to the army at Valley Forge is reconstructed from *G.W.*, XI. 213–14; Elias Boudinot's *Journal* . . . , p. 78; and Ebenezer Wild's "Journal," *Proceedings, Massachusetts Historical Society* (2nd series), Vol. XI (1890–91), p. 107.

17   Monmouth, June 28, 1778

The sketch of Henry Clinton is drawn from Willcox's *Portrait of a General*, a model work of its kind based upon the most extensive papers left by a participant in the Revolution. The largest collection, in the William L. Clements Library, University of Michigan, is most frequently cited. Clinton's frame of mind as he assumed the American command is made clear by Willcox, pp. 201 ff.

The account of the Meschianza is based on André's description to an unknown correspondent in London, May 23, 1778, published in *The Annual Register* for 1778, pp. 267–70.

General von Heister's comment on Howe ("He is as valiant as my sword," etc.) is from William Smith's *Diary*, March 31, 1778, New York Public Library.

The anonymous comments on the lowered morals of Philadelphians during the British occupation are taken from "a late Philadelphia paper" in *Continental Journal and Weekly Advertiser* (Boston), July 30, 1778.

Benedict Arnold's debut as military commander of Philadelphia, which led to his treason, is described in Van Doren's *Secret History* . . . , pp. 168–69.

The guides for this narrative of the Battle of Monmouth were Stryker's *Battle of Monmouth*; *Freeman*, Vol. V, pp. 11–37; Ward, pp. 570–86; Hughes, Vol. III, pp. 357–81; *Carrington*, pp. 433–56; and with emphasis on the role of Charles Lee, Alden's *Lee*, pp. 194–227, and Willcox's *Clinton*. All these sources draw heavily on original documents, but as Alden has pointed out, Stryker's work contains errors, and its contributors accepted hearsay evidence against Lee. Many phases of the battle were vaguely recorded in conflicting testimony by participants—time sequences, troop movements, etc.

The confrontation between Washington and Lee on the battlefield, one of the most familiar scenes in Revolutionary lore, is based chiefly on Lee's testimony in *Lee Papers*, New York Historical Society, Vol. III, pp. 78, 81, 112, 147, 191–92. The charge that Washington swore at Lee did not appear until Lafayette (who was not present) told it in 1812. Alden warns that Lafayette's intensely partisan views must be used cautiously.

The fame of the Molly Pitcher of Monmouth rests upon the lone published contemporary account by Joseph Plumb Martin, *A Narrative* . . . , pp. 96–97.

Lee's travail during his court-martial and its aftermath is skillfully, if sympathetically, treated in *Alden*, pp. 228–75.

18   The Dangerous Season

D'Estaing's problems at the entrance of New York harbor are made clear in *G.W.*, VII, 182, and *passim*. Contemporary accounts of the Rhode Island campaign are in Gordon, Vol. III, pp. 158 ff.; *G.W.*, *ibid.*; Marshall's *Washington*, Vol. I, pp. 306 ff.; and in Sullivan's *Letters and Papers*, Vol. II, pp. 283 ff. (The latter source includes letters of French and American officers.)

Freeman concluded that this document, "one of the ablest that ever appeared over the signature of Washington," resulted from the general's collaboration with his secretary, Col. R. H. Harrison (*G.W.*, XIII, 223 ff.)

Washington's dismay at the effects of inflation and the evidences of corruption and extravagant living in Philadelphia was expressed in a letter to Jacky Custis, January 2, 1779 (*G.W.*, XIII, 478).

Contemporary views on conflict of interest involving army officers engaging in personal business ventures are reflected in Washington's investment in a privateer (with Jacky Custis, Lünd Washington and George Baylor), a vessel that apparently never sailed (sources: Washington's *Writings*, edited by Ford, Vol. VI, p. 197; Charles C. Moore, *The Family Life of Washington* (Boston, 1926), p. 99.

The comment on Benedict Arnold by Benjamin Rush ("His conversation was uninteresting . . .") is in the doctor's *Autobiography*, p. 58.

Arnold's early reports to Washington on the Pennsylvania charges are in *G.W.*, XIII, 392–93. The most exhaustive narrative of the unfolding of Arnold's treason is in Van Doren's *Secret History*.

Greene's report on the marathon dance by Washington and Kitty Greene is quoted in G.W. Greene's *Greene*, Vol. I, p. 377.

Washington's observation that Wayne was "more active . . . than judicious" is in *G.W.*, VII, 281.

The brief summary of Sullivan's punitive expedition against the Six Nations is based largely on *The Sullivan Papers*, pp. 48 ff.

Washington's reports of the hardships of the Morristown winter encampment are found in *G.W.*, XVII, 273–74 and *passim*.

Hughes, in his Vol. III, p. 499, gives an amusing picture of Martha Washington's sufferings at headquarters, based on Lossing, Vol. I., p. 310.

The glimpse of a playful Washington in a relaxed moment is found in *Pennsylvania Magazine of History and Biography*, LXV, pp. 363–69.

Washington's protest over Arnold's presumptuousness in assuming "some civilties I never meant to show him" is in *G.W.*, XX, 370; the general's reprimand of Arnold is in *G.W.*, XVIII, 18, 225.

Washington's tearful reaction to the triumphant letter from the returning Lafayette is in Lafayette's *Memoirs*, Vol. I, p. 251.

19   *Our Enemies the French*

Ebenezer Huntington's bitter remarks on the country's neglect of the army are found in his *Letters* . . . , pp. 87–88.

Washington's urgent pleas that Congress make a final effort to win victory are found in *G.W.*, XIX, 104–5, and Washington's *Writings*, edited by Ford, Vol. VIII, p. 293.

The pessimistic estimate of his prospects in the south was written by Horatio Gates to Lincoln, June 24, 1780 (*Gates Papers*, New York Historical Society).

As previously noted, the story of Arnold's treason is drawn chiefly from Van Doren's *Secret History* . . . ; Hannah Arnold's gossip about her sister-in-law is on p. 265.

Lafayette's proposal that "we cheat a little" in presenting American troops to the French is from *Memoirs* (letter to Heath, June 11, 1780) Vol. I, p. 68.

The report, Vergennes to Lafayette, on the inept American commissioners in Paris was in a cipher letter captured by the British (*Am. Hist. Rev.*, Vol. VIII, p. 507.)

Greene's protest (August 29, 1780) that his successor as quartermaster general, Jeremiah Wadsworth, was a congressional spy is in *The Knollenberg Papers*, Yale University Library.

20   *Arnold and West Point*

The discovery of Arnold's treachery, as retold by Van Doren, depends entirely upon the testimony of witnesses. Arnold's ciphered note to André revealing Washington's secret route is in the *Clinton Papers*, William L. Clements Library, University of Michigan. The note, of September 15, 1780, is accompanied by the original decoding made at British headquarters.

The impoverished state of Washington's party on this journey is documented in Gordon, Vol. III, p. 128.

Axel Fersen's impression of Washington is found in his letters, as quoted in *Magazine of American History*, Vol. III, pp. 303 ff.

NOTES

Washington's purported remark that "All you young men are in love with Mrs. Arnold" is quoted from Lossing's Vol. II, p. 158.

Joshua Hett Smith's trial for his part in the conspiracy dragged on for a month before he was freed, only to be arrested by civilian authorities, from whom he escaped. Smith received a British pension until his death in New York in 1818.

The striking praise of André by American officers is cited in Tallmadge's *Memoirs*, p. 57, and in Meade–Theodorick Bland, in Henry B. Dawson's *Papers Concerning the Capture and Detention of Major John André*, p. 108.

Hamilton's denunciation of Washington for the execution of André in a letter to his fiancée is quoted in Hamilton's *Works* (1904), Vol. IX, p. 208.

Since the only account of Washington's estrangement from Hamilton was recounted only by the latter (in *Hamilton's Works*, Vol. IX, pp. 232 ff.), reflections upon the general and the rather ungenerous estimate of his motives should be accepted with caution.

In later life, according to a secondhand report by Benjamin Rush, Hamilton said of Washington, "He never read a book on the art of war but Simms' *Military Guide*, and his heart was a stone."

The plea of Mary Ball Washington to the Virginia Assembly for a pension, as reported to Washington by Benjamin Harrison, February 25, 1781, is in the *Papers* of G.W., Library of Congress, Vol. CLXVII, p. 14; Washington's response is in *G.W.*, XXI, 341–42.

Washington's critical letter concerning French cooperation in the futile pursuit of Arnold was published in Rivington's *Gazette*, April 4, 1781. Rochambeau's reply, to Washington, is in the *Papers* of G.W., Library of Congress, Vol. CLXXII, p. 25; a later letter from the Frenchman on the same subject (May 5, 1781) is in the *Papers* of G.W., Vol. CLXXIII, p. 19.

The condensed narrative of the Carolinas campaign of 1780–81 is based on the author's previous works, *The Cowpens-Guilford Courthouse Campaign* (Philadelphia, 1962), and *The Campaign That Won America: The Story of Yorktown* (New York, 1970), pp. 91 ff. Both works made use of available contemporary documents. The relationship between Cornwallis and Clinton in this period is shown most clearly in Willcox's *Portrait of a General*.

21 Mutiny

Van Doren's *Secret History* also offers the most satisfactory narrative of the mutiny of the Pennsylvania and New Jersey troops in January 1781. The biographies of Wayne by Stillé and Glenn Tucker, also valuable sources, marshal the pertinent documents.

Wayne's report to Washington on the events of January 1 at Morristown is found in *G.W.*, XXI, 56n.

22 Thunder in the South

The complexities of allied efforts to trap Arnold early in 1781 are thoroughly explored in Freeman, Vol. V, pp. 251 ff.; in the interest of clarity these events have been recounted but briefly in the present narrative. The key document to which misunderstandings traced (Rochambeau–Washington, "I am going this moment," etc.) is found in the *Papers* of G.W., Library of Congress, Vol. CLXIV, p. 139.

23 Lafayette in Virginia, Summer, 1781

The movements of Lafayette in this vital phase of the war are given definitive treatment by Gottschalk in *Lafayette and the Close of the American Revolution*, pp. 209 ff.; Willcox documents the British side of the operations from the point of view of Clinton in New York.

Despite exhaustive research, including that of Freeman and his associates, it is not possible to resolve all conflicting testimony as to the genesis of the Yorktown campaign. Washington wrote numerous letters on several phases of the plans, indicating that both he and Rochambeau were aware of the possibilities from the opening of their Wethersfield conference, but the origin of the strategy is left in doubt. The basic documents, including Rochambeau's letter to Washington, are in Vols. CLXXIII and CLXXV, *Papers* of G.W., Library of Congress, and *G.W.*, XXI, 382 ff., and *G.W.*, XXII, 98 ff. Rochambeau's account is given in his *Memoirs*, Vol. I, pp. 270 ff.

Rochambeau's reluctance to confide French naval plans to Washington stemmed from his personality as well as from his orders. The coded letter of De Grasse to Rochambeau, detailing his plans to sail to America with his fleet, is in the *Papers* of G.W., Library of Congress, Vol. CLXXV, p. 100. It was only after receipt of this letter that Rochambeau revealed the secret to Washington, and plans for the great concentration got under way.

Among the most valuable accounts left by witnesses are Chastellux's *Travels in North America*; Claude Blanchard's *Journal*; and Von Closen's *Revolutionary Journal*.

24 Hoodwinking Henry Clinton

The brief sketch of the French army is based on accounts in Stephen Bonsal's *When the French Were Here* (New York, 1945), Gilbert Chinard's *George Washington as the French Knew Him* (Princeton, N.J., 1951), and on the journals and diaries of Von Closen, Axel Fersen, Blanchard and the Abbé Claude Robin.

The striking scene of Washington's anger upon discovery of the French change of campaign is from Pickering and Upham, *Timothy Pickering*, Vol. II, pp. 54–55.

Details of Washington's deception of Clinton are found in the *Minutes* of Jonathan Trumbull, Jr. (in *Massachusetts Historical Society Papers*, April 1876); Dr. Thacher's *Journal*, the *Memoirs* of Count Mathieu Dumas; the *Journal* of Elias Boudinot; from William Willcox's study of Clinton, *Portrait of a General*; and from Washington himself, notably in his *Diaries*, Vol. II, p. 258; *G.W.*, XXXVI, 183; and *Papers* of G.W., Library of Congress, Vol. XXIII, p. 58.

25 Concentration in the Chesapeake

Memoirs and contemporaneous diary and journal entries of French officers of special value in detailing the story of the allied march southward are the Duc de Lauzun's, Deux-Ponts's, Cromot du Bourg's, Von Closen's and Claude Robin's. Among the most useful American observations are those of Trumbull, Pickering and Washington himself.

The routes of march are taken from W.S. Baker's *Itinerary of General Washington* (Phila., 1892).

The sketch of the battle between the French and British ships is based on *The Graves Papers . . .* , French E. Chadwick, ed. (New York, 1916); *The British Navy in Adversity*, by William M. James (London, 1926); *Admiral de Grasse and American Independence*, by Charles Lewis (Annapolis, 1945); and *Decision at the Chesapeake*, by Harold A. Larrabee (New York, 1964).

The description of Lafayette's emotional greeting of Washington in Williamsburg, recorded by St. George Tucker, is taken from W. C. Bruce's *John Randolph of Roanoke* (New York, 1922), Vol. I.

The graphic sketch of the French latrine at the College of William and Mary is from James Tilton's *Economical Observations On Military Hospitals* (Wilmington, Del., 1813), pp. 63–64.

Jonathan Trumbull Jr.'s *Minutes* (in *Massachusetts Historical Society Papers*, April 1876) document Washington's prolonged absence from Williamsburg on his visit to the French fleet; the exchange between the general and the admiral at this critical meeting is recorded in *Correspondence of General Washington and Comte de Grasse* (Washington, D.C., 1931).

26   The Siege of Yorktown

This account of the siege is a synthesis of well-known secondary accounts, all based on the extensive literature of original source material; Henry P. Johnston's *The Yorktown Campaign* (New York, 1881); Freeman, Vol. V; Hughes, Vol. III; *Ward*, Vol. II; *Carrington*; and B. Davis's *The Campaign That Won America*, pp. 189 ff.

Invaluable details were drawn from the accounts of the Americans Lt. William Feltman, Sgt. Joseph Plumb Martin, and Col. Richard Butler. The Yorktown point of view is offered in the journals of Johann Doehla (*William and Mary Quarterly* (2nd series, Vol. XII, 1942) and Stephan Popp (*American Heritage*, October 1961). Max von Eelking's *The German Allied Troops in the North American War* offers further details. Banastre Tarleton's *A History of The Campaigns of 1780–81 . . .* (Dublin, 1781) is also an important source.

27   Victory

Still other American diarists recorded the final hours at Yorktown, among them Ebenezer Denny, in *Pennsylvania Historical Society Memoirs*, Vol. VII, pp. 246 ff.; James Duncan, in *Pennsylvania Archives*, Vol. II, p. 751; David Cobb, *Massachusetts Historical Society Papers* (1881–82), pp. 68 ff.; and St. George Tucker, *William and Mary Quarterly* (July, 1948).

Tilghman's bizarre journey to Philadelphia with news of the victory is based on Oswald Tilghman's *Memoir of Lt. Col. Tench Tilghman* (Albany, N.Y., 1876) and on an unpublished article by Lee Crutchfield, Jr., on deposit in the Maryland Historical Society. Elias Boudinot reported in his *Journal*, p. 59, attempts to execute Cornwallis.

The burning of Benedict Arnold's effigy, and the sparing of its leg, is from Heath's *Memoirs*, p. 297.

Epilogue   Peace At Last

The allied witnesses Thacher, Denny, Von Closen, Blanchard and Butler, whose reliable accounts cover most of the Yorktown campaign, continued to record events at Yorktown to the last.

Figures on casualties and British losses of arms and equipment are in dispute. The most exhaustive discussion is in Freeman, Vol. V, Appendix V–5, pp. 513–16.

James Armistead, a black who served as Lafayette's informant in the British camp, was probably the man recognized by Cornwallis as a counterspy. James was awarded his freedom by the Virginia Assembly soon after the war, assumed the name Lafayette, and was pensioned in his old age as a war veteran by the state.

The sanguine reception of the news of Yorktown by George III ("I have no doubt . . .") is from Sir Nathaniel W. Wraxall's *Historical and Posthumous Memoirs . . .* (5 vols., New York, 1884), Vol. II, pp. 137–42. The King's draft message of abdication is from Sir John Fortescue's *The Correspondence of King George III . . .* (6 vols., London, 1927–28) Vol. V, p. 425.

Mary Ball Washington's touching letter is from *The Pierpont Morgan Collection*, by permission of the Trustees.

Washington's distressed response to Nicola's proposal that he become King George I is found in *G.W.*, XXIV, 272.

The inflammatory appeal to Washington's officers by Armstrong is found in *Journals of the Continental Congress*, Vol. XXIV, p. 297, and Washington's proposal that the officers discuss their problems in a regular meeting is on p. 298; his emotional speech is in *G.W.*, XXVI, 208. The one reliable account of this scene by a witness is Shaw's in Josiah Quincy's *The Journals of Major Samuel Shaw* (Boston, 1847), pp. 103–5.

Washington's comments on the Treaty of Paris are found in *G.W.*, XXVI, 236, 238; "Washington's Legacy" is from the same source, p. 487.

The bankrupt state of Congress at the time is revealed in Morris–Washington; 221 *Papers* of G.W., Library of Congress, p. 102, and the mutiny of Pennsylvania troops and the move of Congress from Philadelphia to Princeton are detailed in Burnett, *Letters*, Vol. VII, pp. 193–94, 199–200.

Much, perhaps too much, has been made of conflicting evidence on the flag-raising scene as New York was reoccupied. James Riker's *Evacuation Day, 1783*, a booklet issued on the centennial of the event; Henry P. Johnston in *Harper's* (November 1883), pp. 903–23; the *Manual of the Corp. of N.Y.*, pp. 841–44; and *George Clinton Papers*, Vol. VIII, p. 297, offer varying versions of the incident.

The sparse accounts of Washington's farewell to his officers at Fraunces Tavern are based almost entirely on Benjamin Tallmadge's *Memoir*, p. 97.

Washington's expense accounts present special problems today, and their settlement cannot be explained in completely satisfactory fashion. Even disregarding the basic—and virtually insurmountable—difficulties of translating eighteenth-century currency into modern values, these accounts defy accurate analysis in terms of the monetary standards of the 1970's. A major problem is the wildly fluctuating values prevalent during the Revolution. Washington's conversion of paper money to "lawful" currency is a case in point.

To compensate for the erosion in the value of Continental currency during the war, Congress had approved a rate of exchange based on a table that reflected fluctuations on a month-by-month basis. For example, in April 1777 £1000 in currency was actually worth £300 in "lawful money." By September 1778 this value had fallen to £75, and by January of 1780 to about £10. The value had climbed to £75 pounds once more by May 1781.

Making use of this table and other adjustments, Washington billed the United States for $44,467.93 per month between June 1775 and November 1783, a period of eight years and five months.

Much sport has been made of these charges in a recent work of humor, Marvin Kitman's *George Washington's Expense Account* (New York, 1970). In considering the justice of Kitman's amusing assault upon Washington's reputation in light of his expenses of some $50,000 in almost eight and a half years, readers should take into account the fiscal chaos of the times. The basic problem has been discussed in the text.

The final scene, of Washington's surrender of his commission, is based on *Journals of the Continental Congress*, Vol. XXV, p. 280; *G.W.*, XXVII, 285n; and on James McHenry's letter to his fiancée, December 23, 1783, cited in Bernard C. Steiner's *Life and Correspondence of James McHenry* (Cleveland, Ohio, 1907), p. 69.

Index

Active (ship), 309
Adair, Lieutenant, 75
Adams, Mrs. Abigail, 12–13, 14, 57, 68–69
Adams, John, 22, 39, 41–42, 54, 55–56, 88, 90, 116, 196, 198, 207, 213, 224, 257, 296
  admiration of Washington, 6–7
  personality of, 5–6
  Second Continental Congress, 4, 5–7, 9–10, 12–15, 18, 19
  Staten Island conference, 121–22
Adams, Samuel, 207, 257
  Second Continental Congress, 4, 5, 7, 8, 12, 18
Ajax (ship), 405
Albany, N.Y., 58, 90, 206, 246, 349
  Burgoyne's march to, 205–8
Alexander, Lady Kitty, 268
Alexander, William, 79
Allen, Ethan, 308
Allen, Ira, 211
Allen brothers (of Philadelphia), 149
Allentown, N.J., 282
Altenbockum, Captain von, 169
Amboy, N. J., 200–1
American Camps, The (Paine), 149–50
American Philosophical Society, 51
American Turtle (craft), 120–21
Anderson, Lieutenant Enoch, 151–52
Anderson, John, 337–38, 342
Anderson, Captain Richard, 160, 166–68, 222
Anderson, General Robert, 168
André, Captain John, 278, 310, 319, 324, 325, 331, 334, 340–47
  executed, 345–47
  imprisoned, 343–44
Annapolis, 25, 371, 459
Apollo (ship), 205
Armistead, James, 379
Armstrong, Major John, 215, 450, 451
  Germantown battle, 229–30, 235–36
Arnold, Benedict, 45–46, 317–18, 319, 388, 441

address to "The Inhabitants of America," 348
background of, 307–8
Canada expedition, 45–46, 64, 82, 85
feud with Pennsylvania Council, 308–10
marriage of, 309
pension funds of, 348
as Philadelphia military commander, 202, 280, 294, 306–8
promoted to major general, 196
removed from command, 243
treason at West Point, 323–25, 330–331, 334–51
  Clinton and, 313, 325, 334, 341
at Valley Forge, 275
Virginia campaign, 359–60, 362, 364, 365, 366, 368, 370, 371, 372, 373, 378
war profits of, 280
wounded, 64, 243, 308
Arnold, Benedict, Jr., 348
Arnold, Hannah, 324–25
Arnold, Henry, 348
Arnold, Mrs. Margaret "Peggy," 306–307, 309, 310, 324, 331, 336, 339, 341, 347, 348
Arnold, Richard, 348
Arnold family, 348
Art of War (Jomini), 284
Articles of Confederation, 300
  passage of, 363–64
Asia (ship), 79, 120–21
Assunpink Creek, 171, 172, 182, 183, 186
Atlee, Colonel Samuel, 102, 106–7
Augusta (ship), 251–52
Augustine, John, 83, 141
Austin, Ebenezer, 48

Baddeley, Mrs. Mary, 277, 389, 428
Baldwin, Colonel, 81
Baltimore, 25, 150, 194, 372, 403, 459
Bangs, Dr., 81, 90
Barber of Seville, The (Beaumarchais), 198–99
Barnard College, 130

INDEX

Barrington, Lord, 51, 52
Barton, Lieutenant William, 313–14
Basking Ridge, N.J., 153
Bassett, Burwell, 447
Baylor, Lieutenant Colonel George, 173, 197–98, 318
Beacon Hill, 67
Bear Tavern (New Jersey), 165
Beaufort, S.C., 333
Beaumarchais, Pierre Augustin Caron de, 198–99
Bedford Road, 98, 102, 104
Beekman family, 18
Bennington, Battle of, 211
Bergen County, N.J., 334
Bermuda, 46
Berthier, Captain Louis, 383
Bethlehem, Pa., 163, 266
Bettin, Captain Adam, 354
Biddle, General Clement, 316, 319–20
Birmingham, N.J., 165–66
Birmingham Meeting House, 216, 218, 219, 220–21
Blanchard, Claude, 377, 425, 444
Bland, Mrs. Martha, 197
Bland, Colonel Theodorick, 197, 216, 217, 218
Board of War and Ordnance, 84, 241, 259, 262, 263, 399
Bonetta (sloop), 444
Bordentown, N.J., 154, 171, 178, 186
Boston, 4, 5, 12, 21, 25, 31, 82, 114, 201, 244, 247, 248, 302
    American siege, 36–77, 80, 308
        British troop strength, 40, 49, 65
        Canada plan and, 45–46, 55, 62–63, 64
        confirmation of victory, 73
        "Congress" mortar bombardments, 68–69, 70
        desertions, 60
        at Dorchester Heights, 66–73
        first American traitor, 55–56
        food shortages (in Boston), 49–50
        French aid to, 47
        George III's proclamation and, 61–62
        headquarter expenses, 48–49
        Howe's evacuation of the city, 73–77
        munition shortages, 46–47, 53, 57–58, 61
        naval warfare, 53–54
        password, 61
        at Prospect Hill, 61–62
        recruits and reinforcements, 43–44, 60, 63
        regimental strength, 59
        shellings, 43
        spy incident, 54–55
        in the trenches, 43
        troop rivalry, 41, 44
        women and, 42, 44, 50, 54–55
    smallpox epidemics, 49, 75
Boston Cadets, 6, 8
Boston Massacre, 68, 72
Bostwick, Elisha, 166, 175
Boucher, Jonathan, 38
Boudinot, Elias, 228, 272, 273
Bougainville, Commodore Louis Antoine de, 404–5
Bouzar, William, 355
Braddock, General Edward, 10, 15, 40, 45, 51
Braintree, Mass., 9
Brandywine, Battle of, 205–23, 240, 249, 265
    casualties, 216, 223
    at Chad's Fork, 214–15, 216, 217, 218, 220, 222
    reaction to, 224–26
Brandywine Creek, 214
Brandywine Valley, 114
Brantly, John, 233, 236–37
Broglie, Prince de, 383, 385
Bronx, N.Y., 136
Bronx River, 137, 382
Brooklyn, 79, 82, 98, 101, 102–9, 111, 114–15
Brooklyn Heights, 82, 96, 97
Broughton, Nicholas, 53–54
Brown, John, 308
Brown, Joseph, 221
Brown, Nancy, 268
Brown, Lieutenant Philip, 93
Brown, Sergeant William, 424
Brunswick, N.J., 26, 141, 146, 147, 149, 150, 154, 184, 282, 391–92
    British supply base at (1777), 193
Bryant, Dr. William, 161
Bucks County, Pa., 161
Bülow, Baron Heinrich von, 192
Bunker Hill, Battle of, 17, 20, 27, 31, 41, 43, 49, 52, 67, 72, 75, 97, 125, 129, 138
    casualties, 27
    Gage's report on, 52
Burgoyne, General John "Gentleman Johnny," 51, 205, 210–11, 213, 228, 239, 243–44, 248, 308
    in Canada, 85
    captive troops of (in Boston), 247–48
    defeat at Saratoga, 243–45, 247, 249
    at Freeman's Farm, 243
    Lake Champlain flotilla, 205–6
    route to Albany, 205–8
    surrender of, 244–45, 247
Burke, Edmund, 15
Burke, Thomas, 225
Burlington, N.J., 154

Burn's Tavern (Philadelphia), 13
Burr, Aaron, 45, 126, 262, 300
Burr, Mrs. Theodosia, 300
Bushnell, David, 120
Butler, Colonel Richard, 287, 352, 353, 354, 355, 416, 420, 434, 444

Cadwalader, General John, 151, 156, 159, 163, 175, 178, 180, 187, 189
    duel with Conway, 297–98
Cadwalader, Colonel Lambert, 140
Cadwalader, Dr. Thomas, 14
Caesar, Julius, 374
Cambridge, Mass., 6, 9, 19, 27, 29–35, 67, 248, 299, 416
    camp inspection tour, 31–35
    disciplining of army at, 35
Camden, S.C., 332, 333
Campbell, Major, 424
Canada, 45–46, 62–63, 81, 82, 83, 85, 93, 205, 319, 441, 448
    Lafayette's invasion proposal for, 303–4
Cannae, Battle of, 230
Cape Hatteras, 405
Cape's Tavern (New York City), 455
Carleton, Sir Guy, 45, 448, 449
Carlisle, Earl of, 279
Chad's Fork, Pa., 214–15, 216, 217, 218, 220, 222
Charleston, S.C., 25, 79, 83, 94, 214, 319, 322, 333, 368, 433, 445
    British evacuation of, 449
    fall of, 320
Charlestown, Mass., 31, 51–52
Charlotte, Queen, 207
Charlotte, N.C., 350, 366–68
Charlottesville, Va., 406
Charlus, Count Mathieu, 383
Charming Nancy (ship), 307, 309, 317
Charon (warship), 421
Chase, Samuel, 305
Chastellux, Chevalier de, 348–49, 375–376, 383, 395, 396, 403
Chatham, N.J., 354, 391, 392
Chatterton's Hill, 137, 138
Chaudière River, 45
Cheraw, S.C., 333
Chester, Pa., 210, 222, 226, 234, 400, 401
Chestnut Hill, 230
Chew, Benjamin, 232
Chew House, 234, 251
Cheyney, Thomas, 217–18
Church, Dr. Benjamin, 4–5, 29
    treason of, 55–56
City Tavern (Philadelphia), 208–9, 395–396
Clark, Major George Rogers, 364
Clark, William, 188
Clark's Inn (Philadelphia), 3

Clinton, General George, 130, 244, 455
Clinton, Sir Henry, 51, 52, 79, 83, 154–155, 243–44, 247
    Arnold's treason and, 313, 325, 334, 341
    capture of New York City, 117, 122–123, 124, 125, 127
    Charleston defeat, 94, 100
    as Commander in Chief, 253, 273, 282–83, 285–86, 289, 292–93, 382–395
        Cornwallis in Virginia and, 369–370, 374, 376, 378, 381, 393–394, 412, 417–18, 425, 427, 428, 441, 445–46
        Delaware River crossing, 280
        departure from Philadelphia, 277–79
        Hudson River and, 311–13
        military strategy, 303
        Monmouth Battle, 282–83, 285, 286, 289, 292–93
        New Brunswick raid (1782), 448
        in New York, 382–95
        in Philadelphia (1778), 277–79
        at Stony Point, 311–13
    Long Island battle, 100–1, 102, 107
    reaction to André's death, 347–48
    recalled to England, 448
    on Throgs Neck offensive, 135
    at White Plains, 139
Closen, Baron Ludwig von, 391, 393, 401, 410, 442
Cobb, Colonel David, 415
Cobble Hill, 43
Columbia University, 198
Common Sense (Paine), 64–65, 144, 149
Concord, Battle of, 4, 321
Connecticut Assembly, 39
Connecticut Continentals, 123
Continental Army:
    Boston siege, 36–77
    bounty system, 84, 195–96
    first submarine attack, 120–21
    first successful bayonet attack, 312
    miscreants in, 35
    mutinies and defiance of authority, 132, 320, 352–58, 454
    Negro volunteers, 302
    New Jersey campaign (1776–77), 143–204
    New Jersey campaign (1778–79), 277–333
    New York defense (1776), 78–142
    salaries, 14
    sectional rivalries, 41, 44, 118
    Southern campaign (1781), 359–447
    Yorktown victory, 413–41
    See also names of generals; names of regiments

Continental currency, 20, 47–48, 89, 267, 306, 353, 411
  decline in value of, 305, 310, 318, 356, 373
Conway, Major General Thomas, 199–200, 221, 257, 259–60, 296
  army promotion of, 259–60
  Canada expedition, 262–63
  departure from America, 298
  duel with Cadwalader, 297–98
  Germantown battle, 229, 230, 231, 236, 240, 297
  on Washington, 240, 249, 250–51
Conway Cabal, the, 238–53, 259–63, 300
  criticism of Washington, 240, 249, 250
  Gates and, 239, 240, 243–46, 247, 248, 249, 250, 260–61
Cooper, Samuel, 57
Cooper, Mrs. Samuel, 57
Copps Hill, 67
Cornwallis, Lord Charles, 97, 127, 143, 147, 150, 151, 181–83, 184, 187, 190, 191, 192
  at Fort Washington, 140
  Long Island battle, 101, 102, 105, 106
  Monmouth battle, 282, 285, 286
  reaction to Trenton disaster, 181
  recalled, 181
  Southern campaign, 323, 332–33, 350, 359, 363, 366, 368–70, 372, 374, 376, 378–81, 386, 388, 389, 391, 393–94, 395
    Clinton and, 369–70, 374, 376, 378, 381, 393–94, 412, 417–18, 425, 427, 428, 441, 445–46
    decision to surrender, 427
    at Yorktown, 413–41
  at Trenton, 157–59, 181–83, 184
  at White Plains, 139
Council of Massachusetts, 68
Craik, Dr. James, 257, 439
Creswell, Nicholas, 191–92, 204
Crisis (Paine), 157
Cropper, Major John, 223
Crosswicks, N.J., 180
Curtenius, General Peter, 87
Custine, Comte Adam de, 424–25
Custis, Jacky, 21, 56, 80, 310, 403–4, 439, 447
Custis, Martha Dandridge, *see* Washington, Mrs. Martha

Danbury, Conn., 303
Dartmouth, Lord, 19
Davie, William, 333
Deane, Silas, 30, 305
  in Paris, 199, 269
  Second Continental Congress, 4

Dearborn, Lieutenant Colonel Henry, 256
De Barras, Admiral, 375, 387, 397, 414, 434
De Borré, General Prudhomme, 219
  resignation of, 225
Dechow, Major von, 168, 173, 175
Declaration of Independence, 89–90, 203, 238, 300, 407, 454
"Declaration on Taking Up Arms," 41
De Kalb, Baron Johann, 209, 225, 240, 242, 254–55, 274, 332
  death of, 332
De La Montaine, Mrs., 79
Delancey, Oliver, 389
Delaware River, 3, 19, 20, 150, 151, 152, 153–55, 156, 160, 161, 183, 200, 202, 208, 210, 211, 226, 252, 279, 280, 393
  French control of, 301–3
Demont, Ensign William, 139
Denny, Ebenezer, 429, 434, 442
Denyse Point, 96
De Ouray, Baron, 225
Destouches, Chevalier Charles, 358, 360, 362–64, 365, 366, 375
Detroit, 304
Deux-Ponts, Count Guillaume, 383, 384, 390, 391, 400, 423, 424, 432
Diadème (ship), 405
Dickinson, John, 41
Dickinson, General Philemon, 184, 276, 284, 285
Dobbs Ferry, 137, 382
Doehla, Johann, 411, 421, 426, 434, 436
Donop, Colonel Carl von, 97, 161, 183
Dorchester, Mass., 51–52, 66–73
  British attack at (1776), 65
Dorchester Neck, Mass., 31, 74
Douglas, Colonel William, 123, 124, 130
Douglass, Alexander, 184
Douglass family, 184
D'Oyly, Christopher, 203
Drayton, W. H., 297
Drinker, Elizabeth, 440
Du Bourg, Count, 384
Duché, Reverend Jacob, 238–39
Du Coudray, Major General Philippe Charles Tronson, 199
Dumas, Count Mathieu, 383, 385, 437
Dumfries, Va., 404
Dundas, Lieutenant Colonel Thomas, 432
Dunmore, Lord, 62
Duponceau, Pierre, 268, 270
Duportail, Louis, 256, 283, 288
Durham boats, 150, 162–63
Dyer, Eliphalet, 19

Eagle (ship), 91, 92, 93, 95, 115
East River, 79, 82, 101, 107, 117, 119, 120

Eastchester, N.Y., 137
Easton, Pa., 249
8th Connecticut Regiment, 320
Elizabeth II, Queen, 414
Elizabeth, N.J., 303
Elizabethtown, N.J., 354
Elk River, 211, 214, 401
Elkton, Md., 214
Elliott, Lieutenant Governor Andrew, 345
Elmer, Dr. Ebenezer, 221
Elmira, N.Y., 313–14
Emerson, Ralph Waldo, 34
Engelhardt, Lieutenant, 170, 171
Englishtown, N.J., 289, 292
Erskine, Colonel Sir William, 100, 101, 183
Estaing, Comte Jean Baptiste d', 274, 301–3, 308, 311
Eustis, Dr. William, 87
Evelyn, Captain William, 125
Ewing, General James, 159, 169

Faneuil Hall (Boston), 69
Feltman, Lieutenant William, 413, 436
Ferguson, Major Patrick, 350
Ferguson, Sarah Graeme, 238
Fermoy, Brigadier General Mathias de, 181
Ferson, Count Axel, 336, 376–77, 383, 398, 435
1st Connecticut Regiment, 424
First Continental Congress, 149
1st New Jersey Regiment, 313–14
1st Virginia Regiment, 189
4th Connecticut Regiment, 320, 423
4th Continental Artillery, 268
4th Massachusetts Regiment, 456
4th New Jersey Regiment, 290–91
5th Pennsylvania Regiment, 139
5th Virginia Regiment, 166–68
40th British Infantry, 231
45th British Foot Regiment, 292
55th British Regiment, 187, 190
Fischer, Lieutenant Friedrick, 161, 168
Fishbourne, Major Benjamin, 355
Fitzgerald, Major John, 162, 164, 168, 170, 189–90, 262, 288, 289
Flatbush Road, 98
Fleming, Captain John, 189
    death of, 191
Flucker, Lucy, see Knox, Mrs. Lucy
Flucker, Thomas, 52
Forbes, Gilbert, 86
Ford, Mrs. Jacob, 314, 315, 316
Forman, General David, 229, 230, 286, 392, 393
Forrest, Captain Thomas, 170, 173, 178
Fort Arnold, 337

Fort Constitution, 132
    re-christened, 136
Fort George, 57–58, 79, 454
Fort Lee, 136, 141, 143–44
Fort Mercer, 251–52
Fort Mifflin, 251, 252
Fort Putnam, 337
Fort St. John, 45
Fort Stanwix, 210
Fort Ticonderoga, 45, 57, 66, 71, 85, 206, 308
    fall of, 207
Fort Washington, 89, 119, 136, 144
    battle at, 139–42
Foutz, Adam, 48
Fountain Inn (Baltimore), 403
Fowey (ship), 432
Fox, Charles, 369
Framingham, Mass., 58
France:
    aid to America, 47, 198–99, 300, 305, 319, 325, 326–28, 448
        first allied cooperation, 301–3
    American agents in, 207
    recognition of America, 244
    See also names of military leaders
Frank, Major David, 336, 339–40, 341
Franklin, Benjamin, 16, 47–48, 64, 82, 90, 93, 97, 116, 228
    in Paris, 199, 269, 304, 328, 349
    Staten Island conference, 121–22
Fraunces, Peggy, 87
Fraunces Tavern (New York City), 85, 455
Frederick the Great, 269
Fredericksburg, 118, 371, 374, 447
Freeman, Douglas S., 226
Freeman's Farm, Battle of, 243
Freeman's Tavern (Morristown), 194
French Academy, 348
French alliance, 273–75, 303
French and Indian War, 6, 8, 22, 30, 79, 137, 146, 168, 257
    causes of, 24
French Revolution, 383
Froelich, Private, 411
Frye, Captain Ebenezer, 172

Gage, General Thomas, 50–52, 56
    Bunker Hill report, 52
    recall of, 52
Galloway, Joseph, 149
Gardiner's Bay, 360, 364
Gates, General Horatio, 40, 44, 83, 298, 450, 452
    in Canada, 85, 187
    Conway Cabal and, 239, 240, 243–246, 247, 248, 249, 250, 260–61
    at Fort Ticonderoga, 201
    insult to Washington, 246

New Jersey campaign, 153, 156–57, 163
Saratoga victory, 239, 243–45, 246, 248, 249, 323
Southern campaign, 323, 332, 333, 351, 366
at York, 262
Gates, Mrs. Horatio, 56
Genesee, N.Y., 314
George I, King, 52, 92
George II, King, 10, 247
George III, King, 24, 41, 52, 92, 143, 207, 248, 350
death of, 447
message to Parliament (on revolt of the Americans), 61–62
reaction to Yorktown surrender, 446–47
statue of (in New York City), 89
Georgetown, S.C., 333
Gérard, Conrad Alexandre, 311
Germain, Lord George, 52, 107, 192, 208, 213, 252, 253, 348, 350, 445–46
German mercenaries, *see* Hessians
Germantown, Battle of, 224–37, 265, 297
assault columns, 229–30
casualties, 230–31
militia reinforcements, 229
Mount Airy attack, 230
reaction to, 237
Germantown, Pa., 210
Gerry, Elbridge, 19
Gist, Major Mordecai, 106
Glens Falls, N.Y., 58
Glover, Colonel John, 44, 107–8, 109, 112, 137, 158, 163, 171–73, 180
Gouvion, Lieutenant Colonel Jean Baptiste, 334
Governor's Island, 82, 121
Gowanus Bay, 102
Gowanus Road, 98, 100, 104
Grant, General James, 100, 101, 102–3, 106, 154, 161, 183, 231
Grasse-Tilly, Admiral François Joseph Paul de, 376–78, 385–87, 392, 396, 397, 400–1, 402, 404–11, 416, 430, 434, 439–40, 445
Graves, Admiral Thomas, 388, 404–5, 411, 428, 445
Gravesend Bay, 96, 97, 98
Graydon, Lieutenant Alexander, 108, 109, 213–14
Grayson, Colonel William, 285, 286, 287
Great Valley Road, 215, 216
Green Mountain Boys, 211
Greene, Colonel Christopher, 252, 302
Greene, Mrs. Kitty, 57, 268, 311, 316
Greene, General Nathanael, 34, 88, 306, 311, 315, 316, 317, 328–31

Boston siege and, 37–38, 39, 41, 48, 54, 60, 67
expelled from Quaker church, 39
at Fort Washington, 139–41
Harlem Heights battle, 130, 132
Long Island battle, 93, 95, 96
military appointment, 15
military background of, 39
New Jersey campaign, 143, 144, 149, 155, 158, 163, 165, 184, 197, 202
Christmas Eve council (1776), 158
Monmouth battle, 291, 293
Princeton battle, 189
Trenton victory, 163, 165, 166, 168, 170, 171, 172, 174–75
New Jersey campaign (1778–79), 283
New York defence and, 82, 88, 117, 119, 126, 136, 140
Pennsylvania campaign, 207, 242
at Brandywine, 218–19, 220–22, 224–25, 226
Germantown battle, 229, 233, 234, 235
as quartermaster general, 266–67, 315–16, 320, 328–31
replaced, 95
Southern campaign, 351, 360, 363, 366–69, 371, 372, 445
war profit speculations, 305, 329
West Point treason and, 340–41, 343
Greenspring, Va., 378–79
Gridley, Colonel Richard, 82–83
Guadeloupe (ship), 432
Guichen, Admiral Luc Urbain de, 332, 335
Guilford Courthouse, N.C., 369

Hackensack, N.J., 141
Hackensack River, 143, 146, 154
Hale, Captain Nathan, 42, 116
death of, 134–35
Hale, Samuel, 134
Halifax, Nova Scotia, 46
Hallowell, Benjamin, 73–74
Hamilton, Captain Alexander, 165, 170, 171, 191, 198, 224, 246, 261, 269, 270, 291–92, 296, 301, 333–34, 336, 337, 338, 341, 343, 360–62, 422, 449–50
Hampton, Va., 445
Hampton Road, 380
Hancock, John, 55, 66, 75, 84, 223, 229, 240
Boston Cadets colonelcy, 6, 8
Second Continental Congress, 7–10, 12, 13, 19
Hand, General Edward, 360
Hand, Colonel Israel, 109–10, 182, 189
Hannah (schooner), 53
Hannibal, 230, 374

Harcourt, Lieutenant Colonel William, 154, 201

Harlem Heights, Battle of, 119, 120, 125, 126–27, 128–35, 385
   casualties, 130, 131–32
   Ranger scouts at, 129–30

Harlem River, 79, 86, 117, 136, 140, 385, 454

Harris, John, 176

Harrison, Benjamin, 38, 47–48, 209, 242–243, 257, 364–65

Harrison, Robert, 220, 289, 290, 338

Hartford, Conn., 331, 334–36

Harvard University, 6, 29–30, 80

Haskell, Fifer Caleb, 42

Haslet, Colonel John, 103, 106, 119, 137, 138, 139, 151, 187–88
   death of, 188, 191

Hausegger, Colonel, 181–82

Haverstraw, N.Y., 207, 301

Hay, Major Samuel, 227

Hayes, Mary Ludwig "Molly Pitcher," 293

Hazen, Colonel Moses, 216, 217, 220, 390

Heath, General William, 39, 88, 90, 116, 119, 126, 132, 141, 146, 147, 248, 317, 326–27, 387, 441

Heeringen, Colonel von, 104–5

Heister, General Leopold von, 100, 101, 106

Heights of Guan, 96, 97, 98, 105

Henry, Patrick, 11, 14, 257, 396

Herkimer, General Nicholas, 210

Hervey, General William, 26

Hessians, 52, 83, 94, 95, 96, 137, 252, 302
   capture of (at Trenton), 160–76
   at Fort Washington, 140–41
   at Kips Bay, 123, 124–25
   Long Island battle, 94, 95, 96, 97, 100–5, 107, 110, 111
   New Jersey campaign, 154, 155, 158, 159, 178, 182, 192, 203
   White Plains battle, 138

Heth, Lieutenant Colonel William, 225–226, 234

Hewes, Mrs. Deborah, 257

Hickey, Thomas, 86, 87

Hillsboro, N.C., 332, 333

Hitchcock, Colonel Daniel, 187, 189
   death of, 190

Hoboken, N.J., 26

Holy Ground (New York City), 80–81, 90

Homer, 18

Honeyman, John, 146, 158

Honeyman, Mrs. John, 146

Hood, Admiral Samuel, 402, 405, 428, 445

Hopewell, N.J., 165, 282

Hopkinson, Francis, 53

Hopper House, 334

Hortalez et Cie, 198–99

Howard, William, 101

Howe, Lady Caroline, 121

Howe, Admiral Richard, 91, 92–94, 103, 115, 143, 203, 277, 301
   peace proposal to Washington, 93–94, 115–16, 121–22

Howe, General Robert, 325, 357–58

Howe, Sir William, 51, 52, 93–95, 100–101, 134, 143, 238, 239, 248, 252, 253, 293
   awarded Order of the Bath, 201
   Boston siege and, 52–53, 59, 61–77
     Dorchester Heights, 71, 72
     evacuation of the city, 73–77, 80
   capture of New York City, 116–17, 120
     plan of assault, 122–23
   departure from America, 277–79
   Harlem Heights battle, 129, 130, 132, 135
   Lonk Island battle, 96–97, 100–2, 107, 115
   New Jersey campaign and, 146, 154, 191, 194, 200–1
     march to Trenton, 181–83, 184
     retreat, 202–3
   at Pell's Point, 136–37
   Pennsylvania campaign and, 206–208, 210–13, 227, 228
     Brandywine battle, 215, 216–17, 223
     departure from New York, 207–208, 210
     Germantown battle, 231–32, 237
     occupation of Philadelphia, 228, 276
   resignation of, 252–53, 273
   at Staten Island, 87–89, 91, 92, 94–96
   Throgs Neck offensive, 135, 136
   White Plains battle, 136, 137–39

Howell, Richard, 169

Howland, John, 182

Hudson River, 26, 45, 58, 81, 82, 89, 93, 139, 143, 201, 203, 205, 206, 208, 211, 243, 295, 301, 311, 322, 323, 359, 385, 387, 448, 455

Hull, Captain William, 176

Humphreys, Colonel David, 127, 129, 403, 439, 459, 460

Hundred Years' War, 303

Hunt, Abraham, 162

Hunter, Lieutenant Martin, 232

Huntington, Lieutenant Colonel Ebenezer, 34, 321–22

Huntington, Colonel Jeb, 42

Indians, 24, 25, 28, 45, 83, 206, 210, 313–314

Intrepid (ship), 405
Iroquois Indians, 313–14
Irvine, Captain, 73
Irvine, General William, 356

Jacataqua, 45
Jackson, Colonel Henry, 287, 455–56
Jamaica, N.Y., 98
Jamaica Pass, 101, 104
Jamaica Road, 98, 100, 102
James, Lieutenant Bartholomew, 412
James, Lieutenant William, 420
James River, 359, 373, 374, 379, 381, 402–403
Jameson, Lieutenant Colonel John, 337, 341, 342
Jarvis, Stephen, 220
Jay, John, 117
Jefferson, Thomas, 11, 16, 17–18, 23, 148, 304, 359–60, 372, 373, 374, 407
Johnson, Thomas, 12
Johnston, George, 197
Jomini, Baron Henri, 284
Jones, Joseph, 451, 452
Jones, Judge Thomas, 27–28, 53, 79, 154, 201, 206
Jumel Mansion (New York City), 120

Kennebec River, 45, 46
Kerr, William, 288
Ketchum, Isaac, 85–86
Kettel, John, 30
Kilmansegg, Baroness, 52
Kimm, Lieutenant Georg, 169
Kinderhook, N.Y., 89
King's College, 21
King's County, N.Y., 96
King's Ferry, 339
King's Mountain, S.C., 350
Kingsbridge, N.Y., 79, 85–86, 116–17, 119, 125, 132
Kingsbridge Road, 126, 127
Kingston, N.J., 154
Kips Bay (New York City), 117, 119, 123–125, 130, 454
Kleinschmidt, Ensign Karl, 173
Knowlton, Lieutenant Colonel Thomas, 116, 129
  death of, 131
Knowlton's Rangers, 129–30
Knox, Henry, 39–40, 52, 57–58, 93, 94, 126, 133, 141, 156, 163, 164, 170, 171, 175, 183, 190, 191, 199, 222, 227, 232, 266, 280, 288, 296–97, 343, 390, 396, 399, 408, 415, 420, 455, 456
Knox, Mrs. Lucy, 40, 57, 268, 280, 311
Knyphausen, General Wilhelm von, 140, 141, 216, 217, 220, 222, 282, 322
Knyphausen Regiment, 173, 174
Koscuisko, Count Thaddeus, 313

Lafayette, Marquis de, 209, 210–11, 221, 222, 225, 241–43, 268, 301, 302, 308, 318–19, 326, 327, 331, 334, 336, 338, 341, 347, 350, 356, 361, 383, 432, 443
  appeal to friends in France, 349
  arrival in America, 209
  background of, 209
  Canada invasion proposal, 303–4
  created a major general, 243
  friendship with Washington, 210, 242
  Monmouth battle, 283, 284, 286, 287, 290, 291
  in Virginia, 362–63, 365, 370, 371–81, 387, 389, 398–99, 400, 402, 404–7, 412, 424, 438
  wounded, 221, 222, 241
Lake Champlain, 28, 45, 205–6
Lake Erie, 313
Lake George, 57, 208
Lake Ontario, 313
La Luzerne, Chevalier de, 318, 341, 380, 398
Lamb, Colonel John, 337
Lameth, Chevalier de, 424
Lancaster, Pa., 224
Langdon, John, 16
Langdon, Samuel, 29–30
Laurel Hill, 140
Laurens, Colonel John, 233, 242, 258, 263, 269, 270, 273, 275, 287, 288, 294, 296, 297, 301, 304, 306, 350, 356, 361, 378, 399, 423, 424, 432, 433
Lauzun, Duke de, 383–84
Lauzun Legion, 383
Lavoisier, Antoine, 198
Learned, Colonel Ebenezer, 75
Lechmere Point, 43, 65, 69
Lee, Arthur, 199
Lee, Billy, 20, 37, 43, 291, 403, 456, 459, 460
Lee, General Charles, 12, 16–18, 271–73, 323
  Boston siege and, 37, 39, 41–42, 44, 53, 58–59
  at Cambridge camp, 31, 33–34
  court-martial of, 294–99
  death of, 298–99
  Indian name of, 15
  journey north (1775), 20, 27, 29, 31, 33–34
  on loss of Fort Washington, 141–42
  military appointment of, 15
  military background of, 15
  Monmouth battle, 279–99
    controversy over, 294–99
    military orders, 284, 290, 295
  New Jersey campaign, 144, 146–48, 151, 152–54, 156
    capture, 154–55

criticism of Washington, 153–54
insubordination, 147, 152, 153
New York defense and, 59, 78–79, 80, 81
prison quarters (New York City), 200, 271–72
Rhode Island expedition, 58
sobriquet, 18
in the South, 79, 83, 136
at Valley Forge, 271–73
Washington's fondness for, 284
at White Plains, 137, 141
Lee, Sergeant Ezra, 120–21
Lee, Henry "Light-Horse Harry," 314, 318, 351, 362, 437
Lee, Richard Henry, 241
Lee, Robert E., 314
Lee, Thomas Sims, 392
Leggett, Major Abraham, 111
Leitch, Major Andrew, 130
L'Enfant, Captain Pierre Charles, 287
L'Estrade, Baron, 424
Lewis family, 56
Lexington, Battle of, 4
Liberty Tree, The, 49
Lincoln, General Benjamin, 133, 207, 296–97, 403, 408, 415, 437–38, 448
army promotion of, 196
captured, 320
in South Carolina, 318, 320, 323
Litchfield, Conn., 86, 89
Limekiln Road, 229, 233–34
Lispenard, Leonard, 27
Lititz, Pa., 266
Livingston, Robert, 324, 325, 448
Livingston, William, 147, 291
Livingston family, 18
London (flagship), 428, 444–45
London Bookstore (Boston), 39–40
Long Island, Battle of (1776), 92–112, 113, 116, 129, 217
Brooklyn lines, 102–9, 111, 114–15
casualties, 108
division of command, 97
at the Heights of Guan, 96, 97, 98, 105
Hessian troops at, 94, 95, 96, 97, 100–105, 107, 110, 111
Jamaica flank, 98–102, 104, 105, 114
line of American defense, 97–98
retreat of Continental Army, 108–12, 114–15
Long Island Sound, 132, 328
Loring, Mrs. Joshua, 53, 87–88, 201, 206, 231
Louis XVI, King, 199, 209, 244
Loyalty oaths, 58, 79
Lukens, Rifleman Jesse, 45
Luken's Mill, 234
Lutheran Church, 214

Lux, George, 18
Lynch, Thomas, 47–48
Lynnhaven Bay, 408

McConkey's Ferry, 158–59, 162, 176, 178
McCurtin, Daniel, 87
McDonald, Hugh, 230–31
McDougall, General Alexander, 201, 229, 234, 296–97, 455
McHenry, Dr. James, 286, 289, 300–1, 334, 338, 339, 362, 379, 460
Machiavelli, Niccolò, 18
McKean, Jean, 415, 425
McKean, Thomas, 396, 397–98, 440
Mackenzie, Lieutenant Frederick, 142
McLane, Colonel Allen, 264
McMichael, Lieutenant James, 149
McWilliams, Major William, 249
Magaw, Colonel Robert, 140, 141
Maidenhead, N.J., 181
Manatawny Road, 235
Manchester, Duke of, 76–77
Mansfield, Lieutenant John, 423
Marie Antoinette, Queen, 383
Marion, Francis, 333
Marquand (spy), 388
Marshall, John, 165, 266
Martha's Vineyard, 79
Martiau, Nicholas, 414
Martin, Sergeant Joseph Plumb, 103, 106, 123–24, 125, 256, 265, 315, 415, 418–20, 423–24
Maryland General Assembly, 459–60
Mason, George, 11, 304
Mason, John, 356–57
Massachusetts Committee of Safety, 47
Matthews, General David, 86, 87, 140
Maudit de Plessis, Chevalier du, 233
Mawhood, Lieutenant Colonel Charles, 181, 187, 188, 190
Maxwell, General William, 201, 211, 216, 218, 220, 222, 225, 226, 229, 276, 322
Monmouth battle, 284, 285, 287, 288
Maybie's Tavern (New York), 343
Meade, David, 198
Meade, Colonel Richard Kidder, 197, 198, 285, 287, 344
Mease, General James, 280
Mercantilism, 25
Mercer, General Hugh, 158, 165, 169, 170, 184, 187–89
death of, 191
wounded, 188–89, 191
Merlin (ship), 252
Metuchen, N.J., 202
Middlebrook, N.J., 201–3, 303, 308–11
Mifflin, General Thomas, 5, 16, 17, 18, 20, 28, 67–68, 110–11, 126, 147, 178, 180, 184, 196, 198, 207, 249, 250, 252, 257, 264, 296, 328, 459, 460

INDEX

Miles, Colonel Samuel, 98, 104

Minden, Battle of, 373

Minghini, Guiseppe, 78, 299

Miralles, Juan, 311, 318

Mohawk River, 210

Mohawk Valley, 206

Monckton, Lieutenant Colonel Henry, 292

Monmouth, Battle of, 277–99
    beginning of, 284–85
    British infantry charge, 292
    casualties, 294
    Continental Army retreat, 287–90, 291, 292
    controversy over, 294–99
    heroine of, 293
    result of, 293–94
    rum issue, 291

Monroe, Lieutenant James, 165, 172

Montgomery, Richard, 45, 46
    death of, 62–63, 64, 82

Montgomery, Mrs. Richard, 27

Monticello, Va., 406

Montreal, 45, 63, 64, 205, 304

Montresor, Captain John, 219

Moore, Benjamin, 166

Morgan, General Daniel, 43, 45, 202, 211, 228, 229, 243, 246, 247, 252, 284, 323, 368

Morris, Gouverneur, 9

Morris, Robert, 41, 178–79, 192, 295, 305, 331, 361, 386, 392, 396, 399, 400, 401, 448, 454

Morris, Roger, 120

Morris, Captain Samuel, 169

Morristown, N.J., 152, 153, 203, 349, 392
    headquarters (1777), 193–201
    smallpox outbreak, 196–97

Moulder, Captain Joseph, 189

Moultrie, General William, 396

Mount Airy, 230

Mount Kemble, 352

Mount Pleasant (mansion), 309, 324–25

Mount Vernon, 21, 22, 48, 84, 132—33, 371, 389, 403, 404, 447, 455, 457, 458, 460

Moylan, Colonel Stephen, 63, 84, 131, 190

Mud Island, 251

Muhlenberg, General Peter, 214, 221, 222, 226, 234–35

Mullen's Tavern, 16

Munsell, Hezekiah, 105

Murfree, Major Hardy, 312

Murray, Robert, 125

Murray Hill (New York City), 125

Musgrave, Colonel Thomas, 231, 232

Mystic River, 31

Nantucket, 79

Napoleon I, 383

Nash, General Francis, 229, 236

Nassau Hall, 191, 355

Negroes, 25, 48, 302, 384, 412, 417, 421, 442, 444

Neil, Captain Daniel, 188

Nelson, Thomas, Jr., 406, 421, 432

Neshaminy Creek, 210

New Brunswick, Canada, 79

New Brunswick, N.J., 200, 202, 448

New Haven, 28–29, 331

New Jersey campaign (1776–77), 143–204
    atrocities, 148–49
    bounty system, 178–80
    Christmas Eve council (1776), 158–159
    Delaware River crossings, 150–51, 152, 153, 162–65, 178
    Hessians, 154, 155, 158, 159, 179, 182, 192, 203
        capture of (at Trenton), 160–76
    at Middlebrook, 201–3
    Morristown headquarters, 193–201
    night march to Princeton, 177–92
    results of, 203–4
    retreat (1776), 143–59
    spies, 156, 158, 180
    Tories, 146, 149, 158, 162, 174
    victory at Trenton, 160–76
    women and, 153, 178

New Jersey campaign (1778–79), 277–333
    Arnold's treason and, 344–51
    Monmouth battle, 277–99
    optimism and idleness, 300–20

New Jersey Continentals, 221

New London, 29, 58

New Market, N.J., 202

New Orleans, 304

New Utrecht, 97

New Windsor, 313, 349, 355, 363, 364, 374–75

New York, 25, 26–28, 59, 78–142, 300–20, 382–95
    British capture of, 113–27
        Hessians and, 123, 124–25
        at Kips Bay, 123–25
        plan of assault, 122–23
    British evacuation of, 454–56
    civilian evacuation, 91
    defense of (1776), 78–142
        at Harlem Heights and White Plains, 128–42
        Long Island battle and, 92–112
        loss of New York City, 113–27
        Manhattan, 78–91, 92–94, 97
    fire in (1776), 133–34
    Loyalists (in New York Assembly), 26

population, 78
Tories, 79, 84–85, 86, 87, 88, 89, 92, 94, 115, 117
women and, 79, 80–81, 86, 88, 89, 90–91, 105, 110, 114, 142
New York Committee of Public Safety, 78, 89
New York Convention, 108
New York Provincial Congress, 26
Newark, N.J., 147
Newburgh, N.Y., 448, 453
Newburyport, Mass., 46
Newport, R.I., 301, 302, 360, 363, 364, 376, 387
Newport campaign (1778), 301–3
Newtown, N.J., 176
Newtown Inlet, 117, 122
Nicholas, 304
Nicola, Colonel Lewis, 450
Ninety-Six, S.C., 333
Nixon, George, 165
Noailles, Viscount de, 383, 432, 433
Noailles family, 209
Nook's Hill, 74
Norfolk, Va., 360
burning of, 62
North Carolina Line, 229
North Castle, N.Y., 139, 342
Norwich, Conn., 58
Nova Scotia, 79

Ogden, Benjamin, 356–57
O'Hara, General Charles, 381, 437–38
Ohio Valley, 24
Old South Church (Boston), 49
Oliver, Chief Justice Peter, 42
Olney, George, 316
Olney, Mrs. George, 316–17
Olney, Captain Stephen, 183, 422, 423
Oriskany, Pa., 210
Orloff, Alexis, 160
Osborne's Hill, 219–20
Oswald, Colonel Eleazer, 286, 287, 288, 296–97, 299

Page, John, 131
Paine, Robert, 12
Paine, Thomas, 64–65, 149, 157, 235, 256
Painter's Ferry, 216
Paoli Tavern (Pennsylvania), 227
Paradise Lost, 151
Paramus, N.J., 300, 391
Paris, Treaty of, 299, 447
signing of, 452–53
Parke, Elizabeth, 404
Parker, Admiral Peter, 94
Parsippany, N.J., 391
Parsons, General Samuel H., 125, 296–97
Passaic River, 146

Patterson, Lieutenant Colonel James, 94
Patton, General George S., 165
Paulding, John, 341–42
Paulus Hook (ferry crossing), 26, 314, 315, 455
Peale, Charles Willson, 22, 84, 150–51, 165, 193
Peale, James, 151, 165
Peekskill, N.Y., 141, 146, 201, 210, 223, 311, 334, 335
Pell's Point, N.Y., 136–37
Pendelton, Edmund, 12, 13, 304
Penn, John, 306
Penn, William, 3
Pennsylvania Campaign (1777), 205–76
Brandywine defeat, 205–23
casualties, 216, 223, 227, 230–31, 236
Conway Cabal and, 238–53
Germantown defeat, 224–37
spies, 207, 213
Tories, 210, 227, 232, 238
Valley Forge headquarters, 254–76
women and, 213, 238
Pennsylvania Council, 148–49, 307, 347, 352, 454, 456
feud with Arnold, 308–10
Pennsylvania Gazette, The, 274
Pennsylvania Journal, The, 191
Pennypacker's Mills, 235
Pennytown, N.Y., 148–49
Percy, Lord, 49, 140
Peter III, Czar, 160
Philadelphia, 20, 25, 29, 119, 150–51, 153, 210, 211, 223, 226, 229, 277–80, 304–8, 380, 388, 395–402, 416, 440, 448, 455, 456–59
British capture and occupation, 228, 238–53, 279
population, 3–4
Second Continental Congress, 3–19
Tories, 278, 279, 306, 307
Philadelphia Associators, 151
Philadelphia Committee of Safety, 149
Phillips, General William, 370, 373, 378
Pickens, Andrew, 333
Pickering, General Timothy, 198, 214, 222–23, 231, 232, 329–30, 386
Piel, Lieutenant, 168, 169, 170, 172–73
Piscataway, N.J., 202
Pitcher, Molly, *see* Hayes, Mary Ludwig
Pitt, William, 26
Pliarne, 47
Ploughed Hill, 43
Pomeroy, General Seth, 31, 39
Pompton, N.J., 323, 349, 391
Pontgibaud, Chevalier du, 383
Popham, Major William, 401
Popp, Stephan, 411, 412, 417, 425, 434, 436–37
Portsmouth, Va., 360, 365, 380

INDEX

Potter, Brigadier General James, 190, 353

Potts, Stacy, 161

Preakness, N.Y., 323

Prenet, 47

Prescott, Major General Robert, 125, 272

Princeton, Battle of (1777), 177–92, 207
  casualties, 188–89, 191

Princeton, N.J., 150, 152, 154, 196, 354, 356, 392, 430, 454, 459

Prospect Hill, Mass, 31, 61, 62

Providence, R.I., 80

Pulaski, Count Casimir, 215, 236

Putnam, Major General Israel, 6, 30, 31, 246, 317
  Boston siege and, 54, 63, 70, 73, 80
  command on the Hudson, 201
  defense of New York, 80, 83, 84, 85, 86, 117, 119, 126–27
  defense of Philadelphia, 150
  Harlem Heights battle, 130
  Long Island battle, 97, 98–100, 102
  military appointment, 15
  at Peekskill, 223, 228, 229

Putnam, Chief Engineer Rufus, 67, 117

Quaker Bridge, 184

Quakers, 18, 39, 42, 88, 117, 125, 213, 216, 217, 221, 233, 440

Quebec, 45–46, 205, 304

Queen Charlotte (cutter), 408, 409

Queen's American Rangers, 137

Queens County, N.Y., 88

Rabelais, François, 18

Rahway, N.J., 141

Rall, Colonel Johann, 139, 140–41, 158, 177, 192
  death of, 175
  Trenton defeat, 160–62, 168–75
  wounded, 172, 173, 174

Ramsay, Lieutenant Colonel Nathaniel, 291

Randolph, Edmund, 197

Randolph, Mrs. Peyton, 407

Raritan River, 150, 282

Rattlesnake (ship), 445

Rawdon, Lord, 88, 100, 124, 127

Reading, Pa., 249

Red Bank, N.J., 251

Red Lion Tavern (Long Island), 102

Reed, Joseph, 16, 17, 18–19, 20, 28, 56, 59, 60, 63, 66, 80, 82, 84, 93, 117, 120, 129, 130, 131, 133, 144–48, 157, 159, 184, 356, 357, 398

Réfléchi (ship), 405

Reign of Terror (French Revolution), 383–84

Rhea, Lieutenant Colonel David, 290

Rhode Island Assembly, 39

Richards, Samuel, 107

Richmond, Va., 359, 378, 407

Ringwood, N.J., 357–58

Robertson, Archibald, 71, 72, 74

Robertson, General James, 74, 277, 345, 389, 427

Robin, Abbé Claude, 384, 385

Robinson, Beverly, 336

Rochambeau, Comte de, 330, 332, 334, 349–51, 357, 359, 360, 363, 366, 375–78, 379, 382–89, 393, 394, 396–98, 400–3, 406, 407, 411, 416–23, 425, 431, 432, 434–37, 440, 443, 448
  arrival in America, 326–28
  first meeting with Washington, 335–336
  secret orders of, 326

Rochambeau, Viscount de, 375, 388

Roche de Fermoy, General, 158

Rocky Hill, 337

Rodney, Thomas, 155

Roebuck (frigate), 123

Rogers, Major Robert, 137

Rosburgh, Reverend John, 183

Ross, Major Alexander, 432, 433

Ross, Colonel James, 216, 217

Roxbury, Mass., 31, 67, 70, 71
  artillery works at, 40

Roxbury Neck, 74

Royal Navy, 26

Rush, Dr. Benjamin, 5, 16, 116, 141, 157, 182, 191, 193, 225, 240, 296, 306

Rutledge, Edward, 116
  Staten Island conference, 121–22

St. Clair, General Arthur, 158, 174, 184, 190–91, 201, 207, 356
  army promotion, 196
  at Fort Ticonderoga, 207

St. Clair's Brigade, 173

St. Lawrence River, 45, 85, 304

St. Lucia, island of, 303

Saint-Simon, Marquis Claude Henri de, 402, 407

Sandy Hook, N.J., 282, 308, 392

Saratoga, 58, 208, 228, 237, 239, 243–45, 308, 325
  Gates victory at, 239, 243–45, 246, 248, 249, 323

Saratoga Convention, 247

Savannah, Ga., 25, 303, 308, 333
  British evacuation of, 449

Sawmill River, 382

Saxe, Comte Maurice de, 39

Scammell, Alexander, 110, 343, 344, 346–347

Scheffler, Lieutenant Colonel Francis, 173

Schuyler, General Philip, 16, 17, 18, 51, 207, 324, 362
   Canada expedition, 45, 46, 64
   departure from Philadelphia (1775), 20, 27, 28
   at Fort Ticonderoga, 207
   military appointment, 15
   New York command, 28
   removed from command, 207
   resignation of, 310
Schuylkill River, 226–28, 229, 255, 256, 267, 309, 398
Schuylkill Valley, 226
Scott, General Charles, 234, 284, 285, 288, 289–90, 296
Second Continental Congress, 4–19
   commissions, 14, 15, 30–31
   flight to Baltimore, 150
   instructions to the army, 14, 15
   move to York, Pa., 224, 245
   nomination of Washington, 7–12
   return to Philadelphia (1777), 194
2nd Light British Infantry, 231
2nd New Jersey Regiment, 289
7th Connecticut Regiment, 42, 166
7th Virginia Regiment, 189, 223
16th Light Horse Regiment, 154
17th British Light Dragoons, 292
Seneca Indians, 15
Serle, Ambrose, 93, 134, 203
Seven Years' War, 247
Sewall, Jonathan, 50
Shabbakonk Creek, 181, 182
Shakespeare, William, 18
Shaw, Major Samuel, 296–97, 316, 334, 451–52
Sherman, Roger, 12
Shewkirk, Parson, 113, 127
Shippen, Dr. Edward, 307
Shippen, Margaret, see Arnold, Mrs. Margaret
Shippen, Dr. William, 163, 249
Shirley, Sir William, 21
Shreve, Colonel Israel, 289
Shrewsbury (ship), 405
Silliman, 126
Six Nations of Indians, 313
Skippack Creek, 244
Skippack Road, 229, 230, 231, 234, 235
Slavery, 24, 25, 30
Smallpox, 49, 75, 82, 84, 265, 372
Smallwood, Colonel Robert, 126, 127, 138, 151, 229, 230, 236
Smallwood, Colonel William, 103, 106
Smith, Captain Ebenezer, 344
Smith, Joshua Hett, 335, 340, 342
Smith, Lieutenant Colonel Matthew, 232
Smith, Chief Justice William, 345, 388, 446
Somerset Courthouse, 191

Sons of Liberty, 5
Southern campaign, 359–447
   in the Carolinas, 366–70
   Chesapeake Bay area, 359–66
      concentration in, 395–412
   Clinton in New York and, 382–95
   Lafayette in Virginia, 371–81
   at Yorktown, 413–41, 442–47
      British surrender, 429–41
      siege, 413–28
      significance of, 442–60
Spain, American agents in, 207
Spear, Major James, 215, 217
Spencer, Major General Joseph, 31, 39, 88
Spring Hill, Mass., 31
Springfield, Mass., 29, 58
Springfield, N.J., 391
Stamford, Conn., 78
Stamp Act, 5, 24
Stark, John, 172, 211
Staten Island, 87–89, 91, 92, 94–96, 116, 120, 121–22, 201, 203, 315, 390, 392
Stedman, Charles, 115
Stephen, General Adam, 148, 164, 166–168, 169, 243
   at Brandywine battle, 215, 216, 217, 218–20
   drunkenness of, 236, 237
   Germantown battle, 229, 233–34, 236, 237
Steuben, Baron Friedrich Wilhelm, 269–271, 273, 283, 285, 292, 344, 365, 373–374, 378, 443–44, 455, 456, 458
Stewart, Colonel Walter, 287, 291, 320, 352, 353, 354, 355
Stiles, Ezra, 15
Stirling, Lord, 79, 80, 102–3, 104, 136, 141, 268, 295, 317
   army promotion, 196
   Conway Cabal and, 249, 250, 262
   Long Island battle, 98, 102–3, 105, 106, 108
   New Jersey campaign, 146, 151, 158, 202
      Christmas Eve council (1776), 158
      Monmouth battle, 291, 292–93
   Pennsylvania campaign, 229
      at Brandywine, 215, 216, 217, 218–20
   surrender of, 106, 115
Stockbridge Indians, 29
Stonington, British bombardment of, 58
Stony Brook, N.J., 186, 187
Stony Brook bridge, 190
Stony Point, Battle of, 311–13, 314
Stony Point, N.Y., 311–13, 330, 342
Strickland (prisoner), 346
Stuart, Gilbert, 8–9

Suffern, N.Y., 391
Sullivan, Major General John, 43, 88,
116, 122, 301, 302, 307, 396
  Boston siege, 46, 67
  at Brandywine, 215, 217, 218, 219–
    221, 225
  captured, 105, 153
  defense of New York, 80, 82, 86
  Germantown battle, 229, 230–33, 234
  in Iroquois territory, 313–14
  Long Island battle, 95, 97–100, 103–
    105, 108, 114
    retreat, 105
  military appointment, 15
  New Jersey campaign, 153, 155, 165,
    166, 202
    Christmas Eve (1776), 158
    Princeton battle, 186, 186, 190
    Trenton victory, 165, 166, 170,
      171, 172
  Newport campaign, 301–3
  in Philadelphia (September, 1776),
    115–16
  surrender of, 115
Sumter, Thomas, 333
Susquehanna River, 313, 372
Swedenborg, Emanuel, 238
Symonds, Captain Thomas, 434

Tallmadge, Major Benjamin, 109, 111,
  235, 341, 342, 344, 389, 456
Tarleton, Colonel Banastre, 368, 374, 412,
  426
Tarrytown, N.Y., 341–42
Taylor, John, 74
Ternay, Admiral, 326–28, 335, 358
Terrible (ship), 405
Thacher, Dr. James, 36, 314–15, 391, 393,
  397, 415, 421
Thimble Mountain, 194
3rd Maryland Regiment, 291
13th Pennsylvania Regiment, 291
Thomas, General John, 31, 39, 67, 69,
  70, 71
  death of, 85
  Quebec rout, 82
Thompson, General William, 82
  captured, 85
Thompson family, 158
Throgs Neck, N.Y., 135, 136, 385
Tilghman, Tench, 130–31, 290, 330–31,
  361, 439, 440, 441
Tilton, Dr. James, 406
Tories, 7, 26, 27, 48, 50, 53, 58, 73, 137,
  350, 396, 433
  arrest of, 58
  in Boston, 73–74
  denunciations of Washington, 38
  feathering of, 42
  New Jersey, 146, 149, 158, 162, 174

New York, 79, 84–85, 86, 87, 88, 89,
  92, 94, 115, 117
  Pennsylvania, 210, 227, 232, 238
  in Philadelphia, 278, 279, 306, 307
Townshend Act, 24
Trask, Israel, 44–45
Trenton, N.J., 20, 150, 152, 154, 178–82,
  194, 196, 203, 224, 357, 388, 392, 393,
  430
  British advance to, 181–83, 184
  Continental Army capture of (1776),
    160–76, 207, 223, 230, 297
    casualties, 109, 174, 175
    Delaware River crossing, 162–65
    reaction to (in London), 192
Trenton Ferry, 175
Trevelyan, 115
Trinity Church (New York City), 133
Trumbull, Reverend Benjamin, 124
Trumbull, Jonathan, 58, 66, 335
Trumbull, Jonathan, Jr., 42, 57, 155,
  198, 390, 403, 404, 408, 410, 431, 434,
  438–39
Trumbull, Joseph, 267
Tryon, William, 26, 27–28, 78–79, 86
Tucker, Major St. George, 406, 432
Tudor, William, 19, 20
Turenne, Vicomte de, 39
Turtle Bay, 90, 119

U.S. Constitution, 83

Valley Creek, 256
Valley Forge headquarters, 254–76, 279,
  292, 300, 314
  arrival of Steuben at, 269–71
  decision for, 254–55
  disease and epidemics, 264–66
  food shortages, 257, 263–64, 265, 266–
    267
  housing conditions, 256–57, 263
  location of, 255
  news of French alliance, 273–75
Van Cortlandt, Colonel Philip, 390
Van Cortlandt family, 18
Van Rensselaer family, 18
Van Wart, Isaac, 341–42
Varick, Colonel David, 336–37, 339–40
Varnum, Captain, 190
Vassall, Major John, 48
Vaughan, Sir John, 107, 127
Vealtown, N.J., 153
Vergennes, Comte Charles de, 237, 328
Verplanck's Point, 331, 448
Ville de Paris (flagship), 408
Virginia Council, 131
Virginia House of Burgesses, 10–11
Von Lossberg, 161, 170, 171, 172, 177
Vulture (sloop), 340, 342

INDEX

Wachtung Mountains, 201–2
Wadsworth, Colonel Jeremiah, 267, 268, 305–6, 335
Wadsworth Brigade, 127
Wainwood, Godfrey, 54
Waldo, Dr. Albigence, 255, 263, 265
Walker, John, 197, 459, 460
Wall, Jessie, 162
Walpole, Horace, 40
Ward, General Artemas, 6, 12, 30–31, 44, 62, 66, 67, 69, 80, 82
  military appointment, 15
  surrender of command to Washington, 33
Warren, James, 55
Warren, Joseph, 19, 76
Warren, Mercy, 57
Washington, George:
  appointed commander in chief, 3–19, 207
    acceptance speech, 13
    commission and instructions, 14, 30
    first military order, 28
    generals and staff, 15–16
    nomination, 7–12
    opposition to, 12
    preparations for New England journey, 16–19
    refusal of payment for services, 13
  Boston siege (1775–76), 36–60, 80
    victory, 73–77, 80
  Braddock affair, 10
  on *Common Sense*, 65
  denture problems, 84
  French and Indian War, 22, 24, 37
  friendship with Lafayette, 210, 242
  on Jefferson, 23
  journey northward (1775), 27–35
    arrival in New York City, 26–28
    at Cambridge camp, 29–35, 36–60
    in Connecticut, 28–29
  marriage of, 10, 21
  military expenses of, 196, 456–58
  New Jersey campaign (1776–77), 143–204
    march to Princeton (1777), 177–192
    Middlebrook battle, 201–3
    Morristown headquarters, 193–201
    results of, 203–4
    in retreat, 143–59
    Trenton victory, 160–76
  New Jersey campaign (1778–79), 277–333
    Arnold's treason and, 344–51

    Monmouth battle, 277–99
    optimism and idleness, 300–20
  New York (1776) and, 78–142
    defense of Manhattan, 78–91, 92–94, 97
    Harlem Heights and White Plains, 128–42
    Long Island battle, 92–113
    loss of New York City, 113–27
  Ohio property, 24
  Pennsylvania campaign (1777), 205–276
    Brandywine defeat, 205–23
    Conway Cabal and, 238–53
    Germantown defeat, 224–37
    Valley Forge headquarters, 254–276
  physical appearance, 8–9, 36
  plantation and personal life, 21–22
  portraits of, 22, 84
  reputation of, 10, 21
  at Second Continental Congress, 8–9, 10, 12
  Southern campaign, 359–447
    at Yorktown, 413–41, 442–47
  tonsillitis attack, 197
  Tory denunciations of, 38
  view of independence, 11
  in Virginia House of Burgesses, 10–11
  wartime letters of, 17
Washington, Lawrence, 414
Washington, Lund, 21, 49, 132–33, 365, 389
Washington, Mrs. Martha, 10, 16–17, 21, 22, 80, 306, 311, 315–16, 318, 403, 447–448
  in Cambridge, 56–57, 64
  in New York, 84, 88
  smallpox inoculation, 84
  at Valley Forge, 268–69, 272, 275
Washington, Mary Ball, 364–65, 447
Washington, Captain William, 172, 351
Washington Heights, 128
Waterloo, Battle of, 95, 383
Watertown, 29, 55
Wayne, General Anthony "Mad Anthony," 202, 214, 218, 220, 222, 227–28, 314, 349
  army mutiny and, 352–57
  Arnold's treason and, 340–41, 343
  Germantown battle, 229, 231, 232, 234, 237
  Lee's court-martial and, 296
  Monmouth battle, 283, 284, 285, 286, 288, 291, 292
  Southern campaign, 373, 378, 379
  at Stony Point, 312
  at Valley Forge, 254, 265
  wounded, 312

INDEX

Webb, Lieutenant Samuel B., 70, 138, 156

Webster, Noah, 29

Weedon, Brigadier General George, 118, 126, 214, 221, 222, 226, 407–8
    Harlem Heights battle, 128, 130, 131
    at Trenton, 171–72

Wellington, Duke of, 95

West, William, 280

West Point, 303, 311, 313, 323, 349, 355
    Arnold's treason at, 323–25, 330–31, 334–51

Westchester 117

Westfield, N.J., 202

Wethersfield, Conn., 29, 375

Wharton, Thomas, 278

White, Mrs., 153, 154

White, Sergeant Joe, 172, 174

White Horse Tavern, 227

White Plains, Battle of, 136, 137–39
    casualties, 139

Wiederhold, Lieutenant Andreas, 160, 161, 169, 177

Wikoff, Captain Peter, 288

Wild, Sergeant Ebenezer, 256

Wilkinson, Major James, 153, 154, 157, 163, 164, 174, 181, 187, 245, 246, 248–249, 250–51, 262

William and Mary, College of, 406

Williams, David, 341–42

Williamsburg, 25, 378, 402–8, 409, 412, 445, 447

Wilmington, Del., 254, 459

Wilmington, N.C., 369

Wilson, James, 16

Winchester, Va., 444

Windt, John de, 343, 346

Winnsboro, S.C., 350

Winter Hill, Mass., 31

Winthrop, Hannah, 247–48

Wissahickon Creek, 235

Wythe, George, 304, 407

Yale University, 15, 29, 120, 134, 321

"Yankee Doodle," 37

Yeates, Lieutenant Bartholomew, 188

Yellow Springs, Pa., 227, 265

York, Pa., 224, 258, 262, 273

York River, 380, 409, 413, 416, 426, 443
    Washington's picket boat line, 407–408

Yorktown, Va., 380–81, 399, 408, 409–12, 413–41, 442–47
    siege of, 413–28
        American bombardment, 420–21
        British surrender of, 427, 429–441, 442–47
        casualties, 421, 424–25, 443
        French advance at, 424
        Purple Heart citation, 424
        significance of, 442–60